The Conversion of Britain

Religion, Politics and Society in Britain
Series editor: Keith Robbins

The Conversion of Britain: Religion, Politics and Society in Britain, c.600–800
Barbara Yorke

The Post-Reformation: Religion, Politics and Society in Britain, 1603–1714
John Spurr

Religion and Society in Twentieth-Century Britain
Callum G. Brown

The Conversion of Britain

Religion, Politics and Society in Britain *c.*600–800

Barbara Yorke

Routledge
Taylor & Francis Group

LONDON AND NEW YORK

First published 2006 by Pearson Education Limited

Published 2014 by Routledge
2 Park Square, Milton Park, Abingdon, Oxon OX14 4RN
711 Third Avenue, New York, NY 10017, USA

Routledge is an imprint of the Taylor & Francis Group, an informa business

ISBN 13: 978-0-582-77292-2 (pbk)

British Library Cataloguing-in-Publication Data
A CIP catalog record for this book can be obtained from the British Library

Library of Congress Cataloging-in-Publication Data
A CIP catalog record for this book can be obtained from the Library of Congress

Set by 3

Contents

Series Editor's Preface

No understanding of British history is possible without grappling with the relationship between religion, politics and society. How that should be done, however, is another matter. Historians of religion, who have frequently thought of themselves as ecclesiastical historians, have had one set of preoccupations. Political historians have had another. They have acknowledged, however, that both religion and politics can only be understood, in any given period, in a social context. This series makes the interplay between religion, politics and society its preoccupation. Even so, it does not assume that what is entailed by religion and politics remains the same throughout, to be considered as a constant in separate volumes merely because of the passage of time.

In its completed form the series will have probed the nature of these links from c.600 to the present day and offered a perspective, over such a long period, that has not before been attempted in a systematic fashion. There is, however, no straitjacket that requires individual authors to adhere to a common understanding of what such an undertaking involves. Even if there could be a general agreement about concepts, that is to say about what religion is or how politics can be identified, the social context of such categorisations is not static. The spheres notionally allocated to the one or to the other alter with circumstances. Sometimes it might appear that they cannot be separated. Sometimes it might appear that they sharply conflict. Each period under review will have its defining characteristics in this regard.

It is the Christian religion, in its manifold institutional manifestations, with which authors are overwhelmingly concerned since it is with conversion that the series begins. It ends, however, with a volume in which Christianity exists alongside other world religions but in a society frequently perceived to be secular. Yet, what de-Christianisation is taken to be depends upon what Christianisation has been taken to be. There is, therefore, a relationship between topics that are tackled in the first volume, and those considered in the last, which might at first sight seem unlikely. In between, of course are the 'Christian Centuries' which, despite their label, are no less full of 'boundary disputes', both before and after the Reformation. The perspective of the series, additionally, is broadly pan-insular. The Britain of 600 is plainly not the Britain of the early twenty-first century. However, the current political structures of Britain-Ireland have arguably owed as much to religion as to politics. Christendom has been inherently ambiguous.

It would be surprising if readers, not to mention authors, understood the totality of the picture that is presented in the same way. What is common, however, is a realisation that the narrative of religion, politics and society in Britain is not a simple tale that points in a single direction but rather one of enduring and by no means exhausted complexity.

Keith Robbins, November 2005

Acknowledgements

First of all, I would like to thank Professor Keith Robbins for inviting me to contribute to the series Religion, Politics and Society, and for the support he has provided as its General Editor. My research for the volume has been aided by various people who have provided encouragement, kindly discussed aspects of it with me or given me access to their own unpublished work. In particular, I would like to thank Lesley Abrams, John Blair, Nicholas Brooks, Dauvit Broun, Thomas Charles-Edwards, Thomas Clancy, Katy Cubitt, Bruce Eagles, Theresa Hall, Nicholas Higham, Tony King, Aidan MacDonald, Donnchadh Ó Corráin, Sarah Semple, Richard Sharpe, Clare Stancliffe, Nicholas Stoodley, Alan Thacker, Malcolm Todd, Howard Williams and the late Patrick Wormald. I also benefited considerably from attendance at three conferences – *Beyond the Goddodin* (St Andrews), *Britons in Anglo-Saxon England* (Manchester), *Adomnán of Iona* (Lampeter/Iona) – proceedings from which have yet to be published as we go to press. Alex Woolf nobly read the entire first draft, and provided much useful and stimulating feedback, as he has done on many other occasions; many of my views on early medieval Scotland owe much to his insight. Two anonymous referees of the final manuscript also provided me with useful advice and corrected various errors. None of these people, of course, bear any responsibility for any remaining errors or quirks of judgement.

The writing of the book took place largely during a period of study leave provided by the University of Winchester and the Arts and Humanities Research Council through their Research Leave Scheme. I am grateful to both institutions for their support, without which this book would not have appeared, and to my colleagues in the History subject area at Winchester who also made my sabbatical possible. Financial support from the University of Winchester also helped me to attend various relevant conferences. Ryan Lavelle kindly drew the maps for me, and provided much useful advice on them and other technological matters.

The final stages were overseen by Christina Wipf Perry, Tim Parker and Hetty Reid of Pearson Education, and I gratefully acknowledge the help I have received from them. As always, I end by thanking my husband Robert for his moral support and bibliographic advice, and his willingness to visit early medieval sites with me.

List of abbreviations

Adomnán, *V. Columbae*   A.O. and M.O. Anderson, *Adomnán's Life of St Columba* (2nd edn, Oxford, 1991)

Adomnán of Iona, trans. Sharpe   Adomnán of Iona, *Life of St Columba*, trans. R. Sharpe (Harmondsworth, 1995)

Alcuini Epistolae   MGH Epistolae IV, vol. 2, ed. E. Dümmler (Berlin, 1895)

Aldhelm: The Poetic Works   ed. M. Lapidge and J. Rosier (Woodbridge, 1985)

Aldhelm: The Prose Works   ed. M. Lapidge and M. Herren (Ipswich, 1979)

Anon., *V. Cuthberti*   'Vitae Sancti Cuthberti Anonymi' in *Two Lives of Saint Cuthbert*, ed. B. Colgrave (Cambridge 1940)

ASSAH   Anglo-Saxon Studies in Archaeology and History (Oxford)

ASC   The Anglo-Saxon Chronicle, ed. D. Whitelock, with D.C. Douglas and S.I. Tucker (London, 1961)

Asser   *Asser's Life of King Alfred*, ed. W.H. Stevenson (Oxford, 1904)

AT   'The Annals of Tigernach', ed. W. Stokes, *Revue Celtique* 16 (1895), 374–419 and 17 (1896), 6–33, 119–263

Attenborough, Laws   *The Laws of the Earliest English Kings*, ed. and trans. F.L. Attenborough (Cambridge, 1922)

AU   The Annals of Ulster (to AD 1131), ed. and trans. S. Mac Airt and G. Mac Nicoaill, Part 1 (Dublin, 1983)

BAA   British Archaeological Association

BAR   British Archaeological Reports (British Series)

Bede, *Historia Abbatum   Venerabilis Bedae Opera Historica*, ed. C. Plummer (2 vols, Oxford, 1896), vol. 1, 362–87

Bede, *Hist. Eccl.   Bede's Ecclesiastical History of the English People*, ed. B. Colgrave and R.A.B. Mynors (Oxford, 1969)

Bede, *Letter to Ecgbert   Venerabilis Bedae Opera Historic*, ed. C. Plummer (2 vols, Oxford, 1896), I, 405–23

Bede, *V.Cuthberti*   'Bedae Vitae Sancti Cuthberti' in *Two Lives of Saint Cuthbert*, ed. B. Colgrave (Cambridge 1940)

Beowulf   *Beowulf and the Fight at Finnsburg*, ed. F. Klaeber (3rd edn, Boston, 1950)

Blackwell Encyclopaedia   *The Blackwell Encyclopaedia of Anglo-Saxon England*, ed. M. Lapidge *et al.* (ed.), (Oxford, 1999)

Burial, ed. Lucy and Reynolds   *Burial in Early Medieval England and Wales*, ed. S. Lucy and A. Reynolds (London, 2002)

Canones Adomnani   *Handbooks of Penance*, ed. J.T. McNeill and H.M. Garner (rpr. New York, 1979), 130–5

CMCS   *Cambridge/Cambrian Medieval Celtic Studies*

'Continuation of Bede'   *Bede's Ecclesiastical History of the English People*, ed. B. Colgrave and R.A.B. Mynors (Oxford, 1969), 572-7

Councils   *Councils and Ecclesiastical Documents Relating to Great Britain and Ireland: II, The Churches of Ireland and Scotland. III, The English Church 595–1066*, ed. A.W. Haddan and W. Stubbs (Oxford, 1871)

EHD   *English Historical Documents, I, c.500–1042*, ed. and trans. D. Whitelock (2nd edn, London, 1979)

Gesta Pontificum   William of Malmesbury, *De Gestis Pontificum Anglorum Libri Quinque*, ed. N. Hamilton, Rolls Series (London, 1870)

Gildas, *De Excidio*   *Gildas: The Ruin of Britain and Other Documents*, ed. and trans. M. Winterbottom (Chichester, 1978)

Gododdin   *The Gododdin: Text and Context from Dark-Age North Britain*, ed. and trans. J.T. Koch (Cardiff, 1997)

Handbooks of Penance   *Medieval Handbooks of Penance*, ed. J.T. McNeil and H.M. Garner (rpr. New York, 1979)

Historia Brittonum   *Nennius: British History and the Welsh Annals*, ed. and trans. J. Morris (Chichester, 1980)

Historia Regum   *Symeonis Monachi Opera Omnia*, ed. T. Arnold, vol. 2 (London, 1885)

Local Saints   *Local Saints and Local Churches in the Early Medieval West*, ed. A. Thacker and R. Sharpe (Oxford, 2002)

MGH   *Monumenta Germaniae Historica*

Pastoral Care   *Pastoral Care Before the Parish*, ed. J. Blair and R. Sharpe (Leicester, 1992)

Pictish Symbol Stones   RCHM Scotland, *Pictish Symbol Stones: An Illustrated Gasetteer* (Edinburgh, 1999)

RCHM Scotland   Royal Commission for Historical Monuments of Scotland

Spes Scotorum   *Spes Scotorum: Hope of Scots. Saint Columba, Iona and Scotland*, ed. D. Broun and T. Clancy (Edinburgh, 1999)

St Augustine   *St Augustine and the Conversion of England*, ed. R. Gameson (Stroud, 1999)

St Patrick   *St Patrick: His Writings and Muirchu's Life*, ed. A.B.E. Hood (Chichester, 1978)

Tangl   *Bonifatii et Lulli Epistolae, MGH Epistolae Selecta I*, ed. M. Tangl (Berlin, 1916)

Theodore's Penitential   *Handbooks of Penance*, 179–214

TRHS   *Transactions of the Royal Historical Society*

V. Wilfridi   *The Life of Bishop Wilfrid by Eddius Stephanus*, ed. B. Colgrave (Cambridge, 1927)

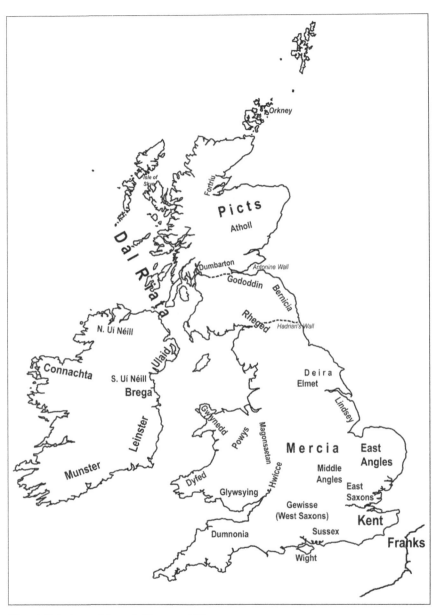

Map 1 Britain and its neighbours c.600

Map 2 The kingdoms of Britain c.800
(with some ecclesiastical and other sites)

Introduction

This book which covers the period *c.* 600–800 is the opening volume in a series which aims to study the interrelationship of religion, politics and society in Britain up to the present day. For the period *c.*600–800, which is the subject of this volume, the links between religion and other facets of the history of the time have always tended to play a major role in studies of it, because most of the written sources on which historians are dependent were produced by churchmen or churchwomen, and so many other aspects of society have perforce to be studied through the opinions of these literate specialists. The range of sources is limited in number and scope, particularly compared to what is available for the later periods of Britain's history, and the problems arising from that produce various distinctive characteristics in the study of the period. Early medievalists have to work very closely with the written sources that have survived and much can depend on the nuanced reading of a relatively short passage of text. Direct use of primary sources is therefore a feature of this volume, and a large part of this introduction is devoted to identifying the major classes of evidence and to examining the work of three authors – Gildas, Adomnán and Bede – who are cited extensively in later chapters.

Not the least of the problems with the sources in the period *c.*600-800 is that not all classes of society nor all areas of Britain are represented equally in what has survived. The problem is particularly acute for the people who inhabited much of northern and eastern Scotland, the Picts, for whom no written records are extant that were produced within Pictland itself except variant versions of a king-list. The Picts are referred to in records produced by their neighbours but, as will become apparent, many details about Pictish political and social organisation remain obscure. Fortunately there are alternative ways of approaching the period through non-written sources of evidence such as archaeological data, sculpture and place-names, and frequent use will be made of such categories of material in the following pages. But anyone seeking to understand the period has to begin by appreciating that they have to live with uncertainty on many key issues. If one enjoys working on the early middle ages it is this very incompleteness of the record that provides part of the fascination as one strives to make sense of apparently contradictory pieces of evidence, but for a newcomer it can be initially disorienting.

The traveller to the period *c*.600–800 has to accept that not only will there be certain aspects of its history that will probably never be fully comprehended, but also that much of what can be known will be unfamiliar. The political map of Britain in this period, for instance, bears little resemblance to that of later periods. Although it can be convenient to refer to England, Wales and Scotland as geographical areas to help orient the reader, it must be appreciated that they did not exist as political or administrative areas at the time, even if the seeds of their emergence as distinctive political and cultural units do lie within the period. Contemporary writers identified four distinct people as living in Britain *c*.600–800 – British, Picts, Irish and Anglo-Saxons. The British and Picts were indigenous inhabitants whose ancestors were living in Britain during the Roman period. The end of Roman control around the beginning of the fifth century was followed by incursions of Anglo-Saxon and Irish settlers into certain areas of the country, though it is possible that Irish settlements in various parts of the west may go back somewhat longer. We can identify certain territories as being under British, Pictish, Irish or Anglo-Saxon control by 600 (Map 1), as long as one does not demand precision over the exact course of boundaries. However, the political map was not stabilised at this point and, as will become apparent in the more detailed discussion of the four peoples in Chapter 1, major changes in the political geography occurred between 600 and 800 (Map 2). It is also not possible to study the period 600 to 800 without appreciating something of what occurred in the turbulent centuries between 400 and 600 when the inhabitants of Britain, like those of other former areas of the Roman empire, had to adjust to life in a post-Roman world. Therefore Chapter 1, which provides an overview of the political and social structures within early medieval Britain, reaches back into the fifth and sixth centuries to seek to explain the origins of structures that continued to evolve in the period after 600. However, it should be noted that no matter how great the problems with sources for the period between 600 and 800, they are nothing compared to the difficulties of understanding the fifth and sixth centuries. In popular works those centuries are often referred to as 'the dark ages' and radically different interpretations have been produced about many key aspects of what may have occurred during that time.

One of the major distinguishing characteristics of the four peoples of Britain, as contemporaries acknowledged, was that they spoke different languages. The languages of the British, Picts and Irish were part of the Celtic group of languages, but fall into different sub-groups thereof. The British and Picts were both speakers of Brittonic, whose modern descendants are Welsh, Cornish and Breton. The Irish, on the other hand, were speakers of Gaelic, from which modern Irish, Manx and Scottish Gaelic descend. The two Celtic groupings are also known as p-Celtic and q-Celtic respectively because words that have an initial 'p' sound in Brittonic have an initial 'q' or 'c' sound in Gaelic; for example the cognate for *Prydain*, the medieval Welsh word for Britain, was *Cruthin* in Old Irish. Old English, the language of the Anglo-Saxons, belongs to a different language grouping, the Germanic, whose present day representatives include, in addition to modern English and German, Dutch and the Scandinavian languages. The Celtic and Germanic languages both belong to the same broader language grouping that is known as Indo-European.[1]

It might be expected that language difference would be emblematic of much broader cultural and organisational differences between these peoples, as contemporary writers appear to have believed, and some of these issues are explored further in Chapter 1. However, it should be made clear from the outset that the matter is not as straightforward as it might at first appear. To identify certain areas as British, Pictish, Irish or Anglo-Saxon is not to say that these were the only languages spoken in their territories, or that all the inhabitants within them were culturally homogenous and had had common histories. Rather what is identified through such labels are the language and culture of the dominant groups within the provinces who might themselves be of much more mongrel origins. The whole question of ethnic identities and the circumstances in which they might change are currently of great interest in early medieval studies, and will be borne in mind throughout this work.

Religion can be one of the ways through which cultural difference is expressed, and the preferences of ruling elites may dictate the nature of the dominant religion in areas under their control. In 600 the British were Christians, as were the Irish, both those living in Britain and those who had remained in their homelands. The Irish had been converted with the aid of British missionaries such as Patrick and through other contacts with areas of Britain, and so the term 'Celtic church' is sometimes applied to describe the common features of the British and Irish churches, though as the seventh century progressed greater divergence of practice was to be found, and many commentators feel that to use a common term can be misleading.[2] In contrast, the conversion of the Anglo-Saxons and Picts to Christianity occurred somewhat later, beginning in the latter part of the sixth century, but gathering increasing momentum in the course of the seventh century. The date 597 would in fact be a more significant one for marking the start of this volume than 600, for that year saw both the death of Columba of Iona, who may have been the first to bring Christianity to the northern Picts, and the arrival in Kent of the mission despatched by Pope Gregory I and led by Augustine which had the express aim of effecting the conversion of the Anglo-Saxons.

Conversion and the Christianisation of the different peoples of Britain are therefore major topics within this book that also enable us to explore the workings of their political systems and the structures of their societies. As will emerge in Chapter 2, whose main topic is the conversion of Britain to Christianity, the decision whether to accept or reject Christianity or to support variant tendencies within the church could be a political one and the cooperation of rulers and the nobility was a prerequisite for establishing the structures that would allow a broader diffusion of Christianity within society. The process of the absorption of Christianity into the societies of early medieval Britain should enable us to study various aspects of them that are difficult to study by any other means. This is because whenever or wherever Christianity has been introduced it has always been adapted and affected, without fatal infringement of its basic tenets, to pre-existing social norms and religious beliefs. The most superficial consideration of Christian communities around the world today reveals how varied they can be in the forms of their worship and expressions of belief even though all draw on the same set of scriptural authority preserved in the Bible and share basic tenets of the faith and their liturgical manifestations. Even in just one branch of the Christian church, for instance that of the Roman Catholics, there are substantial differences in ecclesiastical culture between churches in Central America, Africa and Europe.

With such key issues in mind, Chapter 3 will look at the structures and culture introduced by the church into Britain and Chapter 4 will attempt to assess the impact of the church on native lay societies. In setting out his aims for the series the General Editor has regretted the tendency in many general histories to isolate the topic of religion in its own separate sections and even to view it as marginal in order 'to concentrate on matters which may seem more important to our increasingly secular-minded age'. It is the contention of this volume that such an approach would be completely inappropriate for the early Middle Ages. When the same families, and sometimes the same individuals, who provided the military and political muscle also commanded the churches, we have a period in which there was no simple separation into 'church' and 'state' and in which there was not a straightforward division between ecclesiastical and lay culture. In an early medieval world where death or disaster were never far way for a large percentage of the population, whose lives were closer to those of the third world today rather than that of the affluent west, religion and religious practice were matters of major import through which they might hope to combat crises and to win some control over their environment.

Although in the first part of Chapter 1 the individual histories of the four peoples of early medieval Britain are reviewed, the opportunity is taken elsewhere to compare more directly their societies and the practice of religion, though for some topics, such as the history of conversion, it will be necessary to deal with separate regions in turn. There has been a tendency in the past to study the early medieval histories of England, Wales and Scotland separately, although this series is part of a growing trend to look at Britain as an entity.[3] Rather surprisingly perhaps greater political devolution seems to have been accompanied by a desire among historians to think about Britain as a whole. Bringing together the histories of the four peoples should allow contrasts and comparisons to emerge more clearly. Unfortunately differential survival of evidence means that equal space cannot always be given to all four peoples. There is a greater number of contemporary records for the Anglo-Saxons than for the other peoples of Britain and so inevitably there are certain sections of this study which cannot avoid being dominated by the illustrative material that survives for the Anglo-Saxons. However, an attempt has been made to try to concentrate on certain topics for which evidence, including archaeological and artistic, does survive from all four territories. It is hoped that by placing some evidence which is poorly recorded from one area against the fuller evidence from another it will be possible to suggest further interpretation of fragmentary remains.

Written sources for the study of early medieval Britain

It will be apparent from what has been said already that what one can or cannot say about the early medieval period is restricted because of the nature of the surviving written material.[4] It is evident that what now survives is only a fraction of what once existed although it is difficult to say how representative that surviving material is. All provinces of early medieval Britain have suffered from considerable attrition of their records over time, but the problems seem to have been more severe in Celtic areas than those of the Anglo-Saxons. The reasons for this are no doubt complex, but probably have much to do with the greater continuity of major religious houses with substantial libraries until the Reformation in England, after which official and private collectors ensured that some of their contents were preserved. The poor conditions for survival in Wales are indicated by the fact that none of the few surviving manuscripts produced there before 1000 are preserved in Wales itself.[5] The case of the Picts is particularly desperate, for apart from the king-lists no records or other manuscripts that originated before 800 can be traced at all. This has led to the suggestion that Pictland never possessed a substantial body of written material, a claim which could have severe implications for the standards and effectiveness of the Pictish church.[6] However, brief written inscriptions on stone do survive from Pictland, and the sophisticated iconography of Pictish sculpture suggests the existence of a Christian intellectual and literary culture analogous to that to be found in contemporary Ireland or England.[7] The early loss of Pictish language and culture in the Gaelicised kingdom of Alba in ninth- and tenth-century Scotland probably provides much of the explanation for the disappearance of Pictish records. Without various works that originated in the monastery of Iona, the Irish kingdom of Dál Riata in western Scotland would be almost as poorly represented.

Chronicles and records of administration

The basic chronological framework for the study of early medieval Britain is provided by chronicles, many of which had their origin in annals, that is yearly entries made in the tables which were used to calculate when Easter would fall in any given year, though often the terms have been used interchangeably. A chronicle was kept on Iona from some point in the seventh century at least; there is no agreement on when its entries become contemporaneous. The 'Iona chronicle' does not survive as a discrete text and has had to be reconstructed from later Irish chronicles in which it was incorporated, those known as the *Annals of Ulster* and the *Annals of Tigernach* are the best witnesses to the original text.[8] The 'Iona chronicle' is our main source for events not only in Dál Riata, where the island of Iona was located, but also in Pictland, where the Ionan church had daughter houses. Contemporary annals may have been kept in Wessex from the middle of the seventh century, but are only known from their incorporation in the late ninth-century *Anglo-Saxon Chronicle*.[9] Bede appended chronicles of events to his two works on the reckoning of time, *De Temporibus* of 703 and *De Temporum Ratione* of 725, but greatly extended his coverage in the yearly entries appended to his *Ecclesiastical History*.[10] The latter inspired others to continue the keeping of such records after his death and the so-called 'northern annals', which may have been written in York and have been preserved through their incorporation in later chronicles, are a major source for events in Northumbria and other parts of northern Britain in the eighth century. Some events in Wales and other British areas are briefly recorded in the *Annales Cambriae* which may have been produced at the episcopal centre of St David's in the late eighth or ninth century, and may incorporate earlier annals from one of the northern British kingdoms in Scotland.[11] Annalistic records are characteristically very brief and so contrast with the much more detailed narrative account contained in Bede's *Ecclesiastical History*, which is discussed in greater detail below.

Another very significant category of written information can be broadly termed administrative. Lawcodes contain invaluable details about the organisation of society and the efforts of kings and the church to increase their control, even if the day-to-day administration of the law through local courts and orally transmitted tradition do not survive.[12] For the Anglo-Saxons three early lawcodes exist from Kent, those of Æthelbert (d. 616), Hlothere and Eadric (jointly reigning 679–85) and Wihtred (690–725) and one from Wessex associated with Wihtred's contemporary Ine (688–726); all are written in Old English. A considerably greater number of lawcodes and associated tracts survive from Ireland, written in both Latin and the vernacular during the seventh and eighth centuries, and are testimony to the important role of professional legal specialists there. The Irish laws have traditionally been used to aid understanding of the Irish colonies in Britain, but the wisdom of assuming that somewhere like Dál Riata would have operated in an identical way to Ireland itself has been questioned.[13] In contrast the earliest surviving laws from Wales were written down in the thirteenth century or later, although several claim descent from legal texts produced in the tenth century during the reign of Hywel Dda. It is possible to propose some reconstruction of aspects of earlier British society from the Welsh laws, particularly through a comparison of Welsh and Irish practice, but there are obviously problems in knowing the antiquity of practices and the rate of change.[14] There are also what could be seen as a form of ecclesiastical law, the penitentials that prescribed penances for specific sins. Examples survive from all areas of Britain (except Pictland) and are discussed in greater detail in Chapter 4 in the context of the impact of the church on lay society.[15] From Anglo-Saxon England there are in addition the records of some church councils or synods, and a greater range of other sources originating in ecclesiastical communities, such as letters, than is available for the Celtic areas of Britain.

Charters recorded gifts and other transactions concerning land. Their form came ultimately from the late Roman private deed and its use in British areas in the early Middle Ages can be presumed to indicate an unbroken practice from the late Roman period.[16] In Anglo-Saxon areas the written charter and the late Roman traditions of land tenure embodied within it were introduced as part of the process of conversion to Christianity, and the Anglo-Saxon tradition seems to draw on the practices of several different areas of Europe. There are no charters surviving from anywhere in early medieval Scotland for the period before 800, and it is unclear when the charter tradition was introduced there. Charters were utilised initially to record gifts of land from kings to the church, but in Anglo-Saxon England at least laymen soon acquired the right to hold land on similar terms and their acquisitions and gifts are also recorded. Such tenure was known in Old English as *bocland*, land held by 'book', that is, a charter. Among the useful attributes of charters are the listing of the boundaries of the land granted and the witnesses to the transaction that usually include rulers and important lay and ecclesiastical nobility. Some of the original charters drawn up in Anglo-Saxon England survive, but more commonly one has to work with later copies. Many later cartularies (that is, collections of charters) carefully preserved the original contents as the charters of the early Middle Ages continued to provide title to land, but charters might also be edited or abbreviated and 'improved' to give additional rights or to reflect later changes to estate history. When a religious community had land that had been in its possession for some time, but for which a charter did not actually exist, a complete charter could be forged, although such forgeries are often readily detectable through comparison with genuine texts. The problems that later interference could cause are particularly evident with the largest surviving collection of early Welsh charters incorporated in the *Book of Llandaf* (*Liber Landavensis*) from south-eastern Wales, which was drawn up between 1120 and 1134 as part of Bishop Urban's campaign to establish the boundaries and antiquity of his diocese.[17] The formulae and forms of names prove the antiquity of the charters, though none are dated. Problems arise over the degree of adaptation and editing that has occurred in accommodating the charters to Bishop Urban's overall purposes. One obvious piece of forgery is that the recipients are all designated as bishops of Llandaf, which is impossible as no early see of Llandaf existed; some other editorial changes may not be so easy to identify.

In the absence of adequate sources from the seventh and eighth centuries for the administration and organisation of society it is tempting to try to read back from later sources, but this is something that has to be done with great care. It may well be the case that the arrangement of estates and royal rights recorded in Scottish sources from the twelfth century and later have their origin in the organisation of the Pictish kingdom(s), but it is difficult to identify and date different layers of development with any certainty.[18] Administrative documents that survive only in later editions are also problematic as the discussion of charter collections such as those utilised in the *Book of Llandaf* has suggested. A difficult case is the tenth-century Scottish document known as the *Senchus fer nAlban* (The traditions of the men of Scotland), which is part genealogical tract and part survey of obligations in the province of Dál Riata. It has been argued that it reproduces an earlier document and can be used to reconstruct the organisation of the Scottish province of Dál Riata in the seventh century. However, one cannot rule out the possibility that the *Senchus* may in fact have undergone various stages of amendment to fit changing situations between the seventh and tenth centuries.[19] The organisation is confused, some information seems to have been omitted and figures and totals do not agree.

Education and theological study

Far more survives of the works that were studied and of a range of theological compositions from England and Ireland than from the Celtic areas of Britain, with the exception of Iona which was in any case an Irish foundation. It would be inappropriate to discuss such material in detail here; much of it has no overt historical content although it is very important for understanding the educational standards and culture of religious communities. Britain and Ireland, like other areas of the early medieval west, inherited a system of education that was derived ultimately from that of the late Roman empire for those entering public life, but which had been gradually adapted to the needs of the church, for instance by substituting Christian for pagan authors. The language of the church was Latin so those entering the church had to receive basic instruction in the language, and the more able and privileged would receive a thorough grounding in grammar, rhetoric and dialectic, the *trivium*, to enable advanced composition in prose and verse.[20] A thorough knowledge and understanding of the Bible was a dominant aim of these studies. The novice began by learning by heart the psalms, which had a central role in the liturgy of the church, and would progress to more detailed biblical study and interpretation. The composition of commentaries on the Bible to bring out literal and allegorical meaning was one of the most revered forms of scholarship.[21] It must be appreciated that anyone writing in Latin in this period would have received this type of clerical education and that their minds would be full of biblical allusions and parallels through which they would attempt to interpret their contemporary world.

Genealogies and poetry

All original compositions of the period show their indebtedness to Christian learning, but some reveal something of lay values and attitudes as well. Genealogies, for instance, traced the descent of rulers from founder kings, heroes and gods, and seem to have been valued at both Celtic and Germanic courts. Their origins may lie with oral records, but in the form they come down to us they are literary productions and influenced in their form and construction by the genealogies of the Bible. They are one example of the complex intermingling of oral and written traditions that one finds in societies such as those of early medieval Britain which are perhaps best designated as 'semi-literate'. Genealogies, like other oral records, were not static productions, but could grow or contract to suit new political situations or literary fashions.[22] The date and context in which they were written are therefore vital for correctly interpreting royal genealogies, which are not such archaic or simple productions as they may at first appear. Genealogies for many Anglo-Saxon royal houses survive from the ninth century, and there is a contemporary counterpart for the Welsh royal house of Powys carved on the Pillar of Eliseg, near Llangollen. A major written collection of British royal genealogies, the Harleian Genealogy, seems to have been brought together in the mid-tenth century.

Poetry may provide an important guide to lay ideals that originated outside a Christian context, even if a careful adaptation of these mores may have been made to make them more compatible with a Christian ethos. Two major poems have often been claimed to have had their origins in the period before 800, the Brittonic poem *The Gododdin* and the Old English *Beowulf*, but in both cases the date is controversial and the subject of ongoing debate. *The Gododdin* is not one coherent poem, but a series of verses that survive in two differing versions and which lament the fate of heroes from northern British kingdoms who conducted an ill-fated raid on the Northumbrian centre of Catterick (though even this basic level of narrative has been the subject of controversy).[23] *Beowulf* is not set in this country at all, but in areas of southern Scandinavia from which some of the Germanic settlers may have come to eastern England. Beowulf, in the first section, is a prince from southern Sweden who establishes his reputation by ridding Denmark of the water-monsters Grendel and his mother, and in the second part loses his life protecting his people, the Geats, from a dragon. Both works share an admiration for heroic ideals and describe in loving detail weapons and other gifts of a type represented in the archaeological record. Although *Beowulf* in the form we have it survives in a manuscript from about 1000, there are remnants of more archaic language that suggest it may have originated in the eighth or ninth century.[24] The two versions of *The Gododdin* survive in a manuscript of the thirteenth century and the Welsh in which they are written is largely of that period, but with possible archaisms that are difficult to date. Part of the debate about the poem's date is concerned with whether this has to mean that the versions were composed in a Middle Welsh period or whether it is conceivable that Middle Welsh scribes updated an earlier text. Some Old English poems on more overtly Christian themes, known from later Anglo-Saxon manuscripts, may have been composed before 800, as is usually assumed to have been the case with the version of *The Dream of the Rood* carved on the eighth-century Ruthwell Cross (Dumfriesshire).[25] There are also some early Gaelic verses that may have been written on Iona.[26]

Hagiographies

The ecclesiastical counterparts of the secular heroes of *Beowulf* and *The Gododdin* were the saints.[27] By the seventh century hagiography, the Lives of saints, had become a distinct literary genre for which the *Life of St Martin*, bishop of Tours (d. 397) written by Sulpicius Severus and the *Life of St Anthony*, a hermit in fourth-century Egypt, by Bishop Athanasius of Alexandria (d. 373), known in the west through a Latin translation by Evagrius, were major exemplars for the religious communities of Britain. Latin Lives of the saints were not automatically written in Britain to support the development of a cult, and it would appear that those we do have were produced in response to particular circumstances and crises. One such major stimulus seems to have occurred in

Northumbria in the aftermath of the synod of *Streanæshalch* (usually identified as Whitby) of 664 when it had been decided to reject the methods of calculating Easter introduced by missionaries from Iona, whose Northumbrian centre was at Lindisfarne, in favour of those used in Rome and Canterbury. The controversy had deep repercussions in Northumbria, not least because of the hard-line stance taken by Bishop Wilfrid (d. 709) who had presented the 'Roman' case at Whitby and called the Ionan clergy heretics. He seems to have continued a campaign against any survival of 'Irish errors' and distrusted any communities that remained in contact with Iona or other Irish religious houses which did not follow the Roman Easter, but his influence was intermittent as he fell out with the Northumbrian kings Ecgfrith (670–85) and Aldfrith (686–705) and was exiled from Northumbria for several years. The upshot was that the major religious houses of Northumbria felt a need to justify their positions and the reputations of their leaders who had lived through this turbulent time.[28] An anonymous *Life of St Cuthbert*, bishop of Lindisfarne (d. 687) was produced some time between 699 and 705, and had been substantially rewritten by Bede by 721. Stephen, a monk of Ripon, had written a *Life of St Wilfrid* by 715, but this seems to have been revised subsequently in the 730s. A *Life of Pope Gregory the Great* was written at Whitby, probably between 704 and 714, and a *Life of Ceolfrith*, abbot of Wearmouth and Jarrow soon after his death in 716, and a *History of the Abbots* of Wearmouth and Jarrow was produced by Bede, probably at some point between 725 and 731. The Northumbrian troubles may also have been in part a reason for Adomnán's composition of the *Life of St Columba*, which was completed about 697, for Wilfrid had cast aspersions on Columba's reputation.[29] Adomnán's work may in turn have helped to stimulate the production of the Northumbrian series. In contrast only one *Life* survives from southern England in this period, Felix's *Life of St Guthlac*, a Mercian saint who died in 714, though others may have been lost, for Bede cites a book containing miracles of the nuns of Barking in his *Ecclesiastical History* that does not otherwise survive.[30] Lives were also written for churchmen, such as Willibrord and Boniface, and one churchwoman, Leoba, who went from Anglo-Saxon provinces, principally from Northumbria and Wessex, in the late seventh and eighth centuries to work among the Germanic peoples of mainland Europe.[31] Although following established conventions, many of these early hagiographies are more individualistic than they might at first appear and provide invaluable evidence on how Christianity was absorbed by the societies of early medieval Britain.

In Wales there is no certain evidence that hagiographies were written before the late eleventh and twelfth centuries, though it is possible that some material in the ninth-century *Historia Brittonum* may derive from lost Lives. The earliest Life of St Samson of Dol, who was born and educated in south Wales, was probably written in Brittany in the eighth century (though opinions vary) and preserves traditions of his life in sixth-century Britain.[32] The major stimulus within Wales for producing hagiography of its early saints came from the circumstances of the Anglo-Norman conquest that led to native clergy and Anglo-Norman newcomers writing Lives in order to protect their possessions or to extend their claims to jurisdiction and precedence over their rivals.[33] The *Life of St Cadog* was written by Lifris of Llancarfan probably in the 1080s or 1090s, but is known only through incorporation of part of it into a later version, and the *Life of St David* by Rhigyfarch of Llanbadarn Fawr around 1095. David is said to have been consecrated archbishop by the patriarch of Jerusalem, in preference to his 'rivals' Teilo and Padarn, and to have had the appointment confirmed subsequently by a synod of 118 bishops. The later *Life of St Cadog* countered this claim by stating that Cadog had been absent on a pilgrimage to Jerusalem when the synod was held and that David had declared Cadog was more worthy of the honour than himself. Bishop Urban promoted the claims of Llandaf through including *Lives* of Dyfrig, Teilo and Euddogwy in the *Book of Llandaf* of *c*.1130. Urban was anxious to prove the antiquity and orthodoxy of his see, which was said to have followed the teaching of Rome since its foundation by Pope Eleutherius in the second century AD, and that it had recognised the authority of Canterbury since the time of Augustine. These claims, of course, can have had no genuine basis and run counter to what is known from more contemporary sources. The Welsh hagiographies provide classic examples of the practice of projecting contemporary concerns back into the historic past, and while they are informative about the times in which they were written they are of limited value for those they purport to describe, unless they can be shown to have had access to genuine earlier written material. Rhigyfarch's *Life of St David*, for instance, incorporates extracts from David's monastic rule which seems to accord with the little that can be pieced together about his life and work from earlier sources.[34] However, much of the content of these later Welsh Lives has to be classed as literary embellishment, though they may also incorporate traditions that had evolved over the centuries in localities which had, or were believed to have had, an association with the saint with which they are concerned.

In Scotland the rejuvenation of the church and introduction of Anglo-Norman influences in the reign of King David I (1124–53) seems to have provided a comparable stimulus for the writing of hagiography to protect established interests and proclaim the antiquity of relatively new initiatives. The *Life of St Kentigern* was commissioned in about 1180 by Bishop Jocelyn of Glasgow from Jocelyn of Furness to replace an earlier version written for Bishop Herbert of Glasgow (1147–64), of which only a fragment survives.[35] Jocelyn's version is the skilled work of a major hagiographer which combines oral traditions, borrowings from earlier works and inferences from the dedications of churches, though that does not mean that what he says is any more reliable. One of its prime purposes, and doubtless that of the Herbertian *Life* as well, was to claim that Glasgow had been founded as the see of Kentigern. There is some evidence for an early cemetery at Glasgow, as Jocelyn claims, though the role of King Rhydderch of Dumbarton in the foundation of any church there is suspect because his name may have been taken from Adomnán's *Life of Columba*, and sculptural and other evidence suggest that nearby Govan had been the more significant centre prior to the twelfth century.[36] Other correlations with known figures from early Scottish history produce further problems. Kentigern, whose death is placed in the *Annales Cambriae* between 612 and 614, is said to have studied with St Serf of Culross, but the latter's *Life,* which may also have been produced in the twelfth century, seems to locate him around 700.[37] The *Life* of Serf, and that of his near contemporary Curetán, which is only known in any detail from inclusion in the Aberdeen Breviary that was published in 1510,[38] display an even greater anachronistic and aggrandising use of the past than their Welsh equivalents. Serf is said to have been the son of a King of Canaan and to have been patriarch of Jerusalem and pope before basing himself at Culross, while Curetán (under his religious name of Boniface) was also claimed to have been pope and to have descended from the sister of St Peter and St Andrew! There is clearly a great difference in the potential value for the historian of the seventh and eighth centuries between these Welsh and Scottish Lives written many centuries later with often minimal factual evidence at the disposal of their authors, and those of the Northumbrian saints discussed earlier that were written within living memory of their subjects. There may also have been a propagandic purpose behind the composition of the latter, but it was one rooted in the seventh- and eighth-century concerns of the period in which their subjects had been actively involved.

Gildas, Adomnán and Bede

Because of their value as contemporary commentators these three authors, who were pre-eminent among the early medieval scholars from Britain, have been singled out for particular discussion and their writings will be referred to frequently in the rest of the book. Their main works of historical import are readily available in English translation or, better still, editions with parallel Latin and translated texts, and anyone who wishes to consult them can find additional portrayals of early medieval life to supplement the examples that are utilised elsewhere in this book.

Gildas (d. c.570?)

Very little is known for certain about Gildas beyond his writings which is why questions of when and where he wrote remain controversial. Some scholars, on the basis of the quality of his Latin and the chronology implicit in his major work *De Excidio Britanniae* (Concerning the Fall of Britain), have seen him as writing in the late fifth century,[39] but the broader consensus is that Gildas was primarily a figure of the sixth century.[40] His death is placed in the Irish chronicles and the *Annales Cambriae* as occurring in 570; this must be a retrospective entry, but could be based on accurate information. Arguments have been advanced in favour of both northern and western Britain as the places where he wrote, but his more detailed knowledge is of the west, especially his devastating criticism of the kings of Wales and Dumnonia (Devon and Cornwall) where he refers to events that had taken place during the previous year. An attractive proposition is that he wrote in the south-west, in part of the former Roman province of *Britannia Prima*, but outside the immediate reach of the kings he excoriates, perhaps in Dorset or Wiltshire.[41]

De Excidio has received much attention for the information it provides about the circumstances in which the Anglo-Saxons came to eastern Britain in the fifth century. These were events that occurred before Gildas's birth and there has been dispute over whether he possessed accurate information or if he placed their arrival correctly within his relative chronology. Equally important, and arguably more reliable, is the insight he provides into the political and ecclesiastical circumstances of the time in which he wrote. Relatively little has survived that was written in western Britain between 600 and 800, which is why Gildas has been used as a major witness in this book in spite of falling outside its main timespan. However, in consulting the work allowance has to be made for the style in which it was written and the purposes that lay behind its construction. *De Excidio* was not intended as a work of history, but as a kind of extended sermon in which contemporaries, especially the clergy, were rebuked for their poor Christian standards and a general spiritual regeneration and raising of moral standards urged. It presents challenges for the modern reader as it is written in the rhetorical style of the late Roman classical schools, and has extensive quotations from and references to the Bible, especially the Old Testament. Gildas's style is in itself of value to the historian for it testifies to the high quality of his education and learning that was presumably shared by others among his contemporaries as he expected them to be able to understand and benefit from his work. Gildas can be placed in the context of other major writers in former areas of the Roman empire in the fifth and sixth centuries who strove to direct their contemporaries down the correct road of Christian behaviour in an often violent and unsettled post-Roman world.[42]

Gildas was also the author of a penitential that is only known in part, together with some other pronouncements on matters of ecclesiastical discipline and organisation, through a tenth-century manuscript from Brittany.[43] These works are thought to date from the latter period of Gildas's life when he had become a monastic leader. Gildas seems to have been revered in Ireland and Brittany as one of the major figures of the early British church who had influenced their practices and whose works were studied in later centuries. One of the fragments of his writings shows him to have been in correspondence with the important northern British churchman Uinniau who was also influential in contemporary Ireland and is probably also recorded for posterity under the names Findbarr of Moville and Ninian of Whithorn.[44] Gildas also influenced Anglo-Saxon authors – though in less positive ways. *De Excidio* may have become known to Anglo-Saxon scholars after the West Saxon takeover of western Britain in the seventh century. Bede made extensive use of it in Book 1 of his *Ecclesiastical History* and based his own calculations of the date of the Anglo-Saxon *adventus* on Gildas's information. Gildas's critical view of his British contemporaries contributed to Bede's negative attitude towards the British church of his day that was also fuelled by the refusal of the western British clergy to accept the authority of Pope Gregory's representative Augustine and, as Bede saw it, by the failure of the British church to aid the conversion of the Anglo-Saxons to Christianity.[45]

Adomnán (c.627–704)

Adomnán was the ninth abbot of Iona, the island monastery founded in the Irish kingdom of Dál Riata by Columba in 563. Like most other early abbots of Iona, Adomnán was related to Columba and both were members of the powerful Cenél Conaill, the lineage that regularly provided the overlord kings of the northern Uí Neíll.[46] While Adomnán was abbot his fourth cousin Loingsech became king of Tara in 696, and so head of both northern and southern branches of the Uí Neíll. Adomnán came from a different branch of the dynasty from his predecessors among the abbots of Iona who had been related to Columba and unlike most of them had probably not been educated from an early age on the island. He may have come to Iona during the time of Abbot Failbe (669–79). Adomnán was an influential figure in Ireland and northern Britain who utilised his royal birth and contacts. With the aid of his kinsman Loingsech he persuaded 91 ecclesiastical leaders and kings from Ireland and northern Britain to be guarantors of his 'Law of the Innocents', which aimed to protect women, children and the religious from involvement in warfare.[47] He twice visited, in 686 and 688, the court of King Aldfrith of Northumbria (686–705) whose succession he had aided, and also visited Pictland whose king, Bridei, son of Derilei (697–706) was one of the guarantors of the 'Law of the Innocents'. While in Northumbria Adomnán seems to have become personally convinced on a visit to Jarrow under Abbot Ceolfrith that the forms of calculating Easter as practised there were correct, but he was unable to persuade the community of Iona to change, and seems to have preferred not to press the issue. Adomnán's penitential rulings were collected by his followers and preserved in the *Canones Adamnani*.[48]

Adomnán's two main literary productions were both written on Iona; *De Locis Sanctis* ('The Holy Places') must have been composed by 686 as a copy was presented to King Aldfrith soon after his accession, and the *Life of St Columba* was perhaps produced for 697, the hundredth anniversary of Columba's death, though revisions may have continued to be carried out subsequently. The detailed study of both works has revealed the depth of Adomnán's learning and theological understanding. Both are very original pieces that do not entirely conform to the conventions of the genres they represent. *De Locis Sanctis* was purportedly based on the account a Frankish bishop called Arculf gave to Adomnán of a visit to the Holy Land, Rome, Alexandria and Constantinople. Whatever Arculf may have supplied – and some have seen him as an invented literary device – Adomnán takes the opportunity to resolve various textual contradictions in the gospels through reference to the geography of the Holy Land in a very innovative way.[49] This was the book for which Adomnán was best known in the Middle Ages, and Bede thought so highly of it (though not of Adomnán's intricate written style) that he produced his own version.

Adomnán's *Life of St Columba* was probably written with the intention of protecting the reputation of the saint after the synod of Whitby of 664 when Wilfrid had intimated that he was a false prophet and at a time when Patrick and Brigit, the saints of rival monastic confederations in Ireland, were being actively promoted by Armagh and Kildare respectively.[50] Adomnán made use of an earlier *Life of St Columba* written by Cumméne (abbot of Iona 657–69) who seems to have made a major effort to record traditions about Columba while some who had known him were still alive. We only know about Cumméne's work because an early copyist included an extract from it and it is not clear how dependent upon it Adomnán was.[51] Adomnán is always careful to name the witnesses for the stories concerning Columba and to explain how the evidence had been transmitted in a very legalistic way. The *Life* eschews the normal chronological treatment of the subject's life that characterises contemporary hagiography in favour of a tripartite division into miracles of power, miracles of prophecy and angelic manifestations. The treatment reveals that Adomnán had thoroughly internalised the portrayal of sanctity in continental exemplars, especially the *Dialogues* of Pope Gregory the Great concerning various Italian saints, and by the implied parallels with these exemplars he established unimpeachable saintly credentials for Columba.[52] Columba's miracles are placed amid the daily round of activities on Iona and during his travels to Pictland and Ireland, and it is partly for this incidental background that the work is so valued as a historical source. But one must never forget that it is a very subtle piece of work whose many intricacies are only being gradually unfolded. As a theological commentator (or exegete) Adomnán was used to reading texts on different levels and some of his material may not be as straightforward as it might at first appear. Adomnán was as we have seen an influential figure at contemporary courts and Columba emerges as someone with similar political interests. It can be suspected that some of Adomnán's commentary on politics apparently located in the time of Columba has been shaped in order to be relevant to the situation of his own day. References to Columba's ordination of Aedan mac Gabráin and designation of his younger son Eochaid Buide as his heir may be connected with competition for the throne of Dál Riata between rival kin-groups in Adomnán's own time,[53] and the prominence given to Columba's intervention on behalf of King Oswald of Northumbria seems to recall Adomnán's assistance in helping his nephew Aldfrith to the throne.[54]

Bede (c.673–735)

When Adomnán visited Ceolfrith at Jarrow in c.688, Bede would have been in the monastery as a novice monk in his early teens, and it is therefore possible that memories of Adomnán contributed to Bede's very positive view of the earlier Ionan missionaries to Northumbria and his vivid pen-portrait of their leader Bishop Aidan in the *Ecclesiastical History*.[55] Bede himself provides a brief autobiographical sketch at the end of the *Ecclesiastical History* from which we learn that he was born on one of the estates belonging to Benedict Biscop's monastic foundation at Wearmouth (founded c.673) and that he was entered into the foundation as a boy-monk (oblate) at the age of seven, by which time, or soon after, Biscop had established a second house at Jarrow (founded c.681).[56] He spent the rest of his life at Wearmouth and Jarrow and was ordained a priest at the canonical age of 30 (c.703). Bede never held high office in Wearmouth and Jarrow, or elsewhere in the Northumbrian church, but was influential through his teaching and his many authored works, of which he provides a list. He placed first his 20 or so theological commentaries on books of the Old and New Testament. Although remembered today principally as a historian, Bede would undoubtedly have described himself primarily as a theologian and expert in the art of exegesis, the expounding of the literal and allegorical meaning of the scriptures, and it is important to remember that he approached the history of the Anglo-Saxons through a thorough study of biblical history. In his commentaries Bede drew upon earlier works by Jerome, Augustine and other Fathers of the Church, but expounded and reconciled their traditions with such clarity and skill that his works were in demand throughout the Middle Ages. Also extremely influential were his books of homilies or sermons, and his textbooks on grammar, computus and cosmology. Bede also produced two books of Latin verse, and in addition to the *Ecclesiastical History* his historical works included a book of the lives of the martyrs, prose and verse accounts of the life of St Cuthbert and a history of the abbots of Monkwearmouth and Jarrow.

For the modern historian of seventh- and eighth-century Britain, Bede's *Historia Ecclesiastica Gentis Anglorum*, whose title is generally translated into modern English as *The Ecclesiastical History of the*

English People,[57] is an essential work and although, as its title suggests, its main focus is the history of the Anglo-Saxons, there is also information about the other peoples of Britain within it. It was Bede's last major work, completed in 731, though he may have continued to revise it afterwards. The preface that is addressed to the contemporary king of Northumbria, Ceolwulf (729–37) emphasises that it is a didactic work, providing models of good and bad behaviour. Bede, following the approach for the Romans adopted by Eusebius of Caesarea in his *Historia Ecclesiastica*, casts the Anglo-Saxons as a new Chosen People whose destiny was to lead the other peoples of Britain towards correct forms of Christian observance. The work follows a clear chronological format, beginning with references to Britain in classical writers and proceeding up to Bede's own day, though showing a regrettable – from the point of view of the modern historian – reticence as it approached the period in which he wrote. Although Bede does not discuss contemporary problems directly in the *Ecclesiastical History* that does not mean he did not have them in mind as he wrote. A letter he sent to his former pupil Ecgbert, bishop of York, in 734 addressed the need for reform in the Northumbrian church, a topic Bede had previously addressed more obliquely in some of his biblical commentaries. There were also political uncertainties, and in 731 King Ceolwulf temporarily lost and then recovered his throne, but was forced to abdicate in favour of a rival branch of the royal house in 737.

It is when one begins to contemplate Bede's problems in putting together his wide-ranging survey that one's admiration for his achievements grows. Bede had relatively few written works to rely on and was dependent upon information supplied by correspondents and visitors to Wearmouth and Jarrow, and, like Adomnán, he was careful to name his sources.[58] There was no universal system of dating used in Bede's sources or by his correspondents, and not the least of his achievements was to fit his material into a system of *Anno Domini* dating that had been little used in Britain before he wrote. Not surprisingly some inconsistencies and possible misunderstandings have been noted by modern commentators, but all who follow Bede are dependent upon him for the ordering of events. In providing his exemplars of good and bad behaviour from the Anglo-Saxon past Bede demonstrated his understanding of contemporary attitudes and rooted his accounts in everyday life. For instance, when describing the knife carried by the would-be assassin of King Edwin, he carefully specifies that it was a double-edged dagger,[59] and so brings to mind the detailed attention paid to the weaponry and equipment of the elite in contemporary Old English poetry.

The dominance of one man's view of the early history of Britain produces some undoubted problems, particularly when that man was an exceptionally skilful writer with definite views he wished to promote. Bede's vision of an Anglo-Saxon destiny under God may have led him to downplay or distort the achievements of the other peoples in Britain.[60] Bede has not a good word to say about British churchmen, particularly because he claims they did not try to convert the English to Christianity, a claim some modern commentators would regard as suspect. On the other hand, he is very generous in his praise of the Irish, particularly the missionaries from Iona who played a major part in the conversion of Northumbria and whose abbot Adomnán visited Jarrow in Bede's youth. Although for much of the period he covers both Iona and many British churches were not in conformity with Roman practice over the date of Easter, Bede endeavoured to find the most favourable interpretation of Ionan attitudes, while condemning the British outright. The Picts appear mainly incidentally as a people the Northumbrians fought in battle or who were brought to correct Christian practice by Ionan and Anglo-Saxon intervention.

Bede's view was not simply Anglo-centric; it also favoured Northumbrian achievements over those of other Anglo-Saxon provinces. The plotting on a map of places mentioned in the *Ecclesiastical History* shows the limits of Bede's geographical coverage.[61] Very few places in the western half of Britain are mentioned at all, including those parts that were in Anglo-Saxon hands by 731. In eastern Britain there is a concentration of references to places in Northumbria and intermittent references to other Anglo-Saxon kingdoms in eastern and southern England. Very few places in modern Scotland are mentioned by name and Bede's remarks about the Picts and Irish of northern Britain are often very generalised. To some extent Bede was limited by the geographical spread of his correspondents and the information they chose to provide for him, but this does not seem a completely adequate explanation for some omissions. Bede, for instance, treats the overlordship of Mercian kings as less significant than that of Northumbrians and the former are excluded from a list of the great overlords who held power south of the Humber, a list that may have been composed or extended by Bede himself.[62] Also suspicious is the downplaying of the achievements of certain notable West Saxons. Bede does pay a somewhat muted tribute to the West Saxon Aldhelm, but it is one that scarcely does justice to the depth and originality of his writing or his achievements in incorporating British Christians into the West Saxon church, in spite of the fact that one of his informants was a

Northumbrian bishop who had been with Aldhelm for many years.[63] Bede makes much of Northumbrian missionaries to the continental Germans, but does not mention the West Saxon Boniface who was a major ecclesiastical influence among Germanic peoples recently conquered by the Franks. Some of Bede's correspondents undoubtedly knew of the work of Boniface and it is hard to believe that Bede could not have written about him if he had wanted to do so. Bede may have helped the 'English' to view themselves as an unified people with a common church, but he also undoubtedly believed that the achievements of the Northumbrians were more significant than those of other Anglo-Saxon peoples.

Inscriptions and Pictish symbols

Fortunately there is some compensation for the severe shortage of written sources from western and northern Britain in the form of short inscriptions carved on stone monuments. In the early Middle Ages such carved inscriptions were largely limited to highland areas, where there was a ready supply of suitable stone, but the practice was never universal – it was only utilised in certain areas and by certain groups within society. The ultimate inspiration came from the Roman practice of setting up inscriptions. In the fifth and sixth centuries the production of inscriptions ceased in the more Romanised areas of Britain, but began to be found in the less Romanised areas of the west and in British areas beyond the Roman frontiers.[64] The earliest inscriptions from these areas are in Latin and are clearly based on their late Roman predecessors. Most appear to have been memorials to the dead and were probably grave-markers. In addition to giving the name of the deceased, the inscriptions may indicate their ancestry or status and name whoever was responsible for having the stone erected. Many contain symbolism or phrases associated with Christianity, and the movement beyond the Roman frontiers of Britain of the practice of raising such inscriptions can be presumed to be linked with the spread of that religion (though it was not taken up in all British communities of the far west and north).

Roman inscriptions also had an impact in some areas of Ireland, and the practice seems to have inspired the invention of an alphabet known as ogham that was used for inscriptions on stone in Gaelic, and probably in other contexts as well.[65] Letters were rendered by groups of vertical and horizontal lines arranged around a central staff. The date and circumstances for the development of ogham remain controversial, but it is possible that it too was linked with the spread of Christianity to Ireland from Romanised areas of Britain in the fourth and fifth centuries. Ogham stones generally record the name of the deceased and their paternal descent, and as in Britain may have been raised over inhumation burials, though later Irish writers suggest that in addition to being memorials to the dead they were seen as boundary markers and proof of ownership of an estate, and one can see how these functions might be interrelated. Ogham inscriptions are concentrated in parts of southern Ireland, but are also to be found in parts of northern Pictland and of Wales and the south-west where they are presumed to represent settlement from Ireland. Inscriptions in these areas may be bilingual, and include, in addition to the ogham, inscriptions in Latin in the Roman alphabet.

At this point one can note that the Germanic areas of the North Sea from whence the ancestors of the Anglo-Saxons came to Britain also developed their own alphabet as a result of contact with the Roman world, though without a link with the adoption of Christianity. Early use of the Germanic runic alphabet is known through inscriptions on small portable objects, and it was only after their conversion to Christianity in the seventh century that the Anglo-Saxons erected stone monuments on which, in Northumbria, runic might be one of the scripts used, especially for inscriptions in Old English.[66]

The fourth distinctive form of incised communication in use in Britain in the early Middle Ages is the Pictish symbols. The symbols form a reper-toire of about 50 designs that have survived in various forms of stone-carving and incised on metalwork and other small portable objects. About 30 have been identified as 'core' symbols that are found regularly in pairs.[67] Most of these are abstract or geometric forms such as the cres-cent and V-rod or the double-disc and Z-rod, but some animal symbols were also used regularly in paired combination including representations of stags, boars, fish, eagles and snakes and the probably imaginary 'Pictish beast'. Many of the splendidly naturalistic animal symbols appear on their own as well, or accompanying paired symbols, as do representations of men and other animals such as bulls and bears that are not found in com-bination with symbols. Among the few recognisable objects are a comb and mirror that often accompany paired symbols. The stones are found throughout the area of historic Pictland, including the islands of Orkney and Shetland, though they are rarer in the areas of north-west Scotland that are believed to have been under Pictish control. Some symbols recur throughout the province, but a few have a distinctively regional distri-bution such as the triple-oval symbol that seems to have been limited to Caithness. Categorisation of the carvings with symbols follows that made by Romilly Allen in his major study of 1903.[68] Class I comprises undressed stones, including caves and rocky outcrops, on which symbols have been incised; and Class II are cross-slabs, on which symbols have been carved in relief and are often associated with Christian iconography. The distinction is often seen as a chronological one, and while it is certainly the case that the majority of Class II stones must have been carved after the conversion of the Picts to Christianity, and so date to the seventh century and later, it need not follow that Class I stones were no longer produced after this date.

There have been many attempts to explain the meaning of the symbols that have clustered around ways in which they might have reinforced the rights and position of the Pictish elite.[69] One of the most exciting suggestions to emerge in recent years is that the paired symbols may have been used as a form of writing, a proposal that would fit well with the development of distinctive alphabets among the Irish and Germanic peoples for recording inscriptions in their own language in the fourth and fifth centuries. It has long been suggested that many of the Class I stones were raised as burial markers or other memorials to the dead as were the inscribed stones in other areas of Britain. The most common feature of these stones is a record of the commemorated person's name, and Ross Samson has suggested that this is also how the paired symbols on the Class I stones should be read, that is as representing two words (either two nouns, two adjectives or a noun and an adjective) that together make up a name – on the same principle as Anglo-Saxon names such as Wulfgar 'wolf-spear' or Æthelred 'noble council'.[70] Katharine Forsyth has gone further to explore how the symbols could have worked as a system of writing.[71] These are promising avenues for future research, but some of the forms used as symbols must have been used in other ways as well. The splendid bull plaques from the promontory fort of Burghead in Moray must have had their own specific connotations, perhaps a totem of the tribe or rulers to whom the site belonged or to a god who was honoured there. It is also likely that the use of some symbols goes back further into the prehistoric past. However, these caveats need not rule out the possibility that an existing symbolic system was developed to create a form of writing to record simple inscriptions in the Pictish language at a time when the Picts were developing as a major power in late Roman and post-Roman Britain.

Allen designated other carvings from Pictland with 'Celtic' decoration but no symbols as Class III, but the categorisation no longer seems very meaningful. The cross-slabs of the eighth and ninth centuries, whether with or without symbols, are among the greatest achievements of Pictish art. Abstract art in the insular style is combined with human and animal figures in a similar style to the symbol-designs, sometimes in complex narrative scenes depicting battles, animal hunts and biblical iconography.[72] In the absence of Pictish texts, these sculptures are the closest we can come to statements about facets of their society made by the Picts themselves, and in the following pages they will often be cited as evidence alongside the written texts that survive from other areas of early medieval Britain.

Conclusion

The twentieth century saw major changes in the attitudes to the sources though which one can study seventh- and eighth-century Britain, and as a result studies written at the beginning and the end of the century can appear very different, particularly on the topic of church history. A major development was the realisation that the Lives of Welsh and Scottish saints written in the eleventh and twelfth centuries could not be taken as providing an adequate guide to events many centuries earlier. Much of the narrative of 'the age of the saints' had been derived from these works, and the difficulty of reconstructing an alternative account based on more contemporary records and archaeological evidence has meant that there has been some reluctance to abandon these sources altogether, especially in more popular accounts. Work is ongoing on reaching a more complete understanding of Wales and Scotland in the early Middle Ages, and there has been much innovative work from Scotland in particular in recent years which suggests that a greater understanding will eventually be reached, especially through study of place-names and church dedications as well as reassessments of the written material. However, one has to admit that knowledge is likely to remain incomplete on many important issues and that interpretations may differ widely as a result.

The second half of the twentieth century saw a thorough reappraisal of many aspects of early Anglo-Saxon history, of which there have been many notable studies. The task of studying the Anglo-Saxons has been easier because so many more contemporary written sources survive, but there have been significant changes in attitude towards the sources with the realisation that most early medieval writers had specific aims in writing that addressed contemporary issues. Historians are now less inclined than they once were to take what early medieval authors say at face value, and instead try to consider how the writings were meant to affect their contemporary audience and how different sectors of that audience might have received them. It has also been appreciated that one must not project characteristics of subsequent periods back on to the early medieval past without examining such assumptions carefully, and this has resulted, for instance, in the appreciation that the demarcation between ecclesiastical and lay culture was not as clearly defined as it was to be in later centuries. The substantial amount of archaeological evidence for the Anglo-Saxons has also suggested different approaches to their history and stimulated new readings of the written evidence, although it is also true that historians and archaeologists do not always agree on the relative weight that is to be given to different forms of evidence that seem to offer varying interpretations.

As a result of these changes in approach to the written sources, the increasing contribution from other disciplines, such as archaeology and place-names, and the consideration of parallels from other areas of early medieval Europe, there have been, in the course of the twentieth century, some major shifts in approach to key issues that affect the study of the period 600 to 800. Secondary works written at different times may therefore vary considerably in their treatment of certain fundamental points. Areas of controversy include the effects of the severance of formal links with the Roman empire at the beginning of the fifth century, in which the survival of Christianity is a major issue, and how pastoral care was provided in early medieval Britain and Ireland, which is linked with broader questions of the organisation of the early medieval church in Britain, and whether that of the Celtic-speaking areas in particular differed in significant ways from that of other areas of Europe. Further guidance on such debates will be provided in the appropriate sections, but it is important to appreciate that research is ongoing and the last word has not been said on many of these issues. Such controversies make early medieval Britain an exciting area in which to work, even if it is not always easy to write about or study. This book will attempt to provide a guide through the often conflicting evidence and approaches, and set out the evidence as clearly as possible to allow the reader to draw his or her own conclusions, but, like all historians, the author may sometimes be found promoting views that are peculiarly her own.

A postscript on names

One of the problems confronting the novice studying early medieval Britain is the mass of unfamiliar names that may appear in variant forms in different secondary works. Any names which do appear familiar are likely to be those of saints that were used as Christian names in later centuries, such as Cuthbert and Oswald. Older works would frequently present names from all areas of Britain in anglicised versions, but it is the regular practice today to represent a name in the language that its owner would have spoken, that is Irish names in Gaelic and British names in Brittonic, and that is the convention generally followed here. Usually the forms that command most frequent usage among modern writers have been followed, but there is not always complete agreement on such issues. The case of Pictish names is particularly problematic. For instance, the name of the king who is referred to in this work as 'Onuist' (729–61) appears in a number of variant forms in contemporary or near-contemporary texts: 'to the Gaels he was *Óengus*, to (some) Anglo-Saxons he was *Unust* ... to Picts he may have been *Ungus(t)* or *Oniust*'.[73] Exceptions have been made where an individual is so well known by a particular name form that it might be unnecessarily misleading to render it in another way. The most notable example is Columba of Iona, whose name sometimes appears in modern works in the Irish form of 'Colum Cille'. However, although *columba* is a Latin word meaning 'dove' it was, as Adomnán assures us, applied to the saint from his earliest days.[74] A flexible approach has also been taken with titles of primary sources where clarity for the modern reader has been balanced by the need to ensure ease of cross-reference to other modern works. Many titles of early medieval sources have been translated into modern English and are regularly referred to under these forms in the secondary literature, but others have very rarely been translated (or if they have been there is no agreement on translation). For instance, the *Annales Cambriae* are nearly always referred to under this title rather than as 'Cambrian' or 'Welsh' annals.

Notes

1 For detailed discussion see K.H. Jackson, *Language and History in Early Britain* (Edinburgh, 1953).

2 W. Davies, 'The myth of the Celtic church', in *The Early Church in Wales and the West,* ed. N. Edwards and A. Lane (Oxford, 1992), 12–21; D.E. Meek, *The Quest for Celtic Christianity* (Edinburgh, 2000).

3 See, for example, E. James, *Britain in the First Millennium* (London, 2001); *After Rome,* ed. T. Charles-Edwards (Oxford, 2003); *The Blackwell Companion to Early Medieval Britain,* ed. P. Stafford (Oxford, forthcoming).

4 H. Pryce (ed.), *Literacy in Medieval Celtic Societies* (Cambridge, 1998); R.C. Stacey, 'Texts and society', in *After Rome*, ed. Charles-Edwards, 221–57.

5 P. Sims-Williams, 'The uses of writing in early medieval Wales', in *Literacy in Medieval Celtic Society*, ed. Pryce, 15–38.

6 K. Hughes, 'Where are the writings of early Scotland?', in *Celtic Britain in the Early Middle Ages*, ed. D.N. Dumville (Woodbridge, 1980), 1–21.

7 K. Forsyth, 'Literacy in Pictland', in *Literacy in Medieval Celtic Societies*, ed. Pryce, 39–61; G. Henderson and I. Henderson, *The Art of the Picts: Sculpture and Metalwork in Early Medieval Scotland* (London, 2004), 176–82.

8 J. Bannerman, *Studies in the History of Dalriada* (Edinburgh, 1974), 9–26.

9 F.M. Stenton, 'The foundations of English history', in *Preparatory to Anglo-Saxon England*, ed. D.M. Stenton (Oxford, 1970), 116–26.

10 K. Harrison, *The Framework of Anglo-Saxon History to A.D. 900* (Cambridge, 1976), 76–98.

11 W. Davies, *Wales in the Early Middle Ages* (Leicester, 1982), 200–1.

12 Stacey, 'Texts and society', 226–30.

13 R. Sharpe, 'The thriving of Dalriada', in *Kings, Clerics and Chronicles in Scotland, 500–1297*, ed. S. Taylor (Dublin, 2000), 47–61.

14 T. Charles-Edwards, *Early Irish and Welsh Kinship* (Oxford, 1993).

15 See Chapter 4, especially 219–30.

16 W. Davies, 'The Latin charter-tradition in western Britain, Brittany and Ireland in the early medieval period', in *Ireland in Early Mediaeval Europe*, ed. D. Whitelock, R. McKitterick and D.N. Dumville (Cambridge, 1982), 258–80; P. Wormald, *Bede and the Conversion of England: The Charter Evidence* (Jarrow, 1984).

17 W. Davies, *An Early Welsh Microcosm* (London, 1978); W. Davies, *The Llandaff Charters* (Cardiff, 1979); J.R. Davies, 'The Book of Llandaf: a twelfth-century perspective', *Anglo-Norman Studies* 21 (1998), 31–46; J.R. Davies, *The Book of Llandaf and the Norman Church in Wales* (Woodbridge, 2003).

18 G.W.S. Barrow, *The Kingdom of the Scots* (London, 1973), especially 7–68; A. Grant, 'The construction of the early Scottish state', in *The Medieval State. Essays Presented to James Campbell*, ed. J.R. Maddicott and D.M. Palliser (London, 2000), 47–71.

19 Bannerman, *Dalriada*, 27–156; D.N. Dumville, 'Ireland and North Britain in the earlier middle ages: contexts for *Míniugud Senchasa fher*', in

Rannsachadh na Gàidhlig 2000, ed. C.O. Baoill and N.R. McGuire (Aberdeen, 2002), 185–211.

20 P. Riché, *Education and Culture in the Barbarian West from the Sixth through to the Eighth Century* (trans. J. Contreni) (Columbia, 1976).

21 M. Lapidge, 'Schools', in *Blackwell Encyclopaedia*, 407–9.

22 D.N. Dumville, 'Kingship, genealogies and regnal lists', in *Early Medieval Kingship*, ed. P. Sawyer and I.N. Wood (Leeds, 1977), 72–104.

23 *The Gododdin: Text and Context from Dark-Age North Britain*, ed. and trans. J.T. Koch (Cardiff, 1997); O.J. Padel, 'A new study of the *Gododdin*', *CMCS* 35 (1998), 45–55.

24 P. Wormald, 'Bede, Beowulf and the conversion of the English aristocracy', in *Bede and Anglo-Saxon England*, ed. R.T. Farrell, BAR 46 (Oxford, 1978), 32–95; C. Chase (ed.), *The Dating of Beowulf* (Toronto, 1981).

25 B. Cassidy (ed.), *The Ruthwell Cross* (Princeton, 1992).

26 T.O. Clancy and G. Márkus, *Iona: The Earliest Poetry of a Celtic Monastery* (Edinburgh, 1995).

27 P. Brown, *The Cult of Saints* (Chicago, 1981); A. Thacker and R. Sharpe (eds), *Local Saints and Local Churches in the Early Medieval West* (Oxford, 2002).

28 W. Goffart, *The Narrators of Barbarian History* (Princeton, 1988), 235–328; D. Rollason, 'Hagiography and politics in early Northumbria', in *Holy Men and Holy Women: Old English Prose Saints' Lives and Their Contexts*, ed. P. Szarmach (Albany, 1996), 95–114.

29 A.A.M. Duncan, 'Bede, Iona and the Picts', in *The Writing of History in the Middle Ages. Essays Presented to Richard William Southern*, ed. R.H.C. Davis and J.M. Wallace-Hadrill (Oxford, 1981), 1–42, especially 5–6.

30 Bede, *Hist. Eccl.* IV, 7–11. Barking's links with the continental Irish missionary Columbanus (d. 615), who was also involved in controversy over Easter dating, may have produced a need to protect the house's reputation through a written work.

31 I.N. Wood, *The Missionary Life: Saints and the Evangelisation of Europe 400–1050* (Harlow, 2001).

32 *La Vie ancienne de Saint Samson de Dol*, ed. P. Flobert (Paris, 1997).

33 Davies, *Wales in the Early Middle Ages*, 207–8; Davies, 'Book of Llandaf'; J. Cartwright (ed.), *Celtic Hagiography and Saints' Cults* (Cardiff, 2003).

34 D.N. Dumville, *Saint David of Wales* (Cambridge, 2001).

35 A. Macquarrie, 'The career of Saint Kentigern of Glasgow: *vitae, lectiones*

and glimpses of fact', *Innes Review* 37 (1986), 3–24; D. Broun, 'Kentigern', *Oxford Dictionary of National Biography* (Oxford, 2004).

36 S.T. Driscoll, 'Church archaeology in Glasgow and the kingdom of Strathclyde', *Innes Review* 49 (1998), 95–114; A. Ritchie (ed.), *Govan and its Early Medieval Sculpture* (Stroud, 1994).

37 A. Macquarrie, '*Vita Sancti Servani*: the Life of St Serf', *Innes Review* 44 (1993), 122–52; A. Macquarrie, *The Saints of Scotland* (Edinburgh, 1997).

38 A. MacDonald, *Curadán, Boniface and the Early Church of Rosemarkie* (Groom House Museum, 1992).

39 M. Herren, 'Gildas and early British monasticism', in *Britain 400–600: Language and History*, ed. A. Bammesberger and A. Wollmann (Heidelberg, 1990), 65–83; N.J. Higham, *The English Conquest: Gildas and Britain in the Fifth Century* (Manchester, 1994).

40 M. Lapidge and D.N. Dumville (eds), *Gildas: New Approaches* (Woodbridge, 1984); P. Sims-Williams, 'Gildas and the Anglo-Saxons', *CMCS* 6 (1983), 1–30.

41 N.J. Higham, 'New light on the Dark Age landscape: the description of Britain in the *De Excidio Britanniae* of Gildas', *Journal of Historical Geography* 17 (1991), 363–72; K. Dark, *Civitas to Kingdom: British Political Continuity 300–800* (London, 1994), 258–66.

42 See, for example, R.A. Markus, *The End of Ancient Christianity* (Cambridge, 1990); P. Brown, *The Rise of Western Christendom: Triumph and Diversity A.D. 200–1000* (Oxford, 1996).

43 Gildas, *De Excidio*, 80–6; 143–7.

44 T.O. Clancy, 'The real St Ninian', *Innes Review* 52 (2001), 1–28.

45 C. Stancliffe, 'The British church and the mission of Augustine', in *St Augustine*, ed. Gameson, 107–51; see further in Chapter 2.

46 *Adomnán of Iona*, trans. R. Sharpe, 43–74; M. Herbert, *Iona, Kells and Derry: The History and Hagiography of the Monastic Familia of Columba* (Dublin, 1996), 47–56.

47 T. O' Loughlin (ed.), *Adomnán at Birr, AD 697. Essays in Commemoration of the Law of the Innocents* (Dublin, 2001); see further in Chapter 4.

48 *Handbooks of Penance*, 130–4; see further in Chapter 4, 118–22.

49 T. O'Loughlin, 'The exegetical purpose of Adomnán's *De Locis Sanctis*', *CMCS* 24 (1992), 37–53.

50 J. Picard, 'The purpose of Adomnán's *Vita Columbae*', *Peritia* 1 (1982), 160–77.

51 Herbert, *Iona, Kells and Derry*, 134–50; Sharpe, *Adomnán of Iona*, 40–3, 53–65.

52 Picard, 'The purpose of Adomnán's *Vita Columbae*'; R. Aist, T. Clancy, T. O'Loughlin and J. Wooding (eds), *Adomnán of Iona: Theologian – Lawmaker – Peacemaker* (Dublin, forthcoming).

53 Adomnán, *V. Columbae*, I, 9; III, 5; M.J. Enright, 'Royal succession and abbatial prerogative in Adomnán's *Vita Columbae*', *Peritia* 4 (1985), 83–103; M. Tanaka, 'Iona and the kingship of Dál Riata in Adomnán's *Vita Columbae*', *Peritia* 17–18 (2003-4), 199–214.

54 Adomnán, *V. Columbae*, I, 1.

55 Bede, *Hist. Eccl.* V, 21; III, 5.

56 Bede, *Hist. Eccl.* V, 24; A. H. Thompson (ed.), *Bede: His Life, Times and Writings* (Oxford, 1935); P.H. Blair, *The World of Bede* (London, 1970, rev. edn 1990); G. Bonner (ed.), *Famulus Christi* (London, 1976); I.N. Wood, *The Most Holy Abbot Ceolfrith* (Jarrow, 1995).

57 However, as a reviewer of the typescript has pointed out to me, a more accurate rendition of the Latin might be *The History of the English Nation as a Church*.

58 D. Kirby, 'Bede's native sources for the *Historia Ecclesiastica*', *Bulletin of the John Ryland's Library* 48 (1966), 341–71.

59 Bede, *Hist. Eccl.* II, 9.

60 N. Brooks, *Bede and the English* (Jarrow, 1999); C. Stancliffe, *Bede, Wilfrid and the Irish* (Jarrow, 2003).

61 D. Hill, *An Atlas of Anglo-Saxon England* (Oxford, 1981), 30.

62 Bede, *Hist. Eccl.* II, 5; see further in Chapter 1, 61–4.

63 Bede, *Hist. Eccl.* V, 18.

64 C. Thomas, *And Shall These Mute Stones Speak? Post-Roman Inscriptions in Western Britain* (Cardiff, 1994); M. Handley, 'The early medieval inscriptions of western Britain', in *The Community, the Family and the Saint: Patterns of Power in Early Medieval Europe*, ed. J. Hill and M. Swan (Turnhout, 1998), 339–62; M. Todd, 'The latest inscriptions of Roman Britain', *Durham Archaeological Journal* 14–15 (1999), 53–8; P. Sims-Williams, 'The five languages of Wales in pre-Norman inscriptions', *CMCS* 44 (2002), 1–36.

65 D. McManus, *A Guide to Ogam* (Maynooth, 1991); C. Swift, *Ogam Stones and the Earliest Irish Christians* (Maynooth, 1997).

66 R. Page, *Runes and Runic Inscriptions* (Woodbridge, 1995).

67 K. Forsyth, 'Some thoughts on Pictish symbols as a formal writing system',

in *The Worm, the Germ and the Thorn: Pictish and Related Studies Presented to Isabel Henderson*, ed. D. Henry (Balgavies, 1997), 85–98; RCHM, Scotland, *Pictish Symbol Stones;* Henderson and Henderson, *Art of the Picts*, 166–74.

68 J.R. Allen, *The Early Christian Monuments of Scotland* (Edinburgh, 1903).

69 C. Thomas, 'The interpretation of the Pictish symbols', *Archaeological Journal* 120 (1963), 31–97; A. Jackson, *The Symbol Stones of Scotland: A Social Anthropological Resolution of the Problem of the Picts* (Stromness, 1984); S.T. Driscoll, 'Power and authority in early historic Scotland: Pictish symbol stones and other documents', in *State and Society: The Emergence and Development of Social Hierarchy and Political Centralization*, ed. J. Gledhill, B. Bender and M.T. Larsen (London, 1988), 215–35; Henderson and Henderson, *Art of the Picts*, 170–2.

70 R. Samson, 'The re-interpretation of the Pictish symbols', *Journal of the British Archaeological Association* 145 (1992), 29–65.

71 Forsyth, 'Pictish symbols as a formal writing system'.

72 Henderson and Henderson, *Art of the Picts*, 123–214.

73 K. Forsyth, 'Evidence of a lost Pictish source in the *Historia Regum Anglorum*', in *Kings, Clerics and Chronicles in Scotland 500–1297*, ed. S. Taylor (Dublin, 2000), 19–34, at 25.

74 *Adomnán of Iona*, trans. Sharpe, 242–3.

CHAPTER 1

Politics and Society in Britain *c*.600–800

The main purpose of this chapter is to introduce the four main peoples who lived in Britain in the early Middle Ages – the British, Picts, Irish and Anglo-Saxons – and to explore their political and social structures. In order to understand the situation between 600 and 800 it is necessary to look back further and in particular to consider how Britain had developed from the late Roman period to that of the early Middle Ages.

The British

The End of Roman Britain

The island of Britain was known to Greek travellers and writers from at least the fourth century BC but, after incorporation of a major part of the island into the Roman empire, *Britannia* also came to be used in a more limited sense for what became the British diocese from which the peoples of Scotland north of the Forth-Clyde isthmus were largely excluded.[1] Gildas was aware of both usages, but 'the Britons' to him were his fellow *cives*, that is former citizens of the Roman empire. In the fourth century Roman Britain was a diocese divided into four main provinces within which the main units of local administration were the *civitates*, the 'city states' that were based ultimately on the tribal divisions at the time of Roman conquest; they were subdivided for purposes of administration into smaller units called *pagi* (singular *pagus*).[2] The apparent uniformity of the administrative arrangements masked significant regional variations and different degrees of Roman influence that would affect the early medieval political histories of the British and assist their fragmentation into different groups. The least Romanised areas were in the highland or military zones where native cultural forms continued to dominate and typical Roman features such as villas were absent. The north of England and southern Scotland had originally formed a militarised frontier zone delineated by the Antonine and Hadrian Walls. Although the Antonine Wall and some outlying forts had been used only intermittently, the British peoples of this area were probably retained within the sphere of Roman influence through a mixture of gifts, treaties and intimidation, but by the fourth century the area was not counted as part of the Roman diocese of Britain whose northern frontier was Hadrian's Wall.[3] This too was an area dominated by the military, but large civilian settlements developed around the forts in which imported Roman material circulated more freely than in the native settlements to the north. In many ways it was one of the most cosmopolitan areas outside London as the army units stationed there might be drawn from all over the empire, including from western Asia and north Africa. Veterans would settle in the vicinity of the forts, marry local women and their descendants would continue to serve in the army as frontier troops (*limitanei*). The other major highland zone area of Wales and the south-west was also controlled largely through the Roman military. The area was exploited for its mineral wealth and its inhabitants were presumably integrated into the Roman tax system, but beyond the forts and roads that enabled them to do this overt signs of Romanisation were scarce.[4]

It is in the lowland areas of Britain that we find the familiar accoutrements of Roman life such as villas, towns and temples, but any visitor from the heart of the empire would have found lowland Britain hopelessly provincial and a pale reflection of the life they were familiar with. For instance, although Britain had towns with shops and substantial townhouses of the type one might expect to find elsewhere in the western empire, the Romano-British elite did not apparently invest their wealth in public buildings as did their counterparts further south, and by the fourth century the forum areas of towns such as Silchester and Caerwent had been adapted for more mundane activities such as metal-working. Lowland areas were intensively cultivated during the Roman period and much of the surplus wealth was probably creamed off to support the Roman state and its military and civil apparatus.[5]

As the fourth century progressed there are signs in both the archaeological and historical record that things were beginning to go wrong in the provinces of Roman Britain.[6] Britain only occasionally features in the histories written in other parts of the Roman empire, but enough has been recorded to show that it came under increasing attack from the three other peoples who form part of Britain's history in the early Middle Ages – the Irish, Picts and Saxons. In 367 the three groups apparently joined forces in a 'barbarian conspiracy' that seems to have inflicted major defeats on the Roman forces.[7] The Roman emperors were robust in seeking to counteract these and earlier attacks; armies were despatched, defences strengthened in towns and coastal forts and new fortifications provided for vulnerable western and north-eastern coasts. Such things suggest the value of the profits to be derived from Britain for the Roman centre. But these measures were not as effective as they might have been, not least because the armies despatched to Britain raised a series of emperors and then departed to help them make good their claims. These usurpers included Magnus Maximus who left in 383 and Constantine III whose departure with what remained of the Roman forces stationed in Britain in 407 seems to have precipitated a crisis in relations between British leaders and Rome. The archaeological record seems to show major changes occurring in the latter half of the fourth century with imports decreasing, towns declining and many villas going out of use or being adapted for agricultural purposes. There is a significant shift from building with stone to buildings entirely of timber of sill-beam construction. As one archaeologist has remarked 'we are, in effect, seeing in the late fourth century the beginnings of settlement structures and patterns that would characterize the post-Roman period'.[8]

Perhaps what we can see in the apparent rejection of many aspects of Roman culture in late fourth-century Britain is something of the disillusionment and impatience with Rome among its British citizens that led them in c.410 to declare their independence. Our main source for these events is a sixth-century Byzantine historian called Zosimus who seems to have drawn upon an earlier written source.[9] He states that the British decided they wished to organise their own defence against 'the barbarians' and that they were successful in dealing with a major Saxon incursion which had been made the year before. Gildas provides some confirmation of these events although for him Magnus Maximus (383–8) was the last emperor to rule Britain, perhaps implying changing relations between Britain and the empire after his reign. He also implies that the British – or perhaps one part of them – sought and received further support from the empire after 410.[10] It is possible that to begin with the four British provinces provided some sort of coordinated defence against their Irish, Pictish and Saxon foes. Gildas describes a 'proud tyrant' (identified in later accounts as Vortigern) deciding with the aid of a council to allow some of the Saxons to settle in the east of the country in return for their military support.[11] When they used their military strength to take over part of the country for themselves, Gildas implies that there was a concerted effort to oppose them led by Ambrosius Aurelianus 'the last of the Romans' which culminated in the British victory at Mount Badon (whose location is unknown) in the year of his birth, 44 years before the time that he wrote, so possibly in *c*.500 or a little earlier.[12]

The kingdoms of the former Roman military zone

Gildas himself had grown up in a time of relative peace, but one in which a clear division had become apparent in the histories of the British of the eastern and southern districts, who had had to contend with settlement by groups of Germanic peoples referred to collectively as the Anglo-Saxons, and the British to their west who were able to develop their own new forms of organisation unfettered by foreign intruders apart from some Irish settlement in the west. In the western province of *Britannia Prima* (administered from Cirencester), the northern province of *Britannia Secunda* (administered from York) and the area based on the Hadrian and Antonine Walls kingdoms developed. These areas included the highland/military zones, which as we have seen were the least Romanised parts of *Britannia*, and some adjacent lowland areas that did include Roman towns, such as Exeter and Caerwent, and a more Romanised lifestyle represented by villas and imported Roman goods. These areas may have been left to run their own affairs under Roman rule to a much greater extent than in the two eastern and southern provinces of *Flavia Caesariensis* (probably administered from Lincoln) and *Maxima Caesariensis* (probably administered from London).

Possibly by the fourth century members of the nobility in *Britannia Prima* and *Secunda* had been authorised to collect taxes and keep the peace on behalf of Rome. Similar concessions seem to have been made in the Roman province of Gaul and led to what were in effect private armies controlled by members of the nobility in the name of Roman authority.[13] In the context of the separation of Britain from the Roman empire, with no single authority being able to take command over the whole island, one can see how such controllers of armed bands could come to assert independent control and turn themselves into kings. There are possible indicators in the archaeological record of the growing stature of local 'big men' in the west and north in the late fourth and early fifth centuries. At Wroxeter (Shropshire) the Roman town of *Virconium* underwent major changes in the fourth century that seem to have included the adaptation of the bath complex to make an imposing residence which, it has been suggested, might mark the seat of an emerging local ruler.[14] At Birdoswald on Hadrian's Wall in the fifth century a former granary inside the fort seems to have been replaced by successive phases of a large timber-framed hall, the archetypal early medieval lord's residence.[15] There are signs of comparable developments and continuation of use in forts at Carlisle, South Shields and Vindolanda.[16] Further north still, in what is today southern Scotland, the loyalty of local leaders may have been purchased by gifts such as the great hoard of late Roman silverware recovered from the hillfort of Traprain Law (East Lothian), a major centre of the Votadini.[17]

In his *De Excidio* Gildas castigates five contemporary kings of Wales and the south-west who were at least second-generation rulers at the time he wrote, but whose dynasties may in fact have gone back further.[18] The would-be emperor Magnus Maximus plays a prominent role in Welsh legend of the period and was claimed as the founder of some of its royal houses. It is possible that he authorised local leaders to take over the defence of their territories when he withdrew from Britain in 383 with much of the army.[19] Three of Gildas's rulers can be identified with some confidence as controlling areas that were based on former Roman *civitates* which logically one might expect would form the basis of subRoman polities.[20] These are Constantine of Dumnonia (the south-west peninsula), Vortipor of Dyfed (the Demetae of south-west Wales) and Maglocunus of Gwynedd (the Ordovices of north-west Wales). The existence of kingdoms in these former tribal areas can be confirmed from other sources such as the later pedigrees of Welsh rulers, the Welsh annals and inscriptions. The two other rulers named by Gildas, Aurelius Caninus (possibly a kinsman of Ambrosius Aurelianus) and Cuneglasus, cannot be so easily placed and there is much disagreement about where they should be located. If they too were based on former *civitates* one might expect them to be rulers of the Silures in the south-east of Wales and the Cornovii of the east and the Welsh marches (see Map 1). By the ninth century this latter area was known as the kingdom of Powys, one of the most significant of the kingdoms of the seventh to ninth centuries that was frequently at war with its Anglo-Saxon neighbour, Mercia. By the ninth century, through Welsh annal entries and a useful overview of affairs in Wales provided by Alfred's Welsh biographer Asser, we can see that the south-east area of the Silures had been divided between at least three kingdoms, Brycheiniog, Glwysing and Gwent, and that there was a kingdom called

Ceredigion in the west of Wales, lying between Dyfed and Gwynedd (see Map 2).[21] However, the sources are not sufficient to indicate when and how these kingdoms came into existence.

Kingdoms also developed in the British areas of the north, between the Hadrian and Antonine Walls. This area of the 'Old North' was celebrated in the battle poetry of medieval Wales, and there is much debate about how much of this poetry may have a genuinely early core going back to the period of the sixth and seventh centuries that it describes.[22] From the poetry and genealogical collections preserved in Wales three major kingdoms in the north can be identified (see Map 1). The longest surviving of these northern British kingdoms is that of northern Dumnonii, known as the kingdom of Dumbarton from its fortress on Dumbarton Rock (*Alt Clutha*, 'rock of the Clyde') and sometimes referred to by historians by its later name as the kingdom of Strathclyde.[23] It is possible that King Coroticus whom Patrick denounced for his slave-trading activities was a king of Dumbarton, which would place the origins of the kingdom in the fifth century.[24] Otherwise the earliest reference to a king of Dumbarton is as a contemporary of Columba in the late sixth century.[25] Kings of Dumbarton were a major power in the north in the seventh century, particularly during the reign of Owain, son of Beli, who in 642 defeated and slew Domnall Brecc of the Dál Riata at the battle of Strathcarron. Although often circumscribed by Northumbrian and Pictish power in the eighth century, the Britons of Dumbarton could still prove to be formidable military opponents and in 750 inflicted a major defeat on the great Pictish overlord King Onuist that led to a decline in his power.[26] The kingdom survived into the tenth century, but was adversely affected by Norse attacks and suffered a major setback in 870 when its stronghold of Dumbarton Rock fell to the Norse after a siege of four months.

The poem *The Gododdin* preserves the name of the British people of the south-east lowlands who in the Roman period were known as the Votadini.[27] The poem has generally been interpreted as recording a major defeat at Catterick (Yorkshire) of an army organised by a king of the Gododdin from his base in Edinburgh against his enemies to the south who are usually taken to be the Anglo-Saxons of Northumbria. The territory of the Gododdin does seem to have been taken over by the Northumbrians by the early seventh century. The hero of other poems was the legendary Urien of Rheged who was king at the end of the sixth century and a major opponent of fellow British rulers as well as of the intrusive Irish and Northumbrian dynasties. The origins and location of the kingdom of Rheged are even more difficult to establish. Some would interpret the place-name Dunragit in the Rhinns of Galloway as the 'fort of Rheged' and would see it originating in this region in the lands of the Novantae, though others have suggested origins further south in Cumbria, with a possible centre at Carlisle, while the poetry appears to associate Urien of Rheged with *Catraeth* (usually taken to be Catterick, Yorkshire).[28] Urien appears to have been a very powerful king before being killed by fellow Britons while besieging Lindisfarne in the late sixth century, and may have controlled land on both sides of the Solway Firth.[29] These lands fell to the Northumbrians in the seventh century, perhaps aided by the marriage of King Oswiu of Northumbria (642–70) with Rhiainfellt, reputedly a great-granddaughter of Urien.[30] Other British kingdoms may once have existed in the north. It has been suggested that the two Anglo-Saxon kingdoms, Bernicia and Deira, which were united in the seventh century to make the kingdom of Northumbria, were in origin British kingdoms, but there is no certain proof of this.[31] However, there is better evidence for a British kingdom of Elmet in western Yorkshire that survived into the seventh century before it too was incorporated into Northumbria.[32] Reliable evidence for British kingdoms in the north is in short supply and it is possible to take a much more sceptical view of how much of their early history can be reconstructed.[33]

A feature of the British kingdoms of the western seaboard is that they seem to have maintained links with areas of the former Roman empire. Settlers from the south-west may have helped establish these when they moved into, and arguably came to dominate, the former Roman province of Armorica which became known as *Britannia*, that is Brittany.[34] Roman-style food, pottery and glass were imported into the British kingdoms of the west in the later fifth and sixth centuries not only from northern France, but also directly from the Mediterranean.[35] It is ironical that these western regions have more obvious affiliations with Roman culture in the fifth and sixth centuries than they ever did when under Roman rule. The interest in demonstrating links with the Roman past can presumably be explained through the desire of the new regimes to legitimise their positions by associating themselves with the remnants of Roman power as did many other groups in Europe who came to power in the post-Roman world.[36] It is a development that is demonstrated very well by the commemorative stones with inscriptions which were erected in a manner evidently derived from late Roman practice in the kingdoms of western Britain and some areas of the north.[37] Some of the inscribed stones carry Latin titles that seem to point in the same direction of wanting to establish a link with Roman authority. An inscribed stone in

Penmachno churchyard in Gwynedd, for instance, was raised in honour of one Cantiori, described as a *cives* of Gwynedd and the cousin of Maglus the magistrate.

The central British civilian zone

Not all the British areas that remained outside the earliest Anglo-Saxon settlements may have been controlled by kings. One of the major problems of the subRoman period is writing the history of the British in a large swathe of what had been the lowland/civilian zone that lay between the British controlled areas of the west and the earliest Saxon controlled settlements of the south and east. The inhabitants of this area are particularly difficult to trace in the archaeological record as diagnostic Roman artefacts such as coins, pottery and various forms of metalwork which ceased to be imported or manufactured locally do not seem to have been replaced with comparable items that can be easily detected in the archaeological record. The absence of inscribed stones and imported Roman goods in the central civilian zone serves to emphasise the contrast between it and the western kingdoms and to support the idea that its political organisation in the fifth and sixth centuries may have been managed differently. In a famous passage Gildas wrote 'Britain has kings, but they are tyrants; it has judges (*iudices*), but they are wicked'.[38] It has been suggested that he is referring to two different types of political organisation to be found in the British-controlled areas at the time he was writing, and that the control of *iudices* is to be associated with the lowland zone areas and is an indication of the continuation of a system based on Roman local government involving councils drawn from the local elites.[39] Gildas himself may have lived in one of these areas of subRoman rule in the west, perhaps in Dorset or Wiltshire His own work suggests that at least one aspect of Roman culture continued in the area where he lived, namely education, for it would seem that he not only had a thorough grounding in Latin, but also in the rhetorical skills which were necessary for public life in the Roman world. Such evidence suggests it was possible that aspects of Roman civil administration did continue in the lowland districts even though the archaeological record appears to demonstrate the disappearance of many facets of Roman culture such as towns, villas and decent plumbing.[41]

However, we should not assume that life was static in the former civilian zone. When the Anglo-Saxons recorded their expansion into the Somerset and Dorset area in the late sixth and seventh centuries they believed they had been opposed by armies led by kings. The *Anglo-Saxon*

Chronicle, for instance, records that in 577 the West Saxons fought against three British kings, Conmail, Condidan and Farinmail, who were linked with Gloucester, Cirencester and Bath. Although the *Chronicle* is not a contemporary record, but a compilation of the late ninth century, the precision of the names suggests some concrete written or oral tradition lies behind this entry.[42] It is possible that the British of the west might have organised themselves into militia based on former Roman centres such as the three places named in the 577 annal. Although there was always a potential for military leaders to try to turn themselves into kings, this does not mean that all did so (whatever the Anglo-Saxons may have thought) and in the former civilian zone of Roman Britain some form of consensual control through local councils may have continued. It is possible that the Hadrian's Wall area should be seen as operating in a similar way with many of the forts continuing as centres for local militia, but with a local council (such as we know had existed in Roman Carlisle) continuing to be influential.[43]

One reason for thinking that there may have been developments along these lines is the reoccupation of hill-forts, often with reinforcement of defences, that occurs in these regions between the fifth and seventh centuries. Nor were the Anglo-Saxons the only potential enemies for the kings of the west and north may have also have sought to extend their authority. Gildas refers to fighting among the British, and the hill-forts of the western central zone are concentrated in the region bordering the British kingdoms where reoccupation of hill-forts is also found in this period.[44] Alternatively some districts may have felt that their interests were best served by linking themselves with neighbouring kingdoms. The Iron Age hill-fort of South Cadbury in southern Somerset not only seems to have had a major refurbishment of its defence in the post-Roman period, but also shared in the distribution of table ware from the Mediterranean in the late fifth and sixth centuries which are indicators of direct trade from that area with the western kingdoms of Britain.[45] There have been comparable signs of refortification and acquisition of imports in northern Somerset. Somerset is generally considered to have lain outside the Iron Age and Roman province of Dumnonia, but the archaeological finds raise the question of whether by the late fifth century it (or parts of it) had moved into the Dumnonian sphere of influence with its controllers benefiting from the patronage of the Dumnonian king.

Ultimately fifth- and sixth-century arrangements in the British civilian central zone remain uncertain, and in the late sixth and seventh centuries most, if not all, of this area was absorbed by the westward expansion of Northumbria, Mercia and Wessex. The military strength of the Anglo-Saxons either compelled or encouraged submission. The best indication of what may have happened next is provided by the lawcode of King Ine of Wessex (688–725) in which British, presumably people who had recently come under his control in Dorset and Somerset, are recognised as a distinct group with differing social classes, including a class of noble landowners.[46] They are given legal standing, but as second-class citizens whose oaths and rights to compensation are of lesser value than those of their Anglo-Saxon counterparts. No doubt landowners had to surrender a considerable amount of land to Anglo-Saxons, and British churches seem to have come under Anglo-Saxon control. The laws seem to represent a situation where British incorporated into an Anglo-Saxon kingdom had to accept an inferior position, but where they were not completely oppressed or without hope of redress in courts of law. Such terms may have encouraged submission to Anglo-Saxon rule in preference to facing continual military harassment with the possibility of not retaining anything, not to mention being sold into slavery or other threats worse than death. Although lawcodes do not exist for Mercia or Northumbria, and no clear statement is made of the fate of the British as they expanded westwards, many historians and archaeologists are convinced that such rapid expansion could only be achieved by an assimilation of British and Anglo-Saxon communities.[47] By the end of the seventh century Mercia had three western satellite provinces of the Hwicce, Magonsaetan and Wreocensaetan, that roughly correspond with the historic counties of Gloucestershire and Worcestershire, Herefordshire and Shropshire respectively (see Map 1).[48] The provinces have Old English names and the first two were controlled c.650–c.750 by dynasties apparently of Anglo-Saxon origin that were subject to the Mercian kings. The earliest recorded ruler of the Magonsaetan was Merewalh, whose second element is the word *wealh* (foreigner) that Anglo-Saxons applied to the British. Cenwalh of the West Saxons (642–72) incorporates the same element, while the name of King Caedwalla of Wessex (685–88) is completely British. These names may indicate marriages between leading Anglo-Saxon and British families as part of a negotiated settlement. The archaeological evidence suggests a basic continuity of population and local centres of significance, even if the dominant language and hierarchy seems to have become Anglo-Saxon. The westward expansion of Northumbria into former British areas in the seventh and early eighth centuries may also have been achieved by military aggression leading to agreed terms for surrender and incorporation.[49] The marriage of King Oswiu (642–70) to Rhiainfellt, a princess from Rheged, may have been part of the process.

The British in the areas of early Anglo-Saxon settlement in the east and south

One of the most controversial areas of modern scholarship of the early Middle Ages is the question of the nature of the Anglo-Saxon settlement in eastern and southern Britain, and one facet of that is the role and fate of the British in those areas in which the earliest Anglo-Saxon kingdoms can be traced from the late sixth century. Gildas provides the only detailed written version of events. The one crucial event of which he had knowledge, and apparently a written source, was an appeal for help made to Aetius 'thrice consul' when the British were feeling particularly oppressed by their enemies, whom Gildas identified as the Picts and the Irish.[50] When there was no response to the appeal the British are said to have resorted to hiring Saxons as federates to defend their eastern seaboard. Aetius was consul for the third time in 446 and for the fourth time in 453 so the letter must have been written between these two dates. This appears to be a fixed point and it has been used for all subsequent calculations for the date of the Saxon *adventus*, beginning with that of Bede who dated it to 449, but it is possible that Gildas has not placed the appeal at the correct point in the narrative of events. The appeal to Aetius may in fact have been an appeal for help against the Saxons in the aftermath of their rebellion and this may also be the event referred to in a contemporary Gallic chronicle which records for 441 that 'the Britons, having up to this time suffered various defeats and catastrophes, were reduced to Saxon rule'.[51] Saxon federates may therefore have been in British employ from a much earlier period within the fifth century than Gildas's chronology suggests. There is nothing inherently implausible in the idea that Saxons came to Britain as federates. Various Germanic armies had been utilised as federate troops within the late Roman empire and its successor states, and in describing the treaty arrangements Gildas used appropriate official terminology such as *annonae*, the Latin Roman tax of food and supplies for support of the army, and *epimenia* for monthly supplies.

The fate of the British in the areas of earliest and most intensive Germanic settlement in eastern and southern England is the subject of some dispute, and one that is not easy to determine conclusively, though scientific analysis of DNA and teeth may eventually provide some solutions. Some prefer a version of the acculturation model with a more or less peaceful merger of British and Germans to produce a distinctive Anglo-Saxon culture, and suggest that the majority of the people buried in Anglo-Saxon cemeteries were actually of British descent.[52] Others suspect that Gildas may have been nearer the mark when he said that many British fled or were killed (presumably in particular people of some substance), and survivors were enslaved; that British did survive, but generally as a conquered people.[53] In this context we must bear in mind that in Britain, unlike most former provinces of the Roman empire where Germanic speakers settled, it was the Germanic language rather than a native Latin-based vernacular that became dominant.[54] In eastern England any Latin vernacular seems to have died out; Old English became the language of authority and Brittonic had inferior status.[55] Very little Brittonic vocabulary was borrowed into Old English, but it has been suggested that there was considerable influence on the syntax and phonology of Low Old English, the form spoken by the bulk of the population, which only emerges in written form after the Norman Conquest.[56] The language evidence seems to support the idea of Germanic dominance, but with British survival in the lower levels of society. That many British were enslaved or became the dependants of Anglo-Saxons seems very likely, and the *laeti* of the laws of King Æthelbert of Kent (d. 616) may, as were their counterparts in other former areas of the Roman empire, have been native dependants.[57] A number of casual references to individuals of apparently lower-class status in Northumbrian sources describing events in the latter part of the seventh century refer to them as British or as having British names.[58] When the captured Northumbrian nobleman Imma pretended to be a peasant to escape being put to death he was rumbled partly because of his dress, but also because of his manner of speaking – presumably his English was too good to be that of a British peasant.[59] While we must allow the possibility that some British nobles and freemen made common cause with their Anglo-Saxon counterparts and became indistinguishable from them, such a transition is hard to demonstrate conclusively.

However, one picture does not necessarily fit all the evidence. There are certain areas of eastern Britain where there appears to have been a significant absence of distinctive Anglo-Saxon material culture including in the immediate vicinity of the important Roman towns of London and Lincoln, and in the Chilterns. In the latter not only does the cult of St Alban appear to have survived from the fifth century, but there seems also to have been a general continuity of land use and settlement patterns, and it has even been proposed that the earliest Anglo-Saxon governmental units in the area were based on Roman *pagi*.[60] Place-names that preserve

Latin names or elements may be another indicator of pockets of British autonomous survival in areas where observable material culture was predominantly Anglo-Saxon.[61] Settlement evidence, for instance, of former villa sites is often suggestive of continuity, but difficult to prove. However, radiocarbon dates for a cemetery of unfurnished graves at Queensford Farm, near Dorchester-on-Thames, suggest that it remained in use from the fourth century through to the sixth.[62] The influx of Germanic settlers varied in its intensity in the eastern half of England, and the conditions for British absorption, or survival as a distinctive group of people, would therefore have varied accordingly. What seems clear is that the future was Anglo-Saxon and, although there may still have been a certain amount of apartheid between Anglo-Saxon and British in some areas in the seventh century, greater levelling seems to have occurred under the pressure of Anglo-Saxon royal government, though mixed sexual unions, including those of masters and slaves, must also have played a part in the eventual Anglicisation of the British population.

The Picts

The other main indigenous people of Britain at the start of the early Middle Ages were the Picts. The name itself seems to have been of relatively recent origin and is first recorded in a poem of 297 by the Roman author Eumenius where the *Picti* are linked with the *Hiberni* of Ireland as major enemies of the Britons.[63] Although the etymology of the name is debated, it is possible that it came from the Latin meaning 'painted ones' and could be a reference to the practice of tattooing which may once have been widespread among the prehistoric peoples of the British Isles. It seems to have been a name bestowed by Roman writers that passed from them into regular use by the other early medieval peoples of the British Isles for these northern British peoples, but we do not know what they would have called themselves. Roman writers from the fourth century onwards also regularly refer to two major groupings within the Picts, though not always by the same names, and such a division may have been perpetuated into the early Middle Ages for Bede records a major subdivision into Picts north and south of the Mounth (the Grampian mountains that run east–west from near Aberdeen to Fort William).[64] These two subdivisions of the Pictish peoples had not necessarily always been closely allied or associated for archaeological evidence seems to show some significant differences in the material culture of the northern Atlantic regions with their distinctive brochs and wheelhouses to the more southerly areas where, for instance, hill-forts were a major component of elite and community identity.[65] In the Iron Age the material culture of the early medieval southern Picts was very similar to that of the neighbouring 'British' people and there is no need to think of them as belonging to separate groupings of people at this time. The creation of the Picts can therefore be seen as a product of the Roman period and a coming together of different tribal groupings of northern Scotland, that is the area north of the Forth and the Antonine Wall but excluding the Irish-settled area of Argyll, which was outside the area of Roman control. Roman authorities may have encouraged such a grouping to occur as the empire seems to have found larger units more convenient for political control and diplomatic influence than many smaller ones. However, an even greater stimulus for unity may have been the opportunities provided by raiding into Roman territory and during the fourth century the Picts seem to have become an increasing threat to Roman stability.

Current trends stress the similarities between the Picts and the other Celtic peoples of Britain, but there has been a long historiographical tradition of asserting the opposite and seeing the Picts as the last remnants of a primitive, non-Celtic, prehistoric people within Britain.[66] A central plank of this contention was that the Picts spoke a different language from the other peoples of Britain, one that did not even belong to any of the main language groups of Europe, and it has been claimed that, similarly to Basque, this language was non-Indo-European in origin. In the absence of any lengthy texts in Pictish it is extremely difficult to be categorical about their language, but the conclusion of recent analyses of place-names, tribal names recorded in Roman texts and names of Pictish people in early medieval sources has been that the dominant language among the Picts was a version of Brittonic, that is the p-Celtic used in most of the rest of Britain.[67] As in other parts of Britain there was some survival of an older stratum of names for rivers and other major geographical features, and the survival rate of these is greater in the north of Pictland than in the south. Many of the recorded names of Pictish kings are of Celtic origin, but there are others such as Bridei that seem to be uniquely Pictish and possibly non-Celtic in origin. A non-Indo-European language may have remained in use in northern Scotland longer than any counterpart further south, but it cannot be assumed that it was still in use there as a spoken language in the early Middle Ages.

The Pictish symbols are the best evidence of a cultural form that was shared at least by the elite in much of the historic province in the early Middle Ages.[68] The earlier Class I stones have their greatest concentration in the north of the province, either side of the Moray Firth, and it was within this area, in the vicinity of Inverness, that Adomnán and Bede depict Columba meeting with the powerful king Bridei in the late sixth century. This area is likely to have been the heartland of the northern Picts and Alex Woolf has gathered evidence to suggest that this was the province of Fortriu, a name that probably derives from that of the Verturiones recorded in the Roman period as one of the two major group-ings in what became the territory of the Picts and which has been located previously in the south of Scotland.[69] In southern Pictland there is a con-centration of some Class I symbol stones, and even more of Class II, in Perthshire north of the Firth of the Tay and this can possibly be identified as the centre of southern Pictish power. Our understanding of Pictish geography is complicated by the tradition of seven provinces preserved in a tract known as *De Situ Albaniae* ('Of the Organisation of Scotland') that was probably written in the late twelfth or early thirteenth century and which has often been related to the legend of the seven sons of Cruithne, the alleged founder of the Picts, that is found in the longer version of the Pictish king-list and in Irish tracts.[70] It has been assumed that each of these provinces may at one time have had its own Pictish royal dynasty,[71] but the arrangements described seem to be of greater relevance to the kingdom of Scotland in the twelfth and thirteenth centuries than to its Pictish predecessor. *De Situ Albaniae*, for instance, includes Argyll as a province, which was the territory of the Dál Riata in the seventh and eighth centuries and so was not part of Pictland.

Political arrangements of the Picts are hard to reconstruct with any cer-tainty. The rule of one dominant king at any one time is implied by the successive rulers of the Pictish king-lists and seems to be supported by the narratives of Adomnán and Bede concerning King Bridei (556–84). Other factors could point in the same direction such as the apparent existence of only one bishopric for Pictland that may suggest the province was viewed as one kingdom.[72] Many of the kings of the regnal lists also appear in the Irish annals in which some are designated as kings of Fortriu, perhaps sug-gesting that this province had become dominant. However, the existence of kings or subkings of other areas is sometimes acknowledged. A king in Orkney is recorded for the late sixth century, and a king of Atholl is recorded as having been drowned in 739.[73] An entry in the Irish annals records in 782 the death of Dubthalorc 'king of the Picts, this side of the Mounth', perhaps a reference to the division into northern and southern Picts separated by the Grampian range recorded by Bede. Such references are too few to allow us to say with any certainty how many kings might have been ruling at any particular period or what subdivisions they may have controlled. The geography of Scotland with its many island and mountain ranges creates a number of isolated districts that could have been controlled by different kin-groups, irrespective of whether they had leaders who called themselves kings or not. One such group on Skye, the 'Geonae', probably also known as the '*genus* Gartnait', are referred to by Adomnán and also appear in the Irish annals that were composed originally on Iona.[74]

What has attracted most attention about Pictish kingship are its instances of succession through the female rather than the male line, and these have traditionally been seen as one of the examples of Pictish difference from the rest of Britain.[75] A key text for the concept of matrilineal succession among the Picts is the origin legend cited by Bede where the Picts are said to have travelled to Ireland from Scythia and to have obtained brides from the Irish on the condition that 'in all cases of doubt, they should elect their kings from the female line rather than the male'.[76] His comment that 'it is well known that the custom has been preserved amongst the Picts to this day' reflects contemporary circumstances for King Bridei (697–706) and his brother and successor King Nechtan (706–24) seem to have claimed the throne through their Pictish mother Derilei (perhaps 'daughter of Ilei') and are identified by their maternal descent in the king-lists whereas all other rulers are given patronymics, that is they are identified through their father.[77] The implication of Bede's story is that it was only in unusual circumstances that such matrilineal succession was to apply,[78] but Bridei and Nechtan do not seem to have been the only kings with non-Pictish fathers. Not all examples of such descent that have been identified in the past stand up to scrutiny, as many have depended on the coincidence of similar names, but among instances that do seem to be well attested are Talorcan (653–7), son of Eanfrith of Northumbria and Bridei (672–93), son of King Beli of Dumbarton. It is not entirely without precedent in the broader insular world for a right to the throne to be claimed through a female, and it was most usually to be found when one lineage was taking over another as, for instance, when the Bernicians annexed the neighbouring province of Deira to form the Anglo-Saxon kingdom of Northumbria. But what is more difficult to parallel in Irish and Anglo-Saxon regnal practice is that, until the end of the eighth century, there was apparently no example of a Pictish king with a father who had also been a king of the Picts. In Ireland and Anglo-Saxon England when rival lineages competed for the position of dominant king it was not unusual for successive kings to be only distantly related to one another and for men to come to the throne whose fathers do not appear in regnal lists,[79] but, especially when there are examples of Pictish brothers succeeding one another in the king-lists, the absence of any fathers who had previously ruled does seem unusual. There undoubtedly were rival factions in contention for the dominant position in Pictland. For example, between 724 and 729 four rival kings are recorded in competition with one another, but we do not know if they claimed a common ancestor or came from quite distinct dynasties.

We do not have enough information to enable us to interpret these apparently unusual aspects of the Pictish royal succession. The king-lists and narrative sources encourage us to see a dominant king of the Picts from at least the late sixth century.[80] Their picture may be illusory, and it has been doubted whether Pictland was sufficiently developed to support kingship of this type from such an early date, but the Pictish symbol stones provide some support for the assertion of a common Pictish identity from about this period and for it having originated in the area north of the Mounth. We do not have to see such kingship operating in the same way as a later medieval state. Occasional references and the frequent succession of kings not closely related to one another in the seventh and early eighth centuries could suggest the existence of subkingdoms or other provinces through which a dominant king would have controlled the country. In the eighth century there are signs of greater consolidation of royal power, and after an unsettled period between 724 and 729 when no less than four rival candidates seem to have been in competition, there emerged the most powerful Pictish ruler to date, Onuist (729–61) who from 736–c.750 seems also to have been king of Dál Riata, in addition to being overlord of the British of Dumbarton and in alliance with Æthelbald of Mercia, the Anglo-Saxon overlord.[81] Another sign of Onuist's success is that he was the first Pictish king to have a son who ruled as king for his son Talorcan was also king of the Picts (?780–2), even if he did not succeed his father immediately.

A significant feature of the history of the Pictish kingdom between 600 and 800 is the growing Irish influence within the province and the merging of the Dál Riatan and Pictish dynasties. Pictish and Irish links may go back to the period of raids on late Roman Britain that one suspects may also have provided the circumstances for a Pictish military-based over-kingship to emerge. Ogham stones, distributed throughout eastern Pictland, and some early Gaelic place-names, may suggest some Irish settlement within Pictland from early in the historic period.[82] Links with Dál Riata may also have gone back a long way, and were supported by missions from Iona to both northern and southern parts of Pictland in the late sixth and seventh centuries.[83] The succession of the brothers Bridei and Nechtan whose father seems to have been a member of the Cénel Comgaill dynasty of Dál Riata may mark the point at which the dynasties began to converge. Onuist appears to have made himself king of both Pictland and Dál Riata, but his ancestry is uncertain and so is his relationship to successive kings, though Dauvit Broun has produced the attractive hypothesis that Onuist was the grandfather of Constantine (789–820) and his brother Onuist (820–34), who were also kings of both the Picts and of Dál Riata and appear in the king-lists of both countries.[84] Debate revolves around the identity of their father, whose name is Uurguist in Pictish and Fergus in Gaelic. A rival theory identifies Uurguist/Fergus with Fergus son of Eochaid, the brother of Áed Find who had temporarily restored Dalriadic independence after the overlordship of Onuist (see Appendix 6).[85] Interpretation is complicated by the fact that the king-lists seem to have been distorted at this point and do not make sense as they stand so that they are hard to reconcile. Whatever the origin of these later kings of the Picts and the Scots, their dynasty was brought to an abrupt end after a major defeat by the Vikings in 839 when several members of the family were killed. The position of king of the Picts was taken by Cinaed, son of Alpin, who is of even more uncertain origin,[86] but it was his descendants who consolidated earlier achievements and united the Picts and Dál Riata in the kingdom of Alba in the tenth century.

The Irish

The history of Ireland does not form part of this volume, but the period 600–800 is one of considerable interaction between Ireland and Britain, and many Irish churchmen had a significant role to play in the conversion of the Anglo-Saxons and Picts to Christianity. Close contacts between Britain and Ireland were not a new development in the early Middle Ages, but had been a feature of the prehistoric past of the two islands.[87] Ireland was, of course, not included within the Roman province of *Britannia*, though it has been suggested that there were exploratory Roman expeditions to Ireland. Certainly contact between the two islands did not cease and as in other parts of the empire Rome would have been concerned to keep its nearest neighbours quiescent and may have sought to control activity across the Irish Sea. The Roman historian Ammianus implies the existence of a treaty that was broken in 360.[88] Trade undoubtedly took place, and is one of the ways in which finds of Roman material within

Ireland can be explained. Like other 'barbarian' peoples Irish were recruited to fight for Rome and many of the survivors would eventually have returned home; the earliest recorded Irish name from Britain is on a building-block probably from the third century AD found at Housesteads, one of the forts on Hadrian's Wall.[89] However, during the fourth century relations between Ireland and Roman Britain changed, and raids by *Scotti*, as the Irish were called by Roman writers, became a major problem and provoked the building of forts in vulnerable areas of Wales at sites such as at Holyhead and Cardiff. Trading and raiding were often closely linked in the past, but these raids became more than a bit of piratical activity on the side and the Irish were part of the confederation that inflicted a major defeat on Roman forces in 369. St Patrick was among the human booty seized on one of these raids, probably in the fifth century, and was a slave for six years in Ireland before he escaped.[90] The opportunities provided by a weakening of the Roman hold on Britain seem to have led to, or coincided with, a period of new developments within Ireland in which powerful royal kindreds rose to dominance, especially the Uí Néill in the north and the Éoganacht in the south.[91] The period following the breakdown of Roman rule in Britain also provided new opportunities for Irish in Britain itself.

The kingdom of Dál Riata and Irish settlement in Scotland

The most notable Irish offshoot within Britain was the kingdom of the Dál Riata (Dalriada) based around Argyll in western Scotland. These are the 'Scots', that is people from Ireland, who ultimately gave their name to Scotland. A retrospective record for *c.*501 in the *Annals of Tigernach* records that 'Fergus Mór mac Eirc with the people of Dál Riata took a part of Britain and died there', and this has generally been taken to indicate an Irish conquest and settlement of this area of Britain.[92] Adomnán in his *Life of Columba* makes it clear that the kingdom of the Dál Riata in Scotland was culturally Irish and Gaelic speaking, and it is contrasted with neighbouring Pictish areas in which Columba needed to use an interpreter to be understood. Kings of Scottish Dál Riata in the sixth and seventh centuries were much involved in events within Ireland. The wider province of the Dál Riata included an area of north-east Antrim, which lay in an uneasy position on the northern edge of the province of the Ulaid and bordering that of the increasingly powerful northern Uí Néill.[93] One can see why the royal family of the Ulster Dál Riata might have welcomed expansion into an adjoining area of Scotland, only some 12 miles away at its nearest point. But in recent years archaeologists in particular have been unhappy with this picture of conquest and colonisation. Ewan Campbell has argued that there is no archaeological evidence for either a major colonisation or an elite takeover by Irish at this time.[94] It is possible that Dál Riata had been a Gaelic-speaking area in close contact with Ireland for many generations before the sixth century, and that the origins of the initial link are lost in the unrecorded prehistoric past. Bede knew an origin legend that placed initial emigration much earlier than 500 under an eponymous leader he names as Reuda.[95] Later kings of Scotland claimed descent from Fergus mac Eirc and the entry recording his 'conquest' of c.501 could be an entirely retrospective attempt to give him a historical context.[96] However, one should not rule out the possibility that, whatever the origins of the Dál Riata in Scotland, this particular kin-group might have come to prominence in the province around 500.

By pooling various sources of evidence, it can be suggested that Scottish Dál Riata consisted of the old counties of Argyll and Bute, that is the western mainland of Scotland from Cowal to Ardnamurchan and the adjacent islands (see Map 1).[97] Skye, according to Adomnán, was part of Pictland,[98] but it is possible that Dalriadic control was extended further north up the west coast in the course of the eighth century, or that there were other Irish settlements along it – certainly Irish churchmen were to be found all along the coast of the Irish Sea.[99] Dál Riata was separated from the main part of Pictland by the mountain ranges referred to in early medieval sources as *Druim Alban* (the spine of Britain).[100] There was a major routeway between Dál Riata and northern Pictland via the firth of Lorn through the Great Glen to Loch Ness. To the south, Dál Riata was separated by the firth of the Clyde from the Britons of Dumbarton.

An insight into the internal organisation of Dál Riata is provided by a tenth-century document usually referred to as the *Senchus fer nAlban* ('The traditions of the men of Scotland') which is a mixture of a genealogical tract and a survey of obligations that is generally believed to be based upon an earlier document of the seventh century.[101] The *Senchus* describes the province as divided between three royal kindreds or *cenéla*, beginning with that of the descendants of Fergus mac Eirc who are depicted as subsequently dividing into two segments, Cenél nGabráin and Cenél Comgaill, named after two of Fergus's grandsons, and based in Kintyre with Arran and Cowal respectively. The two other royal kindreds were the Cenél Loairn (based in Lorne) and the Cenél nÓengusa (based on Islay), both supposedly tracing descent from appropriately named brothers of Fergus. On the face of it this information could suggest that Scottish Dál Riata conformed to the theoretical organisation of kingdoms defined in the Irish law tracts and that it had three (and eventually four) minor kingdoms or *tuatha* whose rulers (*ri*) competed for the position of overking (*rí ruiri*) of the whole province of the Dál Riata. However, the *Senchus* is not a straightforward document to use and may have undergone various amendments to fit changing situations that make the organisation of the province appear more static and more conventionally 'Irish' in organisation than was actually the case. Richard Sharpe has urged us not to start from the assumption that organisation conformed to the ideals of the Irish law tracts, but to let the evidence we actually have for the operation of kingship in Dál Riata speak for itself.[102]

The historical horizon of the Dalriadic kings begins in the latter part of the sixth century during the reign of Conall mac Comgaill (the reputed grandson of Fergus) who is recorded as giving the island of Iona to Columba in 563[103] – the fact that Iona is later recorded as being in the territory of the Cenél Loairn is among the reasons for concern about how far back the situation presented in the *Senchus* can be projected. Conall's eventual successor was his first cousin Áedán mac Gabráin (574–608). Áedán became a major power in northern Britain and was successful in campaigns in Orkney (580), the Isle of Man (582) and the territory of the southern Picts (*c.*590).[104] He also seems to have exercised an overlordship in northern Ireland and at a meeting at Druim Cett (near Derry) reached agreement with the Northern Uí Néill overlord that recognised his place in the Irish hierarchy.[105] In 603 Áedán suffered a major defeat at the battle of *Degastan* and lost much of his previous gains. His dynasty continued to rule after him, but the reign of his grandson Domnall Brecc (629–42) was something of a disaster; he fought and lost at least five battles in northern Britain and Ireland. After the battle of Mag Rath (Co. Down) in 637 when he fought against the Northern Uí Néill the price of his defeat seems to have been the permanent loss of the Dalriadic territory in Antrim.[106] His last defeat was at the battle of Strathcarron (Stirlingshire) where he died fighting the British of Dumbarton. His defeat marked a temporary decline in the power of the Cenél nGabráin; kings of the Cenél Loairn are recorded for the first time, and the two dynasties seem to have been in frequent dispute with each other and with rival factions of their own dynasties. Events of 719 give something of the flavour of the period. In that year King Selbach (700–23) of the Cenél Loairn defeated and slew his own brother Ainbcellach (who had previously ruled) and was himself defeated, though not unseated, by Dúnchad Bec of the Cenél nGabráin, described as king of Kintyre in the Irish annals.[107] This is a confused period when it is difficult to reconcile king-lists, genealogies and annals in order to produce a single line of kings over all of Dál Riata, and perhaps it is not appropriate to try to do so. Cenél nGabráin fortunes, and those of Dál Riata too, revived under Áed Find (c.748–78) who turned the tables on the Picts who had dominated the province after victories of their powerful king Onuist in 736.[108] After Áed all is confusion again, but it would appear that from this time the two kingdoms of the Picts and the Dál Riata were frequently ruled by the same individual, although rival views exist over whether the dominant family, descended from Uurguist/Fergus, was predominantly Irish or Pictish in the male line (see Appendix 6).[109] This dynasty suffered a major defeat from the Vikings in 839, and the subsequent history of the Dalriadic province becomes obscure, but part of it at least may have come under Norse control.[110]

The spread of Gaelic to Pictland has often been assumed to have occurred subsequent to the succession of Cinaed mac Alpin (840–58), though his background is far from clear. Current thinking is favouring a more gradual Gaelicisation of the Picts as a result of Irish settlement within Pictland at a much earlier point.[111] One possible indicator of an Irish presence in Pictland are the 29 stone inscriptions in ogham, the script developed in Ireland probably in the late fourth century for the Gaelic language.[112] Ogham script was not used for stone inscriptions in the north of Ireland or in Dál Riata so such use in Pictland could be an indicator of influences from other parts of Ireland. Some stones seem to have a mixture of Gaelic and Pictish names and language that perhaps suggests an earlier adoption of Gaelic by some Pictish speakers than was once assumed. Gaelic place-names are hard to date with any accuracy and many Gaelic names must have been adopted after the formation of the kingdom of Alba in which Gaelic became the preferred language, but there are some that are deemed to have originated before the ninth century. Many of these have ecclesiastical connections and so may be more certainly connected with Irish missionary work rather than with lay settlement.[113] More suggestive of lay infiltration is the name of Atholl (Perthshire), which is mentioned as a Pictish kingdom in an entry in the Irish annals for 739, and may mean 'new Ireland'.[114] Its king Talorcan was the son of Drostan, the half-brother of Nechtan son of Derilei. Their father seems to have been a member of the Cénel Comgaill of Dál Riata, and his branch may have settled in southern Pictland.[115] Strategic political alliances may have stimulated settlement in the seventh century, but one should not overlook the fact that Picts and Scots had apparently worked in close military cooperation since the fourth century when they had attacked Roman Britain. Scottish settlement in Pictland could have a longer history than is often supposed. A final stimulus for a movement east into Pictland may have been provided by Norse conquest of at least part of the Dál Riatan province in the ninth century.[116]

Irish in Wales and the south-west

Irish settlement was also to be found in Wales and the south-west – another area of Britain that bordered the Irish Sea and so had had a tradition dating from the prehistoric period of trade and other contacts with Ireland, and was also an area that suffered in the fourth century AD from Irish raids. Raiding may have led to settlement, or rather seizure of land, but one should also not ignore the possibility that, as seems to have been the case in eastern Britain, there was an attempt to turn poachers into gamekeepers, that is, once official Roman military forces had been withdrawn, some Irish fighters may have been hired to provide a defence instead. Place-names, personal names and ogham inscriptions all reveal the presence of Irish settlers in Wales and south-west England by 600. Stones erected using Gaelic inscriptions or to people with Irish names are concentrated in Anglesey and from Pembrokeshire to Breconshire, with a few outliers in Cornwall and Devon.[117] The greatest concentration of stones and other indicators is in Dyfed in the south-west of Wales. Later traditions from both Ireland and Wales record that its royal house was of Irish origin and that a branch of the Déissi from Munster (modern Co. Waterford) had moved to Wales when expelled by rivals in Ireland.[118] Vortiporius the king of Dyfed is one of the 'tyrants' addressed by Gildas who gives no indication that he saw anything to distinguish him from the other contemporary rulers whom he castigates. However, some confirmation of his probable Irish ancestry comes from one of the stones containing ogham from Dyfed (currently in Castelldwyran churchyard in Carmarthenshire) which was raised to one Voteporix, who from the similarity of their names, was probably related to Vortipor. The stone is bilingual, and has inscriptions in both Latin and Gaelic written respectively in the Roman and ogham alphabets. The Latin inscription reads 'the memorial of Voteporix "protector" ', and the Irish contains only his name in its Gaelic form 'Votecorigas'. Voteporix would therefore seem to have been a man who was open to two cultures; the stone acknowledges his Irish background, but in life he apparently used the Latin title of 'Protector', a term that perhaps suggests a military role in the royal household.[119] There is therefore some circumstantial evidence to support the traditions of the migration of the Déissi, but those surrounding an invasion by the sons of Cunedda from northern Britain into north-west Wales seem more suspect and likely to be retrospective accounts to explain or justify the political situation of the tenth century.[120]

A significant proportion of the inscribed stones erected in Wales in the fifth and sixth centuries seem to have been raised to commemorate men of Irish descent. A conservative estimate would be 35 per cent, but a recent reassessment has suggested between 75 and 80.[121] That is not, of course, a reflection of the proportion of Irish in the population, but only of the Irish who were in Wales and south-west England being particularly keen to have themselves commemorated in this way. The practice suggests that Irishmen were a significant group within the population, even if numbers are impossible to estimate, and that their Irish descent was important to them, though it might also suggest a certain insecurity behind the swagger. There is a possible parallel with incoming Anglo-Saxons displaying themselves in ostensibly 'Germanic' burial customs. The proclamation of Irishness seems to have been less of an issue in the seventh century and one may suspect a greater assimilation with the rest of the population and the disappearance of a distinctive group identity that may in part have been maintained by the speaking of Gaelic. As far as we can tell the Déissi of Dyfed did not maintain involvement in Irish affairs in the way that the Dál Riata of Scotland did. The failure of Gildas to comment on their Irishness or of any Irish settlement in Wales, although he castigated the *Scotti* who had attacked Britain, suggests that he did not associate them with the raiders. Their origins were not an issue for him and there is perhaps an implication that the Irish were already well assimilated with the British population. Nevertheless, the movement into Wales and, to a lesser extent, Devon and Cornwall, of not insignificant numbers of presumably fairly elite Irish needs to be taken into account when considering the nature of the British kingdoms of Wales and the south-west, and we may suspect that they had important roles in the military entourages of the British kings.

The Anglo-Saxons

The term 'Anglo-Saxon' is applied to the Germanic culture that came to dominate in eastern and south-eastern Britain in the course of the fifth and sixth centuries. Bede says that the three major groups involved were the Angles, Saxons and Jutes, the names of continental Germanic peoples from areas bordering the North Sea between southern Denmark (Jutland) and the north provinces of the Netherlands.[122] The sixth-century Byzantine historian Procopius in referring to the Germanic settlement within Britain substituted the Frisians for the Jutes.[123] The Frisian province in modern Netherlands contains the shortest North Sea crossing between these lands and Britain and it would seem that many northern Germanic peoples congregated there before making the journey. Migrants to Britain may in fact have come from a greater range of Germanic peoples. Bede learnt from Anglo-Saxon missionaries who had gone to work in northern Germany that settlers had included 'Frisians, Rugians, Danes, Huns, Old Saxons and Bructeri' (using names current when he wrote in 731).[124] As he says 'there were many peoples in Germany from whom the Angles and Saxons, who now live in Britain, derive their origin' for the emergence of the distinctive groupings he knew as Angles, Saxons and Jutes is something that had occurred within Britain.[125] As Bede informs us the Angles included the East Angles, the Mercians and the Northumbrians, the Saxons consisted of the South, East and West Saxons (the last were based originally in the upper Thames valley), while 'the people of Kent and the inhabitants of the Isle of Wight are of Jutish origin and also those opposite the Isle of Wight, that part of the kingdom of the West Saxons which is still today called the nation of the Jutes' (see Map 1).[126] Although Bede orients his reader with references to the political organisation of the time at which he was writing, the division into Angles, Saxons and Jutes can be seen to have had an earlier existence. It is supported by differences in the dress-sets in which wealthier women were buried that can be interpreted as *tracht*, a form of regional costume. The full version of Anglian women's dress with wrist-clasps, elaborate chatelaines and increasingly baroque cruciform brooches is more ostensibly Germanic and combines practices of a number of different area of continental Germania.[127] Jutish dress was also very showy and in various combinations linked southern Scandinavian and Frankish elements.[128] Saxon female dress, on the other hand, although it too was based around the traditional Germanic *peplos* gown, fastened by brooches on the shoulders, tended to be more restrained and seems to have drawn on Romano-British art for some of its decoration.[129] Although a common Germanic language, usually referred to as Old English, emerged in the Anglo-Saxon provinces, there appear to have been dialectical differences that broadly correspond to the division into Angles, Saxons and Jutes.[130]

It cannot be doubted that some people moved from north Germany into parts of eastern and southern Britain. Burial customs, including forms of both inhumation and cremation, styles of building, jewellery and other metalwork, all characteristic of the North Sea provinces of *Germania*, are reproduced in the areas of Britain identified by Bede as the places of Anglo-Saxon settlement. What is disputed is the scale of that migration, and whether the incomers should be seen as conquerors or settlers alongside a native population who eventually assimilated themselves to their language and culture. The model of a succession of conquests was enthusiastically adopted by prehistorians in the early twentieth century as the explanation for episodes of major changes in material culture that had occurred in the country's pre-Roman past. In the later twentieth century there was something of a reaction against such interpretations, and an emphasis instead on the diffusion of ideas from outside, often coupled with internal stimuli, as a reason for culture change. Some archaeologists have attempted to bring such interpretations to bear on the emergence of Anglo-Saxon culture and to stress the motors for change that came from within late Roman society in Britain.[131] However, many archaeologists and most linguists think the scale of change in material culture and language is too great to be explained without positing a major movement of Germanic peoples into Britain. Historians would stress that at some point written and archaeological evidence needs to be reconciled, and that the testimony of Gildas has to be taken seriously even if he is simplifying a complex situation and reinforcing his case through rhetorical flourishes.

What Gildas tells us, as we have seen, is that some 'Saxons' were recruited as federates, but that the number of settlers grew and eventually rebelled against their paymasters. They would appear to have created a formidable army that looked capable of taking over much of *Britannia*, but they were defeated by determined opposition from the British of the west under the leadership of Ambrosius Aurelianus. It would seem that Britain might at one point have had a similar history to Roman Gaul where a Frankish army was able to take over individual provinces with relative ease.[132] The western British proved more capable of putting up a resistance, perhaps because their leaders had their own military troops who had been hardened by fighting off Irish raiders, and probably each other, and possibly strengthened by the recruitment of Irish warriors. Gildas indicates that up to the time he was writing the Saxons had been restricted to the more easterly part of the island where they had first been established.[133] The earliest concentrations of Anglo-Saxon finds come from the Anglian areas of eastern England where the larger cremation and mixed rite cemeteries are to be found, and the upper Thames valley around Dorchester-on-Thames, the site of the first bishopric of the West

Saxon kings. We have two early focuses here for the development of the Anglian and Saxon confederations of the sixth century. The equation to be found in Bede's *Ecclesiastical History* of the leaders of Gildas's federates with Hengest and Horsa, the legendary founders of the Kentish royal house, is almost certainly a later piece of Kentish propaganda that can be put to one side.[134] Settlement in Kent can also be traced back to the fifth century and was distinguished by early contact with, and perhaps to some extent, domination by Francia.[135] It may have been the first of the Anglo-Saxon kingdoms to have established a royal house, perhaps in the final quarter of the sixth century.

Gildas's account need not be seen as incompatible with the archaeological evidence. The Germanic settlers do not have to be seen as restricted to the members of a federate army, and Gildas implies that once a bridgehead had been created the way was open for much more widespread settlement. The prevalence of male burial with weapons in Anglo-Saxon cemeteries shows the importance of warfare in their culture,[136] but the cemeteries also suggest that not all Anglo-Saxon males were warriors, and that the Anglo-Saxon settlers included women and children as well. The consolidated leadership of a Saxon army implied in Gildas's account need not have survived the army's defeat. Written and archaeological evidence both suggest the emergence of kings and kingdoms among the Anglo-Saxons towards the end of the sixth century,[137] but that does not have to mean that there was an egalitarian society before that date nor one without some overarching form of political organisation. From a relatively early point a hierarchical organisation can be discerned within Anglo-Saxon cemeteries, but it became more pronounced as the sixth century progressed.[138] Perhaps one should look to Old Saxony for parallels with the type of political organisation that may have operated in the Anglo-Saxon areas of eastern Britain for much of the sixth century. The Old Saxons do not seem to have had kings, though they might recognise a dominant military leader for the duration of hostilities, but they did have powerful local families who competed for control within their regions.[139] The increase in displays of wealth through gravegoods seen in Anglo-Saxon cemeteries during the sixth century could be indicative of such competition between dominant families.[140]

Twelve provinces can be traced that are claimed either by Bede or in charters to have been ruled at some point by kings; these are Kent, the East Angles, the Middle Angles, Lindsey, Deira, Bernicia, Mercia, the Hwicce, the Magonsaetan, the South Saxons, the West Saxons (Gewisse) and the Jutes of southern Hampshire and Wight (see Map 1). Significant smaller units of varying size, often called *regiones*, appear in narrative sources and charters,[141] and a number are listed in a somewhat mysterious document of obscure purpose and origin known as the Tribal Hidage.[142] A number have place-names ending in *-ingas*, *-saetan* or *-ware*, all of which indicate the people dwelling in a particular district, or, in the case of some *-ingas* names, identified with a particular individual.[143] These areas might have their own leaders, at least in the seventh century, who might be entitled *duces* or *principes* (in Old English 'ealdormen'), but apparently not *reges* (kings). The *regiones* may take us back to forms of organisation that existed before the formation of kingdoms. In the sources that we have from the seventh century or later they appear principally as districts of administration, and it is possible that some may have had a long history as taxable and organisational units and descend from late Roman *pagi*.[144]

From the point at which kingdoms appear in written records in the seventh century the kingdoms can be seen frequently fighting each other, and the competition for land and resources, and concomitant need to provide defence against external attack, no doubt played a significant role in the development of kingship in the areas of Anglo-Saxon settlement. From an early point there was a tendency for smaller kingdoms to combine or to fall victim to more aggressive neighbours. The royal houses of Bernicia and Deira, for instance, combined to produce the kingdom of Northumbria. The process began when Æthelfrith of Bernicia (592–616) expelled the Deiran princes and married the Deiran princess Acha, but the tables were turned when Edwin of Deira returned from exile to take control of the two provinces (616–33), only for control to pass eventually to Oswald (634–42) who was the son of Æthelfrith and Acha, and so descended from both royal houses (see Appendix 5).[145] The kingdoms that became the most dominant were those with the opportunity to expand westwards by taking in British-controlled territory in the seventh and eighth centuries. Mercia seems to have done this through setting up satellite provinces (those of Hwicce, Magonsaetan and Wreocensaetan) on its western flanks; the first two had their own royal lines, but they seem to have been subservient to their Mercian overlords.[146] Wessex and Northumbria seem to have absorbed the British areas more directly into their main kingdom structures, and in Wessex, as we have seen, the British were given a legally defined, though inferior, position.[147] The kingdoms of the south-east were smaller, but were probably well organised internally and shored up by involvement with well-developed trading networks because of their proximity to the continent; they showed themselves remarkably resilient to intermittent dominance by more powerful neighbours.[148] Nevertheless most of them finally lost their independence during the reign of the mighty Offa of Mercia (757–96),[149] so that by 800 only the royal dynasties of the East Angles, Northumbria, Mercia and Wessex were left in contention (see Map 2). Although it looked in the eighth century as if the Mercians were set to become the dominant kingdom among the English, the failure of Offa to establish a line of successors led to a series of disputed successions and loss of the newly acquired provinces in the south-east that were snapped up by King Ecgbert of the West Saxons (802–39) instead.[150] However, it was only the vigorous activities of the great heathen army between 865 and 872 that saw an end to the royal houses of Northumbria, Mercia and the East Angles and so paved the way for the kings of Wessex to turn themselves into kings of all England in the course of the tenth century.

Overlordship and warfare in early medieval Britain

It will have become apparent from the discussion of the individual peoples of Britain that by 600 they were all dominated by military-based kingships. The failure of the Roman authorities to police the borders of *Britannia* adequately from the fourth century had led to the privatisation of military power and the opportunity for those with the most effective military forces, and so with access to the greatest profits, to declare themselves kings and secure the succession for their descendants. Although there were clashes in which each of the opposing armies was drawn predominantly from one of the four peoples of Britain, as when Ambrosius Aurelianus led a successful resistance of Britons against the Saxon incomers, not all fighting occurred along what could be broadly described as ethnic lines and many armies were much more mixed. One reason for this was the practice of overlordship whereby one ruler recognised the superiority of another through payment of tribute and often, it would appear, through supplying military contingents to fight in the overlord's army. Such tiers of authority are seen as an integral part of the practice of Irish kingship, and so have often been assumed to be inherent among the Scottish Dál Riata as well.[151] In the early seventh century the Cénel nGabráin seem to have dominated the other *cénela* in the territories of the Dál Riata in both Scotland and Antrim, but had themselves to recognise the authority of (predominantly) Uí Néill overlords of a much wider area of northern Ireland. Similar, but perhaps more unstable, tiers of authority can be found among the Anglo-Saxons. For example, in the seventh century the South Saxons seem to have been overshadowed by their more powerful neighbours, Kent and Wessex, and often to have been obliged to recognise the authority of one or the other. However, in c.660 their king Æthelwalh formed an alliance with the rising power Wulfhere of Mercia (658–75) and in exchange for recognising his authority was himself made overlord of the kingdom of Wight that Wulfhere had just conquered (but presumably could have had some difficulties in controlling as it was some distance from his midland base).[152]

Overlordship could therefore operate both at a localised level and over a much wider expanse of territory. By the seventh century the most powerful kings were acting as overlords over large areas of Britain and over different ethnic groupings. To begin with there were two distinct zones of overlordship in the south and north of Britain, but due to the zeal of the Northumbrians they came to overlap. Bede provides a list of seven kings who were overlords south of the Humber in the late sixth and the seventh centuries.[153] The list is repeated in the *Anglo-Saxon Chronicle* of 829 with the statement that King Ecgbert 'was the eighth king who was bretwalda', and so historians sometimes use the term 'bretwalda' (meaning either 'wide ruler' or 'ruler of Britain') for kings holding this authority, although it was far from certain that it was a term in regular use. In the same period we can find similar powerful kings in the north of Britain especially King Áedán mac Gabráin of Dál Riata (574–608).[154] Áedán campaigned widely and established overlordship of British, Picts and some of the kings of northern Ireland (though he recognised the ultimate overlordship of the Uí Néill overlordship with respect of the latter). His involvement with the Britons brought him into conflict with the Anglo-Saxon king Æthelfrith of Bernicia who was also seeking to extend authority into northern British territory, and the two sides fought at the unidentified site of *Degastan* in 603. Áedán seems to have fielded a multi-national army with forces drawn not only from Dál Riata and kingdoms from northern Ireland, but probably from the northern British as well and including a disaffected Northumbrian Hering son of Hussa, whose father had ruled in Northumbria before Æthelfrith. Defeat in this battle was a major setback for further expansion by the Dál Riata.

The Northumbrians appear initially to have been more involved with the northern British overlordship than that of the other Anglo-Saxon dominated kingdoms to the south, with the Humber being, as Bede suggests, a major dividing line between them.[155] However, the exile of Edwin of Deira during the reign of Æthelfrith of Bernicia sent him to seek shelter in the southern kingdoms where he was protected by the fourth of the great southern overlords in Bede's list, Raedwald of the East Angles (d.616x627).[156] Raedwald, when faced with the choice of either handing Edwin over to Æthelfrith or facing the consequences of a refusal, led an army against Æthelfrith in 616 and placed Edwin on the throne instead. Attack was often deemed the best form of defence in early medieval Britain. Edwin was presumably somewhat beholden to Raedwald until the latter's death (which cannot be dated precisely, but must have occurred between 616 and 627), but then became overlord of the southern English in his place. He was followed in this position eventually by his Bernician successors Oswald and Oswiu, though not without intermissions for Mercian overlordship under its kings Penda (?626–55) and his son Wulfhere (658–72). Penda had initially come to pre-eminence through an alliance in which a British king Caedwalla was the dominant partner. Caedwalla has often been seen as a king of Gwynedd, but is perhaps more likely to have been a king from one of the northern British kingdoms that had suffered from Æthelfrith's ambitions.[157] He was responsible for the death of King Edwin in 633 and of King Eanfrith, the son of Æthelfrith, the following year.

Edwin, Oswald and Oswiu sought to dominate the northern part of Britain as well as the south, and gradually increased the extent of Northumbrian overlordship over all the northern peoples. Oswiu's son Ecgfrith (670–85) took Northumbrian self-confidence even further when in 684 he sent a Northumbrian fleet to attack Brega, a centre of Uí Néill power, probably to discourage them from joining a northern coalition against him. In 685 he led an army deep into Pictish territory and was slain together with a large part of his army by King Bridei.[158] This disastrous defeat ended Northumbrian overlordship in the north (though lands in the south of Scotland were subsequently recovered and incorporated into Northumbria). The history of the Northumbrian overlordship in the south had effectively been ended in 679 when at the battle of the river Trent King Aethelred of Mercia (675–704) had avenged an earlier defeat of his brother Wulfhere by Ecgfrith and permanently detached the former kingdom of Lindsey from Northumbrian control.[159] Whether Mercia and the Picts had been acting in concert against Northumbria is not known, but in the eighth century Onuist of the Picts (729–61) and Æthelbald of Mercia (716–57) may well have operated in unison to hold the northern and southern overlordships respectively between them.[160]

There were therefore many occasions on which warriors from the different peoples of Britain fought on the same side and that would have occasioned delegations moving from one kingdom to another. Political alliances were sealed by marriages and might be underpinned by personal friendships and obligations. Dynastic rivalries could drive princes from a kingdom to seek refuge in a different province; mutual interests could be served for, if the host helped the refugee return to power, he could expect to extend the area of his influence. We have already seen how this worked when Edwin sought refuge with Raedwald of the East Angles and how that led to the Northumbrians being drawn into the ambit of the southern English overlordship, apparently for the first time. When Edwin became king in 616, it was the turn of the sons of Æthelfrith to seek sanctuary, and they turned to the other kingdoms of northern Britain for support. The eldest, Eanfrith, who later ruled for a year on the death of Edwin before falling to the British king Caedwalla in 634, went to the Picts and, it would seem, married a Pictish princess for the king-lists include a reign of Talorcan, son of 'Enfret' (653–7) whose reign coincided with part of that of his uncle Oswiu in Northumbria.[161] The two younger sons, Oswald and Oswiu, who were mere boys aged roughly 12 and 4 respectively, went to Dál Riata where in 616 the king was Eochaid Buide (608–29), the son of their father's major protagonist, Áedán mac Gabráin.[162] Oswald may well have fought in Ireland with his Dalriadic hosts either in support of the Uí Néill overking or in disputes with Ulaid kings, and may not have been the first Northumbrian prince to do so. Oswiu played a different role in cementing relations between his Dalriadic hosts and northern Irish allies for he seems to have married (or at least to have had a liaison with) a princess of the Cenél nEógain of the northern Uí Néill. Their son who had the Irish name Flann Fina may have been brought up in Ireland, but later became King Aldfrith of Northumbria (686–705).[163] Although the record may not be so full for other peoples of Britain we need not doubt that political exile was also a significant part of their royal histories and that it may have led to significant alliances

The strength of the involvement of seventh-century Northumbrian kings with the royal families of northern Britain may be a pointer to some significant differences between Northumbria and the southern English kingdoms. In 600 the wider political world with which a number of the southern royal houses were involved was that of Francia. Frankish involvement with southern England may have gone back into the sixth century and have originated in their desire to keep the Channel free of 'Saxon' pirates.[164] Frankish influence in Kent, the Anglo-Saxon province closest to Francia, is relatively well attested, and it may be no coincidence that Kent is the earliest known Anglo-Saxon kingdom. Involvement with

Francia may have stimulated the development of kingship in the Anglo-Saxon provinces. The first king of Kent who can be named (though not necessarily the first to rule) was Eormenric who has a Frankish name. His son Æthelbert married in 580 Bertha the daughter of King Charibert of Neustria.[165] The East Angles also had close Frankish connections. Sigebert, who became king of the East Angles in 630 or 631 returned from exile in Francia, and East Anglian princesses were abbesses of the nunnery of Faremoutiers in the 640s at a time when it was under the patronage of Erchinoald, the powerful mayor of Neustria. A daughter of Erchinoald had married King Eadbald of Kent (616–40) and the royal houses of Kent and the East Angles, and perhaps of other areas in southern England, seem to have been drawn into the complex internal feuding of Neustria.[166] The southern kingdoms are not known to have intermarried with the non-Anglo-Saxon houses of northern Britain, though the appearance of West Saxon kings with Brittonic names may suggest intermarriage with one or more British royal house, perhaps from Wales or the west of England. However, a number of marriages are recorded between Northumbria and the royal houses of Kent, the East Angles, Mercia and the West Saxons.[167]

Thus the contacts formed through obligations of overlordship were underpinned by other ties between the royal families of Britain. Not only was there a considerable movement of princes and princesses around the island, but these would have been attended by other members of the court. Bede tells something of the histories within Northumbria of two East Anglian noblemen who had travelled there when its princess Æthelthryth married Ecgfrith, the son of Oswiu in c.660, and records that the sons of Æthelfrith are said to have gone into exile 'with many young nobles'.[168] No doubt contingents of fit young fighting men, with or without princes, were welcome additions to the armies of kings up and down the country. Such mobile units of men with swords for hire may account for the presence of Irish, as revealed by the distribution of ogham stones, among the Picts and in parts of Wales and the west of England. A contingent of Picts is said to have fought alongside the British in *The Gododdin*, and Columba arranged for an exiled Pictish noble called Tarain to enter the *comitatus* of a Dál Riatan noble on Islay.[169] Many of the armies fielded by kings in early medieval Britain may have been more ethnically mixed than one might at first assume, and this must have led to some commonalties of court culture, especially among the military households in constant attendance on kings.

There are two ways in which such entourages can be viewed; the 'heroic' mode of poetry that may well have originated at the royal courts, and the rather more jaundiced view of the military households from some of the churchmen who encountered them. The Old English poem *Beowulf* and the Brittonic *The Gododdin* present remarkably similar views of loyal nobles whose most ardent desire was to earn a good reputation for themselves fighting, and if necessary, dying in battle for the lord who had housed, wined and dined them and supported them with generous gifts, though one must remember that there are problems in using these poems to illuminate the seventh century as both are known to us only from later texts and have complex histories of transmission.[170] They are the closest we can come to the type of poetry recited in the great halls of the kings and, through the idealisation of their violent world, helped create the bonds that were essential for success when the warriors left the halls to fight.

Others saw the warriors in a more jaundiced light. Gildas characterised the military companions of the southern British kings as 'bloody, proud and murderous men, adulterers and enemies of God',[171] and many Irish churchmen were equally scathing about confraternities of warriors in their society.[172] Although Anglo-Saxon churchmen were rarely as outspoken about their own leaders and their followers, they complained about the brutality of their non-Saxon enemies. The British Caedwalla after his conquest of the Northumbrian provinces in 633 is said by Bede to have ravaged them 'like a savage tyrant, tearing them to pieces with fearful bloodshed',[173] and in the continuation of the chronicle that ended the *Historia Ecclesiastica* it is said of King Onuist of the Picts who died in 761 that 'from the beginning of his reign to the end he perpetrated bloody crimes, like a tyrannical slaughterer'. Battles and their aftermath could be extremely bloody affairs with no quarter given. The greater part of Ecgfrith's army seems to have been slaughtered at *Nechtansmere*, and those who survived were enslaved. The story Bede provides about a Northumbrian noble called Imma, who was captured by a noble from the opposing Mercian side at the battle of the river Trent in 679, implies it was not unusual for any captured warriors to be put to death to avenge deaths of kinsmen in battle.[174]

Although a military household, usually referred to as a *comitatus* in Anglo-Saxon contexts and as a *teulu* in medieval Welsh, would contain some seasoned warriors, a large part of it was made up of young men of the nobility seeking to establish their reputations and future security. The *Lives* of a number of Anglo-Saxon saints make clear that a normal career pattern for an Anglo-Saxon noble was to be in a king's *comitatus* between the ages of roughly 14 and 25, after which they could expect to receive a grant of land on which to establish their own households, but with the obligation to return to fight with their own entourages when called out by the king.[175] The laws of Ine of Wessex (686–726) envisage that all freemen will turn out in response to a royal summons.[176] The right to bear arms, represented in symbolic burial with weapons in the fifth and sixth centuries, may originally have been synonymous with rank as a free Anglo-Saxon, and something that distinguished them from the British population of their provinces.[177] But similar obligations to fight seem to have existed in the Celtic world, though they may have been constituted slightly differently. The flow of young men to a king's entourage was aided in Wales and Ireland by the institution of fosterage, and the landed nobles and freemen were obliged to provide military service by a system of clientage that either involved a grant of land or of cattle and chattels; the workings of such a system are fully recorded in contemporary Irish laws.[178] The *Senchus fer nAlban*, although only preserved in a tenth-century version, may give a glimpse of military and other obligations among the Dál Riata as early as the seventh century.[179] Obligations were laid on households organised into groups of five; for instance, every 20 households were expected to provide two seven-benched ships for a sea expedition.

Ships must have been particularly important to the Dál Riata because of the many islands within their province and their involvement in the political structures of northern Ireland. They were used not only for transport, but also for naval battles; a sea battle is recorded between the rival kindreds, the Cénel Loairn and the Cénel nGabráin in 719.[180] The Picts and the Anglo-Saxons had been, like the Irish, formidable raiders in the fourth and fifth centuries, if not longer, and so can be expected to have continued to have considerable naval know-how, though neither is recorded as having fought at sea. The Pictish stronghold at Burghead, which protects a good anchorage, would have been an appropriate place to host a Pictish fleet.[181] Pictish kings would have needed ships to communicate between their many islands, and seem to have been able to command large fleets for there is a record in the Irish annals of 150 Pictish ships wrecked in 729.[182] Anglo-Saxon overlords also operated outside the mainland of Britain. Edwin of Northumbria, like Áedán mac Gabráin before him, conquered the Isle of Man, and Ecgfrith of Northumbria was able to mount a naval raid on Brega in Ireland.[183] There are no records for the seventh and eighth century of ships being used in warfare among the British or southern English, though the famous Sutton Hoo ship burial, often linked with the overlord Raedwald of the East Angles, is a reminder of their association with royal status in the Anglo-Saxon world.

Although large numbers of land battles are referred to in the sources, and even occasionally depicted in other media such as the sculptures of Pictland, we have frustratingly few detailed descriptions of what actually took place. As far as we can tell warfare and weaponry in Britain seem similar to the practices in other parts of western Europe at this time, and probably owed much to the nature of the late Roman armies with which some ancestors of the early medieval peoples of Britain may have served or come into hostile contact. It may not have been the case that the shield-wall, which is often seen as distinctive of Anglo-Saxon warfare, was a normal mode of fighting among them at this time for it may have been a later development in response to Viking attacks.[184] Like the other peoples of Britain, the Anglo-Saxons probably fought either on foot or horseback as circumstances dictated. Pooling all our information from vernacular poetry, Latin sources, archaeological finds and sculpture, we have impressions from throughout Britain of the elite fighters as mounted warriors equipped with sword, spear, lance and shield, just as were the mobile field armies of the late Roman world. The Pictish sculptures, in comparable ways to the poems *Beowulf* and *The Gododdin*, lovingly depict details of war gear, and may have been erected over the graves of warriors – or at least men who wished to be portrayed as such. Particularly interesting is a stone from Aberlemno churchyard (Angus) which has been interpreted as representing the battle of *Nechtansmere* that was fought in 685 between King Bridei mac Beli of the Picts and King Ecgfrith of Northumbria, and is generally believed to have taken place in the vicinity at Dunnichen. The action is depicted in three registers, each of which features a figure in a distinctive helmet that bears a resemblance to one excavated at Coppergate in York, thus fuelling the interpretation that the figure is the defeated Ecgfrith. In the top register the helmeted figure flees from a (presumably) Pictish horseman, dropping his sword and shield; in the middle he is opposed by foot-soldiers and in the bottom one he is shown as fighting a horseman before finally being depicted as dead with a symbolic raven attacking his corpse.[185]

In spite of these overall similarities there were differences in the equipment of warriors from different parts of Britain and in aspects of their warfare.[186] Although the Picts are sometimes depicted with round shields of the type used by the Anglo-Saxons, and probably the other Celtic peoples, they also had square shields and rectangular ones with notches. Some Anglo-Saxons used the *francisca* or light, throwing axe, which is particularly associated with the Franks, and wore distinctive helmets whereas Picts depicted as engaged in warfare on the sculptures are generally shown bare-headed. On the other hand, most of the Anglo-Saxon kingdoms do not seem to have made use of hill-forts and cliff-top fortifications that were utilised in the Celtic areas of Britain and also by the Bernicians in the late sixth and early seventh centuries, perhaps another indication of their closer connection at this time with the peoples of northern Britain than with the Anglo-Saxons to their south.[187] In consequence, whereas Anglo-Saxon battles were generally fought in the open, though often in the vicinity of Roman roads that were no doubt used to move armies round the country, warfare in the north might involve sieges and direct attacks on the enemy's stronghold. Sieges at the defended Dál Riatan royal centres of Dunadd and Dundurn are recorded in the Irish annals for 683, while a third fortress at Dunollie was burnt in 686, 698 and 701, apparently in internal disputes over the kingship.[188] Drowning as a specific ritual to kill princes is recorded among the Picts. Onuist is recorded as having drowned Talorc, son of Cong in 734 and in 739 Talorcan, son of Drostan, the king of Atholl.[189] Beheaded men are shown on Sueno's stone, and severed heads are apparently displayed hanging on a tree on the Eassie Priory cross-slab,[190] but this method of dealing with defeated enemies is unlikely to have been restricted to the Picts. Penda had the head and arms of King Oswald of Northumbria removed and displayed on stakes after he defeated him in battle in 642.[191]

Behind all the fine sentiments expressed in British and Anglo-Saxon poetry about the ties of lord and warrior, there was a hard economic imperative.[192] Men fought in the expectation of reward; in *Beowulf* a 'good' king not only won his battles, but generously rewarded those who had enabled him to do so. Decisive action might be taken against a king who offended the mores of his followers. King Æthelbald of Mercia was murdered by his *comitatus* in 757 though we do not know the precise circumstances that led to his death.[193] Dissatisfied followers might also vote with their feet. The crucial battle at the river Winwaed fought between Penda of Mercia and Oswiu of Northumbria in 655 was lost for the former because King Oethelwald of Deira (nephew of Oswiu), who should have been fighting on his side, withdrew from the battle.[194] Kings therefore had to take the opinions of their chief supporters into account, especially those who controlled substantial tracts of country and were themselves the lords of men obliged to fight for them. Warlords needed a well-filled treasury if they were to prove more attractive than their opponents. Tacitus, who knew something of a not dissimilar Germanic world in the first century AD, offered an interesting critique of how the need to reward service could lead to an escalating cycle of war if that was the main means of acquiring the necessary resources to do so.[195] Such warfare may have dominated much of the history of kingdoms of Britain in the period 600–800, but the future of kingship lay in strengthening the inherent rights of kings and exploiting the resources of the lands that they ruled.

Economy and society

The majority of the population was involved in supporting themselves and the elites through agriculture. The farming population did not share in the rewards of royal service, but were all too likely to suffer from the effects of living in a society run by military leaders. When one king wished to encourage another to pay tribute he did so by ravaging part of his territory until he either paid up or challenged the intruder. By 'ravaging' one means taking away or destroying any crops, animals or people that were in the invading army's way. The population could also do little to avert the natural disasters that were a recurrent feature of early medieval life. Bad harvests and disease among animals and men are regularly noted in early medieval annals. The *Anglo-Saxon Chronicle* recorded a 'great mortality of birds' in 671, and the 'Continuation of Bede' refers to major droughts in 737 and 741 that 'rendered the land infertile'. Not even the wealthier members of the community might be immune in such circumstances, for a study of teeth and bones from Anglo-Saxon cemeteries suggests that even those buried with an array of gravegoods had often suffered a period of deprivation in their childhood.[196] Plague, which seems to have been endemic in western Europe in the early Middle Ages, also affected the whole population and seems to have first reached Britain in the 540s. Particularly severe outbreaks are recorded in 664–6 and 684–7, in which several Anglo-Saxon and Irish kings and churchmen are recorded as dying, though Adomnán states that the Picts and Irish of Dál Riata escaped because of the protection provided by St Columba.[197] There are references to depopulation in the countryside and it has been suggested that the effects may have been as severe as the Black Death of the fourteenth century, though, if so, the population seems to have recovered rapidly; descriptions of the bubos of the victims suggest that it was the same disease as that known as the Black Death.[198] Early medieval burial grounds (predominantly Anglo-Saxon) suggest a high infant and child mortality, and a high death rate for women of child-bearing age, with something like 70 per cent of the women who had reached adulthood dying by the age of 35.[199] Men fared slightly better, but social class again does not seem to have made a significant difference to mortality rates.

There were other major changes that the bulk of the population would neither be able to control or to understand. The beginning of the early Middle Ages seems to have coincided with a deterioration of the climate after a relatively warm spell in the Roman period, and this has been suggested as a major factor in bringing Anglo-Saxons to England because farming in their North Sea homelands would have become less viable. Climate change therefore coincided with the end of Roman rule in Britain.[200] As we have seen, opinion differs on just how traumatic the ending of Roman authority was for the ordinary inhabitants of the lowland zone of Britain, but population decline, retrenchment and a regrouping of settlements on the most viable land does seem to have resulted, even if one does not want to go as far as envisaging a complete systems collapse. Further changes in settlement patterns occurred in the seventh and eighth centuries in Anglo-Saxon England and have been associated with a need to increase agricultural production again in response to a rising population and the increasing demands upon it from the emergent kingdoms,[201] though it is possible such reorganisation may have been aided by a short-term drop in the population caused by plague in the late seventh century. There is no similar evidence for major changes in the rural settlements of the other areas of Britain in the same period, though a more gradual shifting of rural settlement patterns has been detected in some areas such as Cornwall.[202]

Methods of exploiting the land would have been dictated by climate, underlying geology and tradition. The aim was self-sufficiency, but some surplus would always have been needed for acquisition of necessary commodities that could not be produced in the local community, such as salt, and for payment to lords. Therefore most rural communities would have a mixed farming economy, but the type and proportion of crop and animal husbandry would depend on local environmental conditions.[203] Highland areas would depend more heavily on pastoral farming and hardier crops such as rye, and this is reflected by the high value placed on cattle as signifiers of status as is apparent in later Welsh laws and Scottish records. Pig seems to have been valued, high-status food in these areas as well, but was more widely available in other areas of Britain as were sheep, for wool production was a significant element of lowland economy as it was to be for much of the Middle Ages. There is no obvious sign that Germanic incomers came with their own animals; Roman stock continued to be used, but a gradual decline in its size probably reflects an increase in exploitation. Roman fields also continued in use, but there was a move away in lowland areas from the cultivation of spelt as the main cereal crop to wheat. Many areas used an infield/outfield system of farming with the best land cropped regularly (infield) and the poorer having long periods when it would be fallow and able to recover its fertility. Other crops widely grown were flax for linen, barley for ale and some vegetables such as peas, beans, cabbages and onions. Regular finds such as hand querns and spinning and sewing equipment reveal that most communities would expect to process their own foods and equip themselves with other necessities. The degree to which hunting, fishing and gathering of wild fruits supplemented farming seems to have varied, for bone and pollen evidence suggests that this was more likely to be a feature of highland than lowland communities. Columba was said to have provided an impoverished layman with a sharp stake so that he could provide for his family from the wild animals and fish that would impale themselves upon it.[204]

To make the best of varied resources, communities were grouped for the purposes of agrarian management into larger units that are often referred to in modern literature as multiple estates and for which a variety of different names can be found in the various regions of early medieval Britain.[205] Traces of land organisation of this type have been found throughout Britain and would appear to have been widespread in the early Middle Ages. A multiple estate would typically include a range of different types of land including arable, woodland and waste and several different zones of settlement and types of husbandry. Settlement forms could therefore be very varied and range from relatively large villages in some lowland areas, through hamlets to individual farmsteads. Dwellings would consist of one large house, typically round in areas on the fringes of and outside the Roman province and rectangular within, though distinctive forms were introduced by Germanic settlers, including the sunken-featured building that was probably used for a variety of agricultural and domestic functions such as weaving.[206]

Differences in status can be found among the peasant population who farmed the land. The fullest descriptions of the various subdivisions of the peasant class are to be found in the lawcodes of the seventh and early eighth centuries from the Anglo-Saxon kingdoms of Kent and Wessex.[207] The earliest comparable evidence from Wales dates from some time after our period, but may still be informative especially when compared with the Anglo-Saxon material.[208] Basic distinctions were between peasants who owned land and those who did not, between those who had free status and those who were dependent or unfree. The higher ranked free peasants, the *ceorls* of Anglo-Saxon England, might have their own dependent peasants and owed services directly to the king, whereas dependent peasants often had a median lord to whom rent or labour services, or sometimes a combination of the two were due; the distinction between being a tribute-payer (*gafolgelda*) who had his own land to farm, even if this belonged ultimately to his lord, and a mere labourer (*gebur*) was an important one.[209] The laws recognised reciprocal obligations between a lord and his dependants. In the laws of Ine equivalence is found between British and Anglo-Saxon ranks. The lawcodes recognised differences between landless Britons, tax-payers with varying amounts of land and freemen owing services to the king. However, detailed study of the later Welsh laws suggests some major differences in approach. Welsh law of the twelfth and thirteenth centuries lacked the Anglo-Saxon distinction between nobleman and *ceorl*, and drew only a distinction between free and dependent status, that is between those who owned land and those (*taeogion*) who lived upon the land owned by others in return for various renders.[210] A fundamental distinction was between those who were able to entertain their lord or the king at their own table and those who paid a food render to his vill.

All the peoples of early medieval Britain were slave-owners and slave labour played a very significant role in the economy.[211] Warfare and enslaving went together in the early Middle Ages, and the seizing of men, women and children for a life of slavery was part of the booty that might be taken. Slavery might also be the punishment for various crimes or the result of being unable to pay one's debts or dues. Slaves could be kept for a variety of household or agrarian functions, or sold on to others for profit. When the identity of the Northumbrian nobleman Imma was discovered, his Mercian captor sold him to a Frisian merchant who took him to London as a preliminary to probably selling him abroad, for slaves were one of the commodities from Britain for which there was a market in Europe. Queen Balthild of Francia was in origin an Anglo-Saxon slave who had been shipped to Francia and attracted the attention of the mayor of the palace of Neustria and eventually of his royal master.[212] As Balthild's story rather dramatically shows, the possibility of reacquiring freedom did exist and the category of freedman existed in Anglo-Saxon and Welsh lawcodes though it could take several generations to escape its stigma. Slave-gangs were not a feature of early medieval Britain and many slaves were expected to support themselves on allocations of land that might give them some capacity to make a profit and ultimately purchase their freedom if they were not freed by their masters. But the lot of the slave was not an enviable one; Anglo-Saxon lawcodes show that they had limited rights and could be severely punished for any infringements of the law while any mistreatment of them was lightly punished. If a slave was killed it was his owner who was compensated rather than any of his own dependants.

The basic unit of organisation, even for many slaves, was the family or household. As in modern society it was the nuclear family that was most significant though one should envisage this including elderly relatives and other dependants. Many Anglo-Saxon cemeteries seem to have been organised on the basis of individual plots for different households.[213] Obligations to kin were taken very seriously, and might involve wider groups of kindred on both the male and female side.[214] Kinsmen might seek redress or vengeance for a wronged relative. The nobleman who captured Imma would have killed him to avenge his brothers and other kinsmen who had died in the battle, if he had not taken an oath not to harm him if he revealed the truth. Clearly there was a danger in societies where it was normal for men to carry weapons for all-out feuds to develop and, to prevent such escalations of violence, the peoples of early medieval Britain, as did those in other parts of early medieval Europe, had systems of arbitration to reach agreement between the parties concerned in local courts.[215] Crimes were usually punished by payment of compensation by the guilty party (with the aid of his kin if he could not pay) at recognised rates dependent on the rank of the individuals concerned. Some Anglo-Saxon laws contain long lists of these payments, not unlike the schedules of payments for injuries in modern insurance policies, and the amount payable for a man's life was his wergild. Communities therefore to an extent policed themselves according to customary law, and there is enough evidence to suggest that in the Celtic areas of Britain, as in Ireland, there were specialists in the law with a recognised position in society.[216] Although the Anglo-Saxon lawcodes are not practical documents for use in courts, they show that kings were taking an active interest in promulgating new law and in developing their authority by these means.[217]

There were sharply gendered divisions in early medieval societies that are symbolised by the different ranges of gravegoods given to men and women in Anglo-Saxon cemeteries which correspond in legal and other documents to the designation of the families of an individual's mother and father as the spindle- and spear-side respectively.[218] Female relatives were the responsibility of their male kin who would be compensated at the time a marriage was arranged by payment of a bride-price.[219] They would retain some responsibilities for their kinswoman during a marriage and she would return to them if the marriage was dissolved, for early medieval unions were not necessarily envisaged as lasting the full lifetimes of the two people involved. In fact the later concept of marriage did not exist as such and a variety of legal male–female unions were recognised; wealthy individuals such as kings might therefore legitimately have several contemporary relationships that could produce children who were regarded as legitimate. Women on the whole did not have public roles, but there were occasions in Anglo-Saxon society when they clearly did and one queen, Seaxburh of Wessex, appears in a regnal list.[220] It is a characteristic of 'pioneer' societies, as that of the Anglo-Saxons in Britain might be considered to be, that there were often more opportunities for women than in more established periods because shortage of male personnel might oblige them to take on a greater variety of roles and hence be seen as 'honorary' men.[221] But we must always remember the limits of our sources. Although we know the names of hardly any Pictish women they are depicted on some of the sculptured stones. A notable example from Hilton of Cadboll (Ross and Cromarty) shows a hunting scene with a woman (riding side saddle) in the most prominent position and wearing a penannular brooch, perhaps normally a symbol of male authority.[222] We know the names of hardly any Welsh or Dál Riatan women either, but in all these societies women would have played important role in securing alliances on behalf of their kin and running households.

Taxation and trade

There were two main stimuli for the rural population to produce a surplus – the need to meet royal fiscal demands and the desirability of acquiring goods through trade. In all the areas of early medieval Britain there are traces of the right of kings to claim support from their subjects. Although we cannot trace the origins of such rights, they may have been very ancient and may have been adapted under Roman rule as taxation in order to support the army and the state.[223] A notional unit of land that would support a household, the hide of Anglo-Saxon sources, was used throughout Britain as a basis for calculating the render owed and for other demands such as military service. The ability to contribute to such public obligations through the ownership of hidated land was an important indicator throughout early medieval Britain and Ireland of free status.[224] Households were commonly grouped in units of five or ten for assessment purposes. The *Senchus fer nAlban* has groupings of five households, and the *davach* of the later kingdom of Scotland was probably a very similar measure.[225] The laws of Ine list the food renders that might be expected from ten hides, and give a good idea of the resources of an early medieval 'multiple' estate:

As a food-rent from 10 hides: 10 vats of honey, 300 loaves, 12 'ambers'
of Welsh ale, 30 of clear ale, 2 full-grown cows, or 10 wethers, 10 geese,
20 hens, 10 cheeses, an 'amber' full of butter, 5 salmon, 20 pounds of
fodder and 100 eels.[226]

Such renders might be delivered to the local royal *tun* or vill and be con-
sumed by the king and his court as they made their circuits of the
kingdom, of which we are given glimpses in some of the relatively plentiful sources from early eighth-century Northumbria.[227] The later Welsh
laws distinguish food render of this type (*dawnbwyd*) payable by the *taeo-*
gion (peasant tenants) to a royal *llys* from the hospitality dues (*gwestfa*)
of the land-owning class that seem to have been a substitution for what
was originally an obligation to entertain the king and his court in their
own homes when he visited their vicinity.[228] There seems to have been a
similar distinction in the kingdom of Scotland between *cain* (tribute) and
conveth (hospitality) that probably also stretched back into the earlier
medieval past,[229] and the laws of Æthelbert of Kent recognised penalties
for violation of the king's peace when he was drinking at a man's
house.[230] The itineration of the kingdom and entertainment by nobles
living in different localities implied by these dues would have been
important ways for kings or other lords to forge bonds and make their
power felt throughout their territories. But a lord might not wish to take
all his food renders in this way and there were potentially other ways in
which they could be utilised.

Kings and their subjects both had need of commodities that could not
be provided from their own resources. There could be various ways in
which these might be obtained, through gift-exchange or gift-giving, for
instance, which were of great importance throughout society not just
because of the usefulness of the items acquired, but because they symbolised important social contracts. Local assemblies, which seem to have
occurred for religious, royal or legal purposes throughout early medieval
Britain,[231] would have provided opportunities for such symbolic transactions to have taken place, but presumably also opportunities for acquiring
commodities through trade. There was probably never a period in which
some form of internal trading did not take place, but it can be hard to
detect archaeologically compared to trade in items from outside Britain.
When artefacts of continental manufacture are regularly found on British
sites we can assume that trade was taking place. Two main trading routes
can be discerned in early medieval Britain, one linking areas around the
Irish Sea with western Francia and beyond and the other involving routes

from the eastern and southern Anglo-Saxon kingdoms across the Channel and the North Sea. The Irish Sea trade can be studied through finds of imported glass and pottery containers for a variety of commodities from wine to dyes.[232] These objects can be seen as the remnants of what must have been in fact a much more varied trade with the Mediterranean and western Francia. In the late fifth and early sixth centuries Dumnonia and south-western Wales seem to have been part of a regular trading route from the Mediterranean via Spain in which it is suspected that tin was the major export. Later in the sixth and into the seventh century trade was established between western Francia and a much wider range of areas bordering the Irish Sea, though the south-west does not seem to have participated to the same extent. Adomnán records sailors from Francia in the time of Columba putting in at the *caput regionis* which is probably a reference to Dunadd.[233] Concentrations of finds of imported material have been found at putative centres of local power such as Dunadd, Dinas Powys, Tintagel and South Cadbury, and it would appear that this trade was tightly controlled by the elites. In addition to precious metals, other exports may have included leather, agricultural products such as honey and slaves. The trade was a means by which the kings celebrated in *The Gododdin* could acquire the wine served in glass vessels for their warriors, but it did not directly involve the bulk of the population.

In the Anglo-Saxon provinces matters seem rather different. As in the west, royal courts were able to acquire luxury imports, probably via Francia, and such items can be seen in the princely burials of the seventh century from sites such as Sutton Hoo, Prittlewell (Essex) and Taplow (Bucks.), though traded items cannot be easily distinguished from diplomatic gifts.[234] A much larger group of the Anglo-Saxon population seems to have had access to imported goods than was the case in the west, though as people were not buried with grave goods in the west we lack an important class of evidence from that area. Anglo-Saxon cemeteries of the sixth and early seventh centuries regularly contain items such as amber beads (from the Baltic), elephant ivory rings and cowrie shells (from India).[235] Exactly how and where the objects were traded is not clear, but metal-detecting finds are producing increasing evidence from the seventh and eighth centuries for so-called 'productive' sites in the countryside, perhaps the regular sites of fairs or other communal gatherings, that do not seem to have had detectable counterparts further west in this period.[236] In addition, specialised trading centres (*wíc*) can be identified from the seventh century at London, Ipswich, York and Hamwic (Southampton), but these may have been sites especially under royal control, one of whose functions was to convert royal surpluses into cash or desirable imports.[237]

The patterns between the east and the west coasts were therefore different, and the Anglo-Saxon kingdoms can be distinguished from the Celtic in having far more signs of a developing market economy, which by the tenth century would be manifest in numerous small towns. Another significant difference was coinage that was adopted in all the Anglo-Saxon kingdoms, following Frankish practice, but not utilised in other areas of Britain. By 700, silver coins known as sceatta were being minted in their thousands and seem to have been used by a large segment of the population.[238] The readier access from mainland Europe to eastern and southern England seems to have been to the detriment of the west coast trade, which died out during the seventh century. The Anglo-Saxons not only had access to Frankish trading routes to the Mediterranean, but to a buoyant trade up the North Sea to Scandinavia and their original homelands where similar trading stations were also established. There are several references to Frisian traders in Anglo-Saxon sources, and it was to one of these based in London that Imma was sold. Other factors in addition to the geographical, such as the past history of Roman contacts and marketing and even Roman roads to ease communications, may also have been significant. Greater access to markets may have been responsible for social differences between Anglo-Saxon and other areas of Britain, and to have resulted in greater opportunities for social mobility and a more diverse social structure among the former.[239] The rulers of the Anglo-Saxons also had more opportunities to profit from the burgeoning system and their interest in doing so can be seen in the development of the *wics*, the desire to control trade through royal officials seen in the law-codes and the competition between the greater kingdoms in the seventh and eighth centuries to control London and Kent, which were both much involved in cross-Channel and North Sea trade.

Ethnic identity

There was an expectation in the early Middle Ages, inherited from writers of the classical world, that 'different people differ between themselves in descent, manners, language and laws'.[240] Such judgements encouraged early medieval British authors to record such variations. Bede in his first chapter of the *Ecclesiastical History* provides an overview of the history and geography of Britain that draws upon not only the descriptions of Britain by classical authors such as Orosius and Solinus, but also on their attitudes and expectations. He describes four 'invasions' of Britain by each of its peoples for whom he provides a brief origin legend, beginning with the British emigrating from Armorica (Brittany) and ending with the arrival of the Saxons, who were, in his interpretation, destined to guide all the peoples of Britain down the correct Christian path. One of the authors Bede had drawn upon was Gildas – though he had put matters somewhat differently. For Gildas the British were the rightful inhabitants of the island who suffered attacks from alien peoples whose homelands were outside the island; his viewpoint seems to have included even the Picts as outsiders although they had almost certainly evolved from peoples who had been living in Britain since remote prehistoric times.[241] According to Gildas the Irish (*Scotti*) and the Picts 'were to some extent different in their customs, but they were in perfect accord in their greed for bloodshed',[242] while the Anglo-Saxons were more akin to wild beasts.

Although the recognition of 'difference' may have served various literary and political purposes in the writings of Gildas and Bede, it was not just a literary invention, but one founded in reality. As Bede noted, the four major peoples of Britain in the early Middle Ages spoke different languages, but it would seem that even before someone opened his or her mouth that difference could also be apparent from the way they dressed, wore their hair and the type of jewellery or other ornamentation they preferred. Forms of wearing hair could be a matter of some importance in the medieval world. Gildas continued his discussion of the Picts and Scots by noting they were 'readier to cover their villainous faces with hair than their private parts and neighbouring regions with clothes'. Pictish laymen are shown on the sculptured stones with long beards and hair, and the latter is sometimes shown elaborately curled at the back.[243] Hair and the exact manner in which it was worn was also very significant in the Germanic world, and some early representations of Anglo-Saxon warriors, such as the warrior on a carved stone from Repton, show them with particularly fine moustaches.[244] The 'seizing of hair' (*feaxfang*) was a grievous insult in Anglo-Saxon society that was punished by a fine of 50 sceattas in the laws of Æthelbert.[245] In contrast, the implication of Gildas's remarks could be that the British were clean-shaven.

What also marked out the Anglo-Saxons from their Celtic neighbours was their choice of decorative metalwork. The Celtic areas favoured variations on the penannular brooch, a Romano-British form that continued to be manufactured in Wales and the west in the post-Roman period. By the seventh century variant versions of the style had been adopted in Ireland and among the Picts, often in increasingly elaborate forms in precious metal with glass inlays and elaborate applied and incised decoration.[246] Such brooches were evidently high-status objects, worn, according to depictions on Pictish sculpture, by both men and women. In the Anglo-Saxon provinces the wearing of brooches on the shoulder, often with strings of beads of glass, amber or stone strung between them, was generally the preserve of women.[247] Adornment for men was lavished on items of military gear especially elaborate belt-buckles that seem to have been important signifiers of status. Anglo-Saxon metalwork was decorated with various forms of animal art, shared with other Germanic areas of Europe, that was representational rather than naturalistic and might involve complex interlacing of extended animal bodies, in contrast to the repertoire of spirals and other geometric forms, derived ultimately from Roman abstract decoration, that was favoured by the British and Irish.[248] The Picts had their own distinctive decorative traditions seen in their symbols and strikingly naturalistic animals, but, though different in form, they shared with the Anglo-Saxons a repertoire of animals and birds, such as boars and eagles, that were no doubt considered appropriate symbols for a warrior aristocracy.

Some of the variations between the peoples of Britain can be accounted for by their different past histories. It is apparent that Germanic incomers introduced customs of burial, building and dress that had been current in their North Sea homelands, but circumstances within early medieval Britain led to the evolution of new variants to meet changing conditions; thus the distinctive dress of Anglian, Saxon and Jutish areas in the sixth century drew upon the Germanic repertoire, but it was interpreted differently in each area. It is not clear how far deliberate decisions were made or whether there was a natural evolution from groups of people regularly associating together, for instance in regional assemblies. It was part of the process of 'ethnogenesis', that is the creation of a common ethnic identity or origin for a group of people who had in fact rather more disparate backgrounds.[249]

It was also the practice in early medieval Britain, as it was elsewhere in early medieval Europe, to validate such new developments by projecting them back into the past through origin legends. At its simplest level the legends for early medieval Britain describe how a 'people' crossed from their original homeland and by force of arms took possession of all or part of the country. Sometimes specific leaders are named who were the real or legendary ancestors of royal houses, and it is presumably safe to assume that such origin legends were developed at the royal courts of their descendants. For the origin legend was a flexible form that continued to be adapted throughout the period.[250] The version of a Pictish origin legend known to Bede, in which the Picts were directed by Irish to the north of Britain and received brides from the Irish 'on condition that, in all cases of doubt, they should elect their kings from the female royal line rather than the male', had presumably been developed relatively recently at the courts of the brothers Bridei and Nechtan, who were of Irish descent in the male line and claimed the Pictish throne through their mother.[251] The evolution of a new kingdom of Alba in the ninth and tenth centuries from the former kingdoms of the Picts and Dál Riata led ultimately to the refinement of existing origin legends to accommodate the new political reality.[252] Bede's attempt in the *Ecclesiastical History* to give the 'English' a new identity as a Christian 'Chosen People' is another variant on the traditional use of origin legends, albeit one with its own literary antecedents.[253]

To speak of an area of Britain as 'Irish' or 'Anglo-Saxon' is therefore not to imply that everyone living within its borders literally had ancestors who had emigrated from Ireland or the North Sea, but instead indicates the dominant language and culture of an area at a particular time, an identity that was often defined by the elite in specific political circumstances. Continual conflict between two peoples might lead to increasing stress on the 'difference' between them as may have occurred between the Anglo-Saxon- and British-controlled areas of southern England in the sixth century.[254] The hostility and the sense of an immense divide between their two peoples can be felt in the writings of Gildas and Bede. Ethnicity therefore could matter a great deal, but the degree to which it mattered might depend upon context. St Patrick evidently identified himself all his life as an upper-class Briton in spite of spending the greater part of his life in Ireland; as an 'outsider' it was easier for him to get away with behaviour as a Christian missionary that went against the norms of Irish society.[255] Other British, it has been suggested, faced with adaptation or annihilation, found it expedient to discover their inner Anglo-Saxon. In the laws of Ine there are evidently people who were defined as Saxon and others defined as British, but in the laws of Alfred for the same areas, almost 200 years later, there are only West Saxons.

The boundaries between different peoples were never impermeable. As we have seen, there was considerable movement within Britain of members of the elite from one province to another. Kings may well have welcomed inclusion of peoples of different origins within their entourages as a symbol of their power and wide-ranging connections. 'Foreign' practices might have the allure of the exotic and in the late eighth century the Northumbrian elite were criticised for apparently imitating fashions of their Pictish and Viking enemies.[256] Tangible evidence for movements of people from one region to another or of diplomatic exchanges are the finds of diagnostic artefacts from different provinces of Britain outside their 'home' area. Typical Anglo-Saxon metalwork has been found, for example, at South Cadbury (Somerset) and at Dunadd (Argyll). Bronze hanging-bowls that seem to have been made, on the basis of moulds discovered, in the British areas of the west and north and in Pictland, were to be found throughout Britain with about a hundred known from richer Anglo-Saxon male burials of the late sixth and seventh centuries.[257] The bowls have rings for suspension and may have been used for the washing of hands or had lights floating within them, and evidently became part of the equipment of any Anglo-Saxon noble with pretensions. But it was not just conventions of court etiquette that might be shared, the exchange of desirable objects transferred knowledge of different traditions of decoration and led in the course of the seventh century to common forms appearing throughout Britain that are often referred to as 'insular'.[258] The master craftsman of the regalia of Sutton Hoo mound 1, for instance, combined the curvilinear designs in red enamel and the use of inlays of multi-coloured millefiori glass rods that was favoured in Celtic areas with Germanic interlace forms and gold and garnet jewellery.[259] At much the same time craftsmen in Celtic areas of Britain were integrating aspects of Anglo-Saxon design into their repertoires. The Dál Riatan royal centre of Dunadd has not only produced various finds of Anglo-Saxon metalwork, but also clay moulds which indicate that metalwork was actually being produced on the site based on bird-headed designs that seem to have been copied from Anglo-Saxon brooches.[260] The Picts were also part of this interchange and incorporated aspects of insular decoration into their metalwork and sculpture, and contributed their own tradition of the depiction of naturalistic animals.

The creation of a common form of insular art that was shared by the elites of early medieval Britain is probably emblematic of a much broader exchange of knowledge and concepts. Although ethnic identity clearly could matter, and people who spoke different languages tended to come from different traditions that might be manifested in various material forms, there were also many basic similarities between the early medieval peoples of Britain. Some of these shared features may be attributable to a common Indo-European inheritance, but the general similarities in societal structures may also owe much to the common experiences of living in a post-Roman world where the balance of power lay with the hard men with military might. Warriors needing employment found they could move with relative ease through the different royal courts and language zones, and knowledge of different customs and fashions might move with them and with the peace-weaving princesses who sealed alliances between different kingdoms. Context was all important. Sometimes people of different ethnic backgrounds were allies, sometimes deadly enemies. Foreign styles could be desirable and exotic, or betray an enemy who should be killed.

And so we come to one of the main subjects of this volume that has not yet been considered in any depth, namely the topic of religion. Religion is one of the customs that could distinguish one people from another. Differences in religion, or in practices of the same religion, sometimes mattered a great deal and at other times might be of little consequence; something that still holds true today. But before we can return to such issues we need to consider the basic functions of religion in early medieval societies, and how the different peoples of Britain were introduced to Christianity and absorbed it into their political and social structures. Was the new religion a means of uniting the disparate peoples of Britain, or one of the agencies by which the differences and tensions between them are revealed?

Notes

1 A.L.F. Rivet and C. Smith, *The Place-Names of Roman Britain* (Cambridge, 1979), 39–40.

2 S. Frere, *Britannia: A History of Roman Britain* (3rd edn, London, 1987); P. Salway, *Roman Britain* (Oxford, 1981); B. Jones and D. Mattingly, *An Atlas of Roman Britain* (Oxford, 1990); M. Todd (ed.), *A Companion to Roman Britain* (Oxford, 2004).

3 D. Breeze, *Roman Scotland: Frontier Country* (London, 1996); D. Breeze and B. Dobson, *Hadrian's Wall* (4th edn, London, 2000).

4 C. Arnold and J.L. Davies, *Roman and Early Medieval Wales* (Stroud, 2000)

5 M. Millett, *The Romanisation of Britain: An Essay in Archaeological Interpretation* (Cambridge, 1990)

6 A.S. Esmonde Cleary, *The Ending of Roman Britain* (London, 1989); N. Faulkener, *The Decline and Fall of Roman Britain* (Stroud, 2000).

7 P. Southern, 'The army in late Roman Britain', in *Companion to Roman Britain*, ed. Todd, 393–448.

8 A. King, 'Rural settlement in southern Britain', in *Companion to Roman Britain*, ed. Todd, 349–70, at 363.

9 A. Woolf, 'The Britons: from Romans to Barbarians', in *Regna and Gentes. The Relationship between Late Antique and Early Medieval Peoples and Kingdoms in the Transformation of the Roman World*, ed. H.-W. Goetz, J. Jarnut and W. Pohl (Leiden, 2003), 344–80, at 346–50; I.N. Wood, 'The final phase', in *Companion to Roman Britain*, ed. Todd, 428–42.

10 Gildas, *De Excidio*, Chapters 13–21.

11 Gildas, *De Excidio*, Chapter 23.

12 Gildas, *De Excidio*, Chapter 25; see Introduction, 15–16, for the problems of dating the text.

13 J. Drinkwater and H. Elton (eds), *Fifth-Century Gaul: A Crisis of Identity?* (Cambridge, 1992).

14 R. White and P. Barker, *Wroxeter: Life and Death of a Roman City* (Stroud, 1998).

15 T. Willmott, *Birdoswald: Excavations of a Roman Fort on Hadrian's Wall and its Successor Settlements, 1987–92* (London, 1997), especially 203–31.

16 M. McCarthy, 'Rheged: an early historic kingdom near the Solway', *Proceedings of the Society of Antiquaries of Scotland* 132 (2002), 357–81.

17 I. Armit, *Celtic Scotland* (London, 1997), 101–19.

18 Gildas, *De Excidio*, Chapters 28–36.

19 Southern, 'Army in late Roman Britain', 405.

20 W. Davies, *Wales in the Early Middle Ages* (Leicester, 1982), 90–102; K. Dark, *Civitas to Kingdom: British Political Continuity 300–800* (London, 1994), 74–86.

21 Asser, Chapter 79; J.E. Lloyd, *A History of Wales from the Earliest Times to the Edwardian Conquest*, 2 vols, (3rd edn, London, 1939), I, 324–30.

22 See Introduction, 10–11.

23 A. Macquarrie, 'The Kings of Strathclyde, *c.*400–1018', in *Medieval Scotland: Crown, Lordship and Community. Essays Presented to G.W.S. Barrow*, ed. A. Grant and K.J. Stringer (Edinburgh, 1993), 1–19; A. Woolf, 'Early Historic Scotland to 761', in *The Shorter History of Scotland*, ed. R. Oram (Edinburgh, forthcoming).

24 *St Patrick*, 35–8, 55–9; T.M. Charles-Edwards, *Early Christian Ireland* (Cambridge, 2000), 227–8.

25 Adomnán, *V.Columbae*, I, 15.

26 *AU* sa 749; *AT* sa 750.

27 *The Gododdin: The Oldest Scottish Poem*, ed. K.H. Jackson (Edinburgh, 1969); *The Gododdin: Text and Context from Dark-Age North Britain*, ed. and trans. J.T. Koch (Cardiff, 1997). See Introduction.

28 McCarthy, 'Rheged'.

29 *Historia Brittonum*; K.H. Jackson, 'On the northern British section in Nennius', in *Celt and Saxon: Studies in the Early British Border*, ed. N.K. Chadwick (Cambridge, 1963), 20–62; P. Sims-Williams, 'The death of Urien', *CMCS* 32 (1996), 25–56.

30 *Historia Brittonum*, Chapter 57; Jackson, 'Northern British section in Nennius', 41–2.

31 K.H. Jackson, *Language and History in Early Britain* (Edinburgh, 1953), 701–5; A.P. Smyth, *Warlords and Holy Men: Scotland AD 800–1000* (London, 1984), 19–21.

32 M.I. Faull, 'The post-Roman period', in *West Yorkshire: An Archaeological Survey to AD 1500*, ed. M.I. Faull and S. Moorhouse (Wakefield, 1981), 171–224; for a more speculative discussion about possible other British kingdoms (some of which may be subdivisions of larger units) see P.N. Wood, 'On the little British kingdom of Craven', *Northern History* 32 (1996), 1–20.

33 D. Rollason, *Northumbria 500–1000: Creation and Destruction of a Kingdom* (Cambridge, 2003), 86–9, 101–3.

34 D. Fahy, 'When did Britons become Bretons?', *Welsh History Review* 2 (1964–5), 111–24; P.-R. Giot, P. Guigon and B. Merdrignac, *The British Settlement of Brittany* (Stroud, 2004).

35 E. Campbell, ' The archaeological evidence for external contacts: imports, trade and economy in Celtic Britain AD 400–800', in *External Contacts and the Economy of Late Roman and Post-Roman Britain*, ed. K. Dark (Woodbridge, 1996), 83–96, and see further below, 76–8.

36 *Regna and Gentes*, ed. Goetz, Jarnut and Pohl, *passim*.

37 See Introduction.

38 Gildas, *De Excidio*, Chapter 27.

39 Woolf, 'The Britons', 366–9

40 See Introduction, 22–5.

41 Cleary, *Ending of Roman Britain*.

42 P. Sims-Williams, 'The settlement of England in Bede and the "Chronicle" ', *Anglo-Saxon England* 12 (1983), 1–41, at 31–4. The date is not likely to come from a reliable early tradition.

43 McCarthy, 'Rheged'; Willmott, *Birdoswald*, 203–31, 408–9.

44 For a survey of the evidence, see Dark, *Civitas to Kingdom*, 40–4; L. Alcock, *Kings and Warriors, Craftsmen and Priests in Northern Britain AD 550–850* (Edinburgh, 2003), 179–217; S. Pearce, *South-western Britain in the Early Middle Ages* (London, 2004), 227–42.

45 L. Alcock, *Cadbury Castle Somerset: The Early Medieval Archaeology* (Cardiff, 1995).

46 *Laws*, ed. Attenborough, 36–61, especially Chapters 23, 24.2, 32 and 33; L.M. Alexander, 'The legal status of the native Britons in late seventh-century Wessex as reflected by the Law Code of Ine', *Haskins Society Journal* 7 (1995), 31–8.

47 P. Sims-Williams, *Religion and Literature in Western England, 600-800* (Cambridge, 1990), 16–53; S. Bassett, 'How the West was won: the Anglo-Saxon takeover of the West Midlands', *ASSAH* 11 (2000), 107–18.

48 M. Gelling, *The West Midlands in the Early Middle Ages* (London, 1992).

49 Rollason, *Northumbria*, 57–109 considers a range of possible scenarios.

50 Gildas, *De Excidio*, Chapter 20.

51 Sims-Williams, 'The settlement of England'; Woolf, 'The Britons', 346–55; T. Charles-Edwards, 'Nations and Kingdoms: a view from above', in *After Rome*, ed. T. Charles-Edwards (Oxford, 2003), 23–58, at 24–30. Many other interpretations exist, many of which propose even greater revision to Gildas's text.

52 D. Powlesland, 'Early Anglo-Saxon settlements, structures, form and layout', in *The Anglo-Saxons from the Migration Period to the Eighth Century: An Ethnographic Perspective*, ed. J. Hines (Woodbridge, 1997), 101–24; S. Lucy, *The Early Anglo-Saxon Cemeteries of East Yorkshire*, BAR 282 (Oxford, 1998).

53 Gildas, *De Excidio* Chapter 25; N.J. Higham, *Rome, Britain and the Anglo-Saxons* (London, 1992).

54 B. Ward-Perkins, 'Why did the Anglo-Saxons not become more British?', *English Historical Review* 115 (2000), 513–33.

55 T.M. Charles-Edwards, 'Language and society among the insular Celts, 400–1000', in *The Celtic World*, ed. M. Green (London, 1995), 703–36

56 M. Filppula, J. Klemola and H. Pitkänen (eds), *The Celtic Roots of English* (Joensuu, 2002); H.L.C. Tristram, 'Why don't the English speak Welsh?', in *Britons in Anglo-Saxon England*, ed. N. Higham (forthcoming).

57 L. Oliver, *The Beginnings of English Law* (Toronto, 2002), 68–9, 91–3.

58 N.J. Higham, 'Britons in northern England in the early middle ages: through a thick glass darkly', *Northern History* 38 (2001), 5–25.

59 Bede, *Hist. Eccl.*, IV, 22; Charles-Edwards, 'Language and society', 732.

60 M. Henig and P. Lindley (eds), *Alban and St Albans: Roman and Medieval Architecture, Art and Archaeology*, BAA Conference Transactions 24 (2001); T. Williamson, *The Origin of Hertfordshire* (Manchester, 2000).

61 M. Gelling, *Signposts to the Past: Place-names and History in England* (London, 1978), 87–105.

62 R.A. Chambers, 'The late and sub-Roman Cemetery at Queensford Farm, Dorchester-on-Thames (Oxon)', *Oxoniensia* 52 (1987), 35–69.

63 M.O. Anderson, *Kings and Kingship in Early Scotland* (Edinburgh, 1980), 125–31; Rivet and Smith, *Place-Names of Roman Britain*, 39–40.

64 Bede, *Hist. Eccl.*, III, 4.

65 Armit, *Celtic Scotland*.

66 F.T. Wainwright, *The Problem of the Picts* (Perth, 1955)

67 Smyth, *Warlords and Holy Men*, 50–1; K. Forsyth, *Language in Pictland*, Studia Hameliana 2 (Utrecht, 1997).

68 See Introduction, 23–5, and S. Foster, *Picts, Gaels and Scots* (London, 1996), 73 for distribution map.

69 A. Woolf, 'The Verturian hegemony: a mirror in the north', in *Mercia. An Anglo-Saxon Kingdom in Europe*, ed. M.P. Brown and C.A. Farr (London, 2001), 106–11; A. Woolf, 'Dún Nechtain, Fortriu and the geography of the Picts' (forthcoming).

70 D. Broun, 'The seven kingdoms in *De situ Albaniae*: a record of Pictish political geography or imaginary map of Alba', in *Alba: Celtic Scotland in the Medieval Era*, ed. E.J. Cowan and R.A. McDonald (East Linton, 2000), 24–42.

71 Anderson, *Kings and Kingship*, 139–45

72 See Chapter 3, 153–5.

73 Adomnán, *V. Columbae*, II, 42; *AU sa* 738

74 Adomnán, *V. Columbae*, I, 33; *AT sa* 668 and 670.

75 Smyth, *Warlords and Holy Men*, 58–68; W.D.H. Sellar, 'Warlords, holy men and matrilineal succession', *Innes Review* 36 (1985), 29–43; A. Woolf, 'Pictish matriliny reconsidered', *Innes Review* 49 (1998), 147–67.

76 Bede, *Hist. Eccl.*, I, 1.

77 T.O. Clancy, 'Philosopher king: Nechtan mac Der-Ilei', *Scottish Historical Review* 83 (2004), 125–49. Their father was Dairgart, a member of the Cénel Comgaill dynasty of Scottish Dál Riata, on which see further below, 54–5.

78 Woolf, 'Pictish matriliny reconsidered'.

79 D. Ó Corráin, 'Irish regnal succession: a reappraisal', *Studia Hibernica* 11 (1971), 7–39; B. Yorke, *Kings and Kingdoms of Early Anglo-Saxon England* (London, 1990), 167–72.

80 Anderson, *Kings and Kingship*, 77–118; 165–79.

81 T. Charles-Edwards, ' "The Continuation of Bede", *s.a.* 750: high-kings, kings of Tara and "Bretwaldas" ', in *Seanchas. Studies in Early Medieval Irish, Archaeology, History and Literature in Honour of Francis J. Byrne*, ed. A.P. Smyth (Dublin, 2000), 137–45; A. Woolf, 'Onuist son of Uurguist: *tyrannus carnifex* or a David of the Picts?', *Æthelbald and Offa. Two Eighth-Century Kings of Mercia*, ed. D. Hill and M. Worthington, BAR 383 (Oxford, 2005).

82 See further below, 54–5.

83 See Chapter 2, 128–33.

84 D. Broun, 'Pictish kings 761–839: integration with Dál Riata or separate development?', in *The St Andrew Sarcophagus: A Pictish Masterpiece and its International Connections*, ed. S. Foster (Dublin, 1998), 71–83.

85 Anderson, *Kings and Kingship*, 190–5; J. Bannerman, 'The Scottish takeover of Pictland and the relics of Columba', in *Spes Scottorum*, 71–94.

86 Anderson, *Kings and Kingship*, 196–200.

87 B. Raftery, *Pagan Celtic Ireland: The Enigma of the Irish Iron Age* (London, 1994).

88 T.M. Charles-Edwards, *Early Christian Ireland*, 154–8.

89 P. Sims-Williams, 'The five languages of Wales in pre-Norman inscriptions', *CMCS* 44 (2002), 1–36, at 25.

90 'Confessio', *St Patrick*, Chapters 1–3; Charles-Edwards, *Early Christian Ireland*, 216–17.

91 Charles-Edwards, *After Rome*, 31–4.

92 *AT* 502; Anderson, *Kings and Kingship*, 131–9; J. Bannerman, *Studies in the History of Dalriada* (Edinburgh, 1974), 73–5.

93 Bannerman, *Dalriada*, 1–8; M. Herbert, *Iona, Kells and Derry: The History and Hagiography of the Monastic Familia of Columba* (Dublin, 1996), 9–56.

94 E. Campbell, 'Were the Scots Irish?', *Antiquity* 75 (2001), 285–92.

95 Bede, *Hist. Eccl.*, I, 1.

96 D. Broun, *The Irish Identity of the Kingdom of the Scots* (Woodbridge, 1999).

97   Bannerman, *Dalriada*.

98   Adomnán, *V. Columbae*, I, 33.

99   Smyth, *Warlords and Holy Men*, 104–11.

100 See, for instance, Adomnán, *V.Columbae*, I, 34; II, 31; II, 42; II, 46; III, 14; P. McNeill and R. Nicholson (eds), *An Historical Atlas of Scotland c.400–c.1600* (St Andrews, 1975), 52.

101 See Introduction, 9.

102 R. Sharpe, 'The thriving of Dalriada', in *Kings, Clerics and Chronicles in Scotland, 500–1297*, ed. S. Taylor (Dublin, 2000), 47–61.

103 *AU* sa 573; Adomnán of Iona, trans. Sharpe, 16, 19-20. For more discussion of the context see Chapter 2, 128–31.

104 Anderson, *Kings and Kingship*, 145–9; Bannerman, *Dalriada*, 80–90; Woolf, 'Early historic Scotland'.

105 Adomnán, *V. Columbae*, I, 10–11, 49; II, 46; Bannerman, *Dalriada*, 157–70; Adomnán of Iona, trans. Sharpe, 312–14 for the date.

106 Anderson, *Kings and Kingship*, 152–5; Woolf, 'Early historic Scotland'.

107 Anderson, *Kings and Kingship*, 157–65, 178–84.

108 Anderson, *Kings and Kingship*, 189–91.

109 See nn. 84–5 above.

110 A. Woolf, 'The age of sea-kings, 900–1300', in *The Argyll Book*, ed. D. Omand (Edinburgh, 2004), 94–109.

111 Broun, 'Alba: Pictish homeland or Irish offshoot?' (forthcoming).

112 K. Forsyth, 'Literacy in Pictland', in *Literacy in Medieval Celtic Societies*, ed. H. Pryce (Cambridge, 1998), 39–61, especially 48–9.

113 S. Taylor, 'Place-names and the early church in eastern Scotland', in *Scotland in Dark Age Britain*, ed. B. Crawford (St Andrews, 1996), 93–110.

114 W.J. Watson, *The Celtic Place-Names of Scotland* (Edinburgh, 1926), 228–9.

115 Clancy, 'Philosopher king'.

116 Woolf, 'The age of sea-kings', 94–109.

117 C. Thomas, *And Shall These Mute Stones Speak? Post-Roman Inscriptions in Western Britain* (Cardiff, 1994); Sims-Williams, 'The five languages of Wales'; E. Okasha, *Corpus of Early Inscribed Stones of South-West Britain* (London, 1993).

118 Charles-Edwards, *Early Christian Ireland*, 163–5.

119 R.C. Stacey, 'Texts and society', in *After Rome*, ed. Charles-Edwards, 221–57, at 243–5.

120 Davies, *Wales*, 89.

121 Sims-Williams, 'The five languages of Wales', 27–32.

122 Bede, *Hist. Eccl.*, I. 15.

123 I.N. Wood, *The Merovingian North Sea* (Alingsås, 1983); Sims-Williams, 'Settlement of England'.

124 Bede, *Hist. Eccl.*, V, 9.

125 B. Yorke, 'Anglo-Saxon gentes and regna', in *Regna and Gentes*, ed. Goetz, Jarnut and Pohl, 381–408.

126 Bede, *Hist. Eccl.*, I, 15.

127 J. Hines, *The Scandinavian Character of Anglian England in the Pre-Viking Period*, BAR 124 (Oxford, 1984).

128 B. Brugmann, 'Britons, Angles, Saxons, Jutes and Franks', in *The Anglo-Saxon Cemetery at Mill Hill, Deal, Kent*, ed. K. Parfitt and B. Brugmann (London, 1997), 110–24.

129 T. Dickinson, 'Early Saxon saucer brooches: a preliminary overview', *ASSAH* 6 (1993), 11–44.

130 J. Hines, 'The becoming of the English: identity, material culture and language in early Anglo-Saxon England', *ASSAH* 7 (1994), 49–59.

131 Powlesland, 'Early Anglo-Saxon settlements'; Lucy, *Cemeteries of East Yorkshire*.

132 E. James, 'The origins of barbarian kingdoms: the continental evidence', in *The Origins of Anglo-Saxon Kingdoms*, ed. S. Bassett (Leicester, 1989), 40–52; Ward-Perkins, 'Why did the Anglo-Saxons?'.

133 Gildas, *De Excidio*, Chapter 26.

134 N. Brooks, 'The creation and early structure of the kingdom of Kent', in *Origins of Anglo-Saxon Kingdoms*, ed. Bassett, 55–74.

135 Wood, *Merovingian North Sea*.

136 H. Härke, 'The Anglo-Saxon weapon burial rite', *Past and Present* 126 (1990), 22–43.

137 Yorke, *Kings and Kingdoms*, 1–19.

138 N. Stoodley, *The Spindle and the Spear: A Critical Enquiry into the Construction and Meaning of Gender in the Early Anglo-Saxon Inhumation Burial Rite*, BAR 288 (Oxford, 1999).

139 Bede, *Hist. Eccl.*, V, 10 – 'they do not have kings, but many *satrapas*'.

140 C. Scull, 'Social archaeology and Anglo-Saxon kingdom origins', in *The Making of Kingdoms*, ed. T. Dickinson and D. Griffiths, *ASSAH* 10 (1999), 7–24

141 J. Campbell, *Essays in Anglo-Saxon History* (London, 1986), 85–98; B.Yorke 'Political and ethnic identity: a case study of Anglo-Saxon practice', in *Social Identity in Early Medieval Britain*, ed. W.O. Frazer and A. Tyrrell (London, 2000), 69–90.

142 W. Davies and H. Vierck, 'The contexts of Tribal Hidage: social aggregates and settlement patterns', *Frühmittelalterliche Studien* 8 (1974), 233–93; P. Featherstone, 'The Tribal Hidage and the ealdormen of Mercia', in *Mercia: An Anglo-Saxon Kingdom in Europe*, ed. M. Brown and C. Farr (London, 2001), 23–34.

143 Campbell, *Essays in Anglo-Saxon History*, 99–120.

144 P. Barnwell, '*Hlafæta, ceorl, hid* and *scir*. Celtic, Roman or Germanic?', *ASSAH* 9 (1996), 58–61.

145 Yorke, *Kings and Kingdoms*, 74–81; Rollason, *Northumbria*, 20–53.

146 N. Brooks, 'The formation of the Mercian kingdom' in *Origins of Anglo-Saxon Kingdoms*, ed. Bassett, 159–70; Featherstone, 'Tribal Hidage'.

147 See above, 41–5. For a detailed comparison of the two kingdoms see J.R. Maddicott, 'Two frontier states: Northumbria and Wessex', in *The Medieval State. Essays Presented to James Campbell*, ed. J.R. Maddicott and D.M. Palliser (London, 2000), 25–45.

148 Yorke, *Kings and Kingdoms*, 25–71.

149 F.M. Stenton, *Anglo-Saxon England* (3rd edn, Oxford, 1971), 206–24.

150 B. Yorke, *Wessex in the Early Middle Ages* (London, 1995), 94–132.

151 F.J. Byrne, *Irish Kings and High Kings* (London, 1973); Sharpe, 'The thriving of Dalriada'.

152 Bede, *Hist. Eccl.*, IV, 13; Campbell, *Essays in Anglo-Saxon History*, 85–98.

153 Bede, *Hist. Eccl.*, II, 5. On problems of interpretation see P. Wormald, 'Bede, the *Bretwaldas* and the origin of the *gens Anglorum*', in *Ideal and Reality in Frankish and Anglo-Saxon Society*, ed. P. Wormald *et al.* (Oxford, 1983), 99–129, and S. Keynes, 'Raedwald the Bretwalda', in *Voyage to the Other World: the Legacy of Sutton Hoo*, ed. C.B. Kendall and P.S. Wells (Minneapolis, 1992), 103–23.

154 Anderson, *Kings and Kingship*, 145–56; Woolf, 'Early historic Scotland'.

155 Bede, *Hist. Eccl.*, II, 5; P.H. Blair, 'The Northumbrians and their southern frontier', *Archaeologia Aeliana*, 4th series, 26 (1948), 98–126.

156 Bede, *Hist. Eccl.*, II, 12.

157 A. Woolf, 'Caedualla *rex Brettonum* and the passing of the Old North', *Northern History* 41 (2004), 5–24.

158 Bede, *Hist. Eccl.*, IV, 26.

159 Bede, *Hist. Eccl.*, IV, 21.

160 Charles-Edwards, 'The Continuation of Bede'; Woolf, 'Onuist son of Uurguist'.

161 Anderson, *Kings and Kingship*, 169–72.

162 H. Moisl, 'The Bernician royal dynasty and the Irish in the seventh century', *Peritia* 2 (1983), 103–26.

163 C. Ireland, 'Aldfrith of Northumbria and the Irish genealogies', *Celtica* 22 (1991), 64–78.

164 Wood, *Merovingian North Sea*.

165 Gregory of Tours, *Decem Libri Historiarum*, ed. B. Krusch and W. Levison, MGH Scriptores rerum Merovingicarum I (Hannover, 1951), IV, 26; Brooks, 'Kingdom of Kent', 64–7.

166 I.N. Wood, *The Merovingian Kingdoms 450–751* (London, 1994), especially 198–9; R. Le Jan, 'Convents, violence and competition for power in seventh-century Francia', in *Topographies of Power in the Early Middle Ages*, ed. M. de Jong, F. Theuws and C. van Rhijn (Leiden, 2001), 243–69.

167 Yorke, *Kings and Kingdoms*, 81–3.

168 Bede, *Hist. Eccl.*, IV, 3 (Owine); IV, 22 (Imma); III, 1 (sons of Æthelfrith).

169 *The Gododdin*, 41, 184; Adomnán, *V. Columbae*, II, 23.

170 See Introduction, 10–11.

171 Gildas, *De Excidio*, Chapter 27.

172 R. Sharpe, 'Hiberno-Latin *Laicus*, Irish *Láech* and the Devil's Men', *Ériu* 30 (1979), 75–92.

173 Bede, *Hist. Eccl.*, III, 1.

174 Bede, *Hist. Eccl.*, IV, 22.

175 T. Charles-Edwards, 'The distinction between land and moveable wealth in Anglo-Saxon England', in *Medieval Settlement: Continuity and Change*, ed. P. Sawyer (London, 1976), 180–7.

176 *Laws*, ed. Attenborough, Chapter 51.

177 Härke, 'Anglo-Saxon weapon burial rite'.

178 T. Charles-Edwards, *Early Irish and Welsh Kinship* (Oxford, 1993).

179 Bannerman, *Dalriada*, 27–156.

180 *AU* sa 718; *AT* sa 719; N. Aitchison, *The Picts and Scots at War* (Stroud, 2003), 116–19.

181 Foster, *Picts, Gaels and Scots*, 42–4; Alcock, *Kings and Warriors*, 192–7.

182 *AT* sa 729; Aitchison, *Picts and Scots*, 113–15.

183 Bede, *Hist. Eccl.*, II, 9 (linked also with conquest of Anglesey) and IV, 26, respectively.

184 G. Halsall, *Warfare and Society in the Barbarian West, 450–900* (London, 2003), 180–6.

185 N. Hooper, 'The Aberlemno stone and cavalry in Anglo-Saxon England', *Northern History* 29 (1993), 188–96; Aitchison, *Picts and Scots*, 86–8, 185–7 (though seeing the action beginning in the bottom left of the stone). For arguments against such a literal interpretation see G. Henderson and I. Henderson, *The Art of the Picts, Sculpture and Metalwork in Early Medieval Scotland* (London, 2004), 178–9.

186 Alcock, *Kings and Warriors*, 160–78; Aitchison, *Picts and Scots*, 44–70.

187 Alcock, *Kings and Warriors*, 179–233.

188 Anderson, *Kings and Kingship*, 180–4; A. Lane and E. Campbell, *Dunadd: An Early Dalriadic Capital* (Oxford, 2000), 37–9; Aitchison, *Picts and Scots*, 108–9.

189 Anderson, *Kings and Kingship*, 183–4.

190 Aitchison, *Picts and Scots*, 155–8.

191 Bede, *Hist. Eccl.*, III, 6 and 12.

192 J.R. Maddicott, 'Prosperity and power in the age of Bede and Beowulf', *Proceedings of the British Academy* 117 (2002), 49–71.

193 *ASC* sa 755.

194 Bede, *Hist Eccl.*, III, 24.

195 *Tacitus: The Germania*, ed. J.G.C. Anderson (Oxford, 1938), Chapters 13 and 14; *Agricola and Germany by Tacitus*, trans. A.R. Birley (Oxford, 1999).

196 K. Manchester, *The Archaeology of Disease* (Bradford, 1983); Härke, 'Anglo-Saxon weapon burial rite'.

197 Adomnán, *V. Columbae*, II, 46.

198 J.R. Maddicott, 'Plague in England in the seventh century', *Past and Present* 156 (1997), 7–54.

199 Stoodley, *Spindle and Spear.*

200 K. Randsborg, *The First Millennium AD in Europe and the Mediterranean* (Cambridge, 1991), 23–9.

201 H. Hamerow, *Early Medieval Settlements: The Archaeology of Rural Communities in North-West Europe 400–900* (Oxford, 2002).

202 S.P. Dark, 'Palaeoecological evidence for landscape continuity and change in Britain ca, AD 400–800', in *External Contacts and the Economy of Late Roman and Post-Roman Britain*, ed. K. Dark (Woodbridge, 1996), 23–52.

203 H.P.R. Finberg (ed.), *The Agrarian History of England and Wales 1.2: A.D. 43–1042* (Cambridge, 1972); Davies, *Wales in the Early Middle Ages*, 31–58; Foster, *Picts, Gaels and Scots*, 53–70; Hamerow, *Early Medieval Settlements*, 147–55; J. Hines, 'Society, community and identity', in *After Rome*, ed. Charles-Edwards, 61–101, at 63–70.

204 Adomnán, *V. Columbae*, II, 37.

205 G.R.J. Jones, 'Multiple estates and early settlements', in *Medieval Settlement*, ed. Sawyer, 11–40; G.W.S. Barrow, *The Kingdom of the Scots* (London, 1973), 7–68.

206 Hamerow, *Early Medieval Settlements*, 46–51.

207 Yorke, *Wessex in the Early Middle Ages*, 256–61; Oliver, *English Law*, 89–105

208 Davies, *Wales in the Early Middle Ages*, 59–84.

209 R. Faith, *The English Peasantry and the Growth of Lordship* (London, 1997).

210 Charles-Edwards, *Irish and Welsh Kinship*, especially 364–9, 391–411.

211 Davies, *Wales in the Early Middle Ages*, 64–7; D. Pelteret, *Slavery in Early Medieval England from the Reign of Alfred until the Twelfth Century* (Woodbridge, 1995).

212 J. Nelson, 'Queens as Jezebels: the careers of Brunhild and Balthild in Merovingian history', in *Studies in Church History*, Subsidia 1 (London, 1978), 31–77.

213 Stoodley, *Spindle and Spear.*

214 L. Lancaster, 'Kinship in Anglo-Saxon society, parts I and II', *British Journal of Sociology* 9 (1958), 230–50, 359–77; Charles-Edwards, *Irish and Welsh Kinship*.

215 W. Davies and P. Fouracre (eds), *The Settlement of Disputes in Early Medieval Europe* (Cambridge, 1986).

216 W. Davies, 'Celtic kingship in the Early Middle Ages', in *Kings and Kingship in Medieval Europe*, ed. A.J. Duggan (London, 1993), 101–24, especially 115–21.

217 P. Wormald, '*Lex scripta* and *Verbum regis*: legislation and Germanic

kingship', in *Early Medieval Kingship*, ed. P. Sawyer and I.N. Wood (Leeds, 1977), 105–38.

218 Stoodley, *Spindle and Spear*.

219 C. Fell, *Women in Anglo-Saxon England* (London, 1984), 56–73; W. Davies, 'Celtic women in the early middle ages', in *Images of Women in Antiquity*, ed. A. Cameron and A. Kuhrt (revised edn, London, 1993), 145–66; Charles-Edwards, *Irish and Welsh Kinship*.

220 *ASC* Preface (to manuscripts A and G) and sa 672.

221 C. Clover, 'Regardless of sex: men, women and power in early northern Europe', *Speculum* 69 (1993), 363–87.

222 *Pictish Symbol Stones*, no. 118; Foster, *Picts, Gaels and Scots*, 93–5.

223 Barnwell, '*Hlafaeta, ceorl, hid* and *scir*'.

224 T. Charles-Edwards, 'Kinship, status and the origin of the hide', *Past and Present* 56 (1972), 3–33; Faith, *English Peasantry*, 89–125.

225 Grant, 'Early Scottish state', 51–2.

226 Attenborough, *Laws*, 58–9 (Chapter 70).

227 Campbell, *Essays in Anglo-Saxon History*, 108–16; T. Charles-Edwards, 'Early medieval kingships in the British Isles', in *Origins of Anglo-Saxon Kingdoms*, ed. Bassett, 28–39, at 28–33.

228 Charles-Edwards, *Irish and Welsh Kinship*, 365–9.

229 Grant, 'Early Scottish state', 52–3.

230 Attenborough, *Laws*, 4–5 (Chapter 3); Oliver, *English Law*, 85–7.

231 A. Pantos and S. Semple (eds), *Assembly Places and Practices in Medieval Europe* (Dublin, 2004).

232 Campbell, 'Archaeological evidence for external contacts'; see above.

233 Adomnán, *V. Columbae*, I, 28.

234 M. Carver (ed.), *The Age of Sutton Hoo* (Woodbridge, 1992); Museum of London Archaeology Service, *The Prittlewell Prince: The Discovery of a Rich Anglo-Saxon Burial in Essex* (London, 2004).

235 J.W. Huggett, 'Imported grave goods and the early Anglo-Saxon economy', *Medieval Archaeology* 32 (1988), 63–96.

236 T. Pestell and K. Ulmschneider (eds), *Markets in Early Medieval Europe: Trading and 'Productive' Sites 650–850* (Macclesfield, 2003).

237 R. Hodges, *Dark Ages Economics; The Origins of Towns and Trade* AD *600–1000* (London, 1982); D. Hill and R. Cowie (eds), *Wics: The Early Medieval Trading Centres of Northern Europe* (Sheffield, 2001); Maddicott, 'Prosperity and power'.

238 D. Hill and D.M. Metcalf (eds), *Sceattas in England and on the Continent*, BAR 128 (Oxford, 1984); D.M. Metcalf, *Thrymsas and Sceattas in the Ashmolean Museum, Oxford*, 3 vols (Oxford, 1993–4).

239 W. Runciman, 'Accelerating social mobility: the case of Anglo-Saxon England', *Past and Present* 104 (1984), 3–30.

240 Regino of Prüm writing in the tenth century and cited (with other relevant discussion), in S. Reynolds, *Kingdoms and Communities in Western Europe, 900–1300* (Oxford, 1984) at 257.

241 N. Wright, 'Gildas's geographical perspective: some problems', in *Gildas: New Approaches*, ed. M. Lapidge and D.N. Dumville (Woodbridge, 1984).

242 Gildas, *De Excidio*, Chapter 19.

243 For example, on a slab depicting a king (?) and two warriors from Birsay, Orkney; *Pictish Symbol Stones*, no. 166.

244 R. Bartlett, 'Symbolic meanings of hair in the middle ages', *TRHS*, 6th series (1994), 43–60; M. Biddle and B. Kjølbye Biddle, 'The Repton stone', *Anglo-Saxon England* 14 (1985), 233–92.

245 Oliver, *English Law*, 70–1, 105.

246 S. Youngs, *'The Work of Angels': Masterpieces of Celtic Metalwork, 6th–9th Centuries* AD (London, 1989), 20–2; Henderson and Henderson, *Art of the Picts,* 96–107.

247 G. Owen-Crocker, *Dress in Anglo-Saxon England* (Manchester, 1986).

248 G. Speake, *Anglo-Saxon Animal Art and its Germanic Background* (London, 1980).

249 Reynolds, *Kingdoms and Communities*; P. Geary, *The Myth of Nations: The Medieval Origins of Europe* (Princeton, 2002); A. Gillett (ed.), *On Barbarian Identity: Critical Approaches to Ethnicity in the Early Middle Ages* (Turnhout, 2002).

250 B. Yorke, 'The origin myths of Anglo-Saxon kingdoms', in *Myths, Charters and Warfare in Anglo-Saxon England. Essays in Honour of Nicholas Brooks*, ed. J. Barrow and A. Wareham (Aldershot, forthcoming).

251 See above, 48–9.

252 Broun, *Irish Identity of the Kingdom of the Scots*.

253 N. Brooks, *Bede and the English* (Jarrow, 1999).

254 J. Hines, 'Welsh and English: mutual origins in post-Roman Britain?', *Studia Celtica* 34 (2000), 81–104.

255 Charles-Edwards, *Early Christian Ireland*, 214–33.

256 C. Cubitt, *Anglo-Saxon Church Councils c.650–c.850* (London, 1995), 184–5; *EHD* I, nos 191 and 193.

257 Youngs, '*Work of Angels*', 22, 47–52; M. Brenan, *Hanging Bowls and Their Contexts*, BAR 220 (Oxford, 1991).

258 G. Henderson, *Vision and Image in Early Christian England* (Cambridge, 1999), 19–53.

259 R.L.S. Bruce-Mitford, *The Sutton Hoo Ship-Burial*, 3 vols (London, 1975–83).

260 Lane and Campbell, *Dunadd*, 236–47.

CHAPTER 2

The Conversion of Britain to Christianity

Pre-Christian religion in early medieval Britain

By 600 Christianity had made widespread gains among the British and Irish as a result of its status as official religion of the Roman empire, and had become the dominant religion among them (though that does not mean that all traces of earlier beliefs and practices had been obliterated). Although some individual Anglo-Saxons had adopted Christianity before 600, it cannot be said to have made much headway among them until the seventh century, which was probably also the period in which the religion consolidated its hold among the Picts. The history of how the Anglo-Saxons and the Picts came to adopt Christianity, and the role of the other peoples of Britain in that conversion, is a major concern of this section of the book. Different stages of conversion need to be recognised. Ludo Milis has provided useful identification of three major stages that had to be gone through in the early medieval world before full conversion had been achieved – control of external collective behaviour; control of external individual behaviour; control of internal individual behaviour and consciousness.[1] This chapter will be mainly considering the first stages of conversion that involved the control of external behaviour. At any one point in the conversion process one might expect to find different Anglo-Saxon and Pictish regions at varying stages of progress, and within individual kingdoms different classes or other subdivisions might also proceed at different rates. Nor was it a simple linear progress because not all communities when introduced to Christianity were convinced of its desirability as the only belief system that should be followed. Moreover, whether a group was considered 'Christian' or not in the types of medieval sources we have available might depend on the circumstances and the attitudes of the commentator. When Pope Gregory wrote triumphantly to the bishop of Alexandria that 10,000 English had been baptised on Christmas Day 597, he was clearly making the most of what was presumably a very superficial acquaintanceship with the new religion for most of the congregation who had undergone a mass baptism.[2] When Bede wrote that a substantial proportion of the East Saxon people rejected Christianity at the time of the great plague of 663–4 he may have felt that their behaviour in resorting to various non-Christian religious practices was incompatible with them being considered as Christians, but that may not have been the view of the East Saxons at all who may have wished to draw upon all possible forms of supernatural protection.[3]

Bede would have doubted that Christianity could exist in any meaningful sense without regular pastoral care being provided.[4] While it might seem that a regular supply of priests was a necessity for Christian worship, one can point to instances in the medieval period where people seem to have considered themselves to be Christians without this being the case. There is evidence, for instance, that some families of settlers who went to Iceland from the British Isles as Christians, probably in the late ninth century, continued to regard themselves as Christians up to the time of the great debate on religion at the Althing in 1000, even though there had never been an organised church on the island and even the 'Christian' families seem to have had a limited knowledge of the religion and its rites.[5] These Christian Icelanders would undoubtedly have been seen as *pagani* (pagans) by churchmen for this term was used by early medieval writers not only to designate someone who was not a Christian, but anyone engaged in practices considered incompatible with Christianity. It meant originally someone who was a country-dweller, an inhabitant of an administrative district called a *pagus*.[6]

However much Christian commentators might wish to think otherwise, pre-Christian religious practices and approaches were bound to affect peoples' absorption of the new religion, even if they had formally renounced pagan beliefs. One can envisage a sliding scale on which some facets of pre-Christian belief, such as the worship of other gods, were regarded as completely incompatible with Christianity, but other religious rituals could be absorbed and adapted, an approach that Pope Gregory recommended to his missionaries once he realised the true nature of the circumstances in Anglo-Saxon England.[7] Of course, not all pre-Christian

rituals that people regarded as important had their exact Christian counterparts, and aspects that could not be readily assimilated tended to
survive as what the church designated 'magic' or superstition.[8] Repeated
condemnations by ecclesiastical authorities of such practices as seeking to
cure illnesses by passing children through holes in stones or to see into the
future through various forms of divination show the importance and
deep-rootedness of these self-help remedies to local communities.[9] There
was church disapproval, but they do not seem to have been seen as a
major threat to Christian stability as long as they did not involve the aid
of 'demons' (a category that could conveniently encompass many of the
supernatural beings of the pre-Christian world). Conversion to
Christianity was not simply a matter of substituting one religion for
another because the two forms of religion were different.

The distinction drawn by A.D. Nock between 'natural' and 'prophetic'
religions helps to make the contrasts clearer.[10] 'Natural religion' can be
characterised as the desire to control natural forces and processes, and
was the form of religion that was characteristic of the prehistoric peoples
of Europe. In such societies religion was integrated into the normal processes of daily life, and so was not necessarily viewed as a separate type of
activity. Religious ritual would be part of the way in which success could
be achieved in all essential activities from the growing of crops to protection from disease or defeating enemies in battle; a major function of such
ritual would have been to harness good forces and to turn away the bad.
In prophetic religions, such as Judaism, Christianity or Islam, the focus is
quite different because the emphasis is on achieving salvation for an individual's inner soul through faith and appropriate behaviour. The everyday
concerns of the present world are seen as of minor significance besides this
major enterprise, though many facets of an individual's life might be
affected by the forms of behaviour deemed necessary if eternal salvation
was to be achieved. There are major conceptual and practical differences
between these two religious forms that are central to the issue of conversion and its success. People were not necessarily aware of a need for
salvation until it had been impressed upon them. Nor would they necessarily have assumed that religion came with a specific moral code attached.
This was another major difference between Christianity and older religious practices, for before the advent of Christianity matters such as
marriage and sexual behaviour were governed principally by secular
norms and customs.

It would therefore be misleading to try to evaluate the earlier pre-
Christian religion by contrasting it directly with Christianity for they were

not the same type of religion and did not operate in the same way. Nevertheless that is what many early medieval Christian writers, such as Bede, tended to do, and naturally they also tended to find the early religion wanting, though they were selective – no doubt deliberately – in the facets of the earlier religion that they were prepared to discuss.[11] They also wrote in the consciousness of how non-Jewish/Christian religions and peoples were depicted in the Bible and might frame their accounts accordingly. However, in spite of the major problems in decoding them, we would be unwise to abandon the accounts of Christian commentators altogether as they are the nearest we have to contemporary descriptions of earlier religious practice. Some types of evidence may be very informative indeed, such as the letters between Pope Gregory and the early missionaries from Italy to southern England concerning practices that the latter had seen for themselves.[12] On the other hand, many hagiographical accounts, such as the healing match between Columba and the *magus* of King Bridei of the Picts can appear superficially very informative, but are in fact based so closely on biblical and earlier hagiographical prototypes that they are of doubtful value.[13] Interpretation of early medieval written accounts have been aided considerably by anthropological studies of traditional religions that can help to place ritual in a broader societal context and to suggest some of the purposes behind it. Prehistorians have also made great use of such studies to understand the archaeological evidence for early religious practice and their approaches are, of course, very relevant for the study of religion in the early Middle Ages in some parts of Britain where such practices had probably had an unbroken tradition from the late Iron Age.[14] Archaeologists specialising in the study of early medieval Britain, especially of its Anglo-Saxon regions, have been somewhat reluctant to engage with the issue of pre-Christian religious belief, partly because of some oversimplistic use of the early written descriptions in the past. However, more recently early medieval archaeology has been increasingly influenced by the work of prehistorians that suggests that religion must always have been an integral part of all aspects of early medieval life.

Gods and other religious beings

Accounts of early medieval missionary activity begin with their demand that pagan peoples abandon the worship of their gods, who are envisaged as being depicted as images in wood or stone. 'How can they have power to help anyone, when they are made from corruptible material by the hands of your own servants and subjects?', as Pope Boniface wrote to King Edwin of Northumbria when urging his conversion.[15] No specific images of this type are known from Anglo-Saxon England, but carved figures of prehistoric date are known from the Germanic homelands and from Scotland, and there are, of course, many representations of deities, both native and imported, from Roman Britain.[16] Bishop Daniel of Winchester in a letter of advice sent between 722 and 732 to Boniface, a priest from his diocese who was hoping to work as a missionary among continental Germans, recommended that he undermined their faith in the gods by pointing out additional ways in which they had been formed by men in their likeness, rather than the other way round, such as in the accounts of gods fornicating with goddesses.[17] 'Do they believe that the gods and goddesses still beget other gods and goddesses? Or, if they do not procreate now, when and why have they ceased from copulation and child-bearing?' Daniel was presumably drawing on his own knowledge of Anglo-Saxon pagan beliefs, for when he was a young priest in the latter part of the seventh century there were apparently West Saxons who had not yet converted to Christianity, and it is tempting to think that he was alluding to stories of Germanic gods and goddesses not unlike those that the Icelander Snorri Sturluson drew together in the early thirteenth century.[18] It does seem to be the case that some of the major gods of the Norse pantheon were known in Anglo-Saxon England for Woden, Thor and Tiw are all represented in place-names,[19] but it would be a mistake to assume either that Anglo-Saxon and Norse paganism were identical, or that Snorri's attempt in the thirteenth century to produce a coherent guide to Norse mythology is a reliable indication of even Scandinavian beliefs in the earlier Middle Ages. Germanic mythology probably consisted of a series of stories known in various forms and there would have been no 'scriptural' canon known to all.[20] The Anglo-Saxon carved whalebone box known as the Franks Casket depicts the story of Wayland the Smith known from elsewhere in the Germanic world, but also has other apparently unique heroic or mythological scenes, including the siege of the home of an archer called Egil and a strange half-human, half-horse being labelled 'Hos'.[21]

There are no accounts as comprehensive as those of Snorri for British or Irish mythology, though remnants of their legends may be preserved in vernacular stories that are also only known from problematic later, and therefore Christianised, written accounts.[22] Some of the Pictish carved stones may contain allusions to their lost mythologies. For instance, a number of stones, including examples from Mail in Shetland and Rhynie in

Aberdeenshire, depict a distinctive male figure with pointed teeth who carries a large axe and for whom it is difficult to find any exact analogues outside Pictland.[23] Even if we do not know the mythologies associated with them, inscriptions provide a good overview of the gods and goddesses honoured in Roman Britain. Although Roman imperial cults and others of foreign origin were introduced into Roman Britain, the native deities remained significant even if they were sometimes twinned with a Roman equivalent as at Bath where the shrine based around the hot springs was dedicated to Sulis Minerva.[24] Although some deities, such as the horse goddess Epona, were honoured in more than one place and were known in Gaul as well as Britain and Ireland, most, such as Sulis or Coventina at Carrawburgh on Hadrian's Wall, were associated with a particular location and were often linked with springs or other water. Stone inscriptions erected for Germans either in Britain or the Rhineland also seem to follow a similar pattern of honouring very localised deities such as the goddess Nehalennia who had two shrines on the island of Walcheren at the mouth of the Rhine, an area from which Germanic settlers probably set out in the fifth century to try their luck in Britain.[25] Popular both in the Germanic Rhineland, Gaul and Britain were the cults of three Mother Goddesses, and it is possible that Bede preserves a reference to them in his *De Temporum Ratione* where he refers to the pagan year beginning on 25 December with *Modranecht* (the night of the mothers).[26] Although the Anglo-Saxons may have known some specialist gods such as Thor who controlled thunder, more localised shrines that were associated with unique deities, who presumably resided or could be contacted there, might actually have been more significant, as they apparently had been among the British. Place-names from eastern England indicate the existence of shrines widely spread around the countryside, and sometimes linked with particular population groups or individuals, but we do not know if they had an association with a particular deity.[27] Nor were gods likely to have been the only religious beings. The folklore of Britain reveals the existence of long-standing belief in a wide range of supernatural forces with localised or specialised powers, and though it would be inappropriate to project all these beliefs on to the early medieval past, some of these lesser beings with magical powers are attested in Anglo-Saxon sources, such as the elves who according to surviving charms (recorded in the later Anglo-Saxon period, long after the adoption of Christianity) could bring disease by shooting people with their arrows,[28] and the water-monster Grendel with whom Beowulf battled so memorably. In traditions about Columba preserved outside Adomnán's *Vita,* he is shown having contact with a range of supernatural beings.[29]

Places of worship and practitioners of religion

One of the distinctive forms of monument surviving from Roman Britain is the temple, though most of these bore little resemblance to the impressive classical buildings of the Mediterranean world, but were rather developments in stone of late Iron Age timber shrines consisting of an inner *cella* of circular or rectangular shape and a surrounding ambulatory.[30] Of course, some particularly notable shrines such as that of Sulis-Minerva in Bath were more elaborate, and inscriptions indicate that they were serviced by priests. In spite of the progress of Christianity in fourth-century Britain, pagan shrines continued in use during that century and in the prosperous west country some such as Lydney had major refurbishments. Written records suggest that the Anglo-Saxons also had shrines and priests. The most detailed account comes in Bede's description of the initial conversion of Northumbria in the reign of King Edwin (616–33).[31] Coifi 'the chief of the priests' (*primus pontificum*) is so impressed by the new religion that he deliberately violated taboos by riding into the shrine on a stallion and casting a spear 'for a high priest of their religion was not allowed to carry arms or to ride except on a mare'. The validity of Bede's account has been questioned,[32] particularly because priests and buildings specifically for worship are not considered to be a feature of religion in the Germanic homelands. However, they did continue in use in the former Roman provinces of the Rhineland that came under Germanic control, such as Frisia,[33] and John Blair has identified a class of small square-ditched or fenced enclosure that can be placed alongside the more substantial building identified as a temple at Yeavering, a royal site in Northumberland.[34] The Anglo-Saxons may have been influenced by Romano-British shrines which they found in use on their arrival, and it is possible that some of the shrines identified in place-names in the areas of early Anglo-Saxon occupation may be those of their British inhabitants. The site at Goodmanham violated by Coifi consisted of a shrine with 'idols' of the gods and outer enclosures, and so sounds very similar to a Romano-Celtic temple.

The Irish included religious specialists among their learned orders, and it is usually presumed that among these were *magi* or druids who were similar to the British druids who were suppressed after the Roman conquest.[35] Women recognised as having specialist magical powers were known among the Irish, and probably among the Anglo-Saxons as well.[36] The *magus* of King Bridei of the Picts is depicted by Adomnán as a druid in the Irish hagiographical tradition, but how far he represents actual practice among the Picts seems more doubtful.[37] But though the peoples of Britain may have had religious specialists that need not mean that important religious roles were not carried out by other members of the community as well. The sacral significance of Irish kings has been much discussed,[38] and, even though it is now generally agreed that there has been too much emphasis on this aspect of Irish kingship in the past,[39] it seems likely that Irish kings had important roles in certain religious rituals which one might expect to have been introduced in areas of Irish settlement in Britain. In the territory of the Dál Riata in Argyll there is evidence from the royal fort of Dunadd for a likely site of royal inauguration that includes a footprint in stone.[40] Across 'the spine of Britain' the Pictish royal fort at Burghead has also produced evidence suggestive of ritual activities including a series of 30 stone plaques depicting bulls and a deep stone shaft from which reputedly came a sculpted 'Celtic' head.[41] The suggested temple from the Northumbrian royal site of Yeavering therefore fits into a wider pattern of an association of royal and religious sites in early medieval Britain, and the account of the mass baptism there in the time of Edwin and the large gathering of people earlier in his reign at the temple of Goodmanham when the king was present may suggest that there were festivals during the year in which the king and a wide cross-section of his people might participate.[42] Lesser lords and heads of households may have been responsible for other rituals in their own areas of authority, as seems to have occurred in Scandinavia.

However, while some important places of ritual may have had specific royal associations, the main characteristic of ritual sites that can be identified among the Irish, Picts and British outside the main areas of Romanisation is that they were natural sites such as lakes, springs, groves, standing stones and hill-tops.[43] These are also a major type of religious site in the Germanic homelands as identified by Tacitus, way back in the first century AD, and from archaeological study over a much longer period.[44] Many Romano-British temples were based around springs or located on hill-tops, and can perhaps be seen as an adaptation of native practice.[45] Deposition in water of a range of objects of varying value seems to have been a significant ritual of all the peoples with whom we are concerned.

Another shared feature to be found throughout Britain and Ireland in what could be called the late pagan period is the reuse of earlier prehistoric monuments for ritual and burial. This desire to reconnect with past inhabitants of the land can presumably be connected with a cult of ancestors, something that is also suggested by structures identified as shrines erected around Anglo-Saxons burials.[46] In part the association with visible structures of earlier peoples may be linked with the desire of new regimes to justify and legalise their position, and, perhaps, to give them the appearance of a greater ancestry. Such an interpretation has been suggested for the reuse of sites such as Navan and Tara in Ireland where it seems to have gone hand in hand with a flourishing mythology.[47] Dál Riatan kings at Dunadd may have stepped into the stone footprint to denote that they 'should walk in the footsteps and uprightness of [their] predecessors',[48] and the reuse and imitation of Bronze Age burial mounds for many of the wealthiest Anglo-Saxon burials may also have been a deliberate attempt to associate themselves with powers from the country's past. Recent studies not only of barrows, but also of cremation and of the poem *Beowulf* suggest that ancestors had a key role to play in Anglo-Saxon religious belief and how this was integrated into their understanding of cosmology, of how the world functioned.[49]

Animal symbolism and warrior cults

A feature of all the societies of early medieval Britain was a love of animal symbolism. Animals were regularly depicted on surviving Anglo-Saxon metalwork and on Pictish sculptures, and had also been a major feature of Iron Age art in Britain.[50] Such symbolism need not, of course, have had overt pagan connotations. Animals appear alongside Christian imagery on Pictish sculptures, and so were evidently not seen as incompatible with the practice of the new religion. In *The Gododdin* there is extensive use of animal imagery with men compared to boars, bulls, wolves, stags or bears,[51] all animals that appear in Pictish sculpture and Anglo-Saxon metalwork. The aggression and strength of these animals made comparison to them a fitting compliment for the warriors who are celebrated in these different media, and it was within such a tradition that in the ninth century Asser, the Welsh adviser to the ostentatiously Christian King Alfred, could describe the young Alfred charging like a wild boar at the battle of Ashdown.[52]

However, although animal symbolism could be safely used within Christian aristocratic and court culture that does not mean it could not at one time have had connotations of a different belief system. Many of the animals already discussed have a long history of cultic use, including in the Iron Age practices of both Celtic and Germanic peoples, all of whom sacrificed certain types of animals and ate others in ritual feasts. Some Celtic gods and goddesses could be closely associated with animals.

Figurines of dogs from the Roman shrine of Lydney (Gloucs) which was dedicated to the god Nodens, but for whom no anthropological depictions are known, have suggested that either Nodens carried out his acts of healing for which the shrine was renowned through dogs, or that he himself took the form of a dog.[53] The Frisian goddess Nehalennia is regularly depicted as accompanied by a dog that was evidently an integral part of her identity. But cultic use of animals was not necessarily linked with a specific deity; certain animals may have been valued as possessing their own supernatural powers.

One of the most ubiquitous was the boar. Wild boars have a prominent role to play in the Irish and Welsh mythological literature. In the Welsh story of *Culhwch ac Olwen* we meet the monstrous boar the *Twrch Trwyth* from between whose ears Culhwch with the aid of King Arthur had to snatch a comb and shears as part of the tasks he had to perform to win the hand of Olwen.[54] A more specific role for boars is suggested by the *Germania* of Tacitus and the Old English poem *Beowulf* where boars on helmets are said to have a protective function, and possibly the boar heads that terminate the eyebrows of the Sutton Hoo helmet could be interpreted in this way.[55] It is likely that many of the animals, and birds, that appear on Anglo-Saxon metalwork had a similar apotropaic or protective function. Similar explanations have been favoured for the original significance of the boars and other impressively naturalistic animals depicted by the Picts.[56]

Another animal with widespread associations is the horse. One of the best known and widely venerated of Celtic goddesses, including in Roman Britain, was the horse goddess Epona.[57] The Anglo-Saxons may also have had horse deities represented above all by the supposed founders of the Kentish royal house, the brothers Hengest and Horsa, whose names mean 'stallion' and 'horse', and are also recorded as the names given to paired protective horse emblems in early modern Saxony.[58] Daniel had recommended to Boniface that gods be recast as heroes (euhemerisation) and that is no doubt what had happened to Hengest and Horsa when they were incorporated into the foundation legend of the royal house of Kent. Horses are depicted on Kentish metalwork, including a notable series of brooches that looked at in one way represent a horse's head, but from another perspective seem to take the form of a man.[59] The apparent metamorphosis between human and animal form suggested by these brooches, and the widespread sacrifice of animals in cremation and other rites, has raised the question of whether the Anglo-Saxons were practitioners of shamanism whereby animals might be spirit guides and men could transform themselves into, or take on some of the characteristics of animals.[60] Shape-shifting is a significant element in the Irish myths and may lie behind the animal iconography and hybrid forms of pre-Christian art from Celtic Britain as well.[61]

Neil Price has produced a major study of Viking-age religion in which he argues that shamanistic practices and the sorcery (*seiðr*) associated with them were central to an Odinic cult centred on the successful propagation of war.[62] Battle magic could include warriors acquiring the attributes, or perhaps even taking on the forms, of the most aggressive animals known in the Norse world, the bear and the wolf. Although one should not assume that later Norse and Anglo-Saxon religious beliefs and practice were identical, Richard North has suggested independently from an analysis of Old English literature that the Anglo-Saxons were familiar with the type of sorcery associated in Scandinavia with Odin and the group of deities known as the *Vanir*.[63] What is perhaps more surprising is that behaviour similar to that of Scandinavian *berserkir* is recorded from Ireland, seemingly before the advent of the Vikings there. The *fianna*, bands of landless young warriors, were condemned by churchmen for the continuation of certain pagan practices that seem to have included the type of war sorcery associated with *seiðr*, and, as in Scandinavia, female practitioners were associated with certain aspects of battle-magic.[64]

In genealogies of the Christian era a number of Anglo-Saxon kings claimed descent from Woden (the Old English version of the name Odin) who by the eighth century had been apparently reclassified as a royal hero that even Bede found it possible to acknowledge.[65] But the mere fact that his presence was allowed in Christian contexts, when an individual with a cognate name was apparently being worshipped in areas with which the Anglo-Saxons were in contact, suggests that he was too important to leave out and so that he had had an earlier currency, presumably as a god. Some early Anglo-Saxon rulers may have sought to enhance their status by claiming descent, or a close relationship, with Woden, as had other Germanic leaders from various parts of Europe from whom Anglo-Saxon leaders borrowed other accoutrements of royal status.[66] We do not know the characteristics specifically attributed to Woden, but that he was a specialist in war as was his Scandinavian counterpart seems highly likely.

It may be that the necessary cohesion of early medieval warbands was underpinned by oaths and rituals which were among the facets of paganism that were not easily abandoned. Kings who relied so heavily on the support and muscle of their warriors would have needed to bond with them in any such pre-Christian rituals. The ritual drowning of defeated kings recorded among the Picts, and the pagan Penda's treatment of the body of King Oswald of Northumbria after the battle of *Maserfelth* in 642 when he had the head and hands severed from the body and hung on stakes,[67] may be examples of the offering up of defeated rivals in pagan ritual associated with the successful outcome of war.

Conclusion

Paganism cannot be codified as a single collection of religious beliefs and practices. It was distinguished by a great range of behaviour that was adapted to the needs of different places or classes in any society. There are many common features to the pre-Christian religious practices of the peoples of Britain, but they are also likely to have differed in detail. Many deities were associated with specific localities and the worship associated with them would have reinforced local identities, though the possibility existed of encouraging wider affiliations, for instance through rituals associated with kingship. In the surviving archaeological record religious items associated with elites predominate, but we should expect the pagan culture of lesser people to have been just as significant to them, and occasionally we find traces of it, for instance in the widespread practice of including amulets with Anglo-Saxon inhumations.[68] Pagan practices had evolved to meet the needs of all facets of early medieval life, and when we come to evaluate the impact of Christianity in early medieval Britain we will need to consider how far such practices had been abandoned or adapted to accommodate the new religion.

The conversion of the British and Irish

There are no narratives surviving of the type that we have for the early Middle Ages describing the work of missionaries to convert the Romano-British to Christianity. Britain's involvement with the wider Roman empire made it inevitable that knowledge of Christianity would come to Britain, and there are references to Christians in the island from the third century onwards.[69] As did other areas of the Roman world, Britain had its early martyrs, most of whom were probably victims of Diocletian's persecution of Christians that began in 303. Gildas refers to several 'of both sexes', but names only Alban of *Verulamium*, for whom versions of an account of his death survive, and Aaron and Julius of Caerleon, though these last two may have been victims of an earlier round of persecutions in the third century.[70] However, under Diocletian's successor Constantine there was a major change in attitude, and in the Edict of Milan of 313 Christianity became a legal religion of the Roman empire and advanced rapidly from this point to become the most significant one. In 314 Britain sent three bishops, a priest and a deacon to the Council of Arles. The bishops came from the three provincial capitals of London, York and Lincoln, and the priest and deacon may therefore have represented the fourth, Cirencester; the bishops may have been metropolitans who had the bishops under them in other *civitates* in their provinces.[71] That Britain was able to send bishops in 314 representing all *Britannia* could suggest that the church was relatively well established in Britain before the edict of Milan.

The detailed case for a thorough Christianisation of Roman Britain and for the continuation of that church in the new British regimes after 410 has been made by Charles Thomas,[72] though not all aspects of his thesis have been universally accepted. The archaeological evidence for Christianity in Britain has been seen as insubstantial compared to that from other areas of the Roman Empire, and it has been doubted that Christianity was sufficiently embedded to survive a resurgence of paganism and the political and military crises of the late fourth century that led to Britain ceasing to be part of the Roman empire in *c*.410.[73] It can be seen that the question of the strength of Christianity in Roman Britain and the post-Roman regimes has been affected by wider debates on the degree of Romanisation in Britain and the extent of collapse in the fifth century. It is undoubtedly the case that the evidence for Christianity from Roman Britain is on a different scale from that of the Mediterranean areas of the Roman empire.[74] Such churches as have been identified from late Roman Britain are for the most part small and unimpressive, though Britain is not so different from northern Gaul in this respect.[75] Moreover, as we have seen in Chapter 1, many features of Romanisation in Britain were understated compared to central areas of the Roman Empire. When all available evidence is drawn together there is in fact a strong case for permeation of Christianity at all levels of Romano-British society, from the villa owners at Hinton St Mary (Dorset) who commissioned a mosaic floor depicting the head of Christ to the much humbler artisans who scratched Christian graffiti on newly made tiles. However, it must also be admitted that some of the evidence is rather idiosyncratic and it would appear that as Christianity was absorbed into Roman Britain it was adapted to pre-existing religious practices. In eastern England, in particular, the practice of votive disposition of hoards in pits and water continued with the inclusion of lead tanks and other objects inscribed with Christian symbols, some of which may have been specifically made as offerings.[76] In the west there was a continuation of the reuse of hill-forts and other hill-top sites for burial and erection of churches, with some temples apparently being adapted for Christian use (as had occurred in Rome itself).[77]

Those who believe in a complete systems collapse in fifth-century Britain see the decline and disappearance of the emergent Christian church as part of that equation.[78] But as has been suggested in Chapter 1, this is not a conclusion that seems tenable for the western areas of Roman Britain where continuation of many Christian sites is part of the evidence for a general continuity and gradual evolution in the fifth century of many aspects of late Roman life. That the church was part of that continuity and an integral part of the regimes that controlled western Britain following the disappearance of Roman control is substantiated by the biographical details Patrick provides in his *Confessio* and *Letter to Coroticus*.[79] Patrick is most likely to have been born in the first half of the fifth century into a noble family who held positions of administrative and religious authority in the *vicus* of *Bannavem Taburniae*, which was close to their estate; his father was a deacon and a decurion (a member of the town council) and his grandfather had been a priest. When Patrick returned from his period in Ireland as a slave in his early 20s, he followed his father into the church and became a deacon. Both at this point, and later in his missionary career in Ireland that met with some criticism in Britain, we are made aware of the existence of a church hierarchy in Britain and of provincial synods. Gildas also gives the impression of a continuation and deepening of Christianity without major interruption, in western Britain at least, from the Roman period to the time he was writing, probably in the first half of the sixth century.[80] Gildas does not suggest that survival of pagan practices was a matter of concern, and his complaints about the laxity of the Christian behaviour of his audience are part of his rhetoric that should not be taken completely literally. Archaeological evidence also testifies to the vitality of Christianity in the west of Britain in the fifth and sixth centuries, and to the decline of earlier cult sites.[81] We might therefore conclude that Christianity had increased its hold in the fifth century in the lowland areas of *Britannia* that remained under British control and spread into the highland areas (where it may have made relatively little progress before 400), as the distribution of inscribed stones with Christian symbols or formulae seems also to suggest.[82] The eighth-century Breton *Life of St Samson* describes a journey he made from south Wales across Cornwall, probably in the early sixth century, in which some religious houses have been established, but pre-Christian practices were still continuing, that is until Samson intervened to eradicate them.[83] It seems unnecessary to evoke, as was the norm in the first two-thirds of the twentieth century, a second missionary phase led by monks from Gaul in order to explain the development of Christianity in the British kingdoms during the fifth and sixth centuries.[84] Britain was not cut off from Gaul or other areas of the western empire in the fifth and early sixth centuries, as finds of imported pottery from Gaul and the Mediterranean indicate.[85] British-born clerics such as Bishop Faustus of Riez are attested, Patrick refers to contacts in Gaul and Gildas criticises British clergy who travelled to Gaul for ordination. It is therefore only to be expected that shared facets of Christian culture would appear in Gaul and western Britain during this period (as the inscribed stones indicate) and that this cultural interchange would eventually include monasticism after it had spread from the eastern empire to Gaul and other parts of the west in the late fourth century.

The British church and the conversion of Ireland

Support for the argument that Christianity was well established in Britain by the end of the fourth century also comes from the evidence for the conversion of Ireland. Christians were already sufficiently numerous in Ireland by 431 for Pope Celestine to appoint Palladius as their bishop.[86] That British contacts had a significant part to play in the conversion of Ireland is suggested by some of the earliest Latin ecclesiastical terminology that was absorbed into Irish – words such as *domnach* for a church from *dominicum* 'the Lord's place' – for these words seem to have come through a British dialect of Latin.[87] There are grounds for thinking that Palladius was based in Leinster on the east coast of Ireland, where the memory is also preserved of other foreign missionaries, at least one of whom is likely to have been of British origin.[88] Leinster was well placed for trade with Britain, and this may have been one way in which knowledge of Christianity was spread, but not all links were necessarily peaceful for Leinster is also a prime candidate for an area from which raiders came to Britain and for some of the Irish settlers in Wales. As Patrick's account of his life reveals, British slaves made up part of the early community of Christians in Ireland although it is unlikely that the religion of slaves would have had much impact on their masters. Patrick's work as a missionary began when he decided to return to Ireland some years after his escape from servitude. Patrick's dates are controversial, but it seems most likely that the bulk of his activity fell in the second half of the fifth century, and that the date of 493 for his death in Irish annals could be reliable, or at least a reasonable estimate.[89]

Already by 650 Patrick was revered in Ireland as their 'apostle', and he seems to have evangelised in areas that had been unaffected by earlier contacts with the British church.[90] However, his career is hard to reconstruct in detail and has to be pieced together from his own writings, for the earliest fuller accounts of his life, from the late seventh-century writers Tírechán and Muirchú, date from after his 'adoption' by the church of Armagh and were written to boost and protect Armagh's interests.[91] The context in which he worked was one in which many kings were still pagan, in which his work was often greeted with suspicion and resentment, and his life and those of his converts were threatened. To survive and to ensure the spread of Christianity Patrick had to adapt to local custom and, for instance, gave gifts to rulers to allow him to preach. Conditions were evidently very different from in Britain, and what was seen as unorthodox behaviour led to accusations against him that he sought to counter in his *Confessio*.

Although the details cannot be traced, it would appear that in the course of the sixth century Christianity had made widespread progress within Ireland. Contacts with the British church seem to have remained strong, and so many British preachers seem to have been coming to Ireland in the sixth century that it was necessary to rule that any who arrived without a letter of permission from their bishop would not be allowed to minister.[92] Senior British churchmen such as Gildas and David were respected and their rulings on matters of church discipline regarded as authoritative.[93] A number of Irishmen studied with British teachers. Columba is said to have studied in Ireland in his youth with Bishop Uinniau, whose name appears to be British.[94] The name can also be rendered in a number of different diminutive forms in both British and Irish. Adomnán also refers to him as Finnbarr,[95] and he may have been known as Finnian as well. There has also been much discussion about whether Bishop Uinniau can be identified with individuals bearing these names that appear in any other sources, and, while it might be premature to say that matters have been resolved, there is some consensus that he was the Bishop Finnian of Moville in Ulster (where Columba would have studied with him) and the author, as was Gildas, of a penitential in the British tradition. In addition, a strong case has been made by Thomas Clancy for Uinniau being identical with the individual known in Anglo-Saxon sources as Bishop Ninnian of Whithorn in Galloway, where the presence of a religious foundation in the sixth century has been confirmed by excavation.[96] There are many dedications to 'Finnian' in the vicinity of Whithorn, but none (of early date) to 'Ninian' whose name may have originated as a scribal misreading of Uinniau.

These arguments for the identity of Uinniau, together with the evidence of inscribed stones from Galloway and from excavations at Whithorn and nearby in Hoddom (Dumfriesshire),[97] show that Christianity had also been disseminated to the British provinces of the north in the course of the fifth century. King Coroticus, to whom Patrick addressed his letter, was Christian and probably king of Dumbarton.[98] The shadowy figure of Bishop Kentigern who died between 612 and 614 is associated with this kingdom, though the later hagiographical accounts written after he had become the patron of Glasgow cathedral probably have little historical validity.[99] The British of the poem *The Gododdin* are portrayed as Christian, and are said to have taken communion and done penance in church.[100]

The church in Dál Riata

There is no specific record surviving of the circumstances in which Dál Riata was converted to Christianity and it should perhaps be seen as part of the process by which Christianity spread from Britain to Irish territories. Conversion would seem to have been achieved before the time Columba arrived there in 563 as there are no references to him encountering non-Christian Irish, there or elsewhere.[101] The earliest sources for Columba's life, the Old Irish eulogy known as the *Amra*, which was written soon after his death and Adomnán's *Vita*, portray Columba's decision to leave Ireland as being taken for religious reasons so that he could better serve God as a religious exile, a *peregrinatus*.[102] Adomnán places his departure after the battle of Cúl Debrene in 561, and later accounts of his life developed a connection between the battle and Columba's removal to Scotland. Possibly Columba had been involved in the victory of his Úi Néill kinsmen in a way that he felt compromised his position as a man of religion. However, if his aim in leaving Ireland was to leave behind political entanglements it was not achieved, for Adomnán's account reveals him to have cultivated links with Roderic, the British king of Dumbarton and King Bridei of the Picts as well as being much involved in the politics of Dál Riata and of his family connections in Ireland. Missionary work was a by-product of his wide-ranging contacts in northern Britain, not its primary aim, and Iona may have become more of a missionary station under his successors than it was under Columba. A series of daughter houses of Iona was founded in Columba's lifetime, and included foundations among the Picts and in Ireland, notably Durrow and Derry, as well as several other communities within Dál Riata, including on the islands of Tiree and *Hinba*.[103]

The preponderance of records from Iona and its later reputation in the Scottish kingdom have obscured the activities of other Irish churchmen in Dál Riata. It is apparent from Adomnán's *Life of Columba* that there were other foundations not linked with Iona in its vicinity; other foundations on Tiree, for instance, are mentioned as having been visited by plague when Columba's foundations were spared.[104] There are a number of references in the *Life* to churchmen sailing from Ireland to the Scottish islands in search of suitable refuges, and surviving archaeological evidence suggests that a number of small hermitages may have been established.[105] Significant larger church foundations that were not connected with Iona included Kingarth, the Dál Riatan bishopric, founded by St Blane of whom little is known, and Lismore associated with St Moluag (also known as Mo Luóc and Lugaid) who was probably a contemporary of Columba from the monastery of Bangor (Co. Down).[106] St Moluag's staff (*bachall*) is still in the custody of its hereditary keepers at Lismore. Kildonan on the island of Eigg, on the borders of Dál Riatan and Pictish territory, was a significant foundation of St Donnán, another near contemporary of Columba, whose cult seems to have spread over a wide area of the Hebrides.[107]

The issues of a 'Celtic' church and the dating of Easter

Sometimes the early medieval churches of Wales, Ireland and Scotland are referred to collectively as 'the Celtic church', and there has been much debate in recent years about whether there is any validity in the idea that they shared certain common features in the early Middle Ages.[108] The debate has been complicated by the modern cult of 'Celtic Christianity' that, although takes its inspiration from medieval texts, often draws on these in a selective and ahistorical way.[109] There was certainly no institutionalised pan-Celtic church that recognised the authority of any one representative or synod. On the other hand, as we have seen, there was considerable British influence on the conversion of Ireland, and British churchmen and their teachings were influential there in the sixth century, so that we would expect to find some shared characteristics in the early years of the Irish church. However, as there were also major differences between the societies of Britain and Ireland these can be expected to have affected the nature of ecclesiastical provision. In Ireland the church had been successful in integrating itself with the traditional learned orders that included other professional groups such as lawyers, poets and genealogists; churchmen had in practice taken over the position of druids and other religious specialists within this hierarchy.[110] Roman control would have disrupted any such native traditions in many parts of *Britannia*.

It has been argued, particularly in one recent study, that the early medieval church in Britain and Ireland was strongly influenced by the teachings of Bishop Pelagius on free will which had been proscribed in Roman territories in 418.[111] Pelagius seems to have been of British origin, but had long been resident in Rome, and was one of many contemporary theologians who reacted against Augustine's views on original sin and predestination.[112] As by 418 Britain was beyond the reach of Roman civil authorities, Pelagian sympathisers who risked prosecution in Roman territory seem to have sought refuge in Britain and Ireland, and were a major reason for Pope Celestine's despatch of Bishop Germanus of Auxerre to Britain in 429 and, perhaps, for his creation of Palladius as bishop for the Christians in Ireland in 431.[113] Although Germanus may have had to return to Britain in 444–5, Celestine's adviser, the chronicler Prosper of Aquitaine, seems to have considered that the heretical beliefs had been successfully eliminated, and it can be doubted if Pelagianism was ever a major influence in Britain or Ireland. What have been described as Pelagian characteristics can be seen as more generally characteristic of the ascetic movement in southern Gaul that was the ultimate source of the monastic impulse in sixth-century Britain and Ireland.[114] Monastic leaders such as John Cassian reacted against the Augustinian doctrine of predestination that seemed to deny the value of their own way of life in affecting man's destiny and they are sometimes referred to as semi-Pelagians. What have been seen as peculiarly 'Celtic' characteristics of asceticism, compatible with Pelagianism, can in fact be viewed as part of the wider monastic movement in western Europe in which western Britain and Ireland shared in the sixth century when many of their religious leaders moved between the two islands. If heretical Pelgianism was a defining characteristic of the British or Irish churches one would expect it to have formed part of the criticisms made in the seventh century about religious practice in some of their churches, but it is never mentioned.

Another issue that has been linked frequently with the idea of a Celtic church with its own defining characteristics is the dating of Easter. The calculation of Easter was a complex matter that involved reconciliation of the lunar and solar cycles and the imposition of various rules derived ultimately from Judaic practices for the calculation of Passover and the way they had been adapted to Christian practice. Easter had to fall on a Sunday in the third week of the first lunar month of the year, and the paschal full moon could not fall before the spring (vernal) equinox.[115] Specialised calendars known as Easter tables were produced to indicate when Easter would fall, and in the sixth century the western British and Irish had adopted an 84-year cycle.[116] However, there were different ways in which calculations could be made, including of the date of the spring equinox and of the days between which it was possible for Easter Sunday to fall. When Irishmen began to travel extensively on the continent from the late sixth century they found that the calendar they had been using differed in these respects from others currently in use in Rome and in Gaul, and early in the seventh century some Irish churches switched to the calendar that had been drawn up by Dionysius Exiguus in 525, and which had been introduced by missionaries from Italy and Francia to Anglo-Saxon England.

The use of the Dionysian calendar spread throughout many parts of Ireland in the seventh century, but was not adopted by many British churches or by the Dál Riatan centre of Iona. The conservatism of the western British church became an issue as the Anglo-Saxons spread westwards.[117] Iona's unwillingness to depart from the practice adopted by their founder Columba caused problems in Northumbria whose main bishopric at this time, Lindisfarne, was a daughter house of Iona, but where some churches followed what was often referred to as the Roman method of calculating Easter, introduced into Northumbria in the 620s by the Italian missionary Paulinus. The divergence was a serious issue because in some years the Ionan and Roman churches would celebrate Easter on different Sundays, which affected the rest of the year's liturgy as well, and meant that they were out of step with the practice of Rome and the majority of Christians in western Europe. Matters were resolved at the synod of Whitby in 664, when King Oswiu ruled in favour of the Roman practices.[118] Many of the northern Irish churches that had held out against the Roman Easter adopted it in 704, but Iona resisted until 716 and some Welsh churches until 768. The Easter controversy shows that when it came to religious practice there was considerable divergence in the seventh century within Britain and Ireland, with churches of southern Ireland being the most open to continental influence and some western British churches and Iona the most conservative. Similar patterns are found in examination of other issues such as the liturgy, baptism and the form of the tonsure, with many western British churches and Iona strongly identifying with the traditions known to their founders.[119]

The British church and the conversion of the Anglo-Saxons

In spite of the active involvement of British clergy in the conversion of Ireland, Bede maintained that the British had made no attempt to convert their Anglo-Saxon neighbours, and in a number of places in the *Ecclesiastical History* he contrasts them unfavourably with the Irish who had played a major role in the conversion of Northumbria and some of the other Anglo-Saxon kingdoms.[120] When Pope Gregory despatched his mission to the English in 596 he was not aware of the true political situation and envisaged that the diocese of *Britannia* would be recreated with Augustine as archbishop of all the British and Anglo-Saxons living within it. In 601, or soon after, a meeting was arranged between Augustine and representatives of the British church, perhaps representatives of the former province of *Britannia Prima*, at a site that became known as Augustine's Oak, and was in Bede's day on the border of the Anglo-Saxon kingdoms of the Hwicce and the West Saxons. Augustine urged the British church to abandon church customs (such as the method of calculating Easter, which differed from practice in Rome) and to join him in evangelising the English.[121] The British clergy declined to do so at a second meeting where Augustine reputedly caused offence by not rising to greet the British delegates. From this point relations appear to have broken down irredeemably. Aldhelm, abbot of Malmesbury, in a letter to King Geraint of Dumnonia written in the latter part of the seventh century complained that the clergy of Dyfed refused 'to celebrate the divine offices in church with us and to take courses of food at table for the sake of charity'.[122] Such sources of information combined with Gildas's criticism of the failings of the British church in his day combined to underpin Bede's highly critical view of British Christianity.

However, Bede fails to include in his assessment the long history of warfare between British and Anglo-Saxons and the way in which large swathes of *Britannia* had come under Anglo-Saxon control; such things are likely to have curbed any missionary impulses towards the Anglo-Saxons from British clergy. In his account of the aftermath of the St Augustine's Oak meeting, Bede has Augustine prophesy that if the British clergy would not preach Christianity to the English, they would suffer vengeance at their hands – and saw the prophecy as being fulfilled in 604 when, reputedly, 1,200 monks from the monastery of Bangor-on-Dee were slain by Æthelfrith of Northumbria at the battle of Chester. Æthelfrith was not a Christian and the monks who had come to pray for the army were no doubt seen by him as a legitimate target, but atrocities of this type (no doubt committed by both sides) must have left deep-rooted scars.[123] Evangelisation depends not only on the willingness on one side to preach, but also on receptivity from the other party. Anglo-Saxons were accustomed to see British in their own kingdoms as inferiors and 'foreigners' in their own country.[124] Their language made little impact on the Anglo-Saxons because of such perceptions of status so that it is unlikely the Anglo-Saxons would have been open to overtures of conversion from them. There was a political as well as a religious context to the meeting at St Augustine's Oak. Augustine was under the protection of the Anglo-Saxon overlord Æthelbert of Kent (d.616), and at the time of the meeting Wessex and Mercia were seeking to extend their political control westwards. Therefore although Augustine appeared in one sense as the representative of Pope Gregory in Rome, he was also in alliance with Anglo-Saxon leaders who threatened the independence of the remaining areas under British control. British rulers are likely to have had views on the idea of their church cooperating with Augustine and recognising his superiority. The British must have felt increasingly beleaguered and criticisms of some of their church practices must have been difficult to disentangle from other outside threats.

Some historians have not only seen Bede as prejudiced against the British church, but wrong in asserting that the British played no part in the evangelisation of the Anglo-Saxons. Bede depended on information from correspondents for events in kingdoms outside Northumbria, and it is evident from the distribution of places he mentions that he received relatively little information from western England, though it is also possible that he was not inclined to seek out details of accommodation between British and Anglo-Saxon Christians.[125] One must also beware of making generalisations about the whole British church, when the British were so politically fragmented, and be prepared for shifts in attitude over time. A few instances of cooperation between Anglo-Saxon and British clergy can be cited. The ninth-century *Historia Brittonum* claimed that King Edwin of Northumbria had been baptised by Rhun, son of Urien of Rheged, but the somewhat garbled insertion into a passage taken from Bede's *Ecclesiastical History* is now usually discounted.[126] In 664 Chad is said to have been consecrated as bishop by Bishop Wine of the West Saxons with

the aid of two British bishops (whose sees are unfortunately not ident-
ified).[127] Aldhelm's *Letter to Geraint* reveals that, unlike the clergy of
Dyfed, churchmen in Dumnonia were cooperating with him and even
Bede admitted that Aldhelm had persuaded many British to change to
Roman methods of calculating Easter.[128]

In contrast to the top-down emphasis in conversion narratives, it has
been suggested that the apparent rapid conversion to Christianity of
Anglo-Saxon settlers in areas such as the West Midlands, which had
remained free from Anglo-Saxon control until the early years of the
seventh century, are an indication that Christianity had been acquired
through assimilation with the native British population, rather in the
manner that has sometimes been proposed for the rapid conversion of
Danish settlers in eastern England in the ninth and early tenth centuries.[129]
The hypothesis is a difficult one to substantiate as it depends on negative
evidence; on the one hand, the lack of burial with gravegoods among the
Anglo-Saxon settlers at a time when this practice was continuing in
eastern England, and, on the other, a failure by Bede to mention any
major missionary campaign, though he may have felt the matter was
covered by discussion of the kingdom of Mercia to which these western
areas seem to have been politically subordinate.[130] There are fragmentary
traditions preserved in the West Midlands which suggest that the Hwicce
and the Magonsaetan may have been subject to campaigns of conversion
comparable to those in other Anglo-Saxon kingdoms. Leominster in the
province of the Magonsaetan, for instance, preserved the memory of a
priest Eadfrith or Entfirth who came from Northumbria and converted
King Merewalh in *c.*660, a period when Mercia had a bishop of
Northumbrian origin.[131]

What can perhaps be more certainly said is that the Anglo-Saxon
expansion into areas of western Britain after *c.*600 acted as a spur for conversion. These were areas where the church had been established for
upwards of two centuries and the Anglo-Saxons seem to have appreciated
that their control would be aided by taking over the church structure for
themselves. There are good arguments for bishoprics and other major
churches of the west, such as Sherborne, Exeter, Gloucester, Worcester,
Lichfield and Carlisle, as being British ecclesiastical centres that passed
directly into Anglo-Saxon hands, sometimes with a shift in location for
the main church sites.[132] In Wessex, families (including that of the future
St Boniface who was entered into a monastery in Exeter *c.*680), were
moving into the west country and establishing Anglo-Saxon controlled
ecclesiastical bases before the full conversion of the West Saxon royal

house had been achieved.[133] Agreement on how the British church was to be treated may have been part of the negotiations, which it has been suggested are likely to have aided the apparently swift takeover of some British provinces and may be represented in the laws of King Ine.[134] Such negotiations may in some cases have begun before a final assault was made on a province, and it is possibly in this context that we should understand Aldhelm's letter to Geraint of Dumnonia urging him to amend certain customs in the churches of his province at a time when he may have had to recognise West Saxon overlordship.[135] Aldhelm seems to have accepted British priests who were prepared to cooperate and act in conformity with Rome, and was perhaps able to build on links established by Wine in the 660s.[136]

A rather different issue is the question of the survival of British Christianity in the eastern parts of England where the Anglo-Saxons first settled. There is no evidence of a persecution of Christians as such, but without a church structure and contact with other Christian regions it would have been difficult for any meaningful church organisation to have survived, although, as discussed above, people might still have continued to think of themselves as Christians and kept some Christian customs. Knowledge of the cult of St Alban seems to have been preserved in a district that may have remained independent of Anglo-Saxon control until the seventh century, even if, as Gildas observed, it was no longer possible for British Christians from other areas to visit his shrine.[137] The place-name *eccles*, deriving ultimately from Latin *ecclesia* 'a church', was adopted into Old English as nomenclature for a Romano-British ecclesiastical building, perhaps still in use, but examples are rare from the areas of Anglo-Saxon primary settlement.[138] Kent has one 'Eccles' name for a place which was the site of a Roman villa that was utilised as a cemetery in the seventh century.[139] It is part of the fragmentary evidence for the possible survival of British Christianity in Kent that includes evidence for a cult of a local martyr called Sixtus, though Pope Gregory and Augustine replaced his relics with those of Pope Sixtus II because they felt doubtful about the validity of a cult which was poorly substantiated.[140] It has also been suggested that questions put by Augustine to Pope Gregory on issues of ritual purity arose from the existence of British Christians, or of Anglo-Saxons converted by them, in Kent.[141] However, the question is complicated by there being another direction from which the Anglo-Saxons of Kent could have received knowledge of Christianity, namely from Francia. During the sixth century Frankish kings, who had by this date been converted to Christianity, had considerable influence in Kent, and there were colonies of Anglo-Saxons, probably from Kent within Francia.[142] Augustine was not the first bishop to work in Kent. He had been preceded by a Frankish bishop called Liudhard who came to Kent with the Merovingian princess Bertha who married King Æthelbert in c.580.[143] It was Liudhard who restored or adapted a Roman stone building in Canterbury that had been a church or mausoleum and dedicated it to the Frankish St Martin, and finds from the church site, probably from burials, suggest that he may have made converts.[144] The evidence for survival of British Christians in eastern England and their possible influence on the Anglo-Saxons is tantalising but inconclusive. We should not forget that when the Anglo-Saxons first settled in eastern England they may have found some Romano-British pagan rites still in operation as well as practising Christian congregations, and that the rituals of the indigenous population may have influenced the practice of the Anglo-Saxons' pre-Christian religion. There may have been British who thought of themselves as Christians living in Anglo-Saxon kingdoms in the late sixth century, but their social standing was such that they are unlikely to have been in a position to influence kings and their aristocracies to change their religious beliefs.

The conversion of the Anglo-Saxons

The conjunction of a number of circumstances explain why it was that the conversion of the Anglo-Saxons was achieved in the seventh century, for this was a time when Anglo-Saxon kingdoms, in some cases probably only established relatively recently, were in a position to react positively to Christian overtures and in which there were churchmen ready and willing to make them.[145] Mission was seen as essential in order to complete Christ's ministry, for until Christianity was spread 'to the ends of the world'[146] (which in the world of classical geographers included Britain at the northern extremity) the final consummation of the Second Coming of Christ could not be achieved. Pope Gregory was profoundly convinced of the need for action and took the unusual step of seeking to convert 'barbarians' living outside the territories currently under imperial control.[147] In 596 he despatched 40 monks led by Augustine from his own monastery of St Andrew who arrived at the court of King Æthelbert of Kent in 597.[148] After initial success that led to the establishment of a first Christian bishopric at Canterbury, Æthelbert used his position as overlord to introduce missionaries to the East Saxons and East Angles, and eventually, in the reign of Æthelbert's son Eadbald (616–40) to Northumbria when King Edwin married King Æthelbert's daughter Æthelburh in 625. However, in spite of these early successes, after the death of Edwin in 633 the Gregorian mission was confined to Kent, and had been extremely lucky to survive there after Archbishop Laurence had objected to Eadbald's marriage with his step-mother; only physical evidence that St Peter himself had scourged Laurence persuaded the king to change his mind.[149] Successive archbishops maintained the links with Rome, symbolised by the presentation of a liturgical garment known as the pallium from the pope to each new archbishop, and gradually increased their influence in all churches of the English in accordance with Gregory's original intentions. As Bede observes, Theodore (669–90), a noted theologian from the eastern part of the empire who had been chosen for the post by the pope when the Anglo-Saxon candidate had died in Rome, was the first archbishop whose authority was accepted throughout the whole of England.[150]

The missionary impulse was also a notable feature of the Irish church in the seventh century. The first bishop in Ireland, Palladius, had also been a papal appointee, but he had no immediate successors who are known to have maintained the link with Rome. The man who was more widely acknowledged as the apostle of the Irish by *c.650* was Patrick from Britain who in his own writings stressed his position as an exile in the tradition of St Paul who had taken the gospel to the gentiles, a theme that was developed further in the late seventh-century *Lives of Patrick*. The idea of exile as a way of serving Christ (*peregrinatio*) seems to have found a particular resonance in Irish society where exile was one of the severest forms of punishment and disgrace in secular society.[151] To voluntarily leave not only one's kingdom and kinsfolk, but Ireland itself, came to be seen as the culmination of an ascetic life. Like Pope Gregory, such Irish clergy drew no dividing line between the active and contemplative lives and accepted that exile might bring responsibilities of missionising in appropriate circumstances.

Bede refers to Dicuil, who settled at Bosham among the South Saxons, and Maelduibh, whose name is preserved in that of Malmesbury in the province of the West Saxons, who were probably Irish religious exiles of this type, and perhaps more significant in the Christianisation of these provinces than he was aware.[152] But the most influential Irish religious exile to come to Britain was undoubtedly Columba, who left Ireland for Dál Riata in 563 (even though he may not have come to Britain with the intention of carrying out missionary work).[153] During Columba's lifetime there were at least two Anglo-Saxon followers, Genereus and Pilu, living on Iona.[154] When the future king of Northumbria Oswald was in exile as a young prince in Dál Riata he had been baptised, perhaps on Iona, and sent for monks from there to continue the conversion of Northumbria after his victory over Caedwalla at the battle of Heavenfield in 634.[155] According to Adomnán, the invitation was the result of a vow made by Oswald after Columba appeared in a dream to him before the battle and promised him victory over his enemy.[156] Bede is full of praise for Aidan who (after the departure of a leader of the mission who was deemed too severe) became bishop of Lindisfarne that became part of the monastic confederation of Iona.[157] Oswald's brother Oswiu used his position as overlord to establish missionaries from Lindisfarne in the provinces of the Middle Angles, East Saxons and Mercia.[158] It was also Oswiu who severed the links of Northumbria with Iona when he made the decision at the synod of Whitby to be in conformity with Rome and to accept the authority of the archbishop of Canterbury.[159] It was the death of the appointee to the archbishopric of Canterbury made by Oswiu and Ecgbert the king of Kent that led to the appointment of Theodore.[160]

Other Irish religious exiles went to the continent, and particularly significant for the conversion of southern Anglo-Saxon kingdoms was Columbanus, who in 590 or 591 left his monastery of Bangor in northern Ireland for religious exile in Francia.[161] Although the Franks had been Christian for most of the sixth century, the leading churchmen had tended to come from the Gallo-Roman community. Columbanus was largely responsible for inspiring the Franks themselves into greater involvement with the church, and in particular to extensive foundation of monasteries in northern Francia.[162] This new enthusiasm spilled over the Channel into southern England. A number of key missionaries in southern England were Irishmen or Franks from such Iro-Frankish monasteries (as they are known after the time of Columbanus when, among other changes, they had abandoned the Irish calendar for the calculation of Easter that he had introduced). They included the Irishman Felix who was bishop of East Anglia (c.630–c.647) and the Frank Agilbert who was bishop of Wessex (c.650–c.660) and was eventually followed in that position by his nephew Leuthere (670–6).[163] Agilbert had studied in Ireland before being appointed bishop in Wessex, and when he left his position there he travelled to Northumbria where he advised the 'Roman' party at the synod of Whitby, He seems to have been influential in establishing links between the Northumbrian church and Francia, particularly in the case of Wilfrid, the main spokesman of the 'Roman' party at Whitby who was strongly influenced by subsequent visits to Francia.[164] Agilbert came from a leading

Neustrian noble family and, subsequent to his return to Francia, became bishop of Paris.

It is arguable that it was the Frankish connection that was most significant in the conversion of the kings of southern England.[165] Frankish kings may have exercised some form of overlordship in southern England during the sixth century, but it was only at the end of that century that they can be shown to have interested themselves in the religion of leaders they had dealings with. The despatch of Bishop Liudhard with Bertha presumably signals that Æthelbert was expected to accept Christianity through his ministrations, though it is not known when or by whom Æthelbert was converted. It was the failure of the Franks to send reinforcements, or perhaps a replacement after Liudhard's death (the date of which is unknown), that opened up the way for Pope Gregory's mission which received considerable help from the Frankish courts and episcopacy, including the provision of essential interpreters. King Sigebert of the East Angles (acc. c.630) had been in exile in Francia, perhaps even in one of the Iro-Frankish monasteries, for he retreated into the monastic life in East Anglia at an unknown point after his accession.[166] Around the middle of the seventh century the royal families of Kent and East Anglia seem to have had marriage and other links with the family of Erchinoald, mayor of the palace of Neustria. Erchinoald, like other leading Neustrian nobles of this date, was a patron of the new monasticism. Princesses from the interrelated Kentish and East Anglian families entered and eventually ran the nunnery of Faremoutiers, probably with Erchinoald's connivance at a time of competition for control of the major northern Frankish religious communities.[167] In many ways the adoption of Christianity at the royal courts in the south was an extension of their political links with their neighbours across the channel and part of a desire to emulate their successes.

However, one also needs to take account of the lure of Rome, both as emblem of the Roman empire and in its contemporary manifestation as the seat of the pope, the successor of St Peter and St Paul who were buried in the city. Thanks to the championship of Christianity by Emperor Constantine, the religion had become inextricably linked with the concept of the Roman empire that survived in the seventh century in the remnants held by the Byzantine emperors. The rulers of the successor states in Britain, as did the inheritors of other former Roman provinces in western Europe, looked to the Roman and Byzantine world for ways of expressing their power.[168] One of the most impressive acknowledgements of the lure of Rome is the burial assemblage from the ship-burial in mound 1 at

Sutton Hoo.[169] It is most immediately apparent in the silver objects of late Roman and Byzantine manufacture, such as the great silver dish with the date stamp of the Emperor Anastasius (491–518), but goes much deeper than this. Many of the items decorated with Germanic symbolism and constructed with gold and garnet decoration, such as the helmet, epaulettes, belt buckle and sword harness, were based upon the ceremonial apparel of officials of the late Roman world. Other items interpreted as insignia of office, such as the whetstone and standard, also seem to be based on Roman symbols of power.[170] Some of the silver objects were inscribed with a cross, thus associating the essential symbol of Christianity with imperial splendour. The popes sent desirable gifts of similar late Roman items to the Anglo-Saxon courts where their missionaries were received: a set of eastern robes for King Edwin and a silver mirror and ivory comb for his queen.[171]

As kings came to know more of Christianity so they, like other Anglo-Saxons, were impressed by the idea of Rome as a holy city where one could be closer to God. The deciding factor for King Oswiu at the synod of Whitby was Wilfrid's argument that in heaven St Peter carried more weight than St Columba as Christ had entrusted Peter with the keys of heaven: 'Since he is the doorkeeper I will not contradict him', concluded the king, 'but I intend to obey his commands in everything to the best of my knowledge and ability, otherwise when I come to the gates of heaven, there may be no one to open them'.[172] Wilfrid's own first visit to Rome had been a formative experience and he was to visit the holy city on several other occasions in his embattled career. Oswiu forbade his own son Alhfrith (subking of Deira) from visiting Rome with Wilfrid, but planned to go there himself with the bishop towards the end of his reign, but died before he could do so.[173] The first Anglo-Saxon king to visit Rome, also under the influence of Bishop Wilfrid during one of his periods of exile from Northumbria, was Caedwalla of Wessex who was baptised there shortly before his death in 689 and buried in St Peter's. His successor Ine also abdicated (in 725) in order to end his life in Rome.[174]

As the history of the conversion of the Anglo-Saxon kingdoms indicates the role of the kings was crucial, and it was only when kingdoms had reached a certain degree of stability that the process of conversion began. Only the kings could give foreign missionaries protected status, as Æthelbert of Kent did in his lawcode, and guarantee the permanent establishment of bishoprics and of grants of land. Christianity was spread through royal contacts, especially through the institution of overlordship, and aided by royal strategies such as marriage between kingdoms.[175] The initial baptism of large numbers of the ordinary population also seems to have been achieved through royal involvement, although we only possess detailed information for Northumbria. Bede, for instance, describes how Paulinus spent 36 days at the royal vill of Yeavering catechising people from the districts roundabout and baptising them in the River Glen.[176] He and Bishop Aidan from Iona seem to have travelled with the Northumbrian kings on their royal progresses through the kingdom,[177] an integral part of which seem to have been occasions when local people assembled in the presence of the kings. It may be suspected that pagan religious ceremonies had traditionally taken place at these times, as Bede's description of the meeting at Goodmanham when Coifi defamed the temple and the signs of ritual feasting from the excavations at Yeavering could be taken to suggest.[178] The use of rivers for baptism may, as Bede says, be in part because there were no suitable church buildings, but can also be seen as a bridge between Christianity and the pre-Christian religions of Britain. The regenerative powers of water were probably an element of these religions as well, as is suggested in particular by the healing springs of Romano-Celtic religion and the apparent identification of rivers with goddesses.[179]

Kings continued to regard themselves as leaders of the church once the initial period of conversion was past. It may have been churchmen who presented the case for and against the Ionan Easter at the synod of Whitby, but it was King Oswiu who presided and made the final decision. Bishops could only be appointed with royal approval, and, as Wilfrid discovered, might be dismissed, imprisoned and exiled if they fell from favour.[180] As the abdications to travel to Rome or enter religious communities may suggest, many kings could take their roles as religious leaders very seriously, indeed, perhaps more seriously than many churchmen would have liked, and further ramifications of this potential clash over respective roles will be explored in Chapter 4. However, in spite of an early enthusiasm from a number of kings, in most kingdoms it took some time for the final stage of commitment to be reached and there could be a gap of some 40–50 years between the first conversion and establishment of bishoprics before all public pagan worship ceased and all members of the royal house were baptised.[181] For example, we are told that King Eadbald of Kent (640–64), the grandson of Æthelbert, was the first king to order pagan worship to cease and the idols to be destroyed, over 40 years after the arrival of the Gregorian mission.[182] In Wessex the first king to be baptised was King Cynegils in 636, but it was possible in 685 for Caedwalla to succeed to the throne without having undergone baptism.[183] It would appear that in the different kingdoms Christian and pagan worship coexisted for half a century or so after the first introduction of Christianity, as would seem to be the case in the temple of King Raedwald of the East Angles at Rendlesham (near Sutton Hoo) which contained one altar to the Christian god and another (smaller) altar to pagan deities.[184] It may be that kings hoped, until persuaded otherwise by their bishops, that they could keep both religions going in tandem, something that would seem quite reasonable to anyone brought up in a polytheistic religion. Certainly baptism of a king does not seem to have meant baptism of all of his family. None of the three sons of Saebert of the East Saxons had been baptised and they did not see why they should keep on their father's appointee as bishop (the Gregorian missionary Mellitus), especially when he would not give them the communion bread he had given to their father.[185] Penda of Mercia (d.655) took the opposite approach; he remained pagan himself, but had his son Peada baptised.[186] Although political expediency, the desire to signal independence from overlordship or to follow different policies from a predecessor, may be part of the reason for the oscillation of support for Christianity that can be traced in most of the kingdoms, the history of the conversion of the Anglo-Saxon kings must be testimony above all to the importance of pagan ritual within their kingdoms, perhaps especially to the way it underpinned kingship and war.

The conversion of the Picts

Compared to many aspects of Pictish history we are relatively well informed about the conversion of the Picts, though the evidence is by no means as detailed as that for the Anglo-Saxons and has led to differing interpretations. However, viewing the conversion of the Picts in the light of what is known about that of the Anglo-Saxons may suggest ways in which the limited material that survives can be decoded. Bede believed that the Picts had received two main missions, and that the southern Picts had been converted by Ninian of Whithorn and the northern Picts by Columba from Iona.[187] Such information is likely to have been a simplification of a much more complex situation, and doubts have been expressed about the reliability of Bede's account.[188] If, as seems likely, there were several Pictish provinces, we might expect by analogy with the Anglo-Saxon situation that each would have had its own conversion history involving different missions and individuals over a number of years. That people from both Dál Riata and British kingdoms were involved is only to be expected as these were areas with which Pictish kings had political and diplomatic links. The Christian British king Coroticus to whom Patrick wrote, and who may have been ruler of Dumbarton, had Pictish associates.[189] Picts are also envisaged fighting alongside British Christians in *The Gododdin*. It is therefore likely, as in Anglo-Saxon England, that some Pictish rulers and nobles gained experience of Christianity through association with kingdoms that had already been converted. As with the Anglo-Saxons, pressure on them to convert probably began to build in the late sixth and seventh centuries.

There has been considerable scepticism about Bede's reference to the evangelisation of the Picts by Ninian of Whithorn, though the recent suggestion that he is to be identified with British bishop Uinniau/Finnian, who was one of the most influential churchmen of his day and involved in the early church in Ireland, could be seen as strengthening the case for some involvement in a wider mission.[190] His transformation into 'Ninian' (more correctly 'Nynia') was a result of Whithorn becoming a Northumbrian bishopric as part of the takeover of Dumfries and Galloway that had begun in the reigns of Oswald and Oswiu in the seventh century. Whithorn was a Northumbrian bishopric when Bede wrote in 731. Both Bede and a hagiographic poem called *Miracula Nynie Episcopi*, which was probably composed in Northumbria in the late eighth century, drew upon the same traditions about Ninian/Uinniau, that were further embroidered by Aelred of Rievaulx in the twelfth century.[191] Some of these traditions have rightly been seen as dubious and the result of misunderstandings or of Northumbrian propaganda. The claim that Ninian 'received orthodox instruction at Rome'[192] is particularly suspect and likely to be the result of a Northumbrian desire to divorce Ninian from his association with the British church and give him an impeccable 'Roman' reputation. But does this mean that the tradition of Ninian/Uinniau working among the southern Picts is equally suspect? It is more difficult to see a Northumbrian motivation for the claim as the Pictish church was well established by the time Bede wrote and there is no evidence that the Northumbrian see of Whithorn claimed any Pictish jurisdiction.[193] British missionary work among the Picts is certainly plausible, whether it is associated with Ninian/Uinniau or other unknown clergy. Archaeological evidence may eventually provide additional information, and one possible fruitful line is the appearance in southern Pictland of new forms of burial in long cists and ditched barrows that are also found in northern and western Britain and have been associated with the spread of Christianity.[194] Twenty-five *eccles* place-names in south-eastern Pictland are also likely to represent British Christian influence.[195]

Columba is reputed to have studied with Uinniau so his own work among the Picts could be seen as a continuation of the work of his master if the identification of Uinniau and Ninian is accepted. Two areas of Pictland are particularly associated with traditions of a Columban mission. The *Amra* or eulogy of Columba, that is widely believed to have been composed *c.*600 and so is the earliest surviving account of his life, says that 'he preached to the tribes of the Tay' which presumably means Picts living in what is now Perthshire.[196] His activities there may have been centred on the province of Atholl where place-names suggest a strong Ionan connection by the beginning of the eighth century, as does a cross-slab from an important early church at Dull.[197] Atholl was recorded in the eighth century as a subkingdom associated with the Dál Riatan family of the Pictish kings Bridei and Nechtan.[198] Adomnán stresses Columba's activities in the northern parts of Pictish territory, including at the court of King Bridei near Inverness where Columba is depicted encountering, and bettering, his *magus*.[199] Adomnán has Columba converting individual Picts that he encountered, but does not explicitly say that he converted King Bridei. Confirmation of an early Ionan presence in the Inverness area seems to come from recent excavations of a monastic site at Portmahomack on Tarbat Ness where early grave-markers of Ionan type have been found and radiocarbon dates suggest burial began *c.*560.[200] Adomnán presents the Picts, as like the Dál Riata, as being particularly under the protection of Columba and implies that there were a number of Ionan religious communities in Pictland, although, frustratingly, he does not name any of them.[201]

It may be pertinent to consider aspects of Columba's work with the Picts in the light of the Anglo-Saxon evidence for conversion. The problem of whether Bridei was converted by Columba or not recalls the ambiguity over the conversion of Æthelbert of Kent, and how in the early days of conversion kings might seek to practise both Christianity and aspects of their traditional religion. What was essential if Columba was to make any impact was for King Bridei to give him his protection not only in his own kingdom, but in provinces that recognised his overlordship. One of Adomnán's stories refers to Columba meeting an underking of Orkney at Bridei's court, and obtaining, through Bridei's intervention, permission for an Irish religious exile to settle in his territory.[202] The need for royal protection may lie behind Bede's story of Columba receiving Iona from Bridei.[203] The Pictish king may not have given the land as such, but may have agreed to protect the monastery that lay close to the border with the Picts. The need for such protection is suggested by the fate of St Donnán of Eigg who is recorded as being burnt to death with 150 of his men in 617.[204] It is generally suspected that Picts were responsible and were objecting to these Irish interlopers in what was probably Pictish territory. They may have suspected (perhaps with good reason) that Irish religious encroachment was linked with political ambitions. It is possible that Columba's journeys into Pictland were made not just for ecclesiastical purposes, but also had a diplomatic element either on behalf of Dál Riatan kings or his Uí Néill kinsmen. In view of the complex interrelationship of Dál Riata and Pictland, and the interrelationships of their ruling houses, the Ionan churches of Pictland must often have been in a potentially fraught situation in the seventh and eighth centuries. The account of Bridei's donation of Iona to Columba could also have arisen out of this later context when Ionan abbots were anxious to promote Columba as an apostle to the Picts. Adomnán, who may himself have worked in Atholl and have been influential with the brothers Bridei and Nechtan, may have been actively promoting Iona's Pictish connection in his *Life of Columba* as something that was not just part of Columba's history, but of major importance to Iona in his own day. If so, he seems to have been successful. In the ninth century Columba emerged as the dominant saint of the new dynasty of Cinaed mac Alpin and a substantial portion of his relics was transferred from Iona to Dunkeld in Perthshire in 848 or 849.[205]

As in Anglo-Saxon England, not all Irish ecclesiastics who worked in Pictland would be from Iona, and the concentration of sources we have on Columba may obscure a much broader Irish contribution to the Christianisation of Pictland. Maelrubai who founded a monastery at Applecross in 671, on the mainland opposite Skye, and seems to have played an important role in evangelising that area of north-west Pictland, came from the monastery of Bangor in northern Ireland.[206] St Donnán and his followers seem to have been active over a wide area of the Hebrides. Some Irish missionaries in Pictland are known only from the survival of their relics and very localised traditions or dedications. St Fillan, who is associated with the area of Glendochart (Perthshire), was represented by five major relics in the Middle Ages of which three, a bell, an enshrined crozier and a head-shrine, survive.[207] The dedication of the important Pictish church at Abernethy to St Brigit of Kildare may point to activity by a missionary with links to this important Leinster monastery, even though the contradictory Abernethy foundation traditions do not inspire much confidence.[208] Nor were Irish the only 'foreign' churchmen to work in Pictland. In addition to the possible British involvement mentioned earlier, Anglo-Saxon churchmen visited Pictland, although whether they were involved in basic missionary work is unclear. Cuthbert is said to have visited the *Niduarii* of Fife some time after 664 while he was prior of Melrose, and in 669 Wilfrid was described as bishop 'of all the Northumbrians and Picts, as far as Oswiu's power extended'.[209] In 681 an Anglo-Saxon bishopric for the Picts was established even closer to their territory at Abercorn, but this had to be abandoned after the defeat of Ecgfrith in 685.[210]

We need not doubt that the emergent Pictish church was subject to a variety of different influences, and as in Anglo-Saxon England one result was a crisis over the correct method of calculating Easter. We know about this chiefly from a letter sent from Ceolfrith the abbot of Wearmouth and Jarrow to King Nechtan, son of Derilei (acc. 706) in response to a request from the king for a detailed exposition of the Roman calculation of Easter and form of tonsure.[211] Advice was probably sought from Ceolfrith because Adomnán of Iona had been influenced by his arguments over the Roman Easter while visiting him, probably in 688.[212] Subsequently Adomnán had sought to convince the Ionan clergy that they should change their practices, and met with some success among their daughter houses in Ireland, and possibly in Pictland as well for place-names suggest he was active there, but he was unable to win over the monks of Iona itself.[213] In 717 the expulsion of Ionan monks from Pictland is recorded,[214] but, as in Northumbria after the synod of Whitby, this may refer only to those who refused to accept the Roman method of calculating Easter and the tonsure. In any case Iona capitulated on the Easter issue in 716 and on the tonsure in 718, perhaps stimulated by the threat to their Pictish interests as well as the teaching of Ecgbert, an English religious exile resident in Ireland who had been invited to Iona to advise on these issues.[215] Although the evidence has been interpreted in different ways, it would appear that the Columban churches of Pictland remained influential within the province.[216]

It is interesting to see a number of parallels between events surrounding the synod of Whitby in Northumbria and the adoption of the Roman Easter in Pictland. One is the leading roles of the kings themselves for both Oswiu and Nechtan appear to have been the prime motivators whose decisions were final. Like Oswiu, Nechtan may have been desirous of stronger links with Rome and anxious about the state of his own soul if that link did not exist. Arguments that the decision reflects the rise of a Pictish national church and a desire for independence from Iona may have been overstated, but one can glimpse behind Nechtan at least one of a new generation of native churchmen keen to establish more direct links with Rome itself. The dominant Pictish bishop in the time of Nechtan was Curetán of Rosemarkie (Ross and Cromarty) who seems to have taken the surname of Boniface to mark his Roman allegiance and to have been associated with a number of churches dedicated to St Peter.[217] In 721 a Pictish bishop called Fergustus who was probably his successor travelled to Rome to attend a council.[218] Nechtan was as anxious as his Anglo-Saxon peers to assure himself of St Peter's support and to surround himself with Roman status symbols. Via the envoys he sent to Ceolfrith, Nechtan also requested masons to build a stone church for him 'after the Roman fashion' which would be dedicated to St Peter, and it has often been suggested that the church was built at Restenneth (Forfar), a southern Pictish centre which preserved traditions of a link with Curetán/Boniface.[219] Pictish sculpture and other artwork suggest the increasing influence of art forms derived ultimately from the classical world, as in Northumbria after the synod of Whitby, including at Portmahomack, one of the best candidates for an early Columban foundation.[220] The monasteries founded from Iona in Pictland may have remained significant, and the cult of Columba may have retained its power, but, as in Northumbria, the Ionan churches can have been only one strand of Christian influence. Pictish churchmen were aware of the wider Christian world and, as elsewhere in the insular world, a number of influences contributed to an emergent native Christian culture.

Conclusion

The conversion of Britain to Christianity was a long process, but appears in our sources as a generally peaceful affair. Martyrs are unknown, or at least unrecorded, in the early medieval phase, apart from St Donnán and his 150 companions on Eigg (though the exact circumstances that led to the burning of their monastery are not known). The heroic battling with the forces of paganism that is a feature of many conversion narratives in imitation of the *Life of St Martin* is not characteristic of those which survive for early medieval Britain, though there are elements in Adomnán's accounts of Columba among the Picts.[221] There is no recorded equivalent of the felling of the great sacred oak tree of Gaismar by the Anglo-Saxon missionary Boniface in Germany. The tone of the Anglo-Saxon conversion is set by Pope Gregory's famous letter of advice in which he urged that pagan shrines should be adapted to Christian use and people eased into the new religion by the establishment of links with the old one.[222] Ireland had also undergone what appears to have been a largely peaceful conversion in which Christianity had been successfully integrated into the fabric of society in ways reminiscent of aspects of their previous religious practices, and so Irish missionaries can be expected to have adopted a comparable approach in presenting Christianity to the Anglo-Saxons and Picts.

The letter of advice sent by Bishop Daniel of Winchester (c.705–45) to Boniface on the type of arguments that should be used when preaching conversion must have been based upon his own experiences in Wessex. He suggested contrasting the prosperity of the Christian world 'rich in oil and wine and other commodities' with 'the frozen lands of the north, where the gods, banished from the rest of the world, are falsely supposed to dwell'.[223] Christianity was not a religion in isolation, but part of the legacy of the Roman world to which the peoples of Britain were heirs, as were other provinces of the former Roman empire and its periphery. Christianity therefore came with very attractive connotations, and the Anglo-Saxons and Picts must already have had some familiarity with Christianity before active missionary work began among them; they were in frequent contact with Christian neighbours and many Anglo-Saxon kingdoms may have contained British Christian communities. Christianity was not imposed upon them by a foreign power intent on conquest, as happened with the continental Saxons, and so there was no need for a violent resistance to it. Christianity was introduced with the aid of systems of overlordship prevalent in early medieval Britain, and rejection of an overlord might lead to rejection of his priests as well, but Christianity was not fatally tainted by these associations. The fact that powerful overlords embraced Christianity could have been taken as a sign of its effectiveness as a religion. But unlike many other Germanic peoples who settled within Roman provinces, the Anglo-Saxons were not converted as part of their assimilation with the native population. Relations between Anglo-Saxons and Britons did not work in that way, and there is no certain example of an Anglo-Saxon kingdom being converted to Christianity through British intervention, though British missionaries had been active in the conversion of the Irish and probably of the Picts as well. Instead the Anglo-Saxons came to use the desirability of correcting the conservative practices of the British church as an instrument for extending their political domination over British provinces; British leaders were placed in a difficult situation where a desire to retain independence put them in danger of appearing heretical.

Daniel's letter of advice stressed the superiority of the Christian God over pagan ones and the association of Christianity with the most successful peoples of the known world. He does not seem to have envisaged that it was necessary to enter into the complexities of Christian belief at the preliminary stage of conversion. In Saxony candidates for baptism were required to swear that they rejected belief and worship of three named pagan gods and believed instead in the Father, Son and Holy Ghost, and something very similar may have taken place as a preliminary to the mass baptisms in England described by Bede. Such mass baptisms by foreign churchmen have naturally raised questions about whether initial conversion could be anything but superficial and with resulting 'contamination' of Christian beliefs by pre-Christian religious practices.[224] Such claims will be tested in the two following chapters, but it can be noted that accounts of conversion in early medieval Britain record that instruction was given; Paulinus, for instance, is said to have spent 36 days catechising Northumbrians at Yeavering in which 'from morning till evening, he did nothing else but instruct the crowds who flocked to him from every village and district in the teaching of Christ'.[225] The use of interpreters in the early stages is acknowledged. King Oswald himself is said to have acted as interpreter for the Irish-speaking Aidan and Pope Gregory's missionaries collected interpreters as they passed through Francia – though by the time he moved to Northumbria Paulinus had probably learnt sufficient English to do without them.

It was a lengthy process but by 700 the first stage of conversion had been completed in all the Anglo-Saxon kingdoms and Pictland. Public rituals of paganism had been banned in Anglo-Saxon kingdoms, and native clergy had taken the place of foreign missionaries. But the question remains of how far private practices continued and the extent to which inner conversion based on some understanding of Christian doctrine and ethics had been achieved. Royal courts would have received the most attention, and although the initial attraction may have been to the association of Christianity with worldly success, one should not underestimate the impression that Christianity made as a religion when they found out more about it. Although Bede was no doubt inventing his own dialogue when he has King Oswiu deciding at the synod of Whitby that he wished to follow the practices associated with St Peter because he was the gatekeeper of heaven, it may well have been the Christian teachings on life after death that seemed to distinguish Christianity most sharply from pre-Christian religious belief. The foundation of monasteries, pilgrimage to Rome and even abdication to live a religious life are all testimony to an enthusiasm for the new religion among the recently converted royal houses.[226] But was this enthusiasm shared among their subjects, and did the type of assimilation recommended by Pope Gregory lead to a confusion of Christian and pre-Christian practices rather than a complete replacement of one by the other? Full conversion could only be achieved if there was sufficient church organisation in place for everyone to receive adequate instruction and regular religious provision. So before we can begin to assess the strength of the impact of Christianity on the societies of early medieval Britain, which will be the subject of Chapter 4, we need to consider the ecclesiastical structures and institutions that were introduced as part of the process of conversion, and these will be the subject of the next chapter.

Notes

1 L. Milis, 'La conversion en profandeur: un procès sans fin', *Revue du Nord* 68 (1986), 187–98.

2 *EHD*, I, no. 163.

3 Bede, *Hist. Eccl.*, III, 30.

4 Bede, *Letter to Ecgbert*; *EHD*, I, no. 170.

5 J. Jochens, 'Late and peaceful: Iceland's conversion through arbitration in 1000', *Speculum* 74 (1999), 621–55.

6 P. Jones and N. Pennick, *A History of Pagan Europe* (London, 1995), 1–4.

7 'Letter to Mellitus', Bede, *Hist. Eccl.*, I, 30.

8 V. Flint, *The Rise of Magic in Early Medieval Europe* (Oxford, 1991); K. Jolly, *Popular Religion in Late Anglo-Saxon England: Elf Charms in Context* (Chapel Hill and London, 1996). See Chapter 4, 219–28, 249–56.

9 A.L. Meaney, 'Anglo-Saxon idolators and ecclesiasts from Theodore to Alcuin: a source study', *ASSAH* 5 (1992), 103–25.

10 A.D. Nock, *Conversion* (Oxford, 1933); see also discussions in C. Stancliffe, 'From town to country: the Christianisation of the Touraine 370–600', in *The Church in Town and Countryside*, ed. D. Baker (London, 1979), 43–59, especially 51–3; N.J. Higham, *The Convert Kings: Power and Religious Affiliation in Early Anglo-Saxon England* (Manchester, 1997), 7–52.

11 R. Page, 'Anglo-Saxon paganism: the evidence of Bede', in *Pagans and Christians: The Interplay between Christian Latin and Traditional Germanic Cultures in Early Medieval Europe*, ed. T. Hosfra, L. Houwen and A. MacDonald (Groningen, 1995), 99–130.

12 Bede, *Hist. Eccl.*, I, 30 and 32, and see further below, 101–9.

13 Adomnán, *V. Columbae*, II, 33.

14 See, for instance, R. Bradley, 'Time regained: the creation of continuity', *Journal of British Archaeological Association* 140 (1987), 1–17.

15 Bede, *Hist. Eccl.*, II, 10.

16 I. Armit, *Celtic Scotland* (London, 1997), 87–8; M. Henig, *The Art of Roman Britain* (London, 1995).

17 *EHD*, I, no. 167.

18 A useful introduction to Norse mythology is provided by R. Page, *Norse Myths* (London, 1990).

19 D. Wilson, *Anglo-Saxon Paganism* (London, 1992), 5–21. However, it is not necessarily the case that all such names were formed before conversion or when belief in pagan gods was still active.

20 P. Meulengracht Sorensen, 'Religions old and new', in *The Oxford Illustrated History of the Vikings*, ed. P. Sawyer (Oxford, 1997), 202–24.

21 L. Webster and J. Backhouse (eds), *The Making of England: Anglo-Saxon Art and Culture* (London, 1984), 101–3.

22 M. Green, *The Gods of the Celts* (Gloucester, 1986), 14–17.

23 G. Henderson and I. Henderson, *The Art of the Picts* (London, 2004), 123–5.

24 M. Aldhouse-Green, 'Gallo-British deities and their shrines', in *A Companion to Roman Britain*, ed. M. Todd (Oxford, 2004), 192–219.

25 H.E. Davidson, *The Lost Beliefs of Northern Europe* (London, 1993), 45–50.

26 Davidson, *Lost Beliefs*, 48–9; R. North, *Heathen Gods in Old English Literature* (Cambridge, 1997), 204–30.

27 Wilson, *Anglo-Saxon Paganism*, 5–21.

28 Jolly, *Popular Religion*.

29 J. Carey, 'Varieties of supernatural contact in the Life of Adomnán', in *Saints and Scholars: Studies in Irish Hagiography*, ed. J. Carey, M. Herbert and P. Ó Riain (Dublin, 2001), 49–62.

30 Aldhouse-Green, 'Gallo-British deities'.

31 Bede, *Hist. Eccl.*, II, 13.

32 Page, 'Anglo-Saxon paganism', 105–22.

33 I.N. Wood, 'Pagan religions and superstitions east of the Rhine from the fifth to the ninth century', in *After Empire: Towards an Ethnology of Europe's Barbarians*, ed. G. Ausenda (Woodbridge, 1995), 253–79.

34 J. Blair, 'Anglo-Saxon shrines and their prototypes', *ASSAH* 8 (1995), 1–28; B. Hope-Taylor, *Yeavering: An Anglo-British Centre of Early Northumbria* (London, 1972), 95–118.

35 M. Green, *Exploring the World of the Druids* (London, 1997).

36 J. Carey, 'Werewolves in Medieval Ireland', *CMCS* 44 (2002), 37–72, especially 64–5; T.M. Dickinson, 'An Anglo-Saxon "cunning woman" from Bidford-on-Avon', in *In Search of Cult*, ed. M. Carver (Woodbridge, 1993), 45–54.

37 T. Charles-Edwards, *Early Christian Ireland* (Cambridge, 2000), 185–202.

38 F.J. Byrne, *Irish Kings and High Kings* (London, 1973); D.A. Binchy, *Celtic and Anglo-Saxon Kingship* (Oxford, 1970).

39 D.Ó Corráin, 'Nationality and kingship in pre-Norman Ireland', in *Nationality and the Pursuit of National Independence*, ed. T.W. Moody (Belfast, 1978), 1–35; P. Wormald, 'Celtic and Anglo-Saxon kingship: some further thoughts', in *Sources of Anglo-Saxon Culture*, ed. P. Szarmach (Kalamazoo, 1986), 151–83.

40 E. Campbell, 'Royal inauguration in Dál Riata and the Stone of Destiny', in *The Stone of Destiny: Artefact and Icon*, ed. R. Welander, D.J. Breeze and T.O. Clancy (Edinburgh, 2003), 43–60.

41 S. Foster, *Picts, Gaels and Scots* (London, 1996), 43–4; L. Alcock, *Kings and Warriors, Craftsmen and Priests in Northern Britain AD 550–850* (Edinburgh, 2003), 192–7.

42 Bede, *Hist. Eccl.*, II, 13 and 14. For the importance of assemblies in early medieval Britain, see A. Pantos and S. Semple (eds), *Assembly Places and Practices in Medieval Europe* (Dublin, 2004).

43 Green, *Gods of the Celts*, 3–38

44 Wood, 'Pagan religions'.

45 A. Woodward, *Shrines and Sacrifice* (London, 1992).

46 Bradley, 'Time regained'; Blair, 'Anglo-Saxon shrines'.

47 Charles-Edwards, *Early Christian Ireland*, 469–521.

48 The quotation comes from a seventeenth-century account of the traditional ceremony for the inauguration of the Lord of the Isles that included use of a footprint in stone: D.H. Caldwell, 'Finlaggan, Islay – stones and inauguration ceremonies', in *The Stone of Destiny*, ed. Welander, Breeze and Clancy, 61–76, at 64.

49 H. Williams, 'Placing the dead: investigating the location of wealthy barrow burials in seventh century England', in *Grave Matters: Eight Studies of First*

Millennium AD *Burials in Crimea, England and Southern Scandinavia,* ed.
M. Rundkvist, BAR International Series 781 (Oxford, 1999), 57–86; *idem,*
'Material culture as memory: combs and cremation in early medieval
Britain', *Early Medieval Europe* 12 (2003), 89–128; J. Bazelmans, *By
Weapons Made Worthy: Lords, Retainers and Their Relationship in
Beowulf* (Amsterdam, 1999).

50 G. Speake, *Anglo-Saxon Animal Art and its Germanic Background*
(London, 1980); J. Hawkes, 'Symbolic lives: the visual evidence', in *The
Anglo-Saxons from the Migration Period to the Eighth Century: An
Ethnographic Perspective,* ed. J. Hines (Woodbridge, 1997), 311–44;
Green, *Gods of the Celts,* 167–99.

51 J. Hines, 'Welsh and English: mutual origins in post-Roman Britain?',
Studia Celtica 34 (2000), 81–104, especially 100.

52 Asser Chapter 38; see also the depiction of a boar's head as the terminal of
the Alfred Jewel.

53 Aldhouse-Green, 'Gallo-British deities', 208–10.

54 R. Bromwich and D. Simon Evans (eds), *Culhwch ac Olwen* (Cardiff,
Welsh version 1988; English version 1992).

55 Hawkes, 'Symbolic lives', 315–7.

56 Henderson and Henderson, *Art of the Picts,* 171–2.

57 Green, *Gods of the Celts,* 171–5.

58 N. Brooks, 'The creation and early structure of the kingdom of Kent', in
The Origins of Anglo-Saxon Kingdoms, ed. S. Bassett (Leicester, 1989),
55–74; B. Yorke, 'Fact or Fiction? The written evidence for the fifth and
sixth centuries AD', *ASSAH* 6 (1993), 45–50.

59 D. Leigh, 'Ambiguity in Anglo-Saxon Style I art', *Antiquaries Journal* 64
(1984), 34–42.

60 H. Williams, 'An ideology of transformation: cremation rites and animal
sacrifice in early Anglo-Saxon England', in *The Archaeology of Shamanism,*
ed. N. Price (London, 2001), 193–212.

61 Green, *Gods of the Celts,* 33, 167–99.

62 N. Price, *The Viking Way: Religion and War in Late Iron Age Scandinavia*
(Uppsala, 2002).

63 North, *Heathen Gods.*

64 R. Sharpe, 'Hiberno-Latin *Laicus,* Irish *Läech* and the Devil's Men', *Ériu*
30 (1979), 75–92; K. McCone, 'Werewolves, cyclopes, *díberga* and *fíanna*:
juvenile delinquency in early Ireland', *CMCS* 12 (1986), 1–22; Carey,
'Werewolves', 64.

65 Bede, *Hist. Eccl.*, I, 15; E. John, 'The point of Woden', *ASSAH* 5 (1992), 127–34.

66 L. Headeager, 'Cosmological endurance: pagan identities in early Christian Europe', *European Journal of Archaeology* 1 (1998), 382–96.

67 See above Chapter 1, 69.

68 A.L. Meaney, *Anglo-Saxon Amulets and Curing Stones*, BAR 96 (Oxford, 1981).

69 D. Petts, *Christianity in Roman Britain* (Stroud, 2003).

70 Gildas, *De Excidio*, Chapter 10; M. Henig and P. Lindley (eds), *Alban and St Albans: Roman and Medieval Architecture, Art and Archaeology*, BAA Conference Transactions 24 (2001), *passim*.

71 Petts, *Christianity in Roman Britain*, 36–9.

72 C. Thomas, *Christianity in Roman Britain to AD 500* (London, 1981).

73 W.H.C. Frend, 'Roman Britain, a failed promise', in *The Cross Goes North: Processes of Conversion in Northern Europe, AD 300–1300*, ed. M. Carver (York, 2003), 79–91; D. Watts, *Religion in Late Roman Britain: Forces of Change* (London, 1998).

74 W.H.C. Frend, *The Archaeology of Early Christianity: A History* (London, 1996).

75 Petts, *Christianity in Roman Britain*, 53–86.

76 Petts, *Christianity in Roman Britain*, 118–33.

77 P. Rahtz, 'Pagan and Christian by the Severn Sea', in *The Archaeology and History of Glastonbury Abbey*, ed. L. Abrams and J.P. Carley (Woodbridge, 1991), 3–37; B. Yorke, *Wessex in the Early Middle Ages* (London, 1995), 148–64; S. Pearce, *South-western Britain in the Early Middle Ages* (London, 2004), 77–134.

78 For example, N. Faulkener, *The Decline and Fall of Roman Britain* (Stroud, 2000).

79 Patrick, *Confessio*, ch. 1; Patrick, *Letter*, ch. 10; Charles-Edwards, *Early Christian Ireland*, 216–22.

80 R. Sharpe, 'Martyrs and saints in late antique Britain', in *Local Saints*, ed. Thacker and Sharpe 75–154.

81 N. Edwards and A. Lane (eds), *The Early Church in Wales and the West*, Oxbow monograph 16 (Oxford, 1992).

82 C. Thomas, *And Shall These Mute Stones Speak? Post-Roman Inscriptions in Western Britain* (Cardiff, 1994), 197–208.

83 *La Vie ancienne de Saint Samson de Dol*, ed. P. Flobert (Paris, 1997); Thomas, *Mute Stones*, 223–36.

84 C.A.R. Radford, 'The Celtic monastery in Britain', *Archaeologia Cambrensis* 111 (1962), 1–24; E.G. Bowen, *Saints, Seaways and Settlements in the Celtic Lands* (Cardiff, 1969). For greater discussion of the nature and impact of monasticism see Chapter 3, 156–61.

85 See Chapter 1, 75–8; C. Thomas, '"Gallici nautae de Galliarum provinciis": sixth/seventh century trade with Gaul reconsidered', *Medieval Archaeology* 34 (1990), 1–26.

86 The visit of Bishop Germanus of Auxerre to Britain in 429 was made in this context. D. N. Dumville, 'Some British aspects of the earliest Irish Christianity', in *Ireland and Europe: The Early Church*, ed. P.N. Chatháin and M. Richter (Stuttgart, 1984), 16–24; Charles-Edwards, *Early Christian Ireland*, 182–6, 204–14.

87 K.H. Jackson, *Language and History in Early Britain* (Edinburgh, 1953), 122–48.

88 D.N. Dumville (ed.), *Saint Patrick: AD 493–1993* (Woodbridge, 1993), 89–105.

89 Dumville, *Saint Patrick*, 27–64.

90 Charles-Edwards, *Early Christian Ireland*, 239.

91 R. Sharpe, 'Armagh and Rome in the seventh century', in *Ireland and Europe*, ed. Chatháin and Richter, 58–72.

92 J.F. Kenney, *Sources for the Early History of Ireland: Ecclesiastical* (New York, 1929), 177.

93 R. Sharpe, 'Gildas as a Father of the church', in *Gildas: New Approaches*, ed. M. Lapidge and D.N. Dumville (Woodbridge, 1984), 193–205.

94 Adomnán, *V. Columbae*, I, 1 and III, 4. D.N. Dumville, 'Gildas and Uinniau', in *Gildas: New Approaches*, ed. Lapidge and Dumville, 207–14. P. Ó Riain, 'St Finnbarr: a study in a cult', *Journal of the Cork Historical and Archaeological Society* 82 (1977), 63–82 puts a case for Uinniau being Irish.

95 Adomnán, *V. Columbae*, II, 1; *Adomnán of Iona*, ed. Sharpe, 317–18.

96 T.O. Clancy, 'The real St Ninian', *Innes Review* 52 (2001), 1–28; J. Fraser, 'Northumbrian Whithorn and the making of St Ninian', *Innes Review* 53 (2002), 40–59; P. Hill, *Whithorn and St Ninian: The Excavation of a Monastic Town 1984–91* (Stroud, 1997).

97 Thomas, *Christianity*, 283–4; C.E. Lowe, 'New light on the Anglian minster at Hoddom', *Transactions of the Dumfries and Galloway Natural History and Antiquarian Society* 3rd series, 66 (1991), 11–35.

98 Dumville, *Saint Patrick*, 107–15.

99 See Introduction, 69.

100 *The Gododdin: the Oldest Scottish Poem*, ed. K. Jackson (Edinburgh, 1969), 37.

101 Dumville, *Saint Patrick*, 183–9.

102 M. Herbert, *Iona, Kells and Derry: The History and Hagiography of the Monastic Familia of Columba.* (Dublin, 1996), 1–35.

103 *Adomnán of Iona*, trans. Sharpe, 15–30; A. Ritchie, *Iona* (London, 1997), 31–46.

104 Adomnán, *V. Columbae*, III, 8.

105 Royal Commission on the Ancient and Historical Monuments of Scotland, *Argyll Vol. 3: Mull, Tiree, Coll and Northern Argyll* (Edinburgh, 1980); Ritchie, *Iona*, 81–90.

106 See further on Kingarth in Chapter 3, 152–3; P. Dransart, 'Saints, stones and shrines: the cults of Sts Moluag and Gerardine in Pictland', in *Celtic Hagiographies*, ed. J. Cartwright (Cardiff, 2003), 232–48.

107 A.P. Smyth, *Warlords and Holy Men: Scotland AD 800–1000* (London, 1984), 107–11.

108 W. Davies, 'The myth of the Celtic church', in *The Early Church in Wales and the West*, ed. Edwards and Lane, 12–21.

109 D.E. Meek, *The Quest for Celtic Christianity* (Edinburgh, 2000).

110 R.C. Stacey, 'Texts and society', in *After Rome*, ed. T. Charles-Edwards (Oxford, 2003), 221–57, at 239–40; he suggests similar professional groups may have survived in highland areas of Britain.

111 M. Herren and S.A. Brown, *Christ in Celtic Christianity: Britain and Ireland from the Fifth to the Tenth Century* (Woodbridge, 2002).

112 R.A. Markus, 'Pelagianism: Britain and the continent', *Journal of Ecclesiastical History* 37 (1986), 191–204.

113 T. Charles-Edwards, 'Palladius, Prosper, and Leo the Great: mission and primatial authority', in *Saint Patrick*, ed. Dumville, 1–18.

114 G. Bonner, 'The pelagian controversy in Britain and Ireland', *Peritia* 16 (2002), 144–55.

115 Charles-Edwards, *Early Christian Ireland*, 391–415.

116 K. Harrison, *The Framework of Anglo-Saxon History to AD 900* (Cambridge, 1976), 30–51; W.M. Stevens, 'Easter controversy', in *Blackwell Encyclopaedia*, 155–7.

117 On which, see further below, 118–20.

118 Bede, *Hist. Eccl.*, III, 25; *V. Wilfredi*, Chapter 10.

119 Davies, 'Myth of the Celtic church'.

120 See in particular, Bede, *Hist. Eccl.*, I, 22; V, 22; V, 23; T. Charles-Edwards, 'Bede, the Irish and the Britons', *Celtica* 15 (1983), 42–52.

121 Bede, *Hist. Eccl.*, II, 2; C. Stancliffe, 'The British church and the mission of Augustine', in *St Augustine*, ed. R. Gameson, 107–51.

122 M. Lapidge and M. Herren, *Aldhelm: The Prose Works* (Ipswich, 1979), 140–3, 135–60.

123 Bede, *Hist. Eccl.*, II, 2; compare II, 20 in which the British king Cædwalla ravaged Northumbria 'meaning to wipe out the whole English nation from the land of Britain'.

124 See Chapter 1, 43–5.

125 See Introduction, 18–22.

126 *Historia Brittonum* Chapter 63; N.K. Chadwick, *Celt and Saxon: Studies in the Early British Border* (Cambridge, 1963), 138–66; D. Kirby, *The Earliest English Kings* (London 1991), 78–9; C. Corning, 'The baptism of Edwin, king of Northumbria: a new analysis of the British tradition', *Northern History* 36 (2000), 5–15.

127 Bede, *Hist. Eccl.*, III, 28.

128 Bede, *Hist. Eccl.*, V, 18.

129 P. Sims-Williams, *Religion and Literature in Western England: 600–800* (Cambridge, 1990), 54–86; S. Bassett, 'How the West was won: the Anglo-Saxon take-over of the West Midlands', *ASSAH* 11 (2000), 107–18.

130 I am grateful to Alex Woolf for this suggestion.

131 J. Hillaby, 'Early Christian and pre-conquest Leominster: an exploration of the sources', *Transactions of the Woolhope Naturalists' Field Club* 45 (1987), 557–685, at 563–72; Sims-Williams, *Religion and Literature*, 55–9. Bede, *Hist. Eccl.*, III, 24 for Bishop Trumhere of Mercia.

132 S. Bassett, 'Church and diocese in the West Midlands: the transition from British to Anglo-Saxon control', in *Pastoral Care*, 13–40; Yorke, *Wessex*, 177–81; T.A. Hall, *Minster Churches in the Dorset Landscape*, BAR 304 (Oxford, 2000), especially 24–9; M. McCarthy, 'Carlisle and St Cuthbert', *Durham Archaeological Journal* 14–15 (1999), 59–67.

133 B. Yorke, 'Boniface's insular background', in *Bonifatius Congressband*, (Mainz, forthcoming).

134 See Chapter 1, 41–2.

135 Lapidge and Herren, *Aldhelm: The Prose Works*, 140–3, 135–60.

136 In addition to the above, see Aldhelm's poem describing a visitation he

made to Dumnonia; M. Lapidge and J. Rosier, *Aldhelm: The Poetic Works* (Woodbridge, 1985), 171–3, 177–9.

137   Gildas, *De Excidio*, Chapters 10–11; *Alban and St Albans*, ed. Henig and Lindley; and see Chapter 1, 44–5.

138   K. Cameron, 'Eccles in English place-names', in *Christianity in Britain, 300–700*, ed. M. Barley and R. Hanson (Leicester, 1968), 87–92.

139   A.P. Detsicas and S.C. Hawkes. 'Finds from the Anglo-Saxon cemetery at Eccles, Kent', *Antiquaries Journal* 53 (1973), 281–6.

140   N. Brooks, *The Early History of the Church of Canterbury* (Leicester, 1984), 20.

141   R. Meens, 'A background to Augustine's mission to Anglo-Saxon England', *Anglo-Saxon England* 22 (1994), 5–17.

142   I.N. Wood, *The Merovingian North Sea* (Alingsås, 1983); B. Yorke, 'Gregory of Tours and sixth-century Anglo-Saxon England', in *The World of Gregory of Tours*, ed. K. Mitchell and I.N. Wood (Leiden, 2002), 113–30.

143   Bede, *Hist. Eccl.*, I, 25; N. Brooks, 'The creation and early structure of the kingdom of Kent', in *The Origins of Anglo-Saxon Kingdoms*, ed. S. Bassett (Leicester, 1989), 55–74, at 65–7.

144   Bede, *Hist. Eccl.*, I, 26; Brooks, *Church of Canterbury*, 16–22; Webster and Backhouse, *Making of England*, 23.

145   H. Mayr-Harting, *The Coming of Christianity to Anglo-Saxon England* (3rd edn, London, 1991); J. Campbell, *Essays in Anglo-Saxon History* (London, 1986), 49–84; Higham, *Convert Kings*.

146   *Romans* 10:18.

147   R.A. Markus, *Gregory the Great and his World* (Cambridge, 1997).

148   Bede, *Hist. Eccl.*, I, 23; I.N. Wood, 'The mission of Augustine of Canterbury to the English', *Speculum* 69 (1994), 1–17.

149   Bede, *Hist. Eccl.*, II, 5.

150   Bede, *Hist. Eccl.*, IV, 2; M. Lapidge (ed.), *Archbishop Theodore: Commemorative Studies of his Life and Influence* (Cambridge, 1995).

151   T. Charles-Edwards, 'The social background to Irish *peregrinatio*', *Celtica* 11 (1976), 43–59.

152   Bede, *Hist. Eccl.*, IV, 13 and V, 18; Campbell, *Essays*, 51–2.

153   Herbert, *Iona, Kells and Derry*, 26–30; see further above, 114–15.

154   Adomnán, *V. Columbae*, II, 10; III, 21.

155 Bede, *Hist. Eccl.*, III, 2-3.

156 Adomnán, *V. Columbae*, I, 1; see Sharpe (ed.), *Adomnán of Iona*, 252–3 for discussion of different emphases in accounts of Bede and Adomnán.

157 Bede, *Hist. Eccl.*, III, 5.

158 Bede, *Hist. Eccl.*, III, 21, 22 and 24.

159 Bede, *Hist. Eccl.*, III, 25; see further discussion above, 115–18.

160 Bede, *Hist. Eccl.*, IV, 1.

161 Charles-Edwards, *Early Christian Ireland*, 344–90.

162 E. Prinz, *Frühes Monchtum in Frankenreich* (2nd edn, Munich, 1988); P. Geary, *Before France and Germany: The Creation and Transformation of the Merovingian World* (Oxford, 1988).

163 Campbell, *Essays*, 49–67.

164 I.N. Wood, 'Northumbrians and Franks in the age of Wilfrid', *Northern History* 31 (1995), 10–21; A. Thacker, 'Wilfrid', *Oxford Dictionary of National Biography* (Oxford, 2004), 944–50.

165 Campbell, *Essays*, 53–67; Higham, *Convert Kings*, 53–132.

166 Bede, *Hist. Eccl.*, III, 18.

167 R. Le Jan, 'Convents, violence and competition for power in seventh-century Francia', in *Topographies of Power in the Early Middle Ages*, ed. M. de Jong, F. Theuws and C. van Rhijn (Leiden, 2001), 243–69.

168 L. Webster and M. Brown (eds), *The Transformation of the Roman World* (London, 1997).

169 R.L.S. Bruce-Mitford, *The Sutton Hoo Ship-Burial*, 3 vols (London, 1975–83).

170 W. Filmer-Sankey, 'The "Roman emperor" in the Sutton Hoo Ship Burial', *Journal of the British Archaeological Association* 149 (1996), 1–9; Webster and Brown, *Transformation*, 222–3; B. Yorke, 'The reception of Christianity at the Anglo-Saxon royal courts', in *St Augustine*, ed. Gameson, 152–73.

171 Bede, *Hist. Eccl.*, II, 10 and 11; the mirror and comb are one of the most common paired Pictish symbols and possibly designated a royal or noble woman.

172 Bede, *Hist. Eccl.*, III, 25.

173 Bede, *Hist. Abbatum*, Chapter 2; *Hist. Eccl.*, IV, 5.

174 Bede, *Hist. Eccl.*, V, 7; in 709 King Cenred of Mercia and Offa of the East Saxons had left for Rome and did not return; C. Stancliffe. 'Kings who

opted out', in *Ideal and Reality in Frankish and Anglo-Saxon Society*, ed. P. Wormald (Oxford, 1983), 154–76.

175 Campbell, *Essays*, 69–84; Higham, *Convert Kings*.

176 Bede, *Hist. Eccl.*, II, 14.

177 T. Charles-Edwards, 'Early medieval kingships in the British Isles', in *The Origins of Anglo-Saxon Kingdoms*, ed. S. Bassett (London, 1989), 28–39, at 28–33.

178 Bede, *Hist. Eccl.*, II, 13; B. Hope-Taylor, *Yeavering*; Pantos and Semple (eds), *Assembly Places*.

179 Green, *Gods of the Celts*, 138–66.

180 D. Kirby (ed.), *Saint Wilfrid at Hexham* (Newcastle, 1974).

181 Yorke, 'Reception of Christianity'.

182 Bede, *Hist. Eccl.*, III, 8.

183 *Chronicle* sa 635; Bede, *Hist. Eccl.*, IV, 16.

184 Bede, *Hist. Eccl.*, II, 15.

185 Bede, *Hist. Eccl.*, II, 5.

186 Bede, *Hist. Eccl.*, III, 21.

187 Bede, *Hist. Eccl.*, III, 4.

188 A.A.M. Duncan, 'Bede, Iona and the Picts', in *The Writing of History in the Middle Ages. Essays Presented to Richard William Southern*, ed. R.H.C. Davis and J.M. Wallace-Hadrill (Oxford, 1981), 1–42.

189 Patrick, *Letter*; Dumville, *Saint Patrick*, 107–15.

190 Clancy, 'The real St Ninian', although Dr Clancy is sceptical of the tradition of a Pictish mission.

191 J. MacQueen, *St Nynia* (2nd edn, Edinburgh, 1990); D. Broun, 'The literary record of St Nynia: fact or fiction?', *Innes Review* 42 (1991), 143–50; Fraser, 'Northumbrian Whithorn'.

192 Bede, *Hist. Eccl.*, III, 4.

193 D. Kirby, 'Bede and the Pictish church', *Innes Review* 24 (1973), 6–25.

194 I. Smith, 'The origins and development of Christianity in north Britain and southern Pictland', in *Church Archaeology: Research Directions for the Future*, ed. J. Blair and C. Pyrah (London, 1996), 19–42. See further in Chapter 4, 212–13.

195 G.W.S. Barrow, *The Kingdom of the Scots* (London, 1973), 60–4; *idem*, *Saint Ninian and Pictomania* (Whithorn, 2004).

196 M. Herbert, *Iona, Kells and Derry: The History and Hagiography of the*

Monastic Familia of Columba (Dublin, 1996), 9–12; for a translation see The Triumph Tree: Scotland's Earliest Poetry AD 550–1350, ed. T.O. Clancy (Edinburgh, 1998), 102–7.

197 S. Taylor, 'Seventh-century Iona abbots in Scottish place-names', in Spes Scotorum, 35–70; R. Will, K. Forsyth, T.O. Clancy and G. Charles-Edwards, 'An eighth-century inscribed cross-slab in Dull, Perthshire', Scottish Archaeological Journal 25 (2003), 57–72.

198 See Chapter 1, 54–5.

199 Adomnán, V. Columbae, I, 12, 37; II, 11, 31–5, 42; Adomnán of Iona, ed. Sharpe, 30–4; A. Smyth, Warlords and Holymen, 84–115; J. Fraser, 'Adomnán, Cumméne Ailbe, and the Picts', Peritia 17–18 (2003–4), 183–98.

200 M. Carver, 'An Iona of the East: the early medieval monastery at Portmahomack, Tarbat Ness', Medieval Archaeology 48 (2004), 1–30.

201 Adomnán, V. Columbae, II, 46.

202 Adomnán, V. Columbae, II, 42.

203 Bede, Hist. Eccl., III, 4.

204 AT sa 615; AU sa 616; Smyth, Warlords and Holy Men, 107–9.

205 J. Bannerman, 'The Scottish take-over of Pictland and the relics of St Columba', in Spes Scotorum, 71–94; D. Broun, 'Dunkeld and the origin of Scottish identity', in Spes Scottorum, 95–111.

206 D. MacLean, 'Maelrubai, Applecross and the late Pictish contribution west of Druimalban', in The Worm, the Germ and the Thorn: Pictish and Related Studies Presented to Isabel Henderson, ed. D. Henry (Balgavies, 1997), 173–87

207 Fillan's three surviving relics are on display in the National Museum of Scotland in Edinburgh.

208 A. Macquarrie, 'Early Christian religious house in Scotland: foundation and function', in Pastoral Care, 115–18.

209 Anon., V. Cuthberti, Chapter 4; Bede, V. Cuthberti, Chapter 11; Bede, Hist. Eccl., IV, 3.

210 Bede, Hist. Eccl., IV, 26; Kirby, 'Bede and the Pictish church'.

211 Bede, Hist. Eccl., V, 21.

212 Bede, Hist. Eccl., V, 15.

213 Herbert, Iona, 47–67; Taylor, 'Seventh-century Iona abbots', 57–62.

214 AU sa 716; AT sa 717.

215 Bede, Hist. Eccl., V, 22; Herbert, Iona, 58–60.

216 K. Veitch, 'The Columban church in northern Britain, 664–712: a reassessment', *Proceedings of the Society of Antiquaries of Scotland* 127 (1997), 627–47.

217 A. MacDonald, *Curadán, Boniface and the Early Church of Rosemarkie* (Groom House Museum, 1992).

218 *Councils*, II, 116. He is described as 'Fergustus, episcopus Scotiae Pictus'.

219 Bede, *Hist. Eccl.*, V, 21; Macquarrie, 'Early Christian religious houses', 114–15.

220 Henderson and Henderson, *Art of the Picts*; Carver, 'An Iona of the east'.

221 I.N. Wood, *The Missionary Life: Saints and the Evangelisation of Europe 400–1050* (Harlow, 2001).

222 Bede, *Hist. Eccl.*, I, 30.

223 Tangl no. 23; *EHD*, I no. 167; *Anglo-Saxon Missionaries in Germany*, trans. C.H. Talbot (London, 1954), 75–8.

224 J.C. Russell, *The Germanisation of Early Medieval Christianity: A Sociological Approach to Religious Transformation* (Oxford, 1994).

225 Bede, *Hist. Eccl.*, II, 14.

226 Stancliffe, 'Kings who opted out'.

CHAPTER 3

The Organisation and Culture of the Church in Early Medieval Britain

Bishoprics

In order to assess the impact of the introduction of the church into early medieval Britain we need to review its organisational structures and consider how these related to other aspects of the ordering of society. The chief responsibility for oversight of the church lay with the bishops, and their duties were described in detail in Pope Gregory the Great's *Regula Pastoralis*, a book that seems to have been well known throughout the insular world in the early Middle Ages. It informed, for instance, Bede's views of the role of bishops that he set out in a letter to Bishop Ecgbert of York and exemplified through his portrayals of Aidan and Cuthbert of Lindisfarne as 'model' bishops.[1] Only bishops could ordain priests, who should be men of proven education and moral rectitude, and the bishops themselves had major responsibilities for baptism and for preaching to the people as they toured their dioceses. The effectiveness of episcopal control therefore depended in part on whether there was adequate provision of bishops for the size of population. One of the major arguments made by Bede to Ecgbert was that the number of bishops in Northumbria was not sufficient, even though the province seems to have been better provided for in that respect than many other areas of early medieval Britain.

When Christianity was adopted as the main religion of the Roman empire in the fourth century, its organisation was made to mirror that of the civil administration with a bishop provided for each *civitas* and a chief bishop or metropolitan supervising the bishops of a province. Such a structure for the four provinces of late Roman Britain is perhaps implied by the proceedings of the council of Arles of 314, but cannot otherwise be traced in any detail.[2] On this basis it can be suggested that there could have been some 25 bishops in late Roman Britain.[3] That bishops continued to function in the western areas of Britain in the fifth and sixth centuries is apparent from the writings of Patrick and Gildas. Seven British bishops came to the second meeting with Augustine in *c.*601 on the borders of the kingdom of the West Saxons and the Hwicce, and, as the participants also included monks from the monastery of Bangor-on-Dee near Chester, it is possible that the former province of *Britannia Prima* was still functioning as a unit of church organisation, though there is no indication of a metropolitan.[4] Archaeological evidence may suggest that some former *civitas* capitals such as Exeter and Gloucester continued as major religious centres until they came into Anglo-Saxon hands,[5] and the Anglo-Saxon bishoprics of Lichfield, Worcester and Sherborne (*Lanprobus*) were founded in places which seem also to have been the site of major British churches, though only Lichfield has some written support for it having been the site of a British bishopric.[6] New episcopal sites came into existence to suit the changing circumstances of the early medieval period. We cannot identify with any certainty the majority of episcopal sites in western Britain for the period 600–800, but bishoprics at St David's in Dyfed, Llandeilo Fawr in Ystrad Tywi and Bangor-on-Dee in Powys are recorded.[7] One can presume that the history of bishoprics in the west of Britain was interconnected with the rise and fall of kingdoms, and even in Gildas's day bishops and priests are presented as closely associated with the secular power system. Dumnonia, for instance, had to adapt to the loss of territory to the West Saxons, and in the early ninth century its bishop had his see at *Dinuurrin*, which may have been Bodmin.[8] Identification of Welsh bishoprics is complicated by the fact that the term *sacerdos* could be used for either a bishop or a priest, and by the projection of later claims back on to an early medieval past. By the twelfth century there seem to have been only four Welsh dioceses, with centres at St David's, Llandaff, Bangor and St Asaph, corresponding to the four most powerful kingdoms.[9] The *Book of Llandaf*, compiled on the orders of Bishop Urban between 1120 and 1134, attempted to claim that it had been the centre of a diocese from the fifth century, had been subject to St Augustine and had always followed Roman custom. Although Llandaff may have been a religious community of some antiquity, its promotion as a bishopric seems to have been a relatively recent development, after the jurisdiction and territory of the former bishopric of Llandeilo Fawr had come under its control.[10]

Pope Gregory knew that Britain had been a part of the Roman empire, and his original expectation had been that Augustine would be able to utilise the Roman infrastructure to establish two provinces of twelve bishoprics each with metropolitans at London and York.[11] Gregory's blueprint was never to be fully implemented. Bishoprics were established at London and York, but both lapsed temporarily after the kings who had authorised them died, with the result that the southern metropolitan centre remains at Canterbury to this day. York became the seat of a metropolitan in 735 with Ecgbert as its first archbishop; Bede had pressed for this promotion in his *Letter to Ecgbert*. When King Offa of Mercia fell out with Archbishop Jaenbert of Canterbury he tried to have the see moved to London (which was under his control) in line with Gregory's original intentions, and, after he was unsuccessful, petitioned the pope to allow the establishment of a third see at Lichfield, the main Mercian bishopric, in 787. This third archbishopric was abolished in 803 after Offa's death.[12]

The establishment of bishoprics in the Anglo-Saxon kingdoms, after Augustine's initial successes, was not controlled from Canterbury, but relied on decisions made by individual kings. It seems to have been accepted that the provision of bishoprics would mirror political arrangements and the principle of one bishop per kingdom was followed, with the exception of Kent where there were two bishops from an early date (Canterbury and Rochester), but this also seems to have been dictated by a political subdivision of the province.[13] However, as some of the kingdoms, such as Northumbria, Mercia and Wessex were very large, and growing as the seventh century progressed, the provision of one bishop was barely adequate. When Archbishop Theodore set out to consolidate the nascent Anglo-Saxon church, one of his aims was to increase the number of bishoprics and it was one of the items discussed at the first synod of the whole Anglo-Saxon church held at Hertford in 670.[14] The division of the large Northumbrian see was bitterly contested by Bishop Wilfrid who obtained a papal ruling that Theodore and King Ecgfrith had acted illegally in driving through a division against his wishes in 678, although he was unsuccessful in getting their decision reversed in spite of several attempts to do so.[15] Thereafter subdivision continued in the larger kingdoms as opportunity arose when incumbents died. Bede recorded that in 731 there were 12 bishoprics south of the Humber:[16] Canterbury and Rochester (Kent), London (East Saxons), Dunwich and Elmham (East Angles), Winchester and Sherborne (West Saxons), Lichfield (Mercia),[17] Hereford

(Magonsaetan), Worcester (Hwicce), Lindsey,[18] Selsey (South Saxons), and four in Northumbria at York, Lindisfarne, Hexham and Whithorn. Episcopal lists also survive that give a very full indication of the succession to the various Anglo-Saxon bishoprics from the time of their foundation.[19]

If only such records existed for the northern part of Britain many thorny problems would be solved, but as it is we are very poorly informed about arrangements within the various provinces in Scotland. Among the British kingdoms of the north the most securely attested bishopric is that of Whithorn in Galloway that seems to have been the see of Uinniau/Ninian in the latter part of the sixth century.[20] Excavations at the site have confirmed continuity of use as an ecclesiastical site from origins in the sixth century up to a period of major rebuilding when Whithorn became a Northumbrian see around 731, even if continuity as a British see cannot be conclusively demonstrated.[21] We might tentatively identify Whithorn as a see of Rheged though political boundaries are extremely uncertain in this area. Carlisle has been proposed as a see for the area south of the Solway that has also, rather speculatively, been seen as part of Rheged, but we know very little about Carlisle's status before it came into Northumbrian hands in the 680s.[22] In the twelfth century the bishops of Glasgow presented themselves as the successors of St Kentigern, the first bishop of the see for the kingdom of Dumbarton whose death is apparently recorded in the *Annales Cambriae* for 612 or 614.[23] Two early graves placed by radiocarbon dating in the seventh century provide some support for the existence of an early religious centre at Glasgow where Kentigern is said to have been buried.[24] However, if Glasgow was the centre of Kentigern's see it certainly did not have an uninterrupted history before the eleventh century when undoubted records for bishops of Glasgow begin. The notable collection of carved stones from the tenth and eleventh centuries at nearby Govan strongly suggests that it was the main centre of the kingdom of Strathclyde in that period.[25] The exact nature of arrangements in the earlier kingdom of Dumbarton must remain uncertain, and the tradition that Kentigern was the first bishop of Glasgow may be another example of wishful twelfth-century back-projection, for the historicity of his later Lives is extremely suspect. No traditions of early bishops for Gododdin or any of the even more shadowy northern British kingdoms survive.

The Scottish province of Dál Riata has generally been interpreted as consisting of several small kingdoms or *tuatha* in accordance with the Irish model,[26] in which case one would have expected each of these small kingdoms to have had its own bishop as happened in Ireland. In fact, it is remarkably difficult to discover many bishops based in Scottish Dál Riata in the sources. The Ionan annals only seem to refer to one bishopric, that at Kingarth on the Isle of Bute, founded by St Blane, which would have lain, according to the dispositions of the *Senchus fern Alban*, in the territory of Cenél Gabráin, the royal kindred that was dominant in the late sixth and seventh centuries.[27] It may therefore be the case that when it came to the provision of bishoprics Dál Riata was seen as one single kingdom rather than several. Iona itself does not seem to have been originally the seat of a bishopric, although it provided bishops for Lindisfarne from its community. Two bishops, Coeti and Ecgbert, are known to have been resident there in the late seventh and early eighth centuries, but both may have come originally from outside Iona and were there to try to help solve issues over the celebration of Easter that threatened to disrupt the community during this period,[28] although the possibility could be entertained that the see was moved there as references to bishops of Kingarth are confined to the seventh century.[29] Bishops do not have a major role to play in Adomnán's *Life of St Columba*, though bishops from Ireland were occasional visitors to the foundation, and probably to other religious communities along the west coast that had been founded from Ireland and retained links with the homeland.[30] Columba and other abbots of Iona also travelled to Ireland with entourages, and such visits would have provided opportunities to make use of the services of a bishop, for instance to ordain a monk as a priest. One would dearly like to know how it was arranged for Aidan to be created a bishop before he went from Iona and Lindisfarne, a ceremony that should have involved three bishops, as we would then be in a better position to understand the interaction of bishops with religious communities on the west coast of Scotland.

In spite of the lack of surviving written records from Pictish territories references survive for two Pictish bishops that may be informative when placed in a broader context. Adomnán's *Law of the Innocents* was supported by by the Pictish king Bridei son of Derilei (697–706) and a Pictish bishop called Curetán who, later Scottish calendars reveal, was also known by the religious name of Boniface and associated with Rosemarkie (Ross), situated in the north-east of Scotland just across the Moray Firth from Inverness.[31] The legend of Boniface in the late medieval *Aberdeen Breviary* links him with Bridei's brother and successor Nechtan (706–24) and equates him with Pope Boniface IV (c.608–15), a successor of Pope Gregory the Great who continued to provide support for the Roman mission in England. This latter identification must, of course, be rejected and the legends surrounding Curetán are not to be credited, but a case has been made for a genuine tradition behind his association with Nechtan and an affiliation with Rome through the suggestion that Curetán was bishop of the Picts at the time Nechtan requested information concerning the calculation of Easter from Ceolfrith of Wearmouth and Jarrow, which resulted in the adoption of the 'Roman' Easter in Pictland and the expulsion of recalcitrant members of Ionan affiliated clergy from the province.[32] This link has been supported further by the tradition that a group of Pictish churches dedicated to St Peter had been founded by Curetán, which recalls Bede's statement that after Nechtan's decision the churches of the Picts were placed under St Peter's protection.[33] Curetán's see may have been based at Rosemarkie where he is reputed to have been buried and where there is a notable collection of Pictish sculpture. But he is also said to have founded a church at Restenneth (Angus) in the southern part of Pictland that was dedicated to St Peter and where there are a number of St Peter dedications in its vicinity. There is also a series of Boniface and St Peter dedications on Orkney that may also be linked with his period in office.[34] These various pieces of information combine to suggest that Curetán may have played an active role throughout Pictland and could have been a key figure in giving the Pictish church a common identity after the decisions to adopt the 'Roman' Easter and tonsure and to move into closer contact with other areas of the western church. In 721 there is a record of a Pictish bishop called Fergustus attesting a council in Rome, and he can tentatively be proposed as successor to Curetán who was continuing his policies.[35] Fergustus seems to have been accompanied by a certain Sedulius described as 'a bishop of Britain of Scottish race' who was possibly a bishop of Dumbarton or Dál Riata.

The question remains whether there was only one bishopric for the whole of Pictland or if one should envisage other bishoprics that have not made any impact on the admittedly limited written evidence. As with Dál Riata, this question has implications for how the political system of Pictland worked. If, as is often assumed, there were several kingdoms among the Picts one might have expected them each to have had their own bishop in accordance with practice elsewhere in the insular world. If, however, Pictland was regarded as one ecclesiastical province that could suggest Pictland should be regarded as being politically unified as well, though allowance should be made for changes over time; for instance, Pictland may have been more politically unified and dominated by individual overlord kings in the eighth century than in the seventh. Bede believed that there was a division into northern and southern Picts that he associated with different ecclesiastical traditions stemming from missions of Columba and Uinniau/Ninian respectively.[36] Bede's statement has to be seen as an oversimplification of a much more complex and chronologically extensive situation, but, as we have seen, there may have been different areas of Ionan and British influence within Pictland. Was Bede's concept of a division based on knowledge of different northern and southern dioceses? The church of Abernethy in Fife in southern Pictland preserved traditions of an early foundation and that it had been the chief bishopric of the Pictish kingdom where three elections of bishops had been made when there was only one bishop for the whole of Pictland.[37] When at least part of Pictland was under Northumbrian overlordship in the reign of King Ecgfrith (670–85), a short-lived bishopric was founded at Abercorn that as Bede explains was in English-held territory (in Lothian), but close to the Pictish border and evidently intended to administer to at least the southern Picts as its bishop and clergy had to flee after Ecgfrith's disastrous defeat at Nechtansmere.[38] Should Abernethy be seen as a replacement for Abercorn, or vice versa? Should Abernethy and Rosemarkie be seen as contemporary bishoprics of northern and southern Picts respectively, or was one the successor to the other as a single bishopric for the whole of Pictland? Unfortunately as so often in the history of Pictland it is easier to pose questions than to provide solid answers. Although in the twelfth century there were nine bishoprics for the whole area of Scotland ruled by King David I, these places seem to have become bishoprics after the demise of the kingdom of the Picts and the other kingdoms within Scotland in the seventh and eighth centuries and probably provide little help with the reconstruction of earlier arrangements.[39]

Although there seems to have been a general expectation in early medieval Britain that kingdoms would have their own bishop, so that political and episcopal arrangements were in harmony, the actual imposition led to rather different patterns among the different peoples. The Anglo-Saxons were the only area of Britain to be a united ecclesiastical province under a metropolitan as a consequence of the continuing direct papal involvement with the Anglo-Saxon church. The archbishop of Canterbury could be seen as the episcopal equivalent of Anglo-Saxon overlords, and the raising of York to metropolitan status in 735 came at a time when Northumbria was withdrawing from political involvement with the southern Anglo-Saxon kingdoms. Archbishop Theodore instituted the regular holding of church synods and the subdivision of the larger bishoprics. The Anglo-Saxons therefore moved away from the concept that there could be only one bishop in a kingdom, though their diocesan system preserved the boundaries of some political units which were subsequently absorbed into larger kingdoms. The meetings at Augustine's Oak in *c*.601 seem to show the churches of the former province of *Britannia Prima* coming together to debate important issues, though without any metropolitan. Although evidence is incomplete, that from Wales suggests that it was normal for each kingdom to have had its own bishop, with numbers perhaps rising or contracting with the rise and fall of kingdoms Within Scotland the limited evidence seems to suggest that Dál Riata and the Picts may have had only one bishopric each, and one per British kingdom also seems likely. Therefore, even allowing for a greater density of population, there was a much more generous provision of bishoprics among the Anglo-Saxons than elsewhere and questions arise from this about the degree of control bishops could have exercised in those areas that were less well provided with sees. Such issues seem to have occurred to the Anglo-Saxons as well and a council of Chelsea in 816 declared that it was improper 'to receive the ministrations of foreigners among whom there was no regular organisation under a metropolitan' (because of doubts about where and by whom priests had been ordained).[40] Shortage of bishops may have led to some irregularities in certain areas, but was not necessarily fatal for the provision of pastoral care to the lay community for, as we shall see in the next section, there were a variety of religious communities within early medieval Britain that could have shared this responsibility.

Monasticism and religious communities in early medieval Britain

In the sixth century a major new mode of religious life came to Britain and Ireland that was to significantly shape the way Christianity operated in early medieval Britain. This was monasticism, a movement that had begun in the fourth century as a reaction against the increasing alignment of the mainstream church with secular structures of society by those who wished to devote their lives to the service of God through prayer and abstinence.[41] The pioneers of monasticism had lived as hermits in the deserts of Egypt and Palestine, but some attracted followers whom they subsequently formed into communities of male and female religious living under a common rule under the command of an abbot. The new ascetic movement spread to the western empire through those who had experienced it at first hand and through accounts of early monastic founders such as St Anthony whose *Life* by Athanasius (in a translation by Evagrius) would become a model for the written Lives of many early medieval saints. The earliest monastic communities in the west were established on the Mediterranean with influential centres at Lérins and Arles. This area of Gaul seems to have been one with which areas of western Britain were in contact and the same seaways that brought pottery to Britain may also have helped spread ideas of monasticism.[42] When Gildas wrote his *De Excidio Britanniae*, probably in the first half of the sixth century, monasticism seems to have been a fledgling movement that he hoped to join.[43] By the time he produced two later works, a letter to Uinniau and a 'Preface on Penance', he seems to have done so.[44] By this period, probably in the second half of the sixth century, monasticism seems to have become much more widespread in both Britain and Ireland and to have been followed with different degrees of asceticism. Gildas was highly critical in these later works of those who were ostentatiously ascetic and regarded themselves as superior to those men of God who lived less spartan lives. He criticised their refusal to eat meat and travel on horseback, their excessive fasting and emphasis on manual labour, in fact all things that seem to have been associated with the monastic rule established by his contemporary David.[45] Similar contrasts are implied in the *Life of St Samson* between the regime of Illtud at Llanilltud Fawr (Llantwit Major) and the more vigorous rule at the monastery of Pirus.[46] These references are an important reminder that even in the early days of monasticism in Britain extreme asceticism was only one form that monasticism might take, for the founders of communities were free to draw up whatever rules seemed to them most appropriate. By the end of the sixth century one of the more moderate rules that was ultimately to become extremely influential in medieval Europe was the Rule written by Benedict of Nursia (d. *c*.550), a religious leader who was regarded with especial favour by Pope Gregory the Great.[47]

Gregory himself can be seen as representative of those members of patrician families who saw in the asceticism of Christian monasticism a means of retaining the mores of their class in the post-Roman world;[48] perhaps Gildas should also be seen as a member of this group. Gregory founded a monastery dedicated to St Andrew on a family estate on one of the hills of Rome and it was from this community that Augustine and the other missionaries were despatched to England in 596. In Gaul there was already a tradition of bishops who were also monks, exemplified by monks from Lérins who entered the episcopate and by St Martin, bishop of Tours (d. 397) to whom the church used by Liudhard and Bertha in Canterbury was dedicated. It is important to appreciate that there was a widespread trend in the western church by 600 to combine the active and contemplative lives because the traditional interpretation of British and Irish Christianity had seen the two forms as distinct, and there was at one time widespread acceptance of a hypothesis that saw an original episcopal church in Ireland and western Britain replaced by one based on monastic lines.[49] More recent reassessments have considerably modified this picture to produce one that is closer to that elsewhere in the western church where the combination of the active and contemplative lives was seen as a spiritual ideal and one particularly suited for episcopal and missionary endeavours.[50] When the Anglo-Saxons were converted to Christianity their earliest missionaries and 'foreign' bishops, whether they were Italian, Frankish or Irish, tended also to be monks. The bishop whose see was also a monastery was to become a common phenomenon throughout the insular world.

A religious community was the ideal form of organisation for the nascent church in early medieval Britain for its members could provide mutual support in an ecclesiastical equivalent of the secular kin-group. As a part of Europe where Roman towns had ceased to function as such, or had never existed, a religious community within its own enclosure was a way of creating the ideal of the 'holy city' that travellers from Britain encountered in journeys within the former Roman empire or read about in the Bible and other texts from which the impression would be received that such 'cities' had both a literal and symbolic significance for a Christian society.[51] Roman sites of various types might be reutilised as new religious centres in part because of the expectations of those familiar with churches based in Roman towns in other former areas of the Roman empire, but also because these sites possessed good communications with building materials to hand, and, above all, were ready-made enclosures that helped to separate the religious community from the secular world. Other types of delineated site might be pressed into service including hill-forts and islands, either in the sea as was Iona or in suitable inland watery areas such as the fenland home of Ely.[52] Sites without artificial or natural defining features would be provided with their own enclosures that were usually curvilinear in form such as that excavated from the British monastic phase of Whithorn or those preserved in numerous earthwork examples known particularly from the west of Britain, though the form was probably originally widespread in Anglo-Saxon areas as well.[53]

Religious communities shared many characteristics, but we must recognise that they could be in other ways diverse and it should not be assumed that all, or all of their inhabitants, uniformly followed the type of ascetic way of life traditionally associated with monasticism. Written sources from the period habitually use a 'monastic' vocabulary to describe religious communities, but examination for different parts of Britain of the contexts in which the terminology was applied have demonstrated that not all these sites were 'monasteries' in the sense of uniform celibate communities bound by religious vows and with a daily schedule of religious services and manual labour.[54] The Latin word *monasterium* could be applied not only to communities of monks and nuns, either in single-sex or mixed communities under the command of an abbot or abbess, but also to communities of secular clergy, that is priests, deacons and lesser clergy who had not taken any form of monastic vow and might be married. It would even seem that monks, nuns and secular clergy could be found in the same community, and that lay people may sometimes have resided in religious houses as well. The peasant cultivators attached to a religious community might be designated as 'monastic' members; some may have been similar to the lay brothers familiar from some later monastic communities, but others were probably comparable to the Irish monastic tenants (*manaig*) who lived on monastic estates with their families.[55] Caedmon the herdsman of Whitby nunnery, who miraculously learnt to compose religious verse in Old English, seems to have been representative of this class of monastic peasant.[56] He and other peasant cultivators attached to Whitby who appear in the *Lives* of St Cuthbert seem to have lived lives that were both physically and occupationally separate from the aristocratic nuns and monks of Whitby. There are references to what seems to have been a dependent grange (in later terminology) at *Osingadun*;[57] Caedmon seems to have lived closer to the main site of Whitby, but separate from its monastic quarters. Excavations at the site of Whitby and its dependent house of Hartlepool suggest that the communities occupied large areas of land that seem to have been divided into zones for different activities and groups among the residents.[58] An implicit division into three zones of activity and access has been detected in Adomnán's *Life of St Columba*. The island shores formed an outermost boundary where visitors from the outside world would land and be vetted; the monastic enclosure-wall (*vallum*) defined a more sacred territory to whose public buildings laymen might be admitted under supervision; and a third zone, perhaps delineated by its own bank and ditch, defined the holiest area of all containing the monastic church and cemetery.[59] Agricultural and other practical activities mostly took place outside the *vallum*. Excavations and fieldwork at Iona's daughter houses of Tarbat and Lindisfarne have revealed what could be seen as comparable divisions of space and separation of activities.[60]

The sites of religious communities were marked out as separate from the lay world. The religious of whatever level also had an appearance distinct from that of laymen. Their major distinguishing characteristic was the tonsure, the partially shaved head,[61] though it is also likely that churchmen were expected to eschew the moustaches and beards favoured by many of the lay aristocracy. Different forms of tonsure existed, but the one that increasingly came to be seen as 'correct', and with which we are most familiar today, was the so-called petrine tonsure in which the crown of the head was shaved in symbolic remembrance of Christ's crown of thorns. British and Irish clergy were familiar with other forms that may have been in vogue when Christianity was first introduced into Britain. Irish carvings seem to show the front of the head as shaved, but various interpretations of the written accounts of tonsure among British and Irish clergy have been made and there may have been more than one custom in existence.[62] The form of the tonsure became one of the issues between the Romanists and traditionalists, and the way in which it was worn instantly proclaimed in which camp an individual placed himself. Other forms of dress probably distinguished laymen and religious as well. On the Pictish sculptures clerics are portrayed quite differently from laymen, who are often shown as hunting, riding or fighting. The clerics wear distinctive long, hooded garments and carry or wear equipment appropriate to their profession such as croziers, staffs and book-satchels.[63] Bede drew the line between the religious and secular professions when he contrasted those who performed 'earthly military service' with those who waged 'heavenly warfare' by using their prayers to win God's support.[64] Although, as we shall see, one should not assume a complete separation of ecclesiastical and lay culture, and considerable variations must have existed between the lives of celibate and married clergy, which could apparently include aspects of dress,[65] there clearly were levels where major boundaries existed between the lay and the religious, and these are reflected in the terminology for the latter's communities. The problem remains of how we should describe them today. Many Anglo-Saxon historians advocate use of the term 'minster', from Old English *mynster*, for their religious communities of this period.[66] This term has its own connotations in the later Anglo-Saxon period, and is not generally utilised by historians of other areas of Britain, even though the similarities between their religious houses and those of the Anglo-Saxons were probably greater than any differences. On the whole, in a work of this type, it seems better to apply some generalised term such as 'religious communities' when writing of them as a distinct group, though it would also seem appropriate to describe those such as Iona or Jarrow, where there is good evidence that they followed a monastic rule as 'monasteries', when the context requires it.

Founders and patrons of religious communities

One way in which we can look at how religious communities operated is to consider the circumstances in which they were founded and patronised. What was the relationship between religious communities and episcopal power? Were they independent of lay society or intermeshed in its power structures? In the late Roman world bishops were responsible for evangelisation, and established baptisteries in their episcopal centres as well as dependent baptismal churches in other centres in their diocese to induct those who wished to be received into the church, especially adults who would require instruction. Baptisteries, fonts and lead tanks for baptism have been recognised from Roman Britain.[67] Potential post-Roman baptisteries have been excavated at the early religious house of Hoddom (Dumfries),[68] and in a former Roman villa at Bradford-on-Avon (Wilts), suggesting a continuation of practice established in the Roman period in these British areas.[69] Baptism of Anglo-Saxons by the missionaries sent by Pope Gregory seems to have taken place in rivers bordering royal vills, and there is very little evidence for specialised baptismal churches or even of fonts, raising the possibility that baptism continued to take place at open-air sites with running water long after the initial phases of conversion.[70] However, there are indications that Augustine and his fellow bishops began the process of establishing subsidiary churches away from their episcopal sees, and Bede describes a series of churches established on royal estates by Paulinus as bishop of York.[71]

The disrupted histories of many of the early Anglo-Saxon bishoprics may have affected the imposition of an episcopally directed system of local church provision. Throughout insular Britain the lure of monasticism also complicated the pattern of ecclesiastical provision. Although in the theory of the canon law of the western church bishops had oversight of all religious communities founded within their dioceses and consecrated new churches, in practice in early medieval Britain new religious communities were created in accordance with the wishes of their founders and patrons. The ascetic movement encouraged the emergence of individuals who flouted the conventions of early medieval society and achieved immense charisma as a result. Bede conveys the impact of Bishop Aidan of Lindisfarne's gesture of giving away to a beggar the king's gift of a horse from the royal stud with all its accoutrements, and his general indifference to the type of aristocratic lifestyle that he might otherwise have been expected to follow.[72] Several generations earlier Patrick had had a similar electrifying impact in early medieval Ireland where he had ranged widely drawing followers and founding communities across political and episcopal boundaries to the alarm of local rulers and his fellow bishops in Britain.[73] By the end of the sixth century many geographically widespread monastic confederations existed in Ireland, though these did not necessarily negate, as was once believed, the operation of the many small bishoprics that served individual kingdoms.[74] The Irish monastic confederation that had most impact in Britain was, of course, Iona. Columba himself had founded daughter houses in Ireland and among the Picts, and his successors continued to extend the number of houses that recognised the authority of Iona and enjoyed the protection of Columba.[75] Their scope was considerably enlarged by King Oswald's request that Ionan monks re-establish the bishopric of Northumbria, especially as Lindisfarne subsequently provided bishops for some of the southern Anglo-Saxon kingdoms that were subject to the overlordship of Oswald and his brother Oswiu. However, all this was ended at the decision made at the synod of Whitby in 664 by King Oswiu to recognise the authority of Canterbury instead of Iona.

It is quite likely that there were monastic confederations in the British kingdoms as well. Patrick after all had come from Britain, and Uinniau/Ninian, the teacher of Columba, had possessed religious houses both sides of the Irish see. Traditionally the fifth and sixth centuries is the 'age of the saints' in the Welsh church, but although we can accept that Cadog (of Llancarfan), David (of Mynyw, later known as St David's), Dyfrig (also known as Dubricius), Illtud (of Llanilltud Fawr) and Teilo (of Llandeilo Fawr) were founders of what were probably monastic communities which bear their names, we know remarkably little about most of them.[76] Detailed *vitae* survive only from the eleventh century or later, and, although some genuine traditions may have survived, these are hard to unpick from hagiographical conventions and adaptation of material to fit specific needs when the *vitae* were composed. Using dedications of churches to these individuals or places containing their names to reconstruct their original spheres of influence is also very suspect and is more likely to reflect later developments, as John Davies has shown in his study of the evidence for the cult of Dyfrig.[77] The two *vitae* of Patrick produced at Armagh in the late seventh century are an object lesson in how the life of a monastic founder could be radically reshaped to accommodate the ambitions of a community with which he may have had no original connection, but that had contrived to annex him as their major patron.[78] If anything the problems are more acute for studying the history of early church foundation among the Picts, but, as in Wales, a careful shifting of the evidence for saints' cults provides some evidence for prominent churchmen, in this case from the late seventh century onwards, who seem to have been active in founding churches.[79]

The most impressive monastic empire assembled in Anglo-Saxon England was that of Bishop Wilfrid of Northumbria who, aided by his various periods of exile, founded religious communities in several different kingdoms and dioceses, all of which he kept under his personal control.[80] Wilfrid's character was such that he seems to have been able to attract and infuriate in equal measure, and there was considerable royal and episcopal opposition to his creation of a monastic empire and his willingness to exercise his episcopal powers in other dioceses besides the one to which he had been consecrated. The ruling at the synod of Hertford in 670 'that no bishop intrude into the diocese of another bishop' may have been framed in direct response to the problems that Wilfrid had caused.[81] Although Wilfrid left money to his abbots and abbesses to buy the favour of kings and bishops after his death,[82] his large monastic confederation seems to have broken up after his lifetime, though his main Northumbrian houses at Ripon and Hexham remained two of the most significant religious communities in the province. The collective power of bishops in England seems more likely than those of any other part of Britain to have been able to affect religious communities founded by other ecclesiastics. One of the other clauses of the synod of Hertford forbade bishops from interfering with *monasteria* and taking part of their property, and several monastic founders in England took the precaution of obtaining papal privileges excluding bishops from their foundations – even though some of those obtaining these privileges were themselves bishops.[83]

The founders of religious houses were themselves dependent on the willingness of kings and other secular powers to act as their patrons, above all by guaranteeing the transfer of land for this purpose. From Wales and Anglo-Saxon England charters survive that record the granting of land. In Wales the tradition of using written memoranda to record land transactions may have evolved from late Roman practice, but in England it was introduced by early churchmen familiar with Roman land law.[84] The earliest surviving Anglo-Saxon charters are from the archepiscopate of Theodore, but it is possible that they were used earlier and that there was not just one point of introduction.[85] Anglo-Saxon charters specify that grants were made in perpetuity with rights of free alienation. These conditions seem to have taken a while to implant themselves in Anglo-Saxon practice. Initially kings did not necessarily accept that they had to honour grants of their predecessors; Abbess Æbbe of Thanet seems to have felt the need to acquire charters for the same estates from successive (and rival) kings of Kent.[86] Bede's *Letter to Ecgbert* reveals that part of the problem was that churches were often endowed from the same reservoir of land that was also used to reward military followers who would customarily receive the estate for their lifetime only.[87] Even when the principle of permanent alienation was accepted, there remained the question of whether kings retained rights over the land. This is something that may have varied between kingdoms. King Wihtred (690–725) apparently freed the Kentish churches from all public exactions, but later in the eighth century King Æthelbald of Mercia caused consternation by allowing his officials to requisition men from monastic estates (presumably tenants rather than the religious themselves) to work on public building projects.[88] Those who had taken religious vows were exempt from military service themselves, but there remained the question of whether military contingents should be raised from their lands. In 749 at a synod held in Gumley (Leicestershire) Æthelbald seems to have reached agreement with the religious houses of Mercia that they would be free of all royal exactions except those necessary for the effective defence of the kingdom. Such definitions seem eventually to have been accepted throughout Anglo-Saxon England (though we lack evidence from Northumbria) and the public services to which religious houses were expected to contribute were generally defined as military service, fortress work and the building of roads and bridges. The charters from the Welsh kingdoms sometimes refer to kings granting exemptions, implying they too believed that they retained some rights over lands held by the church, but specific details are not given.[89]

Some kings were not content with supporting the activities of religious leaders, but wanted a more direct involvement with monasticism. The insular world is unusual for the number of kings who, in Clare Stancliffe's felicitous categorisation, 'opted out' and entered monastic communities.[90] Gildas provides two early examples of British kings. Constantine of Dumnonia is said to have personally murdered two princes (presumably political rivals) as they were praying in church and while he was wearing 'the habit of a holy abbot'; the implication seems to be that Constantine had combined the positions of king and abbot.[91] Maelgwn of Gwynedd, on the other hand, had given up his position as king and taken vows as a monk only to renounce them and return to his original role.[92] King Brocfael of Powys may have been living in retirement at the monastery of Bangor-on-Dee when it was attacked by King Æthelfrith of Northumbria in c.604, which may help to explain the ferocity of the latter's attack on the monks.[93] Five Anglo-Saxon kings renounced their thrones in order to become monks in the period before 710, though Sigebert of the East Angles (acc. c.631) seems to have continued to have been regarded as king in spite of his monastic retreat, and Æthelred of Mercia (acc. 675) seems to have retained some political influence after he abdicated to become abbot at his own foundation of Bardney in 704.[94] Kings who combined the office with that of abbot or abdicated to enter monasteries are also known from Ireland, and there is a potential early example from Dál Riata in Domangart son of Fergus who abdicated in 507, but the information dates from the period before contemporary record keeping and so may be suspect.[95]

When seeking to decode what was happening in these instances, it needs to be recognised that there might have been different triggers behind kings opting for monastic retreat. In Francia retreat to monasteries became a way of removing political rivals from active life without actually killing them or could serve as a temporary expedient while explosive situations were resolved through negotiation. Sigebert of the East Angles who had been exiled to Francia had possibly spent that period in a monastery, which could explain his desire to return to the cloister after gaining the throne. Temporary withdrawal to a monastery while political tensions were diffused seems to have been a relatively common insular experience in the eighth century, though in some cases the retreat became permanent. Three examples can be taken from a similar time-frame, though there are further instances especially from Northumbria. Selbach of Dál Riata is reported as retiring into a religious community in 723, and was succeeded by his son Dúngal. However, after Dúngal was deposed in 726 Selbach re-emerged to fight on his behalf.[96] Ceolwulf of Northumbria was 'captured, tonsured and restored to the kingdom' in 731 and opted, apparently on his own volition, to retire permanently to Lindisfarne in 737.[97] King Nechtan, son of Derilei, of the Picts is recorded as retiring into the religious life in 724, which apparently precipitated a competition for the throne between several rival factions and Nechtan's return as king in 728.[98] The British and Irish churches had also developed from a relatively early stage the practice of penitential punishment for serious crimes that might require 'exile' to a monastery until the crime was expiated. Such circumstances may have impelled Maelgwn's retreat for, according to Gildas, he had been guilty of killing his uncle and many of his warband. Such concepts would have spread to Anglo-Saxon England as well and may have influenced some of the recorded abdications in order to enter a monastery, and perhaps occasioned other responses like that of Caedwalla of Wessex who abdicated in 688 to undertake *peregrinatio* to Rome where he was baptised and died soon after.[99]

One can also not rule out the possibility that some kings, especially in initial periods of the introduction of Christianity, were simply inspired by the new religion to want to devote themselves to it entirely, or were overwhelmed by realisation of the number of the ten commandments they had broken, thus imperilling their salvation. But one also wonders, especially in the case of the Anglo-Saxons, whether there might not be a bit more to it than that. It is noticeable that in the southern kingdoms of the Anglo-Saxons abdication for religious purposes tends to occur at the point at which the final commitment to Christianity was made and the worship of the gods abandoned after a period of dualism.[100] Is it possible that such an ostentatious embracing of the new religion was intended to mark the formal transition from the old cults to the new Christian religion? It is one of several pieces of evidence that suggests Anglo-Saxon kings were keen to actively involve themselves, or members of their immediate families, in leading the new religion rather than merely delegating responsibilities to bishops or other clerical leaders. Another manifestation in the Anglo-Saxon kingdoms, after the final commitment to Christianity had been made, was the foundation of royal nunneries commanded by retired queens and princesses of the royal houses. Several of these houses were founded in each of the Anglo-Saxon kingdoms, and at least 30 had been founded before the death of Bede in 735.[101] These royal nunneries formed a significant proportion of the early ecclesiastical foundations in the early Anglo-Saxon kingdoms, and among those for which good written or archaeological evidence survives are Barking, Hartlepool, Minster-in-Thanet, Whitby and Wimborne.

Equivalent royal nunneries are not known from the kingdoms of the other peoples of Britain, though from Ireland there are some comparable examples, especially Kildare with its close links with one of the leading royal houses of Leinster.[102] The lack of royal nunneries in the non-Anglo-Saxon provinces of Britain may be due in part to differences in the legal position of women, particularly with respect to women's ability to own land that may be reflected as well in the small numbers of women referred to on inscribed stones or depicted on Pictish sculpture.[103] The relative prevalence of Anglo-Saxon royal nunneries also owes much to Frankish influences for in the seventh century many leading families of northern Francia, some of which can be shown to have close links with Anglo-Saxon royal houses, founded nunneries on their estates that were controlled by women of the founding family.[104] Such foundations gave a spiritual dimension that must have enhanced the temporal positions of these families, and such considerations were presumably attractive to the rival kin-groups who contended for control in the different Anglo-Saxon kingdoms. Ways in which pre-Christian cult was managed, and the roles of kings and probably of female members of the royal house in the pre-Christian religion, may also lie behind the greater emphasis on provision of royal nunneries in the Anglo-Saxon provinces. That is not to say, of course, that some kings or dynastic segments did not also have particularly close associations with male communities that they founded or patronised. The close links of Ecgfrith of Northumbria (670–85) with the monastery of Jarrow are recorded on its foundation stone. After the troubled succession of his half-brother Aldfrith (685/6–705) both the new king and abbot Ceolfrith of Jarrow seem to have striven to perpetuate the association and to support each other's position.[105]

A number of Pictish rulers are closely associated with the foundation or patronage of individual male religious communities as noted in one of the versions of the Pictish king-list. Abernethy is linked with Nechtan son of Uerb (d. 621), St Andrews with Onuist son of Uurguist (c.729–61) and Dunkeld with Constantine son of Fergus (c.789–820).[106] The close association of Nechtan and his brother Bridei with Curetán/Boniface of Rosemarkie has already been discussed. The St Andrew sarcophagus with its classical depictions of King David may have been the tomb of Onuist himself, or possibly that of a saint favoured by him, and can be compared with a sculpture of an Anglo-Saxon mounted warrior in the guise of a Roman emperor from the nunnery of Repton which may have been a memorial to Onuist's political ally King Æthelbald of Mercia (716–57) who is known to have been buried there.[107] During the eighth century, burial of kings within favoured religious communities seems to have become increasingly common, at least in some areas of Britain. We know relatively little about the interaction of kings and religious communities in Dál Riata and the British kingdoms. The *Book of Llandaf* records grants of land by kings to the church,[108] and the occasional geographical proximity of a major secular site to a major ecclesiastical one, as with Dinas Powys and Llandough (Glamorgan), may be suggestive, but overall we get little sense of the depth of the relationship and how the apparently close association of rulers with some religious communities recorded by Gildas and in Bede's account of the battle of Chester had developed. We can note though that in the eighth century the kings of Brycheiniog seem to have been buried in a religious house at Llangorse (Breconshire), and that from the ninth century onwards kings were actively claiming links for their dynasties with notable religious figures of the past.[109] Iona, of course, did have very close associations with a royal house, but not one that was based in Britain. Columba was a member of the Uí Néill dynasty of northern Ireland, and subsequent abbots were nearly all descended from his kinsmen.[110] The *Life of St Columba* emphasizes the importance of the support of Columba to enable kings of Dál Riata, and other areas of Britain, to be successful, and they were ultimately to establish a mutually beneficial partnership with the dynasty who became kings of Alba.[111]

Royal courts often set fashions that were imitated by the nobility, and from Anglo-Saxon England there is plenty of evidence to suggest that aristocratic families also founded religious communities and churches. One of Bede's major complaints in his *Letter to Ecgbert* was that kings of Northumbria had been too ready to grant land to found religious houses to their nobles so that 'there are innumerable places, as we all know, allowed the names of monasteries by a most foolish manner of speaking, but having nothing at all of a monastic way of life'.[112] These 'family monasteries', as they are sometimes known, have been seen as a rather different form of religious community to the truly monastic foundations such as Wearmouth and Jarrow, and have even been depicted as a form of tax evasion, or at least evasion of military service, on the part of nobility who had no intention of founding genuine religious communities.[113] However, it is probably more appropriate to see them as one end of the same, broad, spectrum that included the foundations of Wearmouth and Jarrow in which Bede passed most of his life at the other.[114] After all, there is no basic difference between the way that Bede describes the communities he deemed unacceptable as being founded and what we know of the circumstances in which Wearmouth came into existence.[115] Its founder, Benedict Biscop, seems to have had the 'normal' career pattern for a scion of the aristocracy. As a young man he served in the *comitatus* of King Oswiu of Northumbria and when he reached the age of about 25 received the gift of an estate. Although he spent two years at Lérins (666–8) where he became a monk and received the name of Benedict and became the abbot of the religious community he founded, he did not hold any other ecclesiastical position. The land on which he founded Wearmouth was granted by King Ecgfrith to whom he acted as adviser. Biscop was particularly anxious that his unsuitable layman brother should not inherit the monastery on his death and obtained a papal privilege that among other things permitted the community to elect its own abbot; nevertheless Biscop appointed his own cousin Eosterwine as co-abbot of Wearmouth during his lifetime. In essentials the only differences between Benedict Biscop and many other nobles who were enabled by royal gifts to found their own houses were that he established a regular monastic life, based on the Rule of St Benedict among others, and was himself a celibate monk – a distinction that was, of course, of vital significance to Bede's perception of what was and was not acceptable in a religious community. Benedict, and thus Wearmouth and subsequently Jarrow, also seems to have acquired exceptional wealth that was partly invested in books, paintings and other religious artefacts he acquired on his many visits to Italy. Once again it was the correct deployment of such wealth for religious purposes that separated to Bede's mind communities such as Wearmouth and Jarrow from those characterised by 'wanton' living and 'overindulgence'.

Charters from southern England illustrate the same processes of royal involvement in the foundation by laymen of religious communities that were subsequently regarded as part of the family's responsibilities and assets. For instance, in the eighth century King Æthelbert of the South Saxons granted an estate at Wittering (W. Sussex) to his nobleman Diozsa so that a religious community could be founded, and he transferred it to his sister who was presumably to oversee the new foundation.[116] The implication of the charters is that the foundation of many Anglo-Saxon religious communities was delegated to leading noble families by kings, with the approval of bishops who subscribed to them. From this come important implications for the nature of such communities and the permeability of the boundary between secular and religious world, and some of the potential ramifications are explored later in the chapter.

Of course, not all communities were necessarily founded on such 'public land' and some nobles (as did the royal houses) may have endowed religious houses from their own inherited estates, sometimes perhaps obtaining charters to confirm what they had done.[117] The evidence from the Llandaf charters suggests Welsh aristocratic families were more likely to endow communities from their own inherited land without the involvement of kings, though many of the examples come from after 800 and relate to endowment of existing houses rather than foundation of new ones.[118] The Anglo-Saxon noble foundations, at least, may have had much in common with patterns in Ireland where a proportion of family land might be set aside to support a church that would be administered by members of the family.[119] Arrangements could be flexible and, for instance, make provision for widows or unmarried sisters as vowed women as needed without the need to establish a separate or permanent nunnery.[120] Anglo-Saxon charters provide some object lessons of the problems in inheritance of the headship of such communities. At Withington in Gloucestershire the abbess on her deathbed assigned the community to an infant granddaughter whose married mother was to be her guardian. When the girl came of age the mother refused to relinquish control and claimed the community's charter had been stolen; the matter was only resolved in the granddaughter's favour at a church synod.[121]

Pictish sculptured stones could suggest that there were close links between noble families and religious communities in Pictland as well. Among the scenes depicted on cross-slabs and grave-covers is a significant sub-group of hunting and other horse-riding themes. As Isabel and George Henderson indicate, scenes of the hunt are based on late antique models and could have an allegorical, Christian significance.[122] However, the scenes go beyond their classical models and are customised for Pictish society with careful delineation of styles of dress, weaponry and horse management that we can presume are those of the Pictish aristocracy. One hunting scene on a cross-slab from Hilton of Cadboll (Ross and Cromarty) depicts a woman wearing a large penannular brooch and riding side saddle. The mirror and comb symbol beside her presumably gives her name or possibly her status.[123] One reasonable conclusion would be that these stones covered the graves or otherwise commemorated members of the lay aristocracy who had particular links with the religious communities in which it is presumed, from concentrated groupings of stones, that many of them were placed. Perhaps surprisingly such depictions of lay people are rare on the sculptures of early Anglo-Saxon England. The main exceptions are the sculptures from Repton and Bewcastle, both of which may commemorate rulers. Closer parallels come from northern England of the late ninth and early tenth centuries when sculptures that also depict hunting or warriors are believed to be associated with the newly converted Scandinavian settlers.[124] This is not to say that there is necessarily a direct link between these sculptural traditions, but rather that both may be manifestations of strong local lordships associated with religious communities.

Religious communities and pastoral care

Kings and nobles can be shown to have become major patrons of the Christian church, and sufficient numbers of the Anglo-Saxon elite entered the church for Bede to express concern about a shortage of men to fight on behalf of Northumbria. The same social groups that provided the fighting men of the early medieval armies, the nobles and freemen, also peopled the new religious communities. But what about those lower down the social scale? Did the early medieval church in Britain have the motivation and capacity to provide a system of pastoral care for the entire population? Such issues have been a major subject of debate concerning the nature of the early Anglo-Saxon religious communities. The so-called 'minster hypothesis' proposed systematic ecclesiastical provision in the *regiones*, the major administrative districts within kingdoms that were equivalent in size to the Irish *tuath*, each of which would have had its own bishop. However, often the evidence that would allow reconstruction of such minster parishes comes from the tenth or eleventh century or later, and there is an alternative view that it represents the regularisation from the ninth century onwards of a much more haphazard earlier system.[125] Prescriptive legislation, such as the canons of the Council of *Clofesho* of 747, stresses the pastoral responsibilities of priests under the supervision of bishops, but does not specify the locations of these priests. Narrative sources, on the other hand, such as Bede's *Ecclesiastical History*, seem more interested in depicting a way of life that can be broadly described as monastic, and on which pastoral responsibilities are rarely shown impinging, so that it has been doubted whether all communities were concerned with the care of lay society.[126] Although some small estates churches did exist, there does not seem to have been, in the Anglo-Saxon provinces in the seventh and eighth centuries, the type of systematic provision of parish churches with their own individual priests that, both archaeological and written evidence indicate, was largely a new development in the tenth and eleventh centuries.[127]

To have contradictory evidence that is difficult to resolve because of an inadequate amount of exemplary evidence is, of course, only too common for the early Middle Ages. It is undoubtedly true that the case for systematic minster provision has relied too much in many cases on relatively late evidence and so has been in danger of producing a circular argument. However, kings accepted a responsibility for ensuring the Christianisation of the people subject to them, seen for instance in the laws of Wihtred of Kent (690–725) and Ine of Wessex (688–725),[128] and presumably local royal agents were meant to see that their orders were followed. Charters in which, with the consent of bishops, kings granted land to nobles to found religious houses may therefore have been part of the policy to ensure that there was adequate ecclesiastical provision to enable the laws to be obeyed. It could, for instance, be suggested that individuals from the same noble families were supervising secular and religious concerns in the subdivisions of kingdoms. There are some districts in which there is suffi-cient evidence for what appears to be a regular topographical distribution of major churches from the late seventh and eighth centuries. In southern Hampshire, for instance, there is evidence from charters, Bede's *Ecclesiastical History* and archaeology for a series of churches in existence during the seventh and eighth centuries that had superior (mother) church status in the later Saxon period.[129] The churches lay in blocks of territory between rivers that drain into the Solent which were utilised as adminis-trative subdivisions (hundreds) in the later Saxon period. This area had been part of a Jutish province taken over by the West Saxons around the middle of the seventh century and it is therefore likely that the imposition of systematic control was part of the process of conquest. This is what seems to have happened later in the seventh century as the West Saxons moved westwards into British-held territory. Anglo-Saxon nobles and other settlers were implanted and British churches placed under Anglo-Saxon control. One of the families which moved into Devon in the late seventh century was that of the future missionary Boniface, who may have migrated from southern Hampshire as others of the family were members of two of the religious houses in the Solent area referred to above.[130] In the families of Boniface and his kinsmen Willibald and Wynnebald some of the male and female members went into the church, but others did not and are depicted as locally based nobles.

It is surely inconceivable that religious communities – even those with the greatest monastic pretensions – would not have been concerned with providing pastoral care for lay populations that were dependent upon them. One explanation for the prevalence of double houses, as opposed to foundations that were simply nunneries, in Anglo-Saxon England is that the monks or clerics were intended to minister to the pastoral needs of dependent lay populations as well as those of the nuns.[131] Even Wearmouth and Jarrow seem to have had extensive *parochiae*, dependent parishes that were not necessarily coeval with lands they actually owned, and there is evidence to suggest that Bede sometimes expected to preach to congregations that included lay people as well as his fellow monks.[132] Bede, following Gregory the Great, believed that monks, especially those who were also priests, had a pastoral responsibility that went beyond their own communities, even if his austere views on the desirability of the extension of celibate and ascetic behaviour to the laity may not have won him a ready audience in the lay world. Preachers from other communities may well have adopted a more accessible approach. Although the story is probably apocryphal, the tradition of Aldhelm singing songs in the vernacular on the bridge into Malmesbury to attract the local population may bring us closer to some of these alternative strategies.[133] By the eighth century the Creed and the Lord's Prayer had been translated into Old English, thus enabling ordinary people to participate in worship in their own language, though the translations also seem to have been envisaged as benefitting priests and monks with little Latin.[134]

However, even if all religious communities were aware of their responsibilities, it would appear that there could be gaps in the system. Bede argued that this was the case in his *Letter to Ecgbert* and wrote of isolated communities that barely saw a priest from one year to the next. He illustrated this point of view in his *Life* of Cuthbert in a story in which local people declined to help monks who had got into difficulties because 'they have robbed men of the old ways of worship, and how the new worship is to be conducted, no one knows'.[135] Religious communities were probably not evenly distributed throughout the whole countryside. There were areas such as southern Hampshire, parts of the west midlands and eastern Yorkshire where they seem to have been relatively thick on the ground,[136] but others such as county Durham and parts of the east midlands where provision seems to have been much thinner and less regular.[137] Surviving records of the synods of the eighth century show that bishops were aware of such problems and were seeking to supervise the activities of all the priests in their dioceses wherever they might be based.[138] The proceedings support Bede's view that the way of life in some religious communities was falling short of acceptable standards and that some places seemed unable to cater adequately for their own pastoral needs, let alone those of a dependent population. The situation may have got worse rather than better as the ninth century approached, for many communities seem to have disappeared or had their activities severely truncated as their lands were reclaimed by kings or absorbed into the other family lands of the nobility, even before Viking depredations may have affected parts of England.[139] However, buoyed up by a resurgence in the church in Carolingian Francia, a spirited rearguard action was fought by the bishops who sought to annex failing religious communities on the grounds that their lands had been granted in perpetuity for ecclesiastical purposes, though there seem to have been considerable regional variations in how successful such arguments were. The bishop of Worcester seems to have been particularly successful in hoovering up communities associated with the former royal house of the Hwicce.[140] Generally throughout England there was much work of repair and extension to be done to the system of pastoral provision in the tenth century.

It is only from Anglo-Saxon England that such detailed contemporary evidence survives, but it can provide some general pointers through which to consider the situation in other parts of Britain. Bede believed that the more remote, upland areas of Northumbria were particularly neglected by the pastoral provisions in place by the 730s,[141] and one would imagine that this was equally a problem in the highland regions of Pictish territory. In Pictland the known religious communities, place-names with an early ecclesiastical element and sculptured stones cluster in the most fertile, and presumably most highly populated areas, on the eastern coast and adjacent river valleys.[142] Adomnán depicts Columba encountering a very poor family in the vicinity of Lochaber who seem to have lived by begging and hunter-gathering, and who benefited considerably from Columba's gift of a sharpened stake for hunting (and presumably would have received some religious instruction as well, though that was not the point of Adomnán's story).[143] It is possible that their descendants would have encountered other religious from Iona for they evidently lived near a routeway from Iona to its Pictish dependencies. But one wonders how often other remote areas of Pictland, especially in the outer Hebrides and the north-west mainland where very little evidence indicative of early medieval Christianity has been found, were visited by a priest, let alone a bishop. The inner Hebrides and adjoining west coast areas in or close to Dál Riata seem to have been relatively well provided for by offshoots of communities from Ireland that were probably not as exclusively eremetical as later traditions might suggest.[144]

One would expect the British areas to be most fully covered by a system of pastoral care as Christianity had been established in the more Romanised parts from the fourth century at least. In spite of a shortage of evidence from the seventh and eighth centuries, there is evidence to support such a supposition. Gildas implies an ordered church in his day and wrote of bishops, priests and deacons; the first two categories are also commemorated on inscribed stones of the fifth to seventh centuries from Dumnonia, the north-west of Wales and the Whithorn area.[145] The Llandaf charters suggest a concentration of some 60 local churches in a relatively small area of south-east Wales (Gwent and Ergyng) by the eleventh century, some of which may have been established in the seventh and eighth centuries.[146] There is an instructive parallel from Cornwall that seems to have had an extensive network of local churches dedicated to local saints before the Anglo-Saxon takeover of the province in the late ninth and tenth centuries.[147] Many of these sites bear the distinctive name-element *lann* indicating a churchtown, a settlement based around a church, that is also common in Wales.[148] The Cornish *lannion* are typically in isolated positions, away from established centres of population and administration, rather than at their centre as was to occur in England in the tenth and eleventh centuries. One explanation may be that some at least developed on the sites of earlier cemeteries (indicated, for instance, by the presence of inscribed stones) for which a marginal situation might have been preferred that then became normative,[149] though it may also have been that those donating the land for founding the churches might have thought it prudent not to surrender the best agricultural areas for this purpose. Cornwall and parts of Wales may have been unusual in Britain for this early provision of local churches, though there are parallels from Brittany and Ireland.[150]

In other parts of Britain, including parts of Anglo-Saxon England and Pictland, open-air sites may have continued to be used for ecclesiastical gatherings as they had been in the initial stages of conversion. Such usage, of course, would have conformed with the expectations of the population of what constituted a sacred site, and, indeed, some of these earlier religious sites may have continued to be utilised for Christian worship, especially if they incorporated running water that might be used for baptism or were where people habitually met for local assemblies.[151] There were ways in which such sites could be Christianised or in which alternative foci could be marked out that need not have involved the construction of a church. St Samson reputedly Christianised a standing-stone in Cornwall where people had habitually gathered for pagan worship by carving a cross upon it (though he insisted upon the destruction of an 'idol').[152] Hugeburh, one of the Anglo-Saxon missionaries to Germany who seems to have been associated originally with a religious community at Bishop's Waltham in Hampshire, recorded that it was the custom for landowners 'to have a cross ... erected on some prominent spot for the convenience of those who wish to pray daily before it'.[153] A lack of local churches need not have equated with a lack of interest in providing pastoral care for local populations, or in a lack of commitment to the new religion from ordinary people. These are issues that will be explored further in the next chapter.

Ecclesiastical culture

The adoption of Christianity meant that the Irish, Picts and Anglo-Saxons needed to acquire Latin and other facets of late Roman learning if their churches were to function correctly and effectively. As we have seen, these peoples had already adopted aspects of late Roman culture before their conversion and the link that Christianity provided with the authority of the late Roman world and its successors was part of its attraction.[154] The Irish and Anglo-Saxons already had specialised alphabets, ogham and runes, that were derived ultimately from Latin scripts and in which simple inscriptions could be made.[155] Development of the Pictish symbol system may also have been stimulated by a similar desire for emulation of a written tradition. The British were, of course, in rather a different position as under Roman rule Latin must have been widely spoken in the more Romanised, lowland areas, and, as in other parts of the Roman world, a secular educational system had existed to equip men for Roman public life. After the severing of the links with Rome, written sources of the fifth and sixth centuries show that, in parts of western Britain at least, the basic three-tier structure of Roman education continued, and thus provides some of the most significant literary evidence for continuation of aspects of Roman culture in the sub-Roman world.[156] Education began in child-hood with basic instruction in Latin from a teacher, from whom one passed to a grammarian to study the best Latin authors. The education of Patrick who was captured by pirates at the age of 16 probably ended at this point, but his writings show that he was able to use language very effectively to manipulate his audience (one of the basic aims of the Roman system of education and one which should be kept in mind when approaching early medieval texts as well). The highest level was instruction in rhetoric and is well illustrated by the style of Gildas. He reveals that Maelgwn of Gwynedd seems also to have been instructed in rhetoric by a notable teacher,[157] a testimony to high standards of education still available in Britain in the sixth century not only for churchmen but apparently for some laymen as well, even in less Romanised areas. Education was increasingly adapted to Christian usage through using Christian rather than pagan writers as the medium for teaching, though moral writers who were also major stylists, such as Virgil, continued to be known, especially through their inclusion in popular grammars and other compendia. Unfortunately, few British Latin writings are known from the seventh and eighth centuries, but the ninth-century *Historia Brittonum* and the work of the notable Welsh scholar Asser from St David's, who was patronised by King Alfred and wrote a biography of the king, suggest the maintenance of high standards within some Welsh religious communities.[158]

Irish, Anglo-Saxons and Picts had to learn Latin as a second language. The Irish and the Anglo-Saxons became so proficient in its instruction and in conveying other basics of learning that they were in demand in Francia in the reign of Charlemagne for their educational skills.[159] By the middle of the seventh century Irish schools were attracting not only students from all over Anglo-Saxon England, such as Ecgbert from Northumbria and Aldhelm's student Wihtfrith from Wessex, but also Franks such as Agilbert who became bishop of Wessex.[160] The generosity of the Irish towards visiting scholars was one of the aspects that endeared them to Bede. However, with the arrival of Archbishop Theodore from Syria and Abbot Hadrian from North Africa in 679 Canterbury acquired two teachers who could impart the best of contemporary learning.[161] They too attracted scholars from all over England as well as from Ireland. Aldhelm, who had studied previously with Irish scholars, wrote of the superiority of the instruction provided by Theodore and Hadrian, and lists an impressive range of subjects he studied in addition to theological interpretation including metrical verse, ecclesiastical computation, astronomy and Roman law.[162] When those who studied at Canterbury returned home they were able to spread the benefits of what they had learnt more widely. John of Beverley recalled for the benefit of the nuns of Watton the advice he had received from Theodore on the best times to bleed the body for medicinal purposes,[163] and Abbot Aldhelm of Malmesbury established traditions for Latin composition in Wessex that were to remain standard for several generations.[164]

Exegesis, the interpretation of the Bible, was the high point and chief purpose of early medieval scholarship for only through such analysis could one reach a full understanding of God and his relationship to man. At the end of the *Ecclesiastical History* Bede provides a list of all the works he had written and pride of place goes to 20 or so works of biblical commentary.[165] No other insular scholar can match the range of Bede's corpus, but before he wrote a substantial body of scriptural commentaries had already been produced in Ireland, reflected for instance in the scholarship of Adomnán, and some of this was known to Bede. The basis for all insular commentaries was the interpretative works of the Fathers of the Church, men such as Augustine, Jerome, Gregory the Great and Isidore of Seville. The writings of the greatest scholars, such as Bede and Adomnán, show that they had access to the major authors in their monastic libraries, and such works were probably among the books that Benedict Biscop purchased in Italy for Wearmouth and Jarrow. The works of Aldhelm and Bede suggest that they each had access to at least 200 texts by classical and patristic authors.[166] Any text of the Bible could be read at a number of different levels. One stage was its literal interpretation, and one reason that Theodore and Hadrian were regarded so highly in the insular world was because they brought not only an extensive knowledge of the Greek Fathers and of a range of scientific disciplines which enabled a fuller interpretation of the text, but also because Theodore in particular could write from personal experience of the biblical lands.[167] For the same reason Adomnán recorded the personal experiences of visiting the east of a Frankish bishop who visited Iona,[168] and some Anglo-Saxons travelled to the Holy Land, including Willibald of Bishop's Waltham (Hants) whose experiences were recorded by his kinswoman Hugeburh.[169] But equally important in biblical commentary were the levels of allegorical interpretation that brought out the typological links between Old and New Testaments and their moral and salvific import. Adomnán showed his mastery of the different levels of interpretation in his portrait of Columba where the saint's own life can be read in a similar multi-faceted way.[170]

These different levels of interpretation were portrayed visually in insular decorated manuscripts and sculpture. The great Anglo-Saxon crosses of Ruthwell and Bewcastle contain narrative scenes that would mean different things to different audiences. At the simplest level for the local lay inhabitants was a visual reminder of some of the key biblical events for any Christian, such as the Annunciation and the Crucifixion. But for the religious community, that it can be presumed was located at Ruthwell, the sequence of scenes could take on added layers of interpretation when the different texts on which they were based were brought to mind.[171] A further layer was provided by extracts inscribed in runes from an Old English poem, *The Dream of the Rood*, in which the cross on which Christ died is made to speak of its experiences.[172] The use of Old English and runes in an area on the northern shores of the Solway Firth that was incorporated into Northumbria in the seventh century, but whose indigenous inhabitants were British, might seem to be deliberately excluding even literate British from this final level of interpretation. A synthesis of the visual and textual messages of the Ruthwell Cross reminds those who have opted for the religious life of the centrality of the eucharist, in which they shared daily in the blood and body of Christ and re-enacted his sufferings on the cross, for the salvation of themselves and of mankind.

Consideration of the iconography of sculpture enables the Picts to be brought into the discussion of intellectual life in the insular religious communities. The lack of surviving textual evidence from Pictland has naturally raised questions about the degree of literacy and scholarship that might have been encountered in their religious communities,[173] though the lengthy letter from Abbot Ceolfrith of Jarrow to King Nechtan demonstrates his confidence that the king had scholars who could read Latin without difficulty and follow complex arguments about the computation of Easter.[174] The sculptures provide evidence of a lost scholarly culture comparable with that of other areas of the insular world. A fragment of an inscription from Tarbat is in a type of display script used in some insular manuscripts and argues for the existence there of a scriptorium as well as a school of sculptors producing an impressive range of interrelated works in surrounding areas of this part of north-east Scotland.[175] Two cross-slabs from this group, from St Vigean's and Nigg, have representations, though with different iconography, of one of the non-biblical scenes that also featured on the Ruthwell Cross in which, as described in the Latin *Life* of St Paul the Hermit, he and a fellow hermit shared a meal of bread that had been miraculously provided by a raven.[176] The scene symbolised in its desert setting the monastic way of life and in the breaking of the bread the celebration of the eucharist. As on the Ruthwell Cross other carvings on the Pictish slabs provide additional commentary, including a highly original scene on the St Vigean's slab in which a sinister figure with a knife licks blood from an ox, perhaps a reference to Psalm 68, verse 31 in which the prayers of the faithful are said to be more pleasing to God than the traditional sacrifice of an ox – the latter may have been a feature of the pre-Christian practices of the Picts as well as earlier Jewish practice. Sculpture from Tarbat suggests that the community had close links with Iona, but that by the eighth century there were also direct contacts with Northumbria, possibly with the very masons which Ceolfrith agreed to dispatch to King Nechtan.[177] The sculpture illustrates the participation of the Picts in the complexities of scriptural exegesis that was such a significant feature of the learning of early medieval Britain and Ireland, and how the Pictish church was energised by contact with different centres within the insular world. Pictish art also contributed to the development of insular art, and the animal symbols of some of the evangelists in the Books of Durrow and Echternach, for instance, seem to derive from the traditions of animal depiction in Pictish sculpture.[178]

From the letters of Aldhelm one receives an impression of someone full of enthusiasm for the new world of learning opened up by the adoption of Christianity, and that had enabled a man whose parents had probably been raised as pagans to achieve mastery of the Latin language and theological teachings. Insular authors also seem to have delighted in forms of mental gymnastics. Several Anglo-Saxon authors, including Aldhelm, produced Latin riddles or *enigmata* that may have been in part classroom exercises based on classical models, but at their best in the work of Aldhelm are closely observed descriptions of the world in which they lived.[179] It may not be too fanciful to suggest that the delight in hidden meanings, whether in riddles or exegesis, represents some continuation from pre-Christian modes of thought which manifested itself in the deliberate ambiguity of Anglo-Saxon animal art that was itself adapted to Christian use in decoration of insular gospel books such as the Lindisfarne Gospels.[180] The complex numerology of the so-called 'biblical style' of Latin prose that has been studied among British writers in particular may have continued in a different medium the love of geometric construction which lay behind the abstract art that was part of the Celtic contribution to the insular art style and which is also displayed to such good effect in the Lindisfarne Gospels. [181]

Scholars in Irish and Anglo-Saxon communities might also write on sacred subjects in the vernacular; Bede was working on a translation of St John's Gospel into Old English at the time of his death and some of the earliest Gaelic poetry on Christian themes seems to have been composed on Iona.[182] But there is less certain evidence for the early appearance of written Brittonic languages though debate still rages over the date of the composition of *The Gododdin*.[183] The differences in scholarly use of the vernacular may reflect the status of the languages in secular society.[184] In this respect Old English and Irish were status languages used for conducting business at the royal courts, and in the case of the Irish also used by the learned classes into which Christian priests and scholars were assimilated. In British areas Latin may have continued in use much longer as the language for official business though this might be less likely to have been the case in the more northerly areas where *The Gododdin*, if it is of early date, is likely to have been composed. The appearance of Pictish symbols alongside Christian ones and biblically inspired scenes could suggest that the Picts are more likely to have followed the Irish and Anglo-Saxons in promoting the vernacular as a written language, even if sadly no Pictish texts of any substance survive.

But while we can identify centres of great scholarship such as Iona and Wearmouth–Jarrow, how far can they be used as an indication of standards at the greater number of lesser communities from which no written records survive? Certain basic standards of literacy and learning would be essential for any religious house to function effectively even though many essential texts would have been learnt by rote. One reason for so many citations from the Psalms in insular writings or allusions to them in sculpture was because the Psalms were a major part of the church services held at regular intervals during the day in religious communities and were learnt by heart; the young Wilfrid after entering Lindisfarne 'learned the whole Psalter by heart and several books'.[185] In theory this initial learning of oral transmission would be followed by instruction in reading and writing, though this may not have been achieved by all clerics. That many communities were highly literate is suggested by sources such as the correspondence between Boniface and other Anglo-Saxons who worked abroad with members of religious communities within England.[186] Although few of the communities are identifiable, it is apparent that a considerable number were involved in which there were religious men and women fluent in written Latin. Some of these communities would almost certainly have been the type of 'family monastery' of which Bede disapproved. Not all had the low standards of clerical culture that he implies, though his concerns are echoed in the Council of *Clofesho* of 747 where it is envisaged that some priests could be ignorant of Latin and unable to explain the meaning of the words they repeated in the services or to be in a position to instruct the laity.[187] In the ninth century, King Alfred famously lamented how learning had decayed so far in his kingdom 'that there were very few men ... who could understand their divine services in English, or even translate a single letter from Latin into English'.[188] Even allowing for some rhetorical exaggeration on Alfred's part, it does appear that there had been a severe decline in ecclesiastical learning from the first half of the eighth century when Boniface had many literate correspondents in Wessex. The emphasis that Alfred was to place on learning in the vernacular rather than in Latin is a sign of the failure of Latin culture to lay down permanent roots in England in spite of its early success, and contrasts with the situation at St David's from which Asser was recruited.

But one must also remember that learning for its own sake was not necessarily conceived as one of the prime purposes of a religious foundation. The procurement of God's favour for current concerns and for salvation in the next world, both for individual members and the wider groups they represented, were major reasons for the huge investment made in supporting religious communities. The original ideal of desert monasticism had been for an ascetic life devoted to the service of God, and the strict traditions associated with St David seem to reflect such early monastic asceticism.[189] His monks had a strictly vegetarian diet and when not involved in religious activity followed a regime of hard physical work in which, for instance, his monks pulled the ploughs themselves with no help from oxen. Such asceticism has often been seen as particularly characteristic of 'Celtic' monasticism. One should, of course, be careful of such crude generalisations – after all Gildas seems to have disapproved of David's holier-than-thou attitudes, which to him smacked of spiritual pride (it was to avoid such inherent dangers in extreme asceticism that St Benedict had promoted a milder regime).[190] One might think that the choice to live on islands in the Irish Sea world, exemplified above all by Iona, in itself demonstrates a robust asceticism, though this may be to misunderstand the desirability of islands as places of habitation in a world where the sea was a major route of communication and the source of many desirable foodstuffs and commodities. However, the difficult crossings to Iona must have helped to control access to the island and so aided the community to keep its distance from the outside world, as well as obliging it to follow a self-sufficient and often arduous regime.

The surviving sources suggest a greater incidence of individuals opting to live as hermits in Irish and British tradition than in that of the Anglo-Saxon (apart from the areas of England influenced by Iona). Individuals searching for a suitable island retreat appear in the pages of Adomnán's *Life of St Columba*, though the fact that they were not always successful in finding them may indicate that Adomnán himself believed that more eremetical forms of life should be organised through a religious community rather than as an independent act.[191] Iona had dependencies on other nearby islands, such as *Hinba* to which Columba withdrew on occasion, perhaps to live a life of greater monastic retreat. That was the tradition Cuthbert followed at Lindisfarne where he would withdraw to the tidal St Cuthbert's Isle for Lent, and he spent his last months in a hermitage on the remote Farne Islands.[192] Some other Anglo-Saxon hermits are known, most notably St Guthlac who began his ecclesiastical career as a cleric in the double house of Repton and subsequently retreated to take up residence in the fens of Crowland,[193] but it does not seem to have been a dominant form of religious life among them, at least as reflected in surviving written sources.

Lay culture in the religious communities

An examination of the ecclesiastical culture of the religious communities of early medieval Britain will only reveal part of their characteristics, for it is apparent that the line between secular and religious life was far from being clear-cut or impermeable and that religious communities also shared to a greater or lesser extent in the culture and mores of the lay world. There were individuals such as Bede who entered monasteries as oblates, that is as children, and so had the greatest opportunity to become immersed in ecclesiastical culture, as Bede's career triumphantly showed. Bede was 7 when his kinsmen placed him in the monastery of Wearmouth; Ælfflaed of Whitby was even younger, having been vowed as an infant to the religious life by her father Oswiu in thanks for his victory over King Penda of Mercia at the battle of the River Winwaed in 655.[194] However, the experiences of Bede and Ælfflaed were far from being the norm, and people might take vows as monks, nuns or clerics at any age and as a second career. Wilfrid entered Lindisfarne in his early teens, at an age when he might otherwise have joined the king's comitatus, as the attendant of a nobleman called Cudda who was retiring from the active life of a lay nobleman because of a paralytic infirmity.[195] Women, especially members of royal houses, who were widowed or wished to separate from their husbands frequently retired to the many female communities of Anglo-Saxon England, and were such a common feature of them that Aldhelm in his tract *On Virginity* felt the need to stress how formerly married women who had embraced chastity were almost as pleasing to God as those who had remained virgins.[196]

It was therefore possible to find men and women who had held the highest positions in secular society living in some early medieval religious communities, and not all of them were necessarily there because of a genuine religious commitment. Æthelwulf, the author of *De Abbatibus*, a poem written in the early ninth century about the abbots of a Northumbrian community, possibly to be identified as Bywell, reveals that the house was founded by a nobleman who had been forced to give up his position as ealdorman and withdraw from secular life by King Osred (705/6–16).[197] We have already seen how retirement to a religious community could be either a temporary or permanent respite for embattled kings and discussed the examples of Maelgwn of Gwynedd, Ceolwulf of Northumbria and Nechtan of the Picts among others.[198] Ireland seems to have developed an early tradition of exile to a religious community as a penitential punishment for kings and other noblemen who had exceeded the acceptable norms of bad behaviour and a number of such individuals appear in Adomnán's *Life of Columba*, though they appear not to have been admitted to the main religious community on Iona, but were instead corralled in a dependency at Mag Luinge on the nearby island of Tiree.

The layman Librán, for instance, was housed temporarily in the guest house of Iona before Columba assigned him to Mag Luinge for seven years' penance, and another religious community on Tiree housed Áed Dub, former king of the Dál nAraide of County Antrim, who had been obliged to live a penitential life as a cleric because he had slain the Uí Néill overlord in 565.[199] Adomnán himself as abbot of Iona had taken in Aldfrith, the son of King Oswiu, prior to his elevation to the kingship of Northumbria in 686.[200] Aldfrith is a rarer example of a prince who had had a clerical education before he succeeded to the throne and had acquired the grade of *sapiens* or learned scholar in Ireland. Entry to the church had presumably been arranged through his mother's family in Ireland, and it appears that it was not until his younger half-brother King Ecgfrith (670-85) had failed to produce any male heirs that he was considered as a possible candidate for the Northumbrian throne.[201]

Other lay people might be more transient visitors. Kings expected to be housed with their entourages at the larger religious communities as they travelled the countryside, and these visits could evidently be extremely onerous and disruptive. King Æthelbald of Mercia is said to have freed the nunnery of Gloucester from the necessity of receiving him for seven years in recompense for the murder of a kinsman.[202] This remission may have been all the more valuable because of Æthelbald's reputation for sleeping with nuns that earned him a letter of censure from Boniface and other missionary bishops safely out of his way in Germania.[203] This may, one hopes, be an extreme example of how the morals of the lay world might invade a religious community (though Æthelbald is not the only Anglo-Saxon king who is said to have violated nuns), but it does seem to have been the case that religious men and women remained part of the kin and social networks into which they were born and so retained obligations to family and monarch that were not invalidated by entry into a religious life. Columba and Benedict Biscop remained the advisers of kings after they became abbots, and Benedict found that so much of his time was taken up with secular affairs that he had to appoint a co-abbot.[204] Columba was himself a prince of one of the leading Uí Néill families and remained involved in their affairs, while apparently being sought out by members of other Irish dynasties and moving easily within the courts of British, Irish and Pictish kings in Scotland.[205] The involvement of religious leaders and many of their communities in secular politics will be examined in greater detail in the next chapter; lesser clerics can be expected to have been no less involved in the lives of their secular kinsmen.

With so many members who had lived an active life in secular careers and who continued to move in the outside world and to receive visitors from it, it is not surprising that many of the pastimes and fashions of the lay world were also to be found in the religious communities. Many of the accusations of inappropriate behaviour in religious communities revolve around two very significant aspects of aristocratic secular life, namely feasting and apparel.[206] Problems of excessive eating and drinking by those who had taken religious vows are recurrent in early medieval penitentials, and the generally mild tariffs assigned to these offences perhaps suggests that they were a common occurrence. The Preface attributed to Gildas, for instance, deals with the problems of monks too drunk to be able to sing the psalms who were merely to be deprived of their supper (which one might think was a wise precaution in any case), and of those who vomited up the host because of previous overindulgence at the dinner table.[207] Finds of large numbers of animal bones from Glastonbury Tor led initially to an assumption that the site must be a lay one, but they have subsequently been reinterpreted as a sign of the good living to be found in some British religious communities.[208] The Penitential of Theodore begins with chapters on the drunkenness of clergy of all degrees from a bishop downwards, but accepted that a certain amount of indulgence was only to be expected at major feast days.[209] Other Anglo-Saxon ecclesiastical legislation was concerned with the type of entertainments that might accompany feasts. The synod of *Clofesho* of 746/7 condemned the retention of poets, harpists, musicians and jesters in religious communities,[210] and in a famous letter Alcuin suggested that too many secular entertainments might be one of the reasons why God had allowed Viking attacks on Anglo-Saxon religious communities:[211]

Let the word of God be read at the priestly repast. There should the reader be heard, not the harpist; the sermons of the Fathers, not the songs of pagans. What has Ingeld to do with Christ? The House is narrow: it cannot hold both.

Another criticism from the synod of *Clofesho* was that some clerics were celebrating religious festivals inappropriately by staging horse races, which recalls a vignette provided by Bede of the young men of the household of Bishop John of Beverley amusing themselves by racing their horses.[212] Aldhelm warned his pupil Æthilwald against too much aimless riding about, as well as too many drinking parties and banquets, and Alcuin criticised clerics who went fox-hunting.[213]

The internal critics of the Anglo-Saxon church were particularly exercised by the lavish dress of male and female religious that was evidently in many cases following secular fashions and this was specifically condemned at the synod of *Clofesho* of 747.[214] The luxuriance of clerical dress was a sign, Boniface warned Archbishop Cuthbert in 747, that the anti-Christ was come among them, and his reference to garments embroidered with dragons may indicate the wearing of Byzantine silken robes. [215] Anglo-Saxon female religious were castigated by Bede and Aldhelm for their fashionable clothes and hairstyles; the unsatisfactory behaviour of the nuns of Coldingham that brought down the wrath of God in the form of fire included the weaving of elaborate clothes 'with which to adorn themselves as if they were brides'.[216] We can get some idea of the clothes they might have worn from the wardrobe that the Frankish queen Balthild, who was of Anglo-Saxon birth, left at the nunnery of Chelles where she spent her last days.[217] It included silk robes and a linen 'chemise' embroidered with a representation of jewelled collars in the Byzantine fashion. Excavations at the nunneries of Barking and Whitby have revealed a range of decorated dress and hair accessories as well as toilet instruments suggesting that dress and appearance in secular styles were of great importance to female religious as the more critical commentators maintained.[218] What these examples show is that many aspects of the aristocratic secular world were retained in the Anglo-Saxon religious communities, leading James Campbell to characterise monasteries such as Lindisfarne as 'a special kind of nobleman's club'.[219] Aldhelm, who was one of those concerned by too much retention of lay mores, nevertheless felt it appropriate to recommend to the clergy of Bishop Wilfrid that they should follow him into exile like members of a comitatus accompanying an exiled lord.[220] This may have been a particularly barbed comment as Wilfrid, although described as personally ascetic, travelled with large retinues of laymen as well as religious and where appropriate entertained on a lavish scale.

Certain Irish sources give anything but a positive connotation to the mores of the warband, and instead portrayed it as the last refuge of pagan practices that were perhaps intended to help bind together a sworn brotherhood.[221] It would appear that in Ireland churchmen distanced themselves more completely from lay society and probably distinguished themselves to a greater extent through forms of dress and their general manner of life. The creation of such a gulf in Ireland was aided by the existence of learned orders in pre-Christian Irish society, into which the Christian ecclesiastical hierarchy was assimilated, and which already possessed traditions that separated them from the ordinary lay world.[222] Although major churches were dominated in Ireland, as in Anglo-Saxon England, by kinsmen from royal houses there was a more noticeable tendency, aided by the more complex segmentation of Irish royal families, for a whole kin-group to become the ecclesiastical arm of a particular royal lineage. Something similar may have occurred in British areas where a system akin to the learned orders of Ireland may have continued through the Roman occupation, especially in the less Romanised areas. It would appear that St David's was dominated by a close-knit group of kinsman of whom Asser was one, and further examples from Wales of prominent clerical families associated with particular religious communities are known from later sources.[223] Asser's observation that Anglo-Saxon churchmen had abandoned recognisable monastic forms of living for more luxurious lifestyles suggests a contrast with the way of life he was familiar with at St David's where the asceticism favoured by David himself seems to have left a lasting legacy, though, as Asser also observed, the difference was in part caused by the greater wealth of Anglo-Saxon England.[224] Something of the contrast between Anglo-Saxon and Celtic areas emerges from Bede's account of the impact of Aidan at the Northumbrian court, perhaps inspired by the impression made on him as a teenager when Adomnán of Iona visited Abbot Ceolfrith at Jarrow.[225] Iona would have brought the same standards to its daughter houses in Pictland, but we are less able to assess the dominant cultural forms in the Pictish religious communities, though one might be inclined to think from the loving depictions of hunting scenes on Pictish carvings, in which pictorial exemplars have seemingly been customised to depict Pictish practices, that at least some of the craftsmen employed by religious communities were familiar, like as were their Anglo-Saxon counterparts, with such lay pastimes.[226]

One part of lay culture that did become embedded throughout the religious communities of Britain was the abstract curvilinear and animal art which made such an important contribution to insular illuminated manuscripts and sculpture. As we have seen, these different facets of insular decoration first seem to have been brought together as a result of interaction between the royal courts as exemplified by finds from sites such as Sutton Hoo and Dunadd.[227] It evidently seemed entirely appropriate in insular society that decorative forms which had been used to honour earthly kings should also honour the King of Heaven. By assimilating abstract insular art with the late antique traditions of illustrated Bibles, scribes were able to give it a new significance as exemplified above all by the spectacular decorated initials and carpet pages of the Lindisfarne Gospels.[228] The raptors, boars and dragons that dominated aristocratic animal art are replaced in the Lindisfarne Gospels by more peaceable birds, some of which seem to be modelled on the ducks and cormorants that would have been found in abundance around Lindisfarne itself. Their intertwined bodies help to reveal hidden crosses within the carpet pages and may have had added numerological significance for the initiated. The conventions of heroic verse were used to original effect in the Old English poem of *The Dream of the Rood*, a version of which was carved on the Ruthwell Cross (Dumfriesshire) probably in the eighth century.[229] In the poem the Cross is made to describe its own sufferings, as if it were a retainer forced to be the instrument of the death of its lord. It had to commit a shameful act, which would bring opprobrium upon it, in order for its lord to achieve a great triumph. The Cross is represented as wrestling with a dilemma of the type that was at the heart of Old English heroic verse. The influence of lay practices could lead to great, original artistic creations as well as to abuses that concerned some contemporary commentators. As Patrick Wormald has argued, the culture of Anglo-Saxon religious houses in the eighth century provided the milieu from which *Beowulf*, the greatest of all early medieval epic poetry, could emerge.[230]

The cult of saints

One further topic that remains to be explored is that of the cult of saints in early medieval Britain. It will enable us to examine another example of how aspects of contemporary ecclesiastical culture were absorbed by the insular religious communities and to trace regional variations in how the cult of saints manifested itself among the different peoples of Britain. The concept of the holy man or woman who could act as a mediator between heaven and earth, and was able, after his or her death, to move between these two worlds, had proved particularly suited to the needs of the aristocracies of the late Roman empire as they struggled to maintain their positions and that of the Christian church in the post-Roman world.[231] Such cults also proved suited to the needs of the conversion period of Britain and were adapted to suit the political and social situations that characterised the island at that time.

The cult of saints among the British and the Scottish Dál Riata

The earliest saints were the martyrs who had died for their faith before the Edict of Toleration in 311. Martyrs seem to have been the only type of saint known to Gildas and he refers to 'St Alban of Verulamium, Aaron and Julius, citizens of Caerleon, and the others of both sexes'.[232] St Alban was apparently Britain's proto-martyr (though there are problems in establishing the exact date of his death) and his cult seems to have been active when Bishop Germanus of Auxerre visited his shrine in 429.[233] In authenticating or perhaps relaunching Alban's cult at a time of heresy and Saxon attack, Germanus deposited other relics including some apostolic ones presumably imported from Rome. These latter were likely to have been secondary or contact relics, that is objects which had been in contact with the tombs of the saints and so had absorbed the imprint of their holiness; strips of cloth might be used in this way, but some secondary relics might be more exotic, such as the filings from the chains of St Peter that were sent by Pope Honorius to Queen Eanflaed of Northumbria in a golden cross.[234] Such devices enabled a widespread circulation of relics from Rome, and may also have been utilised in the conversion of Ireland and less Romanised parts of Britain, as they were to be in the conversion of the Anglo-Saxons in the seventh century. An early inscribed stone from Whithorn, for instance, proclaims it as the *locus* of the apostle Peter and suggests the value placed on these connections with Rome as Christianity was spread within the British kingdoms; such links were to become somewhat embroidered and elaborated in the developing cult of St Ninian.[235]

By the end of the sixth century, communities in Britain and Ireland had begun to follow continental trends in promoting local confessors as saints, that is those whose lives were deemed sufficiently holy could be said to have imitated Christ without undergoing his martyrdom.[236] Religious leaders and founders of communities were particularly likely to be honoured as saints, and cults provided an important means for their successors to consolidate their work and to establish local centres of religious power. This was, of course, 'the age of the saints' in Britain and while we can be reasonably certain that the likes of David, Cadog, Teilo, Illtud, Winniau and Kentigern were the founders of major communities in which they were honoured as saints, we know, as has been remarked before, very little about them. What has been demonstrated by recent research is that the widespread distribution of dedications to these individuals does not reflect the sphere of their contemporary activities, but the much later diffusion of cults from the tenth century onwards.[237] This is well illustrated by the cult of Uinniau/Ninian whose earliest dedications are in his true form as Uinniau, but who was culted on a much wider scale in his later guise at Ninian in the later Middle Ages when he became one of Scotland's national saints (after the incorporation of Galloway) and Whithorn became a major pilgrimage site patronised by the kings of Scotland.[238]

It is apparent from church dedications and place-names that in the British regions there were many extremely localised saints' cults about which little reliable information has been recorded. That many, perhaps the majority of these, were created in the early Middle Ages is suggested by the example of Cornwall where more local saints' names exist as prominent features of local toponomy and church dedication than anywhere else in the country. Cornwall was incorporated into Wessex in the ninth and tenth centuries, and it seems likely that many of the native saints' cults had been established before this conquest, a conclusion that is supported by written records of the tenth century that confirm the existence of a number of the dedications by that date.[239] It would appear to have become an established custom in early medieval Cornwall that places were named from and churches dedicated to individuals who, one can presume, were their founders, either as patrons or first incumbents, and that at some point there was an ascription of sanctity to these people.[240] Although the process may have begun in the sixth and seventh centuries, it is likely that the pattern of naming was spread over many centuries, a conclusion that is supported by comparison with neighbouring Devon, the eastern parts of which came into West Saxon hands in the seventh century. Relatively few local British saints are recorded from Devon,[241] and while this is likely to be evidence of the thoroughness of Anglo-Saxon colonisation, seen also in the ubiquity of Old English place-names, it could also be an indication that the creation of local saints in the southwest was a continuing process throughout the eighth and ninth centuries and beyond. There are signs of similar patterns in Wales where very localised dedications and place-names with the name of a saint and the element, *llan* 'church settlement' are also found, though with greater disruption from later developments and the spread of dedications to the major monastic saints. In these localised saints' cults of the west the saints' bodies generally seem to have remained in the graves in which they were originally buried, and there is less evidence for the continental trend, from the seventh century onwards, for the elevation and translation of the bodies to more accessible shrines that became a normal feature of Anglo-

Saxon cults.[242] The British seem to have adhered to the preference for not disturbing dead saints that was prevalent in the western church in the period in which they were converted to Christianity. This conservatism and respect for the customs of their founding fathers was, as we have seen, a characteristic of the British church by the seventh century. The desire not to disturb or divide the body was compensated for by an emphasis on secondary relics, especially portable objects that had belonged to the saints themselves such as books, staffs and bells.[243]

Such conservative attitudes were also retained in some of the Irish churches, and are exemplified above all by Iona. There is surprisingly little written about Columba's burial or tomb in Adomnán's *Life*,[244] and possibly this was a deliberate policy on the part of the community who may not have wanted the island to have become a centre of pilgrimage. Instead there was an emphasis on relics associated with the saint that could be more readily utilised in a variety of situations both on Iona itself and further afield. Adomnán describes how at a time of drought Columba's tunic and books that he had written were carried in procession around the fields of the island with predictably successful results.[245] The precedent for the procession seems to have come from the account of Italian saints written by Pope Gregory the Great in his *Dialogues*. It was part of Adomnán's purpose in writing to demonstrate that Columba exemplified the virtues and behaviour of continental saints, but we presumably also have here an instructive example of how ritual surrounding saints might be developed through an accretion of traditions. Relics of Columba were, of course, to continue to have major ritual roles to play in medieval Scotland when the *Cathach* (psaltar), *Breccbennach* (Monymusk reliquary) and *Cathbuaid* (crozier) were carried by armies hoping for victory through the intervention of the saint. The cult of Columba drew upon the Irish tradition of the *érlam* or patron saint that may have had its ultimate origins in older ideas of protective deities or ancestors of different kindreds.[246] Columba could be evoked as protector not only of his community at Iona, who were buried with him in the monastic churchyard, but of those of his daughter houses who were linked to him by confraternity of prayer and other members of his kindred. Even sinful laymen might be saved by evoking Columba's name, as is claimed in Adomnán's account of brigands who sang Gaelic songs in praise of Columba and escaped the determined attempts of their enemies to kill them.[247] Columba was not, of course, the only Irish saint to have lived and died in Scotland and to be culted there, and many other abbots and leading figures from Iona were regarded as saints including Adomnán himself. Dedications are once again a treacherous source to use as they might have been given at various points in the history of the medieval Scottish church and widespread dedications to Irish saints may reflect a broader Gaelicisation after the creation of the kingdom of Alba. But the existence of some cults is confirmed by early sources, and some dedications or place-names incorporating a saint's name such as that to St Blane at Kingarth on Bute, the site of the religious house and bishopric with which he was associated, undoubtedly do preserve genuine traditions. The martyrdom of St Donnán of Eigg, for instance, is recorded in the Irish annals, and four other saints from Eigg are known from early Irish sources.[248] The traditional founder of the monastery on Lismore, St Molaug from Bangor, was remembered through the survival of his crozier, the *Bachall Mór*, that remains in the possession of its hereditary keepers on the island.[249] The cult of Columba was one of several among the Dál Riata in the seventh and eighth centuries for it seems likely that all the major religious communities had their own patron saints who were their founders or subsequent notable men from the foundations.

Anglo-Saxon saints

A detailed review of a wide variety of evidence has enabled John Blair to produce a substantial list of Anglo-Saxon saints, the majority of whom seem to date from the pre-Viking period, enabling him to raise the possibility that there had once been 'a saint for every minster'.[250] The tendency that we have already seen in Celtic areas where the founders or first leaders of communities came to be regarded as saints seems to have been the practice in Anglo-Saxon England as well. The developments of the cults of Cuthbert and Wilfrid can be traced in some detail through their surviving Lives that were written not long after their deaths by people who had known them.[251] Consideration of the contexts in which they were written in the somewhat turbulent church politics in the aftermath of the synod of Whitby suggests the need of the communities associated with the two saints to actively promote their founders in order to protect their positions.[252] However, there are also some features of the early Anglo-Saxon cults that differ from those of other areas of Britain. Local Anglo-Saxon saints very rarely appear in place-names or early church dedications for the normal practice of the Anglo-Saxons was to dedicate their churches to universal saints, something that reflects the desire to stress their orthodoxy and patronage from Rome which were dominant features of the Anglo-Saxon reception of Christianity from an early stage.[253]

Perhaps even more striking is the prevalence of female and royal saints compared to other areas of Britain. These two characteristics are, of course, related because the majority of saints from the female-led communities were of royal birth. But the Anglo-Saxons were also unusual in having a category of saints consisting of kings or princes who had died violent deaths. The prototype of this type of royal saint was King Oswald of Northumbria who died in battle against the pagan Penda of Mercia in 642.[254] Although Bede takes some pains to stress that Oswald was not a martyr, the evidence he records about the early stages of the cult suggests that Oswald's violent death in battle was a significant aspect, for the site of his death, and particularly the earth on which blood had been spilt, became early centres of devotion. What is particularly notable is the role that lay members of the royal house played in the promotion of the cult. It was Oswald's brother Oswiu who launched the cult in Bernicia itself when he retrieved his brother's head and hands from somewhere in Mercia where Penda had displayed them on stakes (perhaps in some form of pagan offering). Oswiu sent the head to his episcopal centre at Lindisfarne and the arms to his royal chapel at Bamburgh. The body itself was retrieved from the battlefield at *Maserfelth*, whose site was either in Lindsey (Lincs) or at Oswestry (Salop), by Oswiu's daughter Osthryth who placed it in the monastery of Bardney (Lincs) that had been founded by herself and her husband King Æthelred of Mercia (son of Penda) and where subsequently both of them were also to be promoted as saints. At about the same time Osthryth's sister Ælfflaed, who was abbess of Whitby, arranged the translation of the body of their grandfather King Edwin, who had been slain by Penda in 633, to her monastery with the intention of launching his cult, though ultimately this was not to be as successful as that of Oswald.[255]

There are other known cults of kings and princes who were murdered from early Anglo-Saxon England and which were generally nurtured in nunneries or other houses with strong royal connections.[256] Examples include the cults of the seventh-century princes Æthelbert and Æthelred at Thanet (Kent) and King Oswine of Deira at Gilling (Yorks). The contests between different branches of the Mercian royal house at the end of the eighth and first half of the ninth century resulted in the murder of the princely rivals Cynehelm and Wigstan, and the subsequent nurturing of their cults at the nunneries associated with their respective lineages at Winchcombe and Repton. There are a number of ways in which the cults of these male royal saints who had died violent deaths can be interpreted, including as examples of the church acting as mediators in lay society, a topic that will be explored further in the next chapter.[257] But it would also appear that they address something much deeper and older within early medieval societies that can be linked with the earlier interest in the burial places of heroes and the creation of significant royal ancestors.[258] These were not just features of Anglo-Saxon societies, and, indeed, a travelling Briton is shown as playing a significant role in the generation of cult at the place where Oswald had fallen in battle. Violent death was just as likely to be the fate of rulers of other areas of early medieval Britain, but as far as we know the spilling of their blood did not result in a comparable series of saints' cults. The difference must lie with Anglo-Saxon kings having a closer involvement with the organisation of the churches in their kingdoms than was apparently the case in British and Irish areas where there were embedded traditions of learned orders with their own distinct spheres of activity. Oswiu, who had grown up a Christian in Ireland and so could have learnt at first hand how saints' cults operated, seems to have been prepared to take the initiative in launching cult of his brother. After the royal nunneries had been founded, kings had ecclesiastical specialists from their immediate families who could organise saints' cults without any need to involve local bishops or abbots. The independence of action of royal abbesses is indicated very well by Seaxburh, abbess of Ely and former queen of Kent, who arranged the translation of her sister Æthelthryth, her predecessor as abbess and a former queen of Northumbria. The ceremony is described in some detail by Bede and was evidently based closely on similar ceremonies in Francia about which Seaxburh could have learnt from the nunnery at Fâremoutier-en-Brie where a third sister and a half-sister were abbesses and in which her own daughter had been a nun.[259] Adomnán was certainly interested in promoting Columba as a powerful saint who could lend his support to kings, but would have balked at the idea of binding kings more closely to the community by promoting their immediate predecessors as saints.

The *Lives* of Columba, Wilfrid and Cuthbert may have been written in consciousness of major debates within the wider church that might threaten their communities, but their main intended audiences must have been the members of those communities themselves. A substantial part of the saints' activities and miracles in the *Lives* takes place within their monasteries and daughter houses and many inmates are mentioned by name. The commonest type of local cult from early medieval Britain was that shaped by a monastic community and such cults must have played a major role in providing a corporate identity, especially at times of potential stress.[260] From such considerations arise issues about whether those managing saints' cults were concerned to involve ordinary lay people.[261] Although miracles that involve ordinary lay people may be in the minority, they are present in the *Lives*. Columba is portrayed as more concerned than his Anglo-Saxon counterparts to help lesser people solve the problems of daily life. In the Anglo-Saxon *Lives* the peasants tend to be there to serve the saint in various ways, as in the story of the British woman whose child is restored to life by Wilfrid so that it can enter his service, which demonstrates that it is impossible to conceal someone the saint has claimed for himself.[262] However, Cuthbert warned that unless his body was left in a remote place, such as the Farne Islands where he was to die, the community was likely to be bothered 'on account of the influx of fugitives and guilty men of every sort, who will perhaps flee to my body',[263] an early reference to churches as places of sanctuary. It may be, as Catherine Cubitt has argued, that saints' cults operated on different levels, and that the written *Lives* reflect primarily the interests of the monastic audiences for which they were intended while other focuses were developed for ordinary lay people that were more in keeping with their interests and traditional places of worship.[264] Consideration of the sites associated with St Oswald seem to fit with this type of analysis. His bodily relics, conveniently divided by the intervention of Penda, went to the royal chapel at Bamburgh, an episcopal see and a royal monastery. We can suspect that at all of these ordinary lay involvement was limited, if not excluded. But the site of the battlefield was open to all and its soil was used to heal a sick horse and an innkeeper's daughter. There was also popular devotion at another battlefield site associated with Oswald at Heavenfield where he had raised a large wooden cross before the battle that won him the kingdom in 634. Splinters from the cross placed in water were believed to heal sick men and beasts. Such open-air sites were, of course, much more in keeping with the traditional sites of early medieval pre-Christian religion and a wooden cross might inherit some of the sanctity associated with holy trees. No doubt those responsible for pastoral care might help to develop the Christian associations of such sites, as did the priest who went to live at the site where Edwin had first been buried after he died in battle and would have liked to build a *monasterium* there.[265] However, in the account told by Bede of the early popular cult of King Oswald there appears to be an implication that it had arisen spontaneously among local British and Anglo-Saxon inhabitants of the areas where his battles had been fought.

Pictish saints

The Picts too shared in the insular enthusiasm for saints. There must be an expectation that saints with apparently Pictish names are likely to have been established before the demise of the Pictish kingdom. Any discussion of Irish saints who may have worked in Pictland is more complex because the later Gaelicisation of the province is suspected to have led to the introduction of established Irish cults, though the form of many place-names that include names of Ionan saints seems to be early, which is, of course, compatible with other evidence that Ionan daughter houses had been established in Pictland probably from the time of Columba himself.[266] Such Pictish saints as can be identified appear to have been prominent churchmen and monastic founders including Bishop Curetán and Serf/Servanus of Culross (Fife), for both of whom relatively late *Lives* survive that unfortunately seem to contain little reliable historical detail and attempt to give both foreign origins.[267] Other native saints with relatively widespread cults in Pictland include Ethernan, who according to the Annals of Ulster died in 669 and was traditionally believed to have been buried on the Isle of May, which became an important medieval pilgrimage site and where a sequence of early chapels and burials has been excavated.[268] Two saints associated with the monastery of Deer in Buchan (Aberdeenshire), but who were also culted more widely are Drostan and Nathalan/Nechtan.[269] Other apparent Pictish saints are more localised and probably reflect the pattern of local church founders being culted as occurred in other parts of Britain; ongoing research may eventually allow more information to be recovered. In spite of the traditions of churches in Pictland being founded by kings, which seems to recall the prominent role played by Anglo-Saxon kings in church foundation, there is no tradition of saintly Pictish kings or princesses as in Anglo-Saxon England, though one can note that both Drostan and Nechtan are names used in royal lineages. However, with such poor written sources for Pictland any conclusions can only be tentative.

Conclusion

The widespread foundation of religious houses in Britain implies the enthusiastic adoption of Christianity among the elites of the different provinces who provided the lands and personnel for the new communities once the work of foreign missionaries was ended. That contemporary ecclesiastical culture, with its art and learning, was imported into Britain cannot be doubted and these islands produced some of the leading scholars of their day in western Christendom. However, it would be a mistake to think that our most eloquent and accomplished writers were typical of the whole range of ecclesiastical communities. Nor did all live up to the rigorous standards that would have been preferred by contemporary critics such as the Anglo-Saxons Bede and Boniface. Anglo-Saxon churches in particular seem to have followed aspects of contemporary lay culture, and nothing illustrates this better than the current debate about whether certain excavated sites for which no clear documentary evidence exists, such as Flixborough (Lincs), should be interpreted as secular or religious communities.[270] As Bede feared it seems to have been sometimes hard to tell the two apart. The greater wealth of the Anglo-Saxons and the Celtic traditions of a separate learned class may have made the infiltration of lay values more of a feature of the Anglo-Saxon provinces than of other areas of Britain, though wealth and a love of native culture were not necessarily completely incompatible with carrying out expected church functions. Churches were firmly embedded in the landscape of Britain by 800, and if the Anglo-Saxons were better provided with bishops to supervise pastoral care, this was offset in some British areas at least by a greater number of local churches. There is therefore the potential for the church to have touched the lives of both the elites, from whose ranks the leading churchmen would have been recruited, and the peasantry, some of whom would have been tenants or possessions of religious communities. The task remains in the final chapter to explore how far observance of the new religion and its moral precepts can be said to have penetrated the lives of those who remained in the lay world.

Notes

1 Bede, *Letter to Ecgbert*; Bede, *Hist. Eccl.*, III, 5 and 17, IV, 28–9; Bede, *V. Cuthberti*.

2 See Chapter 2, 109–12.

3 C. Thomas, *Christianity in Roman Britain to AD 500* (London, 1981), 191–8.

4 Bede, *Hist. Eccl.*, II, 2; C. Stancliffe, 'The British church and the mission of Augustine', in *St Augustine*, ed. R. Gameson (Stroud, 1999), 107–51.

5 P. Bidwell, *The Legionary Bath-House and Basilica and Forum at Exeter* (Exeter, 1979); S. Bassett, 'Church and diocese in the West Midlands: the transition from British to Anglo-Saxon control', in *Pastoral Care*, 13–40,

where he suggests in addition that Wroxeter, Worcester and Lichfield were the centre of sub-Roman dioceses.

6 Basset, 'Church and diocese'; H.P.R. Finberg, *Lucerna* (London, 1964), 95–115.

7 W. Davies, *Wales in the Early Middle Ages* (Leicester, 1982), 97–8, 142–62 *passim*.

8 L. Olson, *Early Monasteries in Cornwall* (Woodbridge, 1989), 52–6.

9 T. Charles-Edwards, 'The seven bishop-houses of Dyfed', *Bulletin of the Board of Celtic Studies* 24 (1970–2), 247–62.

10 J.R. Davies, 'The Book of Llandaff: a twelfth-century perspective', *Anglo-Norman Studies* 21 (1998), 31–46; and see Introduction, 8–9.

11 Bede, *Hist. Eccl.*, I, 29.

12 N. Brooks, *The Early History of the Church of Canterbury* (Leicester, 1984), 111–28.

13 B.Yorke, 'Joint kingship in Kent c.560 to 785', *Archaeologia Cantiana* 99 (1983), 1–19.

14 Bede, *Hist. Eccl.*, IV, 5.

15 D. Kirby (ed.), *Saint Wilfrid at Hexham* (Newcastle, 1974); A. Thacker, 'Wilfrid', *Oxford Dictionary of National Biography* (Oxford, 2004), 944–50.

16 Bede, *Hist. Eccl.*, V, 23. Selsey was vacant at the time Bede wrote.

17 A second bishopric for the main Mercian province was created at Leicester in 737.

18 The location of the see of Lindsey has not been securely identified; see S. Basset, 'Lincoln and the Anglo-Saxon see of Lindsey', *Anglo-Saxon England* 18 (1989), 1–32, and A. Vince (ed.), *Pre-Viking Lindsey* (Lincoln, 1993).

19 S. Keynes, 'Episcopal lists', in *Blackwell Encyclopaedia*, 172–4.

20 See Chapter 2, 113–14.

21 P. Hill, *Whithorn and St Ninian: The Excavation of a Monastic Town 1984–91* (Stroud, 1997).

22 M. McCarthy, 'Rheged: an early historic kingdom near the Solway', *Proceedings of the Society of Antiquaries of Scotland* 132 (2002), 357–81.

23 A. Macquarrie, 'The career of Saint Kentigern of Glasgow: *vitae, lectiones* and glimpses of fact', *Innes Review* 37 (1986), 3–24; D. Broun, 'Kentigern', *Oxford Dictionary of National Biography* (Oxford, 2004); and see Introduction, 14.

24 S.T. Driscoll, 'Church archaeology in Glasgow and the kingdom of Strathclyde', *Innes Review* 49 (1998), 95–114.

25 A. Ritchie (ed.), *Govan and its Early Medieval Sculpture* (Stroud, 1994).

26 See Chapter 1, 51–4.

27 *AU* sa 659 death of Daniel, bishop of Kingarth; *AU* sa 674 the death of Noah, Bishop Daniel's son; *AU* sa 688 Iolan, bishop of Kingarth died.

28 M. Herbert, *Iona, Kells and Derry: The History and Hagiography of the Monastic Familia of Columba* (Dublin, 1996), 48–62; B. Yorke, 'Adomnán at the court of King Aldfrith', in *Adomnán of Iona: Theologian – Lawmaker – Peacemaker*, ed. R. Aist, T. Clancy, T. O'Loughlin and J. Wooding (Dublin, forthcoming).

29 I am grateful to Alex Woolf for this point.

30 For example, the visit of Bishop Crónán of Munster to Iona in I, 44.

31 A. MacDonald, *Curadán, Boniface and the Early Church of Rosemarkie* (Groom House Museum, 1992).

32 Bede, *Hist. Eccl.*, V, 21, and see Chapter 2, 131–2.

33 MacDonald, *Curadán*.

34 R. Lamb, 'Pictland, Northumbria and the Carolingian empire', in *Conversion and Christianity in the North Sea World*, ed. B. Crawford (St Andrews, 1998), 41–56 (though with a rather differently nuanced interpretation); S. Foster, *Picts, Gaels and Scots* (London, 1996), 90–1.

35 *Councils*, II, 116; G. Donaldson, 'Scottish bishops' sees before the reign of David I', *Proceedings of the Society of Antiquaries of Scotland* 87 (1952–3), 106–17, at 108–9.

36 Bede, *Hist. Eccl.*, III, 4; and see Chapter 2, 128–33.

37 Donaldson, 'Scottish bishops', 108–9; A. Macquarrie, 'Early Christian religious houses in Scotland: foundation and function', in *Pastoral Care*, 110–33 at 115–18 (with differing interpretations of the evidence).

38 Bede, *Hist. Eccl.*, IV, 26.

39 Donaldson, 'Scottish bishops'; Macquarrie, 'Early Christian religious houses', 118–29.

40 *Councils*, III, 581 (Chapter 5); Donaldson, 'Scottish bishops', 116–17; the ruling is said in the first instance to apply to clergy of the *Scotti* (i.e. Irish), but a reference to 'foreign nations' suggests that ecclesiastics of other peoples who might be in contact with the English were also considered problematical.

41 P. Brown, *The Rise of Western Christendom: Triumph and Diversity* AD

200–1000 (Oxford, 1996); R.A. Markus, *The End of Ancient Christianity* (Cambridge, 1990)

42 See Chapter 1, 76–8.

43 Gildas, *De Excidio*, Chapter 65; see Introduction, 15–17.

44 Gildas, *De Excidio*, 80–6, 143–7; M. Herren, 'Gildas and early British monasticism', in *Britain 400–600: Language and History*, ed. A. Bammesberger and A. Wollmann (Heidelberg, 1990), 65–83.

45 D.N. Dumville, *Saint David of Wales* (Cambridge, 2001), especially 12–22.

46 *La Vie ancienne de Saint Samson de Dol*, ed. P. Flobert (Paris, 1997), I, 14, 16–21; Davies, *Wales in the Early Middle Ages*, 149-57.

47 R.A. Markus, *Gregory the Great and His World* (Cambridge, 1997), especially 69–82.

48 Brown, *Rise of Western Christendom*.

49 K. Hughes, *The Church in Irish Society* (London, 1966); Thomas, *Christianity in Roman Britain*, 346–55.

50 R. Sharpe, 'Some problems concerning the organisation of the early medieval church in Ireland', *Peritia* 3 (1984), 230–70; C. Etchingham, *Church Organisation in Ireland AD 650–1000* (Maynooth, 1999); T. Charles-Edwards, *Early Christian Ireland* (Cambridge, 2000); W. Davies, 'The myth of the Celtic church', in *The Early Church in Wales and the West*, ed. N. Edwards and A. Lane (Oxford, 1992), 12–21.

51 J. Blair, *The Church in Anglo-Saxon Society* (Oxford, 2005), 221–2, 246–51. For Augustine's recreation in Canterbury of aspects of the ecclesiastical topography of Rome see A. Thacker, 'The making of a local saint', in *Local Saints*, 45–74, at 52–4.

52 Blair, *Church in Anglo-Saxon Society*, 182–95.

53 N. Edwards and A. Lane (eds.), *The Early Church in Wales and the West*, Oxbow monograph (Oxford, 1992); Blair, *Church in Anglo-Saxon Society*, 196–204.

54 S. Foot, 'Anglo-Saxon minsters: a review of terminology', in *Pastoral Care*, 21–25; H. Pryce, 'Pastoral care in early medieval Wales', *Pastoral Care*, 41–62, especially 49–51; Sharpe, 'Organisation of the church', 260–5; Etchingham, *Church Organisation*, 47–99.

55 Etchingham, *Church Organisation*, 363–454; Blair, *Church in Anglo-Saxon Society*, 212–14.

56 Bede, *Hist. Eccl.*, IV, 24; the form of his name suggests he could be of British origin.

57 Anon. *V. Cuthberti* Chapter 10 (recording the death of 'one of the brothers from the shepherds' huts'); Bede, *V. Cuthberti*, Chapter 34.

58 R. Cramp, 'Monastic sites' in *The Archaeology of Anglo-Saxon England*, ed. D. Wilson (London, 1996), 202–52, especially 223–9 (reinforced by recent unpublished excavations); R. Daniels, 'The Anglo-Saxon monastery at Church Close, Hartlepool, Cleveland', *Archaeological Journal* 145 (1988), 158–210.

59 A. MacDonald, 'Aspects of the monastic landscape in Adomnán's *Life of Columba*', in *Saints and Scholars: Studies in Irish Hagiography*, ed. J. Cary, M. Herbert and P. Ó Riain (Dublin, 2001), 15–30.

60 M. Carver, 'An Iona of the east: the early medieval monastery at Portmahomack, Tarbat Ness', *Medieval Archaeology* 48 (2004), 1–30; D. O'Sullivan, 'Space, silence and shortages on Lindisfarne: the archaeology of asceticism', in *Image and Power in the Archaeology of Early Medieval Britain*, ed., H. Hamerow and A. MacGregor (Oxford, 2001), 33–52.

61 E. James, 'Bede and the tonsure question', *Peritia* 3 (1984), 83–93.

62 N. Venclová, 'The venerable Bede, druidic tonsure and archaeology', *Antiquity* 76 (2002), 458–71.

63 G. Henderson and I. Henderson, *The Art of the Picts: Sculpture and Metalwork in Early Medieval Scotland* (London, 2004), 153.

64 Bede, *Hist. Eccl.*, III, 24.

65 C. Cubitt, 'The clergy in early Anglo-Saxon England', *Historical Research* 78 (2005), 273–87.

66 Foot, 'Anglo-Saxon minsters'; Blair, *Church in Anglo-Saxon Society*, 3–5.

67 Thomas, *Christianity in Roman Britain*, 202–27.

68 C.E. Lowe, 'New light on the Anglian minster at Hoddom', *Transactions of the Dumfries and Galloway Natural History and Antiquarian Society* 3rd series, 66 (1991), 11–35.

69 M. Corney, *The Roman Vill at Bradford-on-Avon: The Investigations of 2003* (Bradford-on-Avon, 2004).

70 See Chapter 2, 126–8; S. Foot, ' "By water in the spirit": the administration of baptism in early Anglo-Saxon England', in *Pastoral Care*, 171–92; Blair, *Church in Anglo-Saxon Society*, 201–2.

71 Blair, *Church in Anglo-Saxon Society*, 69–70.

72 Bede, *Hist. Eccl.*, III, 14; Campbell, *Essays*, 93, 96–7.

73 Charles-Edwards, *Early Christian Ireland*, 214–40

74 Op cit., 241–63.

75 Herbert, *Iona, Kells and Derry*, 1–67.

76 Davies, *Wales*; 141–68; J.R. Davies, 'The saints of south Wales and the Welsh church', *Local Saints*, 360–95.

77 Davies, 'Saints of south Wales', 370–6; and see Introduction, 13.

78 R. Sharpe, 'Armagh and Rome in the seventh century', in *Ireland and Europe: The Early Church*, ed. P.N. Chatháin and M. Richter (Stuttgart, 1984), 58–72; Charles-Edwards, *Early Christian Ireland*, 9–67.

79 See below for discussion of early Pictish saints, 196.

80 Kirby (ed.), *Saint Wilfrid at Hexham*; Thacker, 'Wilfrid'.

81 Bede, *Hist. Eccl.*,IV, 5.

82 *V. Wilfridi*, Chapter 63.

83 W. Levison, *England and the Continent in the Eighth Century* (Oxford, 1946), 15–44; P. Wormald, 'Bede and Benedict Biscop', in *Famulus Christi*, ed. G. Bonner (London, 1976), 141–69, at 146–9.

84 See Introduction, 7–8.

85 P. Wormald, *Bede and the Conversion of England: The Charter Evidence* (Jarrow, 1984).

86 *Charters of St Augustine's Abbey, Canterbury and Minster-in-Thanet*, ed. S. Kelly (Oxford, 1995), 139–53.

87 Bede, *Letter to Ecgbert*, 414–15.

88 *EHD* I, no. 177; N. Brooks, 'The development of military obligations in eighth- and ninth-century England', in *England Before the Conquest*, ed. P. Clemoes and K. Hughes (Cambridge, 1971), 69–84.

89 Davies, *Wales in the Early Middle Ages*, 128–9.

90 C. Stancliffe, 'Kings who opted out', in *Ideal and Reality in Frankish and Anglo-Saxon Society*, ed. P. Wormald (Oxford, 1983), 154–76.

91 Gildas, *De Excidio*, Chapter 28.

92 Gildas, *De Excidio*, Chapters 33–6; possibly this was also what Constantine had done.

93 J.R. Davies, 'Church property and conflict in Wales, AD 600–1100', *Welsh History Review* 18 (1996/7), 395–6.

94 Bede, *Hist. Eccl.*, II, 15 and III, 18 (Sigebert); V, 19 and 24 (Æthelred); Stancliffe 'Kings who opted out', 154–8.

95 M.O. Anderson, *Kings and Kingship in Early Scotland* (Edinburgh, 1980), 137–8; Stancliffe, 'Kings who opted out', 163–4.

96 Anderson, *Kings and Kingship*, 181–2.

97 Stancliffe, 'Kings who opted out', 155–6.

98 T.O. Clancy, 'Philosopher king: Nechtan mac Der-Ilei', *Scottish Historical Review* 83 (2004), 125–49, especially 143–5.

99 Bede, *Hist. Eccl.*, V, 7; Stancliffe, 'Kings who opted out'. Bishop Wilfrid seems to have inspired a number of kings to travel, or plan to travel, to Rome.

100 B. Yorke, 'The adaptation of the royal courts to Christianity', in *The Cross Goes North: Processes of Conversion in Northern Europe, AD 300–1300*, ed. M. Carver (York, 2003), 243–58.

101 B. Yorke, *Nunneries and the Anglo-Saxon Royal Houses* (London, 2003), 17–46.

102 C. Harrington, *Women in a Celtic Church: Ireland 450–1150* (Oxford, 2002).

103 W. Davies, 'Celtic women in the early Middle Ages', in *Images of Women in Antiquity*, ed. A. Cameron and A. Kuhrt (revised edn, London, 1993), 145–66; M. Handley, 'The early medieval inscriptions of western Britain', in *The Community, The Family and The Saint: Patterns of Power in Early Medieval Europe*, ed. J. Hill and M. Swan (Turnhout, 1998), 339–62.

104 P. Geary, *Before France and Germany: The Creation and Transformation of the Merovingian World* (Oxford, 1988), 171–85.

105 I.N. Wood, *The Most Holy Abbot Ceolfrith* (Jarrow, 1995).

106 Macquarrie, 'Early Christian religious houses', 115–22.

107 S. Foster (ed.), *The St Andrews Sarcophagus: A Pictish Masterpiece and its International Connections* (Dublin, 1998).

108 W. Davies, *An Early Welsh Microcosm* (London, 1978).

109 Davies, 'Saints of south Wales', 385.

110 Herbert, *Iona, Kells and Derry*, 35–41, 57–67.

111 Bannerman, 'The Scottish take-over of Pictland and the relics of Columba', in *Spes Scottorum*, 71–94; D. Broun, 'Pictish kings 761–839: integration with Dál Riata or separate development?', in *St Andrew Sarcophagus*, 71–83.

112 *EHD* I, no. 170.

113 E. John, *Land Tenure in Early England* (Leicester, 1960), 44–5.

114 P. Sims-Williams, *Religion and Literature in Western England: 600–800* (Cambridge, 1990), 115–43; Blair, *Church in Anglo-Saxon Society*, 100–8.

115 Bede, *Hist. Abbatum*; Wormald, 'Bede and Benedict Biscop'.

116 *Charters of Selsey*, ed. S. Kelly (Oxford, 1998), no. 7, 37–40.

117 Wormald, *Bede and Conversion*, 20–3; Blair, *Church in Anglo-Saxon Society*, 104–5.

118 Davies, *Welsh Microcosm*, 111–16.

119 T. Charles-Edwards, 'Érlam: the patron saint of an Irish church', in *Local Saints*, 267–90.

120 S. Foot, *Veiled Women*, 2 vols (Aldershot, 2000), vol. 1.

121 Sims-Williams, *Religion and Literature*, 130–4.

122 Henderson and Henderson, *Art of the Picts*, 125–9, 179–82.

123 Op. cit. 46; *Pictish Symbol Stones* no. 118. Other symbols are displayed more prominently in a separate panel immediately above her.

124 R.N. Bailey, *Viking-Age Sculpture in Northern England* (London, 1980).

125 E. Cambridge and D. Rollason, 'The pastoral organization of the Anglo-Saxon church: a review of the "minster hypothesis" ', *Early Medieval Europe* 4 (1995), 87–104; J. Blair, 'Ecclesiastical organization and pastoral care in Anglo-Saxon England', *Early Medieval Europe* 4 (1995), 193–212.

126 S. Foot, 'Parochial ministry in early Anglo-Saxon England: the role of monastic communities', *Studies in Church History* 26 (1989), 43–54; C. Cubitt, 'The 747 council of *Clofesho*' in *Pastoral Care*, 193–211.

127 Blair, *Church in Anglo-Saxon Society*, 368–425.

128 Attenborough, *Laws*, 24-61; *EHD* I, nos 31–2.

129 P. Hase, 'The mother churches of Hampshire', in *Minsters and Parish Churches*, ed. J. Blair (Oxford, 1988), 45–66.

130 B. Yorke, 'Boniface's insular background', in *Bonifatius Congressband* (Mainz, forthcoming).

131 J. Godfrey, 'The place of the double monastery in the Anglo-Saxon minster system', in *Famulus Christi*, ed. G. Bonner (London, 1976), 344–50.

132 A. Thacker, 'Monks, preaching and pastoral care in England', in *Pastoral Care*, especially 140–2.

133 *Gesta Pontificum*, Chapter 191; William of Malmesbury, *The Deeds of the Bishops of England*, trans. D. Preest (Woodbridge, 2002), 227–8.

134 Bede, *Letter to Ecgbert; Councils*, III, 366 (clause 10).

135 Bede, *V. Cuthberti*, Chapter 3.

136 Sims-Williams, *Religion and Literature*, 115–76; R. Morris, *Churches in the Landscape* (London, 1989), 121–38.

137 Cambridge and Rollason, 'Pastoral organization'; Blair, *Church in Anglo-Saxon Society*, 149–52.

138 C. Cubitt, *Anglo-Saxon Church Councils* c.650–c.850 (Leicester, 1995).

139 Yorke, *Nunneries*, 52–60; Blair, *Church in Anglo-Saxon Society*, 291–340.

140 Sims-Williams, *Religion and Literature*, 144–76.

141 Bede, *Letter to Ecgbert*.

142 See maps in Foster, *Picts, Gaels and Scots*, figs 4 and 47.

143 Adomnán, *V. Columbae*, II, 37.

144 A. Ritchie, *Iona* (London, 1997), 81–90

145 Pryce, 'Pastoral care', 47–8; C. Thomas, *And Shall These Mute Stones Speak? Post-Roman Inscriptions in Western Britian* (Cardiff, 1994), 305–26.

146 Davies, *Early Welsh Microcosm*, 122–4, 134–8.

147 Olson, *Early Monasteries in Cornwall*.

148 O.J. Padel, 'Local saints and place-names in Cornwall', in *Local Saints*, 303–60, especially 308–13. The use of an asterisk before *lann* is a linguistic convention which indicates that the word is known only from place-names and does not appear in other contemporary records.

149 A. Preston-Jones, 'Decoding Cornish churchyards', in *Early Church in Wales and the West*, ed. Edwards and Lane, 104–24.

150 W. Davies, 'Myth of the Celtic church' 12–21, at 19–20.

151 Blair, *Church in Anglo-Saxon Society*, 166–86, 221–45; A. Pantos and S. Semple (eds), *Assembly Places and Practices in Medieval Europe* (Dublin, 2004).

152 Olson, *Early Monasteries in Cornwall*, 9–12; Thomas, *Mute Stones*, 10–13, 229–30.

153 'The Hodoeporicon of St Willibald', in *The Anglo-Saxon Missionaries in Germany*, trans. C. Talbot (London, 1954), 153–77, at 155.

154 See Chapter 2, 125–6.

155 See Introduction, 22–3.

156 M. Lapidge, 'Gildas's education and the Latin culture of sub-Roman Britain', in *Gildas: New Approaches*, ed. M. Lapidge and D.N. Dumville (Woodbridge, 1984), 27–50; D. Howlett, *The Celtic Latin Tradition of Biblical Style* (Dublin, 1995); A. Orchard, 'Latin and the vernacular languages', in *After Rome*, ed. T. Charles-Edwards (Oxford, 2003), 191–219

157 Gildas, *De Excidio*, Chapter 36.

158 D. Howlett, *Cambro-Latin Compositions: Their Competence and Craftsmanship* (Dublin, 1998).

159 P. Riché, *Education and Culture in the Barbarian West from the Sixth through to the Eighth Century*, trans, J. Contreni (Columbia, 1976).

160 D. Ó Cróinín, *Early Medieval Ireland 400–1200* (London, 1995), 169–232; Bede, *Hist. Eccl.*, III, 7 and 27; *Aldhelm: The Prose Works*, 154–5.

161 M. Lapidge (ed.), *Archbishop Theodore: Commemorative Studies of his Life and Influence* (Cambridge, 1995).

162 *Aldhelm: The Prose Works*, 152–3; see also Bede, *Hist. Eccl.*, IV, 2.

163 Bede, *Hist. Eccl.*, V, 3.

164 A. Orchard, *The Poetic Art of Aldhelm* (Cambridge, 1994).

165 Bede, *Hist. Eccl.*, V, 24; see Introduction.

166 M. Lapidge, 'Libraries', in *Blackwell Encyclopaedia*, 285–6.

167 Lapidge (ed.), *Archbishop Theodore*.

168 T. O'Loughlin, 'The exegetical purpose of Adomnán's *De Locis Sanctis*', *CMCS* 24 (1992), 37–53; O'Loughlin suggests that the Frankish bishop may be a literary device rather than a real figure.

169 Talbot, *Anglo-Saxon Missionaries*, 153–77.

170 J. O'Reilly, 'Reading the scriptures in the *Life of Columba*', in *Studies in the Cult of Saint Columba*, ed. C. Bourke (Dublin, 1997), 80–106. See Introduction.

171 B. Cassidy (ed.), *The Ruthwell Cross* (Princeton, 1992).

172 É Ó Carragáin, 'The Ruthwell crucifixion poem in iconographical and liturgical contexts', *Peritia* 6–7 (1987–8), 1–71.

173 K. Hughes, 'Where are the writings of early Scotland?', in *Celtic Britain in the Early Middle Ages*, ed. D.N. Dumville (Woodbridge, 1980), 1–21.

174 Bede, *Hist. Eccl.*, V, 21.

175 J. Higgitt, 'The Pictish Latin inscription at Tarbat in Ross-shire', *Proceedings of the Society of Antiquaries of Scotland* 112 (1982), 300–21.

176 Henderson and Henderson, *Art of the Picts*, 137–42.

177 Carver, 'Iona of the east'; Henderson and Henderson, *Art of the Picts*, 215–21.

178 Henderson and Henderson, *Art of the Picts*, 31–5; the place(s) of origin of these gospel books is hotly debated, but they may derive from a Columban milieu.

179 *Aldhelm. The Poetic Works*, 61–9; A. Orchard, 'Engimata', in *Blackwell Encyclopaedia*, 171–2.

180 M. Brown, *The Lindisfarne Gospels: Society, Spirituality and the Scribe* (London, 2003); for animal art see Chapter 1, 79–80.

181 Howlett, *Celtic Latin Tradition*; for Celtic abstract art see Chapter 1, 79–80.

182 'Cuthbert's letter on the death of Bede', Bede, *Hist. Eccl.*, 380–7; T.O. Clancy and G. Márkus, *Iona: The Earliest Poetry of a Celtic Monastery* (Edinburgh, 1995).

183 See Chapter 1, 10–11.

184 T. Charles-Edwards, 'Language and society among the insular Celts, 400–1000', in *The Celtic World*, ed. M. Green (London, 1995), 703–36; Orchard, 'Latin and the vernacular languages'.

185 *V. Wilfridi*, Chapter 2.

186 Talbot, *Anglo-Saxon Missionaries*; Sims-Williams, *Religion and Literature*, 211–42.

187 Bede, *Letter to Ecgbert*; *Councils*, III, 366 (clause 10); Cubitt, '747 council of *Clofesho*'.

188 *Alfred the Great: Asser's Life of King Alfred and Other Contemporary Sources*, trans. S. Keynes and M. Lapidge (Harmondsworth, 1983), 124–5.

189 Dumville, *Saint David*, 12–26.

190 See above, 156–61; Davies, 'The myth of the Celtic church', 12–21.

191 For example, Adomnán, *V. Columbae*, I, 6 and 20.

192 Bede, *V. Cuthberti*, especially Chapter 16 and 17; O'Sullivan, 'Space, silence and shortages'.

193 *Felix's Life of Saint Guthlac*, ed. B. Colgrave (Cambridge 1956).

194 Bede, *Hist. Eccl.*, III, 24

195 *V. Wilfridi*, Chapter 2.

196 *Aldhelm: The Prose Works*, 55–69; Yorke, *Nunneries*, 153–5.

197 Æthelwulf, *De abbatibus*, ed. A. Campbell (Oxford, 1967) Chapters 2–4; D. Howlett, 'The provenance, date and structure of *De Abbatibus*', *Archaeologia Aeliana* 5th series 3 (1975), 121–30.

198 See above, 164–8.

199 Adomnán, *V. Columbae*, II, 39 and I, 36.

200 Anon., *V. Cuthberti*, III, 6.

201 C. Ireland, 'Aldfrith of Northumbria and the Irish genealogies', *Celtica* 22 (1991), 64–78; Yorke, 'Adomnán in Northumbrian context'.

202 Sims-Williams, *Religion and Literature*, 123–4.

203 *EHD* I, no. 177; Tangl no. 73; Yorke, *Nunneries*, 150–6.

204 Bede, *Hist. Abbatum*, Chapters 7–8; Wormald, 'Bede and Benedict Biscop'.

205 Herbert, *Iona, Kells and Derry*, 9–35.

206 R. Fletcher, *The Conversion of Europe* (London, 1977), Chapter 6.

207 *Handbooks of Penance*, 174–8 (Chapters 7 and 10).

208 P. Rahtz, 'Excavations on Glastonbury Tor', *Archaeological Journal* 127 (1971), 1–81; P. Rahtz, 'Pagan and Christian by the Severn Sea', in *The Archaeology and History of Glastonbury Abbey*, ed. L. Abrams and J.P. Carley (Woodbridge, 1991), 3–37, at 19–34.

209 *Handbooks of Penance*, 184–215 (Chapters 1–4)

210 *Councils* III, 360–76, Chapter 20 .

211 *Alcuini Epistolae* 124; translated with further discussion in P. Wormald, 'Bede, "Beowulf" and the conversion of the Anglo-Saxon aristocracy', in *Bede and Anglo-Saxon England*, ed. R.T. Farrell, BAR 46 (Oxford, 1978), 32–95, at 43.

212 *Councils*, III, 360–76, Chapter 16; Bede, *Hist. Eccl.*,V. 6.

213 *Aldhelmi Opera*, 499–500; *Aldhelm: Prose Works*, 168.

214 *Councils* III, 360–76; Chapter 19.

215 Tangl no. 78; Talbot, *Anglo-Saxon Missionaries*, 129–34; J. Campbell, 'Elements in the background to the Life of St Cuthbert and his early cult', in *St Cuthbert, His Cult and His Community to* AD *120*, ed. G. Bonner, D. Rollason and C. Stancliffe (Woodbridge, 1989), 3–19, at 13–14.

216 Bede, *Hist Eccl.*, IV, 25; *Aldhelmi Opera*, 317–18 (*De Virginitate*); *Aldhelm: The Prose Works*, 127–8.

217 J.-P. Laporte and R. Boyer, *Trésors de Chelles: Sépultures et Reliques de la Reine Bathildis et de l'Abbesse Bertille* (Chelles, 1991).

218 L. Webster and J. Backhouse (eds), *The Making of England: Anglo-Saxon Art and Culture* AD *600–900* (London, 1991), 96–100, 141–3; Yorke, *Nunneries*, 147–50.

219 Campbell, 'Elements in the background', 12.

220 *Aldhelmi Opera*, 500–2; *Aldhelm: The Prose Works*, 168–70.

221 See Chapter 2, 106–9.

222 D. Ó Corráin, 'Nationality and kingship in pre-Norman Ireland', in *Nationality and the Pursuit of National Independence*, ed. T.W. Moody (Belfast, 1978), 1–35; Charles-Edwards, *Early Christian Ireland*, 264–81.

223 Asser Chapter 79; Davies, *Wales in the Early Middle Ages*, 77, 157–64; Davies, *Welsh Microcosm*, 128–30.

224 Asser Chapter 93.

225 Bede, *Hist. Eccl.*, III, 14; Yorke, 'Adomnán in Northumbrian context', and see Introduction, 19.

226 See above, 170, for their possible allegorical significance.

227 See Chapter 1, 79–83.

228 Brown, *Lindisfarne Gospels*.

229 *The Dream of the Rood*, ed. M. Swanson (2nd ed,, Exeter, 1987); Ó Carragáin, 'The Ruthwell Crucifixion Poem'; Cassidy (ed.), *Ruthwell Cross*.

230 Wormald, 'Bede, Beowulf and conversion'; for problems of date see Introduction, 10–11.

231 P. Brown, *The Cult of Saints: Its Rise and Function in Latin Christianity* (Chicago, 1981).

232 Gildas, *De Excidio*, Chapter 10; Sharpe, 'Martyrs and saints in late antique Britain', in *Local Saints*, 75–154.

233 M. Henig and P. Lindley (eds), *Alban and St Albans: Roman and Medieval Architecture, Art and Archaeology*, BAA Conference Transactions 24 (2001).

234 Bede, *Hist. Eccl.*, III, 29; D. Rollason, *Saints and Relics in Anglo-Saxon England* (Oxford, 1989), 3–20; A. Thacker, '*Loca sanctorum*: the significance of place in the study of the saints', in *Local Saints*, 1–44, especially 17–20.

235 The inscription seems likely to be earlier than the Northumbrian acquisition of Whithorn to which it is ascribed in Hill, *Whithorn and St Ninian*, 38.

236 Thacker, '*Loca sanctorum*', 20–31.

237 Davies, 'Saints of south Wales', 361–80; see above.

238 T.O. Clancy, 'The Real St Ninian', *Innes Review* 52 (2001), 1–28; T.O. Clancy, 'Scottish saints and national identities in the early Middle Ages', in *Local Saints*, 397–421, especially 399–404.

239 B.L. Olson and O.J. Padel, 'A tenth-century list of Cornish parochial saints', *CMCS* 12 (1986), 33–71; Padel, 'Local saints in Cornwall', 316–26.

240 Thacker, '*Loca sanctorum*', 32–3.

241 *Nicholas Roscarrock's Lives of the Saints: Cornwall and Devon*, ed. N. Orme, Devon and Cornwall Record Society, new series 35 (1992).

242 Thacker, 'Making of a local saint'.

243 N. Edwards, 'Celtic saints and early medieval archaeology', in *Local Saints*, 225–65.

244 T. O'Loughlin, 'The tombs of the saints: their significance for Adomnán', in *Saints and Scholars: Studies in Irish Hagiography*, ed. J. Carey, M. Herbert and P. Ó Riain (Dublin, 2001), 1–14.

245 Adomnán, *V. Columbae*, II, 44; T.O. Clancy, 'Columba, Adomnán, and the cult of the saints in Scotland, in *Spes Scotorum*, 3–34.

246 Charles-Edwards, 'Érlam'.

247 Adomnán, *V. Columbae*, I, 1; Clancy, 'Columba, Adomnán and the cult of saints', 18–19, 21–5.

248 A. Smyth, *Warlords and Holy Men: Scotland AD 80–1000* (London, 1984), 107–12.

249 Ritchie, *Iona*, 81–2.

250 J. Blair, 'A saint for every minster? Local cults in Anglo-Saxon England' and 'A handlist of Anglo-Saxon saints', in *Local Saints*, 455–565.

251 Kirby (ed.), *Saint Wilfrid at Hexham*; G. Bonner, D. Rollason and C. Stancliffe (eds), *St Cuthbert, His Cult and His Community to AD 1200* (Woodbridge, 1989).

252 W. Goffart, *The Narrators of Barbarian History* (Princeton, 1988), Chapter 4; Rollason, *Saints and Relics*, 105–14; and see Introduction, 11–12.

253 C. Cubitt, 'Universal and local saints in Anglo-Saxon England', in *Local Saints*, 423–54.

254 Bede, *Hist. Eccl.*, III, 9–14; A. Thacker, '*Membra disjecta*: the division of the body and the diffusion of the cult', in *Oswald: Northumbrian King to European Saint*, ed. C. Stancliffe and E. Cambridge (Stamford, 1995), 97–127.

255 *The Earliest Life of Gregory the Great*, ed. B. Colgrave (Lawrence, 1968), Chapter 18–19.

256 Rollason, *Saints and Relics*, 115–29; C. Cubitt, 'Sites and sanctity: revisiting the cults of murdered and martyred kings', *Early Medieval Europe* 9 (2000), 53–83; Yorke, *Nunneries*, 118–22.

257 See Chapter 4, 231–6.

258 See Chapter 2, 106–9.

259 Bede, *Hist. Eccl.*, IV, 19; Thacker, 'Making of a local saint', 45–8, 54–62.

260 Cubitt, 'Universal and local saints', 432–8.

261 Rollason, *Saints and Relics*, 101–4.

262 *V. Wilfridi* Chapter 18.

263 Bede, *V. Cuthberti*, Chapter 37, which is just the type of problem that the

monks of Iona may have sought to avoid through their low-key treatment of the burial place of Columba.

264   Cubitt, 'Sites and sanctity'.

265   *Life of St Gregory*, Chapter 19.

266   S. Taylor, 'Seventh-century Iona abbots in Scottish place-names', in *Spes Scotorum*, 35–70.

267   MacDonald, *Curadán*; A. Macquarrie, '*Vita Sancti Servani*: the Life of St Serf', *Innes Review* 44 (1993), 122–52.

268   P. Yeoman, 'Pilgrims to St Ethernan: the archaeology of an early saint of the Picts and Scots', in *Conversion and Christianity in the North Sea World*, ed. B. Crawford (St Andrews, 1998), 75–92. It is possible that Ethernan was of Irish origin.

269   Clancy, 'Scottish saints', 414–15.

270   C. Loveluck, 'Wealth, waste and conspicuous consumption: Flixborough and its importance for middle and late rural settlement studies', in *Image and Power*, ed. H. Hamerow and A. MacGregor (Oxford, 2001), 79–130; Blair, *Church in Anglo-Saxon Society*, 204–12.

CHAPTER 4

Religion, Politics and Society in Early Medieval Britain

Death and burial

In the previous chapter we saw that the capacity existed in most areas of early medieval Britain for the church to have had a significant impact on the lives of all sectors of society. The task remains in this chapter to consider whether it in fact did so, and in what ways and to what extent lay society was affected by the practices and ideals of Christianity. Aspects of the issue have already been touched on through consideration of how lay and ecclesiastical culture blended within religious communities. The topic of death and burial has been chosen to begin the investigation because it is an aspect for which some evidence survives from all areas of early medieval Britain and for a cross-section of its societies. Although it has often been observed that there are no clear rulings from the early medieval church about what burial practices should be followed,[1] by 800 we can identify characteristics of burial that were common throughout early medieval Britain and which by that date we can confidently identify as being those of followers of Christianity. These common features include extended supine burial in dug graves with the head oriented to the east and with any grave-goods the exception rather than the rule. The degree of adherence to these basic characteristics is all the more striking because of the much greater variation in practice that existed within Britain in 600, with, at one extreme, the furnished and clothed inhumation and cremation burials of the Anglo-Saxons, which must often have involved extremely elaborate funerary rites, and, at the other, the apparent scarcity of burial practices that left visible remains among the Picts.

Characteristics of early medieval Christian burial can be observed first within Britain in the fourth century in the 'managed' cemeteries attached to some Roman towns, although there is some debate over whether all those so buried were converts to Christianity or not.[2] By the late fourth century distinctive types of rural cemetery have been observed in which the basic early medieval characteristics of Christian burial were followed. In the fifth and sixth centuries, and beyond, this type of rural cemetery came to be found throughout western and northern Britain, including the south-eastern lands of the Picts.[3] These cemeteries were generally unenclosed and not associated with churches, but might make use of prehistoric monuments or lie among apparently abandoned Roman buildings. Although the basic form of burial was the simple inhumation, there could be a considerable range of monuments and grave-structures in which the body was placed including use of square and penannular ditched enclosures, graves lined with stones (cists) or planks, and use of coffins. Special graves could be picked out with even more elaborate structures such as the late Roman mausolea with traces of painted wall-plaster excavated in the cemetery of Poundbury (Dorset) that seem to have continued to be visited after the cemetery went out of use.[4] The identity of the individuals in the graves might be indicated by various forms of inscribed stone.[5] Other distinctive grave-forms or associated monuments such as long cists and square barrows, which possibly imitate Roman mausolea, are found in south-eastern Pictland as well as in British areas of the west and north,[6] and provide support for the idea of a British role in the conversion of southern Pictland that is encapsulated in the traditions surrounding Ninian (while leaving open the question of personal involvement by Uinniau/Ninian himself).[7]

The burial traditions associated with the Anglo-Saxons had their own distinctive features, but in the course of the seventh century there was a radical change in practice with an abandonment of cremation and a gradual move away from clothed inhumations with grave-goods towards the forms of early medieval Christian burial that have already been discussed.[8] However, some shifts in Anglo-Saxon burial ritual seem to have begun before the written sources suggest that conversion had been achieved, and it would appear that some changes in burial practice were connected with the major upheavals in Anglo-Saxon society which accompanied the emergence of kingdoms rather than to changes in religion.[9] The two competing explanations need not be starkly opposed for they are likely to have been interrelated in quite complex ways. The emergence of kingdoms saw the breaking down of former Anglian and Saxon alliances and the creation of wider overlordships, probably under Frankish influence or pressure.[10] One consequence seems to have been the replacement of the Germanic female burial dress with its prominent brooches that might symbolise Anglian and Saxon or other allegiances with forms that had more in common with fashions of Francia and other Christian areas of Europe, including the wearing of necklaces and head-coverings whose presence is suggested by gold braids and the pin-suites which fastened them. Such shifts are part of the greater changes that provided the circumstances in which Christianity could be introduced to the Anglo-Saxon provinces in a way and at a time they were willing to accept.

When Christianity did begin to make an impact in the Anglo-Saxon areas there are likely to have been some burial practices that the missionaries would find completely incompatible with accepted Christian practice, but others which could be tolerated. Cremation is likely to have been on the immediate hit-list and does seem to have become rapidly obsolete in the seventh-century (making allowance for the different timetables of conversion in the various Anglo-Saxon kingdoms).[11] Cremation ran counter to the belief apparently current in seventh-century Europe that an inhumed body was necessary for salvation, and the complex rituals associated with cremation may have included aspects that were deemed unacceptably pagan. The social display that was a key part of furnished inhumation burial was not necessarily seen as problematic, as is indicated by elaborate seventh-century Frankish burials within the cathedrals of Cologne and St Denis, though the ceremonies surrounding such burials, which may have left no physical traces, are likely to have changed.[12] Such elaborate burials have not been found within any Anglo-Saxon church, but the richest 'princely' burials in barrows from the seventh century, such as Sutton Hoo (Suffolk), Prittlewell (Essex) and Swallowcliffe Down (Wilts), include objects with Christian symbolism and could well have been of people who considered themselves to be Christian.[13] But although such conspicuous display may not have been incompatible with burial as a Christian, nor was it in accord with the spirit of such biblical pronouncements as 'we brought nothing into this world, and it is certain we can carry nothing out'.[14] In fact, the church could provide its own forms of conspicuous display and expenditure that also aided salvation. Some royal houses were quick to adopt these new practices. King Æthelbert of Kent, for instance, endowed the church of St Peter and Paul 'so that the bodies of Augustine himself and all the bishops of Canterbury and the kings of Kent might be placed in it'.[15] But in many other kingdoms there seems to have been a longer transition period in which it would appear Christian burial took place in established burial grounds and utilised some traditional forms of burial such as barrows. It was probably only towards the end of the seventh century, when many family minsters were founded by kings and nobles, that location and modes of burial began to change on a significant scale. What the new practices could entail has been suggested by excavations at the Mercian royal nunnery of Repton where a conspicuous mausoleum and sculpture of an Anglo-Saxon ruler as a victorious warrior in the classical style may be associated with King Æthelbald who was buried there after his murder in 757.[16]

The irrelevance of many traditional forms of burial to the workings of Christianity seems also to have been accepted by the bulk of the population in the Anglo-Saxon provinces by about 700. Although unfurnished burials are obviously hard to date, the cemeteries in the West Saxon *wic* of Hamwic are a useful guide as at least eight small burial grounds have been found that date from its foundation in the late seventh century to the severe decline of settlement in the ninth century.[17] Apart from minor exceptions in some of the earlier burials, overlain by later phases of Middle Saxon occupation, burials are without grave-goods and on an east–west alignment. Comparable small unenclosed cemeteries are increasingly being recognised in the countryside of central and eastern England from a similar period,[18] and have several features in common with those already discussed from the western areas of Britain. What is particularly significant is that the changes in burial custom established throughout Britain by the eighth century can be presumed to be linked with a widespread absorption of one of the fundamental tenets of Christianity, namely the doctrine of salvation. The burial of early medieval Christians facing east has generally been interpreted, although this is not explicitly stated in any contemporary text, as indicating the belief that Christians would rise to meet Christ coming from the east (i.e. Jerusalem where he was buried) to enjoy eternal salvation on the Day of Judgement. Adomnán implies that all those who had been properly buried in tombs would be resurrected when their souls would be reunited with their bodies, but if there was no tomb there could be no resurrection.[19] The adoption of tomb burial by the Picts, who would appear to have disposed of their dead in other ways previously, may therefore be evidence for the impact of Christian beliefs in the importance of having a body to be resurrected. The eastern alignment of graves may have been established each year by reference to the rising sun at Easter, the feast of the sacrifice that Christ made so that all his followers would be saved.[20] The Christian doctrine of life after death is likely to have been substantially different from any concepts of what happened after death in pre-Christian religions and can be presumed to have formed one of the major attractions of the new religion. The promise held out in the New Testament that heaven was open to all who lived a virtuous life and that those who were poor or had suffered on earth would be rewarded in the kingdom of heaven has meant that Christianity has always spoken to the whole of society.

The burial evidence therefore suggests that the missionaries and native clergy who succeeded them had been successful in getting over funda-mental ideas about the new religion to a wide sector of the population and that people felt sufficiently confident in Christian ritual to abandon many of their traditional forms of burial. How far understanding went on more complex ideas concerning the human soul is difficult to assess and there was not necessarily agreement on all matters. Adomnán apparently believed that judgement was made on the soul's destination immediately at the time of death and could not be affected by any form of interven-tion,[21] while Bede followed Augustine and Gregory the Great in expounding the doctrine of purgatory. His story of Imma explains why masses should be said for the dead and may provide an insight into how such ideas were presented to a wider audience. He relates how the Northumbrian thegn Imma was taken into captivity after the battle of Trent in 679, but that his brother who was an abbot assumed he had been killed and so celebrated 'many masses for the absolution of his soul' with the result that the earthly chains with which his captors had sought to bind Imma repeatedly fell off and, as Imma observed, 'if I had now been in another world, my soul would have been loosed from its punishment by his intercessions'.[22] Bede also provided a vision of the world after death as seen by a Northumbrian called Dryhthelm,[23] and a comparable vision reported by a monk of Wenlock is also known.[24] Dryhthelm was shown the extremes of heaven and hell, to which the very perfect or imperfect might be immediately assigned on death, but also holding areas where the bulk of the Christian people would wait until the Day of Judgement. Those with sins to their name would have to work out their time suffering some of the agonies of extreme heat and cold to be found in hell, but prayers, masses and acts of charity could buy their release.

However, burial ritual in early medieval Britain did not entirely conform to later medieval practices that were established by about 1000. Churches did not, or were not able to claim the type of jurisdic-tion over the dead that was a feature of later parochial practice in which burial in a churchyard or consecrated burial ground became the norm and payment for such burials was a major source of church income.[25] Some lay people were undoubtedly buried in the cemeteries of minsters. Excavations at some of the northern English monastic sites such as Whitby and Hartlepool have revealed evidence of burials of mixed populations of men, women and children which can be suspected of being those of lay people, but it would appear that they had their own burial places separate from those of the members of the religious communities.[26] There was also a long tradition of lay people being buried on Iona, even though lay people did not apparently live on the island. Adomnán records the saint's prophecy to two laymen that their two sons would ultimately be buried on the island,[27] and a number of different sites of burial have been located in excavations on Iona, where the cemeteries of the monastic community and lay people also seem to have been kept separate.[28] Members of monastic communities apparently believed that the fellowship they had enjoyed in life would continue after death and that even if they were buried in separate locations they would be reunited.[29] Laymen buried within monastic territory could presumably not expect necessarily to enjoy the same degree of intimacy, any more than they had in life, but would benefit from the association and the prayers of the community. It is likely that only certain categories of lay people were buried at minsters. Among the most favoured would have been members of the families especially associated with the foundation and related to its abbots and abbesses. Imma's brother, Abbot Tunna, retrieved a body from the battlefield that he took to be his and gave it an honourable burial at his minster.[30] Excavation of a timber church associated with a cemetery at the nunnery of Nazeing (Essex) revealed four burials, three of women and one male, possibly King Swaefred who had given the land on which the nunnery had been founded.[31] Other lay people buried in cemeteries associated with minsters are likely to have been tenants. It would appear that, as with the Irish *manaig*, those who actually lived on minster estates were entitled to a greater degree of pastoral care than those who merely lived in the same vicinity or, to put it another way, were subject to a greater degree of supervision in death as in life.[32]

Burial for the majority of lay people throughout early medieval Britain was in unenclosed, rural cemeteries, and so reflects what has been suspected from the evidence for preaching that much Christian ritual for ordinary laymen occurred at traditional open-air sites. Some of the cemeteries were close to settlements, but others had probably been chosen because of other, traditional associations, and incorporated, or were placed within, prehistoric and later monuments. Some cemeteries had clearly begun as burial grounds in the pre-Christian past and simply continued in use. Such continuity enabled the circumvention of a problem that could be a stumbling block to conversion in early medieval Europe: namely the question of what happened to one's pre-Christian ancestors after conversion.[33] One king of Frisia reportedly changed his mind on the brink of conversion when he discovered that if he went to heaven he would be separated from his pagan ancestors.[34] This was not just a sentimental attachment. Descent from certain ancestors, real or acquired, and perhaps their continuing active support from their places of burial, was essential for royal claimants and probably for other landowners. Irish laws refer to burial on boundaries as having a protective function, and that ownership of land could be proved by riding over them (perhaps because their inhabitants would rise up in indignation if the claims were false).[35] Such concepts may explain why many of the latest Anglo-Saxon furnished burials are to be found in border positions; it may have been one of the traditional associations of burial that was hardest to abandon in the face of new practices.[36]

However, concerns were raised about the continuation of such burial traditions, and particularly the intermingling of pagan and Christian dead. Irish ecclesiastical laws beginning in the seventh century sought to discourage burial in ancestral cemeteries and to promote burial at churches and at places of burial of the saints instead.[37] Irish churchmen, through close perusal of the Old Testament in particular, developed concepts of sacred space and enclosure in advance of other areas of Europe.[38] *Theodore's Penitential* was concerned with the rather different problem of pagans having been buried within churches, something that might easily have arisen in the early conversion period in Anglo-Saxon England when families might contain both converted and unconverted members.[39] The foundation of minsters, particularly those run by their own relatives, would have helped to persuade Anglo-Saxon royal and noble families to abandon traditional forms of burial and to embrace the new opportunities for ostentatious display in a Christian setting. New ancestors were created, some of whom had saintly credentials and could intervene for their families. The new literacy that came in with Christianity could find new ways of remembering ancestors and demonstrating the links between the present and the past, for instance in the construction of genealogies in which gods and pre-Christian heroes were incorporated as founders of the dynasties.[40] Burial with members of the family who had entered minsters united the family in death. However, elite practices had not trickled down to the whole of lay society by 800. For many ordinary people within Britain churchyard burial, or even burial in an enclosed cemetery that had been consecrated, was a process which belonged to the tenth century and later when the church extended control over many matters that had been more a matter of custom in the period up to 800. [41]

Traditional customs and Christian practices

Study of burial practices suggests that basic tenets of Christian faith, in this case the doctrine of Resurrection, were implanted fairly rapidly among the lay population, but that the way in which they were absorbed was affected by traditional customs. Changes in traditional behaviour were not necessarily adopted, or imposed, on the whole of society according to the same timescale, for, as we have seen, burial in a cemetery attached to a church or a consecrated graveyard was not the norm any-where in Britain by 800, but was restricted to members of religious communities and lay people who had a close association with them.[42] It is a moot point whether the church lacked the capacity to impose greater control over the burial places of the ordinary population, or whether churchmen as well as laymen considered certain aspects of burial custom were not appropriate areas for ecclesiastical intervention. Such consider-ations arising from the evidence for burial are likely to be relevant to many other aspects of Christian practice in early medieval Britain where one can expect the reception of new concepts to have been tempered by people's expectation of how such matters would be managed within their societies. There were many areas where there was uncertainty about what should be expected of lay people and how traditional customs were to be accommodated with Christian practice. The series of questions apparently sent by Augustine to Pope Gregory, the *Penitential* attributed to Theodore and the Irish *Collectio Canonum Hibernensis* all provide evidence of how churchmen were battling to solve some of these issues in the seventh and early eighth centuries. Augustine and Theodore found themselves when they became archbishops of Canterbury suddenly projected into complex pastoral issues that are unlikely to have concerned them in their previous more contemplative or scholarly lives. The Irish missionaries may have been particularly successful in Britain because they had already had to deal within their own society with many of the issues of adapting tra-ditional lay behaviour in a Christian context, and when Anglo-Saxon missionaries went to went work in continental Germany they could in turn draw upon their own experiences of Christianisation.

Early medieval peoples were probably already familiar before conversion with the idea that religious ritual might demand certain forms of behaviour from them. Pope Gregory in his letter of advice to Mellitus refers to festivals involving the erection of temporary huts at sacred sites and the feasting on sacrificed animals which he felt could be continued providing that the sites were Christianised and the festivals were Christian ones, such as the feast day of a saint.[43] Rogationtide, the three days before the Ascension, was according to the council of *Clofesho* of 747 a time when the laity might be expected to join the clergy in their liturgical processions with the relics of saints.[44] This was meant to be a solemn, penitential occasion, and the council refers with disapproval to the clergy joining in the horse racing and feasting with which it was concluded, presumably an example of the combination of Christian and traditional celebration that Gregory had suggested should be promoted. Whether there was also a tradition in pre-Christian practice of one day a week being set aside for ritual practices is perhaps less likely, for the observance of Sunday as a day on which no work should be done had to be specially enjoined in the laws of Wihtred of Kent and Ine of Wessex.[45] It is particularly stressed that if lords ordered their men to work that day then they, rather than their workmen, were at fault. It is unlikely that the capacity existed to provide services for all every Sunday, though minsters were enjoined to invite laymen to their services on Sundays in the canons of the Council of *Clofesho*, but, as with burial, only those with privileged access may have received the invitations.[46]

In Christian practice the layman's preparation for a major church festival would have involved fasting: *Theodore's Penitential* suggested three main periods of fasting for laymen: at the festivals of Easter, Christmas and Pentecost (Whitsun).[47] The idea of ritual fasting was not necessarily a new concept, and in Ireland at least seems to have been a traditional way in which subjects might bring matters to the attention of their rulers. When the Irish-trained Cedd sought to cleanse the site of Lastingham in preparation for the foundation of a monastery he undertook a regime there of prayer and fasting that may have owed something to older Irish practices.[48] Fasting is used in the *Life of Columba* in a number of different circumstances in addition to being an integral part of the monastic regime where two days of fasting a week on Wednesdays and Fridays appears to have been the norm, as is clear from the Irish names for those days of the week.[49] On one occasion, for instance, Columba is said to have organised the prayer and fasting of a married couple to resolve a quarrel between them.[50]

A major preoccupation in Irish ecclesiastical legislation was the issue of ritual purity and pollution and many areas of concern were as relevant to lay people as to religious.[51] The penitential writings attributed to Adomnán are predominantly concerned with which animals could be eaten and the circumstances in which they must be deemed polluted and so rejected. 'Hens that taste the flesh of a man or his blood are in a high degree unclean, and their eggs are unclean; but their chicks are to be preserved', but 'marine animals cast upon the shores, the nature of whose death we do not know, are to be taken for food in good faith, unless they are decomposed'; the latter was presumably a matter of some interest to a community based on Iona.[52] Irish authors paid close attention to Old Testament rulings, but seem to have sought to adapt these to traditional Irish practice so that, for instance, the eating of pork – a staple of the Irish diet – was permitted, but the eating of horseflesh was forbidden (perhaps because its consumption had a role in pagan Irish practices).[53] Other major areas of concern included the ideas of impurity associated with certain bodily functions, especially concerning women who were menstruating or had given birth. Such issues also formed part of the questions that Augustine posed to Pope Gregory, and Rob Meens has suggested that Augustine was reacting to practices of British Christians.[54] That the British church had strict attitudes to ritual purity as did the Irish, is suggested by Aldhelm's experience of the priests of Dyfed who purified church vessels with ash if there was a danger of pollution (caused in this case by taking communion with Anglo-Saxon clergy) and apparently expected visiting Anglo-Saxon clergy to undergo 40 days of penance before they were fit to mingle with them.[55] There were admittedly particular reasons for the hostility of British clergy to Anglo-Saxons, but it is certainly possible that the extreme fear of pollution was a shared feature of the British and Irish churches that stretched back to their period of common origin. What is less certain is the extent to which such ideas connected with taboos that existed within their societies before conversion and how far they stemmed from close reading of the Old Testament. It is perhaps the case that the British and Irish were drawn to the prohibitions of the Old Testament because they recognised similarities between their societies in these as in other matters. In Anglo-Saxon society the use of polluting substances such as blood, urine and semen seems to have been associated with what came to be seen as unacceptable magical practices.[56]

Whatever may have been the expectation of Anglo-Saxon lay people on such matters as the taboos surrounding women who had just given birth, we can see that after conversion they might be exposed to a confusing variety of advice on how they should conduct their daily affairs. The views of the Irish laws were stricter and more restrictive than those promulgated in the contemporary Frankish church, and those held by Pope Gregory who stressed that Old Testament views were not to be taken literally but should be interpreted, as in the New Testament, in a spiritual sense; the inner state was more important than the outer bodily one so that there should be no objection to the baptism of a pregnant women as some (presumably British or Irish) apparently believed.[57] The lengthy citation of Gregory's views in Bede's *Ecclesiastical History* presumably suggests that Bede believed the Anglo-Saxons should follow Pope Gregory's approach. Archbishop Theodore, on the other hand, seems to have endorsed many of the provisions he found in Irish writings, perhaps because they fitted with his preconceptions from the eastern church, though unlike the Irish he did not see the unintentional consumption of polluted food or drink as sinful.[58]

We might therefore expect to find considerable variation within early medieval Britain on many aspects concerning the correct ways in which lay people should conduct themselves as Christians, and that quite variant attitudes could be deemed as 'correct' by different authorities. Possibly such variation would encourage the retention or development of traditional views on many matters of conduct. However, as with burial there would be some forms of behaviour that would no longer be tolerated. Infanticide seems to have been one example. Infanticide was apparently regarded as a legitimate way of restricting the population in both Celtic and Germanic societies, but it was not acceptable after conversion when all infants were expected to be baptised (within 30 days of birth according to Chapter 2 of the laws of Ine) and so were deemed to have souls. The visible result is a greater incidence of infant burials in Christian than in pagan cemeteries.[59] However, infant burials might continue to be treated in special ways. In Anglo-Saxon cemeteries burials of infants might be particularly likely to be accompanied by amulets, and where there was early burial beside churches infants might be crowded under the eaves of the church, as in the pre-Anglian phase at Whithorn. There were other ways as well in which older ideas of the potentially problematic nature of the dead, or some dead, were perpetuated. The prevalence of rural cemeteries away from settlements may have owed something to the wish of the living to avoid contact with the potentially polluting dead, views which would have been in accord with Roman hygiene laws that saw the dead banished to the outskirts of towns. Conservative Irish clerics – and no doubt British ones too – believed that priests risked defilement if they came into contact with the dead, a ruling that had support from Leviticus, but could also have had older roots. Such attitudes are reflected in Adomnán's account of how Columba removed himself from the bedside of a dying monk so he would not be present when he died,[60] and may explain the apparent antipathy in conservative British and Irish churches to the cult of corporeal relics.[61]

Marriage and sex

Marriage, even more than the issue of burial, is an example of a very important area of early medieval life on which church law had clear rules and regulations, but for which Germanic and Celtic societies had well-established social customs that were governed by traditional law rather than by religious considerations. Rules concerning marriage were a major concern of contemporary Anglo-Saxon and Irish law, and of the later medieval Welsh laws that are likely to reflect early medieval practice among British communities. All these laws show that there were many broad similarities in practice between the different communities of Britain with regard to marriage customs, even though there might be variation in detail.[62] Various forms of sexual union were regarded as legally acceptable and gave varying status and rights to the women involved. The lesser forms of union tended to be recast by the church as concubinage, and so undesirable, and it was the more formal arrangements that were promoted as appropriate for Christians. Formal marriages were arranged between the bridegroom and the male kindred of the bride who acted as protectors of her interests. A payment was usually made by the bridegroom to the bride's kindred and part of this, or separate provision by both parties, would be made to the bride herself. Where property was involved, the husband and wife might have joint control of certain properties while they were together, and arrangements might be made at the time of marriage for the woman's 'dower' when she was widowed or separated from her husband. Although death brought an end to many marriages, and as in other comparable societies there was a particularly high death rate among women as a result of childbirth, it also seems to have been relatively easy for marriages to have been dissolved in the early Middle Ages. In these circumstances the woman would generally return to the protection of her male kin. Widows and separated married women may have been the class of women who enjoyed the greatest personal freedom in the early Middle Ages. The terms of their marriage contracts might allow them to live on their own property at this stage, even if they might only have a life-interest in it. Anglo-Saxon widowed or separated women of royal birth seem frequently to have been prominent members of their families, especially those former queens who controlled royal nunneries and continued to perform public as well as familial roles.[63]

Marriage was therefore frequently not so much a question of a love match between two individuals, as an alliance between two kin-groups in which major issues such as the ownership of property were also concerned. In marriages between royal houses these issues took on a wider political significance. Marriage could seal an alliance between kingdoms, as in a series of marriages between the royal houses of Northumbria and Wessex in the seventh century that were probably motivated at least in part by a desire to work together against their common enemy, the kingdom of Mercia, which lay between them.[64] Marriages might also be part of the negotiations to end hostilities between rival kingdoms – though not always with the desired results. Osthryth of Northumbria married King Æthelred of Mercia after a period of several bitter battles between the two kingdoms in which many members of the two houses had been killed, only to be murdered herself by members of the Mercian nobility.[65] The exact reason for her murder is not known, but the tensions for a bride and her entourage in such circumstances are one of the topics of Old English verse and are vividly evoked in the fragmentary *Battle of Finnsburh* and the Freowaru/Ingeld episode in *Beowulf*.[66] Although we lack specific details about laws governing marriage in Pictland, and those followed by the royal houses have been the subject of much dispute, it is nevertheless evident that Pictish royal marriages had a major significance in directing the course of the Pictish royal succession.[67] A series of endogamous marriages of Pictish women with princes from other provinces of northern Britain brought members of Anglo-Saxon, British and Irish royal houses to the Pictish throne. The principles on which marriages were conducted were of major political concern in early medieval Britain, and also affected matters concerning the transfer of property and the integrity of family lands for a much wider sector of the population.

By the time the Christian church came to Britain it had established its own rules concerning marriage.[68] The Old Testament set out various prohibitions against marriage with close relatives that reinforced similar, though less extensive, prohibitions under Roman law which also influenced the development of the canon law of the early medieval church. Clashes between ecclesiastical and traditional secular practices were inevitable, particularly as the latter recognised marriage between close relatives, whether actual kin or kin by marriage, especially where this facilitated retention within a particular kin-group of landed property or control of a kingdom. Among Gildas's complaints about King Maelgwn was that he had married the widow of a nephew, though admittedly his concerns also included the fact that the king had had both his nephew and his own first wife murdered so that both he and his niece by marriage were free to remarry.[69] The Gregorian mission almost lost its tentative hold within England when it objected to King Eadbald wishing to marry his stepmother, the widow of his father and predecessor Æthelbert. On this occasion the king backed down, convinced by his own epileptic fits and the apparent scourging of Archbishop Laurence by St Peter that the marriage was ill-omened.[70] However, in the longer term the church in Britain found ways to accommodate many aspects of traditional secular practice.

The gap between ecclesiastical theory and secular practice was the subject of one of the questions Augustine is stated to have put to Pope Gregory, and he asked in particular whether it was lawful for a man to marry a stepmother or a sister-in-law.[71] Gregory forbade such marriages and those of first cousins, but apparently allowed those of second or third cousins, a ruling that subsequently surprised Boniface because such unions were not recognised by many in the church because they ran counter to the detailed prohibitions in the Old Testament, particularly as laid out in the Book of Leviticus. In Ireland it appears that the marriage of first cousins was traditionally allowed, one of its advantages being that it meant that property was retained within the family unit.[72] Irish lawyers carefully combed the Old Testament and a close reading of the Book of Numbers enabled them to find biblical support for first cousin unions, for the concerns of the tribal society of the Children of Israel with regard to the transmission of property had many parallels with those of the traditional societies in early medieval Britain. Divergent views within the Old Testament and among those responsible for their own conversion may have aided the Anglo-Saxons and Picts in retaining those features of traditional marriage that were most important to them. In spite of Archbishop Laurence's stand against the marriage of Eadbald with his stepmother, it was still possible for King Æthelbald of Wessex to marry his father's widow in the ninth century, even though Alfred's biographer Asser professed himself as shocked by this as Gildas had been by the irregular unions of some contemporary kings.[73]

Although progress was gradual, it can be seen that Christian views on marriage had begun to have an impact in early medieval Britain by 800, though we are limited for any detailed information to various high-profile marriages. Polygamous unions of varying status that had been normal, at least among leaders, in pre-conversion Ireland, and it is suspected was also practised by their Anglo-Saxon and Pictish counterparts, became unacceptable, though in practice one can suspect redefinition rather than significant changes in behaviour, with leaders having many mistresses or practising serial monogamy rather than blatant polygamy. The Kentish king Wihtred (690–725) can be shown from charters to have had three wives in succession, but Theodore was apparently aware that there could be people who embarked on fourth or fifth marriages.[74] The retreat of ex-queens into nunneries provided a Christian legitimisation for the traditional expectation that marriages could be dissolved if the parties concerned so desired. Archbishop Theodore conceded that this established Anglo-Saxon practice could continue.[75] A stricter interpretation of church law would have ruled that both partners should remain unmarried while the other was still alive, and such a ruling was associated with Adomnán in the *Canones Adomnani*.[76] One of the best recorded instances of the build-up to such a separation concerns the East Anglian princess Æthelthryth who, reliable informants told Bede, had remained a virgin in spite of contracting two marriages.[77] Her second marriage was to King Ecgfrith of Northumbria (670–85) who may have been several years younger than Æthelthryth when he married her. Its non-consummation became an issue, and Ecgfrith at first tried to persuade Bishop Wilfrid of Northumbria, who had been encouraging Æthelthryth to remain chaste, to advise her to perform her marital duties. When the marriage remained unconsummated, Æthelthryth was first allowed to retreat to the nunnery of Coldingham that was ruled by Ecgfrith's aunt Æbbe, and then to return to her native East Anglia where she founded the nunnery of Ely, while Ecgfrith married Iurminburh.

A Christian ceremony became part of the legitimisation of a marriage; according to *Theodore's Penitential* there should be a mass and a blessing.[78] Unfortunately details of relatively few wedding ceremonies are recorded, but the marriages of the Northumbrian kings Æthelwold and Æthelred in 762 and 792 respectively are both said to have taken place at Catterick (Yorks), an important royal vill, but also a significant church site with associations with the Gregorian missionary James the deacon who had remained in Northumbria when Bishop Paulinus withdrew from the see of York on the death of king Edwin in 633.[79] The concept of legitimate and illegitimate marriage, and of legitimate and illegitimate children, began to enter the political discourse. Such issues seem to have been aired when Aldfrith became a candidate for the Northumbrian throne on the death of half-brother Ecgfrith in 685.[80] Aldfrith appears to have been the son of King Oswiu and an Irish princess, in a union of uncertain status from Oswiu's period as an exile in Ireland. Aldfrith seems to have been passed over initially as a possible candidate for the Northumbrian throne in favour of sons by marriages contracted by Oswiu after he succeeded as king in 642. There were clearly circles within Northumbria in which Aldfrith was regarded as illegitimate, as Bede reports, but he also had powerful ecclesiastical backers in the form of Bishop Cuthbert of Lindisfarne and his own half-sister, Abbess Ælfflaed of Whitby, who presumably held him to be a legitimate heir. The papal legates who visited England in 786 urged acceptance of the view that anyone who was illegitimate could not succeed to the throne and linked this with their unsuitability to be anointed as king (another Christianised ceremony that was being promoted at this time).[81] King Offa, who received the legates, had already given an unusually high profile to his queen Cynethryth, presumably to help emphasise the superior claims of their son Ecgfrith to succeed him, and had his son anointed as king in the following year.[82]

The church sought not only to regulate marriage, but also sexual relations both within and outside marriage. Sex was a potential pollutant, and the preparation that laymen were urged to make before major church services and festivals included abstention from it. In fact many churchmen felt it would be better if married people, let alone the unmarried, gave up sex altogether, a view we can see Bishop Wilfrid promoting when he urged Æthelthryth to remain chaste within her marriage. Bede promoted similar ideals in his historical works and theological commentaries.[83] One of his exemplars was the exceptionally pious layman Dryhthelm who lived a religious life with his household, but after his near-death experience and vision of the afterlife separated completely from his wife and entered a religious community.[84] Such extreme antipathy from celibate clergy to the married state cannot have been helpful in making Christian mores acceptable to the bulk of the population, but presumably there were other teachers who promoted more accommodating views, especially as many priests and others in lesser orders were themselves married (something else that met with Bede's disapproval). Aldhelm, for instance, who undoubtedly believed that it was most desirable for those who entered the monastic life to be virgins, nevertheless was at pains to point out in his work *On Virginity* that widows who lived a chaste life after the end of their marriages could also be pleasing to God and less likely to fall into the sin of spiritual pride than the smug virgins.[85] The book was written for the nuns of Barking, many of whom had probably been married and would have been grateful for this reassurance – and potentially extremely annoyed if it had not been forthcoming.

If there were reservations about what could be regarded as legitimate sex within marriage, there was obviously outright condemnation of sex outside marriage. British, Irish and Anglo-Saxon penitentials suggest that many forms of sex were indulged in not only by the laity, but also by those in holy orders, including homosexuality, for both men and women, incest and bestiality. It is unclear whether before conversion the peoples of Britain had been more sexually liberal than they were being urged to be after conversion. Adultery and defilement of virgins were certainly treated as serious crimes in the early Anglo-Saxon lawcodes, partly because they affected rights and honour of the families concerned.[86] It has also been claimed that Germanic paganism involved ceremonies in which sexual activity had a role.[87] Early medieval Britain was probably no exception to the rule that those in positions of power often felt they were beyond normal rules of behaviour. Æthelbald of Mercia received a stinging letter of rebuke from Boniface and other missionary bishops in Germania for many aspects of his behaviour, including his sexual laxity that included sleeping with nuns.[88] Other Anglo-Saxon rulers were also said to have violated nuns, and this is perhaps an indication of the sort of *droit* de *seigneur* they expected to enjoy among the daughters of the nobility. Although basic human nature did not change, the criticisms of churchmen at a time when the Christian responsibilities of kings and kingship as a form of holy office was being promoted, especially in Carolingian Francia in the late eighth and ninth centuries, do seem to have had some impact. Æthelbald's successor Offa promoted himself as a model family man (apart from the murder of some unwelcome relatives),[89] and a century later the young prince Alfred was so troubled by lust that he asked for a discrete disease that would dampen his ardour.[90]

Penance and the expiation of sin

An important aid to the permeation of Christian ideals within insular society was the concept of penance whereby sins could be expiated by appropriate penitential behaviour such as fasting and prayer.[91] For example, from *Theodore's Penitential*, 'if one commits fornication with his mother, he shall do penance for fifteen years and never change except on Sundays', and 'whoever has stolen consecrated things shall do penance for three years without fat and then be allowed to take communion'.[92] The insular world seems to have played a major role in developing private penance for laymen out of the traditions of monastic penance that were the subject of the early penitential literature associated with Gildas, though in the penitential of Uinniau there was already a concern with extending the system to lay people.[93] The Irish were also active in the development of such rulings for laymen, and their penitentials were studied by Archbishop Theodore when he took control of the English church and brought his own experiences of the penitential literature of the eastern church to bear on the topic. Copies of his rulings then circulated in Ireland, perhaps taken back by his Irish students, and informed further developments there.[94] The penitential rulings attributed to Theodore and Adomnán seem to have been records of their pronouncements collected by and from those who had studied with them. The Ionan involvement with penitential literature makes it likely that the penitential system was introduced into Pictland as well, where the Columban church played a significant role throughout the period.

The penitential rulings with their spiritual tariffs were ideally suited to the societies of early medieval Britain that were used to the concept of reparation of crime in their secular legal systems. Instead of compensation being paid to an injured party or their representatives, there were spiritual penalties that, though often severe, were achievable and would enable individuals to rehabilitate themselves in the eyes of God. The whole penitential system must have played an important part in helping laymen to reflect upon the significance of their religion and how it should inform their daily lives. Sins would be privately confessed to a priest, thus preventing the loss of face that was dreaded in the early medieval world and avoiding the possibility of feud if certain crimes were made public. However, for the most serious crimes there was public penance which was an altogether more formidable matter that not only involved public exposure, but exclusion from society and the adoption of a monastic mode of life. We meet such penitents in Adomnán's *Life of Columba* where they were to be found on the subsidiary island of *Hinba* (whose modern identity is unknown) and within the community of Mag Luinge on Tiree.[95] Public penance was not unknown in the early Anglo-Saxon church, but does not appear to have been at all common and it may be significant that the only reference to it is from Northumbria where Irish influence had been for a time dominant.[96] It is possible that some of the early abdications by kings to enter monasteries or to undertake pilgrimage to Rome could be seen as penitential; Caedwalla of Wessex, for instance, who gave up the throne of Wessex in 688 to go to Rome to be baptised (where he subsequently died) certainly had many sins to work off after his brutal treatment of the Jutes of the Isle of Wight.[97] However, such an explanation does not seem appropriate in all cases.[98] Nor was it necessarily convenient or desirable for kings to have to give up their positions because they had infringed Christian laws. Other ways were derived whereby the sins of the most influential members of society could be mitigated to the benefit of the church without loss to their dignity or interruption of their secular roles. When King Oswiu of Bernicia arranged the murder of his fellow ruler Oswine of Deira in 651 he atoned for the crime by founding a monastery at Gilling (Yorks) where, as Bede writes, 'prayers were to be offered daily to the Lord for the redemption of the souls of both kings, the murdered king and the one who ordered the murder'.[99] The foundation of the church at Gilling provided a way of dealing with the murder of Oswine for which it would have been difficult to provide a satisfactory solution by traditional secular means. Oswine was related to Oswiu's queen Eanflaed and as the surviving relative of the highest status she might under traditional expectations have been obliged to prosecute a feud against her husband. As it was, Bede specifically states that it was Eanflaed who requested this form of reparation from Oswiu and that another kinsman be installed as the first abbot.[100] A comparable example is the granting of land by King Ecgbert of Kent (664–73) to his kinswoman Æbbe in compensation for his murder of her two brothers that she used to found the nunnery of Minster-in-Thanet.[101] In such ways the church established its value in early medieval society by finding a way of mitigating potentially serious crime that could otherwise have been solved only by further bloodshed and instability.

The ability to commute penance did, of course, lessen its impact upon the more powerful and wealthy of society who could afford to pay others to say prayers, or even to fast, on their behalf. Concern that some laymen apparently believed that generous almsgiving allowed them to sin with impunity was expressed at the synod of *Clofesho* in 747, and Bishop Boniface was at pains to point out in his letter to King Æthelbald in the same year that his generosity as an almsgiver did not offset other grave deficiencies in his behaviour.[102] But there were limits to how far churchmen could or had the will to make fundamental changes to an unequal society where the rich and powerful had inherent advantages over the poor and weak. The church was, of course, a major beneficiary of the need of rulers to expiate sin, as we have seen from the examples of the foundation of churches in compensation for murder, and so lacked the incentive to change a system that worked to its advantage and persuaded leaders of the church's utility for ensuring their own well-being.

War and peace

Bede when he wished to give an impression of the benefits King Edwin of Northumbria had brought to his people through conversion to Christianity stressed the gift of a peace so great that 'a woman with a new-born child could walk throughout the island from sea to sea and take no harm'.[103] Such peace was no doubt profoundly wished for by many in society who could thereby get on with their everyday lives without risk of their crops and worse being destroyed or requisitioned by enemy forces, or even by their own side, and it provided the conditions that the church needed to function effectively. But war, as we have seen, was fundamental to the aristocratic way of life in early medieval Britain and so was a factor which had to be incorporated into the way Christianity was presented to, and absorbed by, that influential sector of society. Although one could see pacifist tendencies in the teaching of the New Testament, the Old Testament was full of fighting and interventions by God on behalf of his favoured forces. Ever since the successful incorporation of Christianity as the main religion of the Roman empire, there had been the promotion of the concept of a 'just' war as defined by St Augustine. Gildas had condemned the 'unjust' wars of contemporary British kings that were fought against each other rather than directed towards the pagan Saxon threat.[104] In his *Ecclesiastical History* Bede provides an exposition of Anglo-Saxon, and above all Northumbrian, history as that of a new Children of Israel with a careful explanation for the success and failure of many military enterprises in the tradition of the Old Testament. King Oswald is said to have declared that he was fighting in a 'just cause' when he set up a wooden cross as his standard before his decisive victory over the British king Caedwalla in 634 'and gained the victory that their faith merited' in spite of fielding the smaller army; Adomnán attributed Oswald's victory to St Columba's intervention on his behalf.[105] On the other hand, King Ecgfrith's disastrous defeat at *Nechtansmere* in 685 was judgement on him for despatching a raiding force to Ireland which attacked churches and monasteries of 'a harmless race that had always been most friendly to the English'.[106] In such ways could God's temporary desertion of his Chosen People be explained in line with Old Testament interpretations and kings be provided with an object lesson in how wrong behaviour on their part might have dire consequences. In plotting war the wise king would be advised to consider the advice of his churchmen. Oswald was successfully able to expand his overlordship in Britain by acting in concert with Bishop Aidan from Iona,[107] whereas Ecgbert's fatal expedition against the Picts had been made against the advice of Bishop Cuthbert. In addition to any divine inspiration that Cuthbert may have enjoyed, he had contacts in Pictland and had himself visited the province, and so may have been able to assess the likelihood of success or defeat.[108] The wise king gave thanks to God for his victory, as did Oswiu of Northumbria, who vowed his daughter to the church and to give 12 estates to found monasteries if he was successful in defeating Penda of Mercia at the battle of the River Winwaed in 655.[109] Perhaps Bede felt Oswiu could have been even more generous for he mentions twice that the estates were 'small'; Bede must have been well aware that the wealthy Northumbrian monasteries such as his own Wearmouth and Jarrow had flourished on the back of Northumbrian military successes in the seventh century.

The worst excesses of Anglo-Saxon warfare that Bede admits to are said to have been carried out by pagans such as Æthelfrith of Northumbria (d. 616) and Caedwalla of Wessex (685–8). The savage harrowing of Northumbria in 633 by the British king Caedwalla, when he behaved like 'a savage tyrant' in sparing neither women nor children, was all the more shocking because he was a Christian and should have known better, whereas civilised behaviour could not have been expected from his ally, the pagan Penda of Mercia.[110] Bede was clearly concerned that there should be a recognition of Christian rules of engagement in war and that the innocent who were especially under God's protection – women, children, the old and infirm, and churches – should not have to suffer its consequences. Aldhelm of Malmesbury, whose monastery was extremely close to the border of West Saxons and that of the Mercian protectorate of the Hwicce, benefited from patronage from both powers, but his foundation would also have become vulnerable if hostilities broke out between them – and there was already a long tradition of such occurrences when Aldhelm was in control of Malmesbury in the last decades of the seventh century. To try to ensure recognition of Malmesbury's neutrality, Aldhelm obtained a grant of privileges from Pope Sergius I and persuaded Ine of Wessex and Æthelred of Mercia to agree that Malmesbury should not be attacked or made to suffer in other ways as a result of wars between their two kingdoms.[111] Concern with increasing royal violence that affected the security of churches in Wales is also expressed in the Llandaf charters, though there are problems in knowing exactly when these sections were written.[112]

The most noteworthy attempt to modify the harsh realities of warfare for the civilian population in line with Christian ideals was Adomnán's enactment of the *Law of the Innocents*, which is also known as the *Cáin*

Adomnán, at a meeting in the monastery of Birr in Munster in 697 that combined an ecclesiastical synod with a royal assembly.[113] The text survives in two early modern manuscripts that contain accretions of different dates, but a reconstruction has been made of the core version of 697. The participants were persuaded to recognise that warfare should not involve innocent parties including the church, the young and, above all, women. The meeting in effect, as Máirí Ní Dhonchadha has argued, redefined peace as a pact (its original Latin meaning) in which the entire population recognised the obligation that women, youths and clerics would be protected from the effects of violence and from any need to resort to violence themselves in self-defence. In fact the *Law* went further to outlaw any acts of violence against women, and is generally noteworthy for its sympathy with the plight of women in the male-dominated world of the early Middle Ages. A preface added in the tenth or eleventh century refers to women being forced to take part in battles and being driven before the main line of troops to receive the brunt of an enemy's attack, a chilling indictment that, if true, casts a very different light on the supposedly 'heroic' world of early medieval warfare, about which Irish commentators were inclined to be less rose-tinted than their Anglo-Saxon counterparts. Penance and fines were to be imposed on guilty parties, and there was also provision for a chanting of selected psalms in a ritual to excommunicate malefactors.

Ninety-one guarantors agreed to support the *Law of the Innocents*, not all of whom were necessarily present at Birr in 697. In addition to leading churchmen and rulers from within Ireland, who naturally made up the bulk of the guarantors' list, there were representatives from the province of the Dál Riata in Scotland, and also Bishop Curetán and King Bridei mac Derile of the Picts, a testimony to the dominant influence of the Columban connection in the Pictish church at this time. There was therefore the potential for warfare in northern Britain to have been modified by the views promoted by Adomnán. Anglo-Saxon kingdoms were not represented at Birr, though the English bishop Wictbert of the Northumbrian Columban community at Clonmelsh (*Rath Melsigi*) in Ireland was present. But Adomnán also had influence with King Aldfrith of Northumbria (686–705) who had stayed with him on Iona immediately before his accession to the Northumbrian throne. Adomnán visited Northumbria in 686 and 688, and was able to perform another humanitarian act in arranging the release of hostages who had been taken after Ecgfrith's raid on the southern Uí Néill territory of Brega. According to the Middle Irish preface to the *Law of the Innocents*, Adomnán had been in part persuaded to draft his *cáin* because of his mother's horrified reaction to the sight of dead and dying women on a battlefield of Brega, which could be a reference to the Anglo-Saxon attack. Aldfrith, who had been educated in the Irish church and obtained the rank of a *sapiens*, is in any case likely to have held different views on warfare from his predecessor and is not known to have taken part in any battles. Unfortunately Bede's judgement on his reign is frustratingly opaque and he merely records that 'he ably restored the shattered state of the kingdom although within narrower bounds'.[114]

The *Law of the Innocents* undoubtedly benefited the Columban church in the sense that it was to provide the judges for cases of infringement and received the fines that were imposed. It must have increased the personal standing and influence of Adomnán himself, aided by his kinship with Loingsech who had become Uí Néill overlord in 696 and whose own position would have been boosted by the hosting of the meeting at Birr. However, none of these things detract from the humanitarian basis of the *Law* and the attempt made within it to bring Christian values to bear on the cult of violence inherent in early medieval aristocratic culture that could blight the lives of the rest of the population. The substitution of church foundation for escalating feud, as seen in the examples of Gilling and Minster-in-Thanet discussed above, also played an important role in reducing levels of internal violence. Another significant intervention was that of Archbishop Theodore following the battle of the River Trent in 679 fought between King Ecgfrith of Northumbria and King Æthelred of Mercia. Ecgfrith's young brother Ælfwine had been killed in the battle; he was also the brother-in-law of Æthelred who had married his sister Osthryth. Perhaps with the aid of this relationship, Theodore was able to reconcile both parties with his 'wholesome advice' so that, in the words of Bede:

Peace was restored between the two kings and between their peoples and no further lives were demanded for the death of the king's brother, but only the usual money compensation which was paid to the king to whom the duty of vengeance belonged.[115]

Theodore no doubt intended that this public reconciliation would serve as a model for other members of the community, for in the penitential rulings attributed to him the penance of seven to ten years for a man involved in a revenge killing on behalf of a kinsman is halved if a wergild was paid.[116] All killing was a sin, and even those who fought in armies were meant to do penance for any deaths they caused; in *The Gododdin* members of the army are depicted going to church before the raid to do penance for any sins they are going to commit.[117] However, in *Theodore's Penitential* the penance for a killing that was part of a public war is the relatively light 40 days.[118]

Concepts of protected space within religious communities allowed the development of the idea of sanctuary whereby wrongdoers or victims of feud could receive temporary protection and a cooling-off period that might lead to a peaceful solution through negotiation.[119] Such concepts were able to draw on existing ideas of 'protection' enshrined in secular laws of both the Anglo-Saxons and the Welsh, and which, for instance, turned anywhere where the king was present into a type of neutral space and where any infringement of its peace brought severer fines. The first law of the code of King Æthelbert transferred such concepts to the church as well, and doubled the compensation payable for a breach of the peace in a church or public meeting-place. Rights of sanctuary granted by kings to early saints, and so to their successor churches, figure prominently in the earliest Welsh saints' lives from the twelfth century, but once again we have the problem of how far we can project such information back into an earlier period.[120] The retreat of kings and nobles to religious houses can often be explained through such ideas of the ecclesiastical community as a kind of neutral space to which individuals could withdraw as an alternative to more brutal solutions.[121] Such ideas may have been developed in Ireland in the seventh century, but in the disturbed politics of eighth-century Northumbria the sanctuary of religious communities was repeatedly violated, probably because these houses were seen as being too partisan. [122]

As bishops and some other leading churchmen were included among the advisers of kings they had many opportunities to influence the outcome of decisions in accordance with Christian ethics, though their opinions may not, of course, have always carried the day. Lawcodes are one area where we can see an increasing Christian influence including a stress on internal peace and attempts to reduce violence in society. The preface to the laws of Ine, which are notable in this respect, specifically mention the contribution of his bishops Haedde and Eorcenwald, and it is possible that other leading churchmen such as Aldhelm also had an input.[123] One would like to know whether the relatively humane treatment accorded to his British subjects in the lawcode, especially when compared to the apparently brutal treatment of the Jutes of Wight by his predecessor Caedwalla, owed anything to an intervention by churchmen. Aldhelm was actively and successfully persuading British Christians of the west at this time to abandon their disputed church customs and can be expected to have promoted charity towards fellow Christians.[124] However, warfare remained a major element in early medieval society, and the advent of the Vikings at the end of the eighth century, with their penchant for attacking wealthy churches, produced a 'pagan' threat that churchmen and laymen agreed needed to be curtailed by force of arms. Nevertheless there are signs that by the end of the seventh century rulers had been made to reflect on their obligations in matters of war and peace as Christian rulers.

Kingship and politics

Because of their pivotal role in the control of their societies, and the pro-tection and patronage they could provide, kings had been a focus of missionary endeavour, and both the Gregorian mission and those associ-ated with Iona had established working relationships with kings as a prelude to reaching wider elements of the population. There was no shortage of role models held up to kings to emulate from the Bible and the early Christian world.[125] Æthelbert was urged by Pope Gregory to model himself on Constantine, the Roman emperor who had ensured that Christianity became the major religion of the Roman empire, and Bede's description of Oswald choosing the cross as the standard under which he would fight Caedwalla was meant to recall Constantine's use of the same symbol at the battle of the Milvian Bridge that was also won against the odds through divine intervention.[126] Non-Christian Anglo-Saxon kings who were nevertheless part of the divine plan were compared by Bede with Old Testament rulers, notably King Æthelfrith of Northumbria (d. 616) who was equated with Saul.[127] Other writers from the insular world had regular recourse to the Old Testament with its galaxy of good and bad kings that could cover most facets of the behaviour of contemporary rulers. Gildas drew heavily on the rebukes of the prophets to feckless rulers to continue their work in his own day.[128] Stephanus threw out par-allels with good and bad biblical rulers depending on how contemporary kings treated his hero Wilfrid, for whom repeated comparisons are made with Old Testament prophets; Ecgfrith was as strong as David when he supported Wilfrid, but became a Herod when he ordered Wilfrid to prison.[129] Pictish kings were probably invited to reflect on the models of kingship provided by the Bible in a similar way, and one object that seems to show the use of positive biblical parallels for a Pictish ruler is the St Andrew sarcophagus that has been linked with the patronage of King

Onuist (d. 761), the founder of the community.[130] The sarcophagus portrays a number of Davidic scenes and is dominated by an arresting image of a David in Roman dress protecting his flock by rending the jaws of a lion. As a preliminary to this event David is also shown, this time with Pictish dress and equipment, participating in a lion-hunt, a scene which draws ultimately from late antique models of Sassanid Persia that have also provided griffins and other exotic animals. David is evoked on other Pictish box-shrines and cross-slabs in similar guises, and also as the composer of the psalms with careful delineation of his harp in native form. David was a particularly appropriate model for an insular king. He was a major warrior-figure, who experienced both successes and failures, the latter because all too human weaknesses sometimes led him to stray from the path of righteousness. King Alfred who translated the first 50 psalms was no doubt struck by parallels between David's lamentations to God when he failed to defeat his enemies and his own difficult progress against the Vikings.[131] David was also the Old Testament type, that is paralleled figure, of Christ who was descended from him. Davidic imagery is found throughout the insular world, but Pictish craftsmen were notably inventive in linking him with images of classical and Pictish rulership through evocation of the hunt whose iconography seems to have been particularly meaningful in the Pictish province.

The models of good and bad behaviour held up to Christian kings incorporated some facets that many would have found irksome, such as the reining in of sexual appetites, and others which called for a shift in emphasis, such as the desirability of peace. But there were many aspects of the Christian model of kingship that echoed existing expectations of good lordship or could be adapted to encompass them. A good illustration of the merging of Christian and traditional expectations of rulers is to be seen in the Irish tract *De duodecim abusives saculi* (Concerning the twelve abuses of the world) that probably dates to the seventh century.[132] Sections in the work that reflect on good and bad rulership stress some expected Christian virtues such as the need to rule with justice, but also link good royal behaviour with such concepts as fertility of the soil, good weather and calm seas which seem to come from older notions of Irish kingship in which the ruler was responsible for the prosperity and good fortune of his people. The Old English poem *Beowulf*, on the other hand, contains a skilful exposition of how the ideals of warrior leadership could be compatible with Christian teachings and how the latter could provide a leader with the type of 'wisdom' he needed to make ethical and informed decisions, as Alfred sought to discover for himself in the ninth century.[133]

Such links were made easier by the fact that key words from the Old English vocabulary of lordship were used for Latin equivalents. Thus *dryhten,* an Old English word for a 'lord' of a warband, such as Beowulf, was used to translate the biblical 'Lord' that is Christ or God himself.[134] Such equations could lead to what seems to us an anachronistic confusion of ideas as in the poem 'Descent into Hell' from the tenth-century Exeter book where Christ is the leader of a *comitatus* of apostles and leads a raid on hell to liberate his loyal kinsman and follower, John the Baptist.[135] Such linkages may have served to disguise from Anglo-Saxons some of the differences between Christian and traditional attitudes, but also led to some original and arresting contemplation of Christian episodes and teachings in such poems as *The Dream of the Rood.*[136] They were also of undoubted importance in demonstrating that Christianity could be compatible with key elements of the ethos of a warrior society.

We have seen plentiful evidence that kings became convinced of the importance of Christianity to themselves and the success of their kingdoms from the extent of their patronage of the church. In some cases the personal commitment was apparently so strong that it led to a renunciation of the throne for retirement to a monastery or religious pilgrimage.[137] The extent to which kings were motivated by religious belief and concern for their own salvation is hard to evaluate, and no doubt varied between individuals, but should not be left out of any discussion about why kings decided to support the church. At the same time it can be recognised that there were ways in which Christianity supported and enhanced the position of kingship which helped to demonstrate the continuing utility and effectiveness of the new religion at a temporal level. Although Christian interpretations presented kingship as a divinely ordained office whose holders were expected to discharge certain responsibilities, it also stressed that a king's subjects had a religious duty to respect the king and obey his commands. Christianity had already demonstrated its utility as a state religion during the Roman empire, and among the attractions of Christianity in the post-Roman world was its association with the Roman past which provided a rhetoric that supported the position of princes, but also an inheritance of practical value such as that of learning and literacy.

In the Anglo-Saxon kingdoms of the seventh and eighth centuries, and perhaps in those of the Picts as well, royal and ecclesiastical power advanced together and their structures supported one another. In the laws of the Kentish and West Saxon kingdoms of the seventh and early eighth centuries we can see increasing royal demands that people act as Christians, baptising their children, observing the sabbath and making payments of churchscot to support their minsters. At the same time royal officials were increasing their intervention in temporal affairs through supervision in the local courts of the maintenance of law and order and an increasing provision for the intervention of royal justice in more serious cases.[138] The westward advance of Wessex provides a very good example of the way the church could facilitate political expansion by breaking down the barrier to integration that was presented by the British adherence to various church customs regarded as dangerously separatist by Rome, but which had become an integral part of British identity and independence by the seventh century. The will of the British to offer resistance was assailed from two fronts, the military strength of the West Saxon forces on the one hand and the force of the arguments for communion with Rome and of dangers to the soul from aberrant practices advanced by churchmen such as Aldhelm on the other. Capitulation on both fronts may have meant defeat, both actual and psychological, but also survival.[139]

By the eighth century we are justified in saying that Christianity had become an integral part of court culture. Of course, the degree of emphasis might vary from ruler to ruler. Aldfrith of Northumbria (686–705) who had been educated as a scholar in Ireland was presumably exceptional in his love of books and the establishment of a royal library.[140] Æthelbald of Mercia (716–57) may have been more typical of royal interests, but his reign ended with the rebukes of Boniface and other missionary bishops and murder by his own *comitatus*. Æthelbald seems to have offended against both acceptable lay and ecclesiastical norms of behaviour, and perhaps by the mid-eighth century these were not so far apart. His successor Offa (757–96) was not above questionable behaviour, but in the letters of Alcuin in particular we have glimpses of a court which had at least some aspirations to emulate that of his great Frankish contemporary Charles the Great whose patronage was so important to the revival of Christian learning and the arts, known as the Carolingian Renaissance.[141] Letters and individual ambassadors travelled between the two courts, and also those of Wessex and Northumbria.

There is a danger that in looking separately at topics such as 'kingship' and 'the church' we drive artificial barriers between them. When many monasteries were managed by members of royal houses, or depended on their patronage, and might be among the places visited by itinerant kings, we need to recognise that they were part of both 'royal' and 'ecclesiastical' worlds. The previous chapter has already explored the distinctive aristocratic character of many minsters that were not so much proto-Benedictine communities in isolation from the world but places where lay and ecclesiastical culture intermingled. Excavation of the royal Dalriadic site at Dunadd that was occupied in the seventh and eighth centuries has revealed some finds such as weapons that are indicative of its secular function, but also others such as a quern marked with a cross, a stone with a Christian invocation and material connected with the production of decorative metalwork that would not be out of place on a contemporary ecclesiastical site, and are evidence of literacy or the type of craftsmanship which could have been utilised for either lay or ecclesiastical artefacts.[142] In England there is currently debate about whether certain sites can be classed as minsters or royal palaces, and whether objects such as the early Anglo-Saxon sceatta coinage, which often bears a religious iconography, should be seen as the product of royal or ecclesiastical production.[143] Perhaps we are following the wrong line in seeking to label them as one or the other. Many minsters were strongly identified with ruling houses and could be seen as extensions of the royal court. Anglo-Saxon kings have been shown as following their own inclinations in founding monasteries or promoting saints' cults, and there is no reason why they could not have initiated other forms of ecclesiastical patronage in ways they felt promoted their interests. Pictish sculptures of the eighth and ninth centuries that depict scenes with a strong secular resonance, such as the battle scenes on Sueno's stone and the Aberlemno cross-slab, and the traditions associating particular Pictish kings with the foundation of major churches suggest they too may have taken the initiative in utilising the skills and rhetoric of the church for their own advantage.

In a period of much political upheaval it was inevitable that churchmen, who might be related to leading families or dependent on their patronage, would be drawn into factional competition and that ecclesiastical considerations could be utilised to try to influence the desirability of one candidate over another. The death of one king and the succession of another was always a potentially fragile period for a kingdom when disputes about the throne could threaten the *status quo* and lay the province open to external attack. There were no guaranteed rules of succession, though practice is likely to have varied within the provinces of Britain, but there were various ways in which a kin-group already in power could seek to manipulate the succession. However, in most provinces, as we have seen, there were rival dynasties or royal segments, and if there was a change in regime those who acquired the throne would be anxious to legitimise their actions and adopt strategies that would persuade or compel other powerful individuals in a kingdom to recognise their authority. In all these situations there were opportunities for the church to influence or validate events that would often be of great consequence to the ecclesiastical hierarchy as well as to the lay elite. The church could offer both ideological and practical support. The former could include interpretation of the will of God and stress the dangers to one's mortal and immortal well-being in not following it. There has been much debate about whether a formal act of designation or ordination of kings was adopted in the insular world before the end of the eighth century.[144] Gildas refers to contemporary British kings being anointed in God's name,[145] and there is a particularly suggestive passage in Adomnán's *Life of Columba* in which he describes Columba's ordination of Áedán mac Gabráin as king, though many would see the account as indicative of Adomnán's own aspirations rather than an actual practice of Columba's day.[146] The Old Testament precedent for early medieval ordination was the anointing of Saul by the prophet Samuel, and an early promotion of the ceremony in the British and Irish churches could be seen as consistent with the type of detailed study of the Old Testament to provide norms of behaviour that can be seen in their early penitential literature. Irish ecclesiastics may have been particularly anxious to find a Christian substitution for, or addition to the traditional royal inauguration ceremonies that may have incorporated concepts of the king 'marrying' the goddess of the land. Traces have been identified in Scottish Dál Riata, above all at Dunadd, of inauguration sites comparable to those that have been studied in Ireland.[147] Although in England some ecclesiastical element to royal inauguration ceremonies might be expected from the seventh century, the first undoubted reference to a royal anointing was to that arranged by Offa of Mercia for his son Ecgfrith in 787, no doubt in an attempt to ensure his succession.[148] It is usually accepted that Offa modelled his ceremony for Ecgfrith on the anointing of Pepin as king of the Franks in 751, which marked the final overthrow of the Merovingian dynasty and its replacement by the Carolingians (named after Pepin's father Charles Martel). After this point there was a considerable development of royal coronation ceremonies both in Francia and England, and references to royal ordinations also begin to appear in Irish annals, suggesting that whatever practices Adomnán may have been keen to promote from Iona in the seventh century were by no means universal in Irish milieu by that date.

Churchmen could not only bear testimony to the will of God but could often bring substantial resources from their landed wealth to aid a favoured candidate. Bishop Wilfrid was said to have possessed 'a countless army of followers arrayed in royal vestments and arms' and left a quarter of his wealth 'to purchase the friendship of kings and bishops'.[149] The importance of the support of a prelate such as Wilfrid is suggested by events after the death of King Aldfrith in 705. Aldfrith, as had his brother Ecgfrith before him, had fallen out with Wilfrid and expelled him from the kingdom, so it is not surprising that Wilfrid is initially found supporting not Aldfrith's son Osred but a rival candidate called Eadwulf whose own son was apparently in his household. However, Eadwulf rebuffed Wilfrid and lost his throne to Osred a couple of months later. Stephanus implies, but does not spell out that the two events were related and it is apparent from what he goes on to record that the accession of Osred had been achieved by a reconciliation of his supporters with Wilfrid, for as Ealdorman Berhtfrith recalled 'when we were besieged in the city of Bamburgh ... we vowed that if God granted our royal boy his father's kingdom, we would fulfil the apostolic commands concerning Bishop Wilfrid' which was sufficient to win over troops on the opposing side (perhaps warriors provided by Wilfrid himself).[150]

The relatively detailed sources from Northumbria for the late seventh and eighth centuries enable us to see how deeply involved churchmen became in the many disputes between rival branches of the royal house.[151] There were ideological tensions in the Northumbrian church in the aftermath of the synod of Whitby that affected the relationship of individual prelates and kings and are very apparent in the career of that hardliner on the calculation of Easter and related issues, Bishop Wilfrid. But it is also clear that the allegiances of many abbots and bishops were decided by their family connections and the patronage ties of their communities. Lindisfarne, for instance, maintained long-standing links with the family of Oswald their founder. Cuthbert of Lindisfarne, with the aid of Adomnán of Iona, had played a significant role in assisting the return of Oswald's nephew Aldfrith from Ireland to succeed his half-brother Ecgfrith in 686. In 750 Lindisfarne gave sanctuary to Aldfrith's son Offa, but the reigning king Eadbert (brother of Archbishop Ecgbert of York to whom Bede had addressed his letter) laid siege to the principal church, took Bishop Cynewulf of Lindisfarne prisoner and had Offa forcibly removed from the relics of St Cuthbert 'almost dead with hunger'. Lindisfarne seems to have been frequently involved in royal politics. King Ceolwulf retired there in 737; in 793 Ealdorman Sicga who had been responsible for the murder of King Ælfwold in 788 committed suicide, but was received for burial at Lindisfarne. In 796 another ealdorman called Osbald retreated there and then sailed to the kingdom of the Picts with some of the brothers. Meanwhile Wilfrid's foundations of Ripon and

Hexham can be shown to have supported some of the kings attacked by those who were given succour at Lindisfarne. King Ælfwold who had been killed by Ealdorman Sicga in 788 was buried at Hexham, which seems to have nurtured a cult of him as a martyr. In 790 Ealdorman Eardwulf was left for dead on the orders of King Osred II outside the gates of Ripon, but was restored to health by the monks and subsequently became king; it is possible he was related to the Eadwulf who had initially been supported by Wilfrid in 705. Osred II himself was forcibly tonsured in York in 790, and in 791 the sons of King Ælfwold (who had been murdered in 788) were lured from sanctuary in the principal church at York and killed. Alcuin warned Archbishop Eanbald II of York of the dangers he faced in harbouring the enemies of King Eardwulf (he who had been left for dead at Ripon in 790) and adding them to his own substantial secular household.[152]

These relatively full details from the eighth-century northern annals allow us to see how the major churches of Northumbria had become mired in the cycle of violence which accompanied the factional politics of that time. The enmity between Wilfrid and Cuthbert that had its origins in the Easter controversy of the seventh century appears to have been continued by their foundations in the eighth century through support for rival factions, with the church of York seemingly favouring other contestants. The right of sanctuary that should have eased reconciliation was not respected and Bede, who had probably seen how things were moving, put into Cuthbert's mouth a speech in which he feared that the community would be disturbed by an 'influx of fugitives and guilty men of every sort' who sought sanctuary at his tomb. If we had more information we would no doubt be able to trace a similar involvement of religious communities with secular politics in Dál Riata and the Pictish provinces where there are hints of similar patterns of behaviour. The emphasis that Adomnán places on Columba's support for the Cenél Gabráin may be an indication of Iona's support for that dynasty at the time he was writing when it had entered a period of contest for the throne with the Cenél Loairn.[153] The Pictish king Nechtan son of Derilei renounced his throne in 724 to enter a monastery, only to re-emerge and eventually resume his reign in 728 in a period of intense rivalry for the throne.[154] In 733 the Dál Riatan king Dungal violated the sanctuary of the religious community on Tory Island in Donegal in order to forcibly remove the Pictish prince Bridei (son of King Onuist) who had taken refuge there.[155]

Churchmen could make a different sort of contribution to factional dispute by framing cases on the acceptability of individuals for the kingship founded on Christian principles, as with the claim that King Aldfrith was an illegitimate son of King Oswiu. Criticism from the church might help to undermine a tyrannical king. It is, for instance an interesting question whether the castigation of Æthelbald of Mercia by Boniface and other missionary bishops may have emboldened his *comitatus* to rise up against him and kill him (though that presumably had not been Boniface's intention). King Coenwulf of Mercia (796–821) found a convenient pretext for deposing Eadbert Praen as king of Kent in 798 on the grounds that he had formerly been a priest and so could not take secular office; Eadbert was imprisoned in Coenwulf's family monastery at Winchcombe (Glos) where his daughter was abbess.[156] Conversion to Christianity can therefore be said to have added new dimensions to the competition between the royal houses of the different provinces of early medieval Britain, but without changing the nature of factional politics fundamentally and, in spite of some notable attempts, their involvement did not reduce the level of internal violence associated with them.

The disadvantaged: the poor, slaves and women

Churchmen lavished much attention on trying to influence the behaviour of the leaders of the community, with some success in perceptions of kingship as an office and on candidates (particularly in the initial periods of conversion), but with rather less impact on royal and noble behaviour in general. Native church leaders were drawn from the ranks of the aristocracy and the introduction of Christianity had provided new opportunities for families at this level to acquire land and offices. How far did these church leaders want or were able to change the lot of the more disadvantaged members of society? It will already have become apparent from previous discussions that the introduction of Christianity to Britain did not call for or cause any radical changes within society. After it had become the major religion of the Roman empire Christian rhetoric had supported the status quo and the established order of society while seeking to modify morals and aspects of behaviour. As God was held to have created the world, to criticise its structures would have been to risk criticism of God himself. Evil and unfairness had come into the world through the fatal flouting of God's instructions by Adam and Eve. It therefore became every individual's duty to fill whatever station in life had been allotted to them in accord with Christian principles and to the best of their ability. Christ's preaching promised that those who had been most disad-

vantaged in this world would be honoured in the next, and this seems to
have been a message that did bring solace to such individuals for when
Christianity spread to new areas in the Roman world it was often women
and the poor who were the first to embrace it.[157]

We should not, therefore, expect the introduction of Christianity to
early medieval Britain to have led to any radical changes in the lives of the
underclass, but there were aspects to the new religion that could have
encouraged more humane treatment. It was clearly the intention that the
whole of society should embrace the new religion. Anglo-Saxon lawcodes,
for instance, make it clear that all sectors were to have their children baptised and observe the sabbath, and that it was the duty of those who were
lords of men to ensure that they were able to practise their faith correctly.
The recognition that all humans had souls was of particular importance
to slaves who lacked many of the basic rights of even the poorest peasants.
Slaves could be bought and sold as if they were farm animals, but
Christianity insisted on the recognition of a major distinction between
man and beasts for only the former had a soul and slaves had to be
allowed access to religion as fellow Christians.[158] The church did not dis-
approve of slavery as such and was a major owner of slaves; in the
Domesday Book the greatest concentration of slaves was to be found on
church lands. Anglo-Saxon lawcodes did not seek to end trade in slaves as
such, but were concerned that slaves should not be sold overseas where
they might come into the ownership of non-Christians and so not be able
to practise their faith.[159] The church did recognise that slavery was one of
the evils that had come into the world as a result of the Fall of man, and
the freeing of slaves, manumission, was a charitable act that aided the
redemption of the person doing the freeing and might be formally carried
out at an altar. Bishop Wilfrid is said to have freed the 250 slaves he was
given with an estate at Selsey (Sussex)[160] – they would have continued to
work for him as freedmen – and one of the few contemporary written
accounts to have come down from early medieval Wales is a record of
manumission added to the Lichfield Gospels in the ninth century when
they were at the religious house of Llandeilo Fawr.[161] Adomnán records
how the Pictish *magus* Broichan was stricken with illness when he refused
to release an Irish slave-girl at the request of Columba.[162]

Protection of the poorer and weaker members of society was one of
the injunctions laid upon Christian kings and enacted in Anglo-Saxon
lawcodes; it may well have been a traditional responsibility. The giving
of alms to the poor and other charitable acts was one of the duties
expected of Christians in Britain from the writings of Gildas onwards.[163]

Bede illustrated the point with a story about the charity of King Oswald who was interrupted at an Easter feast by an officer 'whose duty it was to relieve the needy' who informed him that a large number of poor people had arrived from all over Northumbria asking for alms. The king at once ordered a great silver dish – perhaps like the one of Byzantine manufacture discovered in the mound 1 ship-burial at Sutton Hoo – to be broken up and given to the poor.[164] In addition to a rare vignette of the impoverished appearing at the royal court, the aftermath of this charitable act is also instructive because Bishop Aidan, moved by the king's generosity, grasped his right hand saying 'may this hand never decay'. The arm was kept as a relic in the royal chapel at Bamburgh (after it and other body parts had been retrieved by Oswald's brother Oswiu following Oswald's death in battle) and the story of its miraculous preservation because of Oswald's charity to the poor was evidently preserved with it. It is a reminder that the deeds of the saints, although they might have a predominantly aristocratic background, were also meant to have a relevance for the more disadvantaged members of society.[165]

There has been much debate about whether the introduction of Christianity improved the position of women or added another layer of misogyny to that inherent to the patriarchal society that was already a dominant feature of early medieval Britain.[166] It is important not to let later medieval developments affect assessment of the early Middle Ages. Both Cuthbert and Adomnán acquired later reputations of hostility towards women that is belied by contemporary sources, and seems particularly unjustified in the case of Adomnán who in his *Law of the Innocents* maintained that women should be treated with greater respect and sought to shield them from physical violence. He argued that the respect due to Mary as mother of God should be translated to all women who were formed in her image. Some of the earliest Marian iconography with the Christ-child is to be found on crosses from Iona and on the coffin of St Cuthbert from its daughter house of Lindisfarne.[167] Although reservations about all sexual relationships can be found in the writings of some early medieval celibate authors from Britain, this does not seem to have been translated, as in later works, in laying undue blame on women for providing sexual temptation as part of the legacy of Eve. One of Bede's main exemplars of the virtues of chastity first in lay life and then in the monastic was a woman, St Æthelthryth of Ely. He not only told the story of her life in some detail, but included a Latin hymn he had composed in her honour some years before.[168] Bede several times observes of individuals in the *Ecclesiastical History* that nobility of birth was matched by nobility in virtue. Former princesses and queens who went into the church were the highest ranked members of lay society within the church (for very few of their male counterparts followed suit) and Bede's personal respect for Æthelthryth may have been underpinned by the deference he would naturally have felt as a member of the Northumbrian nobility for a princess of the East Angles who had been a queen of Northumbria.[169]

The large number of religious communities controlled by women in early Anglo-Saxon England seems to be an example of new opportunities provided for women to play a public role following the introduction of Christianity. Some of these female-led communities can be seen to have been very influential indeed in both ecclesiastical and secular politics. Whitby, for instance, was the location of the famous synod of 664 and a place where a number of future Northumbrian bishops were trained. Its princess-abbesses Hild and Ælfflaed are both credited with playing decisive roles in aspects of Wilfrid's career, and Ælfflaed also had a significant alliance with Cuthbert and emerges as a king-maker on the deaths of her brother Ecgfrith and half-brother Aldfrith.[170] Stephanus described Ælfflaed as 'the comforter and best counsellor of the whole province'.[171] But we can also see these influential princess-abbesses as indicative of one of the principles that seems to have been characteristic of the introduction of Christianity to early medieval Britain, namely that it was adapted to existing structures within society. The Anglo-Saxon abbesses received their opportunities as part of the way in which the Anglo-Saxon ruling houses adopted Christianity rather than through any advancement of the status of women inherent in the church organisation that they inherited. As far as we can tell there was no equivalent to the Anglo-Saxon double houses in the other provinces of Britain (though there were significant nunneries and mixed communities in Ireland and presumably women who took vows as religious in the other areas of Britain). The fact that women could not be priests and bishops meant that there were limits to the authority they could exercise within the church, and the repercussions of this are already apparent in the way that Ællflaed is presented in relation to St Cuthbert in his Lives.[172] Christianity has therefore often been seen as providing less scope for major public religious roles for women than the pagan religions, though we do not know enough about the latter to be certain of this. There were certainly some powerful goddesses in Celtic and Scandinavian mythology whose general behaviour was quite different from that of the Virgin Mary, whose promotion in seventh-century Ireland has sometimes been linked with the need to provide a substitute female holy figure. The popularity of female saints in Ireland and England may also have owed something to a pre-existing expectation that there would be localised female representatives of divine power, though in Anglo-Saxon England their prevalence is also a reflection of the widespread distribution of female-led religious communities.[173] The question of the impact of the introduction of Christianity on the position of women is therefore a complex one, but it could be argued that in the period which is the subject of this book it was more notable for stressing respect for women and, in some cases, providing new opportunities for them, than for those elements that reinforced patriarchy which are certainly there in this period, but received greater stress after 800.

Christian 'magic': medicine and protection

We are now in a position to revisit some of the issues raised at the beginning of Chapter 2 about the compatibility of Christianity with the pre-Christian religions of Britain that are relevant to the questions of the receptivity of the lay population to the new religion and of how the reception of Christianity might have been affected by pre-existing religious beliefs and practice. Although as 'natural' and 'prophetic' religions respectively paganism and Christianity differed in many significant ways, there were also areas of overlap. One of the aims of the pre-Christian religions of early medieval Britain had been to establish some control over the natural world, in particular to safeguard against the ravages of disease and natural disasters. Christianity taught that as God had created the natural world it was in his power to control all its elements as he wished, and the Bible contained many examples of God, the prophets, who were his agents, and Christ exercising such control by sending various forms of plague, parting the sea, walking on water and so on.[174] The traditions of saints' lives inherited by the churches of early medieval Britain assumed that divine grace had enabled exceptional holy men and women to perform similar miracles both in their lifetimes and after death, and many of the accounts of these were closely modelled on biblical counterparts or exemplary hagiographies such as the *Life of St Martin* by Sulpicius Severus and the *Dialogues* of Pope Gregory the Great. Therefore Christianity had its own means of achieving some of the main desiderata of pre-Christian religious practice. Insular saints' lives include miracles which were particularly relevant to the hazards that faced local populations. Bede's *Ecclesiastical History*, for instance, contains several examples of saints intervening to stop fires from spreading, a particular

hazard when practically all buildings were made of wood or other inflam-
mable materials. Adomnán's *Life of St Columba*, on the other hand, has
the saint frequently intervening to deflect storms or to control large wild
animals.

The prevention and cure of illness was a major concern of the early
medieval world, and was part of Christian and pre-Christian religious
practice. Medicine was one of the subjects that was taught at the school
of Canterbury established by Theodore and Hadrian. John of Beverley
recalled advice on the best times to let blood – a staple remedy of classical
and medieval doctors – that he had received while studying with
Theodore. The group of miracles Bede provides for John of Beverley contains several concerned with healing and gives a good overview of the
approaches that might be found after conversion. Prayer and the intervention of John himself are efficacious in a number of cases, though the cleric
Herebald, who was injured falling from a horse, needed to be rebaptised
as his initial baptism had been performed by an incompetent priest.
However, after this ceremony Herebald was handed over to a physician to
deal with his fractured skull, and John's own 'cure' of a dumb boy seems
to have consisted of elementary hygiene and some practical instruction.[175]
There is a combination here of divine intervention, through prayer and
John's personal intercession, and a practical knowledge of medicine
gained through experience and ultimately from the medical traditions of
the antique world. A number of medical texts in Old English survive from
the ninth century and later, and suggest that medical knowledge from the
Mediterranean world was combined with well-established native practice
that had its origins in the pre-Christian past.[176] Both traditions made considerable use of homeopathic, plant-based remedies that could have been
of genuine medical benefit. Bishop Cyneheard of Winchester complained
in a letter of about 754 of the difficulty in acquiring many of the foreign
ingredients listed in the medical books in his library, but the surviving
literature shows that native plants were used in a number of cases and
many such cures were probably the result of long-established traditional
knowledge. Medical knowledge was not confined to clerics for lay physi-
cians are recorded from both Ireland and Anglo-Saxon England.

Lay and clerical doctors probably both made use of prayer and incantation to assist their practical treatments or as the main remedy if no
effective cure was known, and no doubt both forms of approach were
considered necessary to effect a cure. The Old English medical texts
contain not only both types of remedy, but (in varying degrees) both
Christian and non-Christian incantations, even in one notable case a

calling upon Woden to intervene. Traditional, pre-Christian approaches were retained for certain types of illness, including the belief that some illnesses were caused by worms or flying venoms and that short, sharp pains such as stitches were caused by elves jabbing with their spears; there are parallels for such beliefs from other Germanic areas.[177] However, remedies could include some impressive Christianised rituals:

Against flying venom, slash four strokes in the four quarters with an oaken brand; make the brand bloody; throw it away; sing this on it three times; [making the sign of the cross as drawn in the manuscript]: Matthew guide me, Mark protect me, Luke free me, John aid me, always, amen. Destroy, O God, all evil and wickedness; through the power of the Father and the son and the holy Spirit sanctify me; Emmanuel, Jesus Christ, free me from all attack of the enemy; the benediction of the Lord [be] over my head; mighty God in every season. Amen.[178]

The use of prayer, both public and private, to invoke the protection of God and his agents had a long tradition in the insular world. Works of this type are attributed to St Columba, but are probably of slightly later date and from the seventh century, as was the much anthologised and imitated *lorica* or breast-plate of Laidcenn (d. *c.*665).[179] Repetition of such prayers on rising and when going to bed was believed to provide protection by day and night. The Irish church seems to have had an important role in developing both the practice of private prayer and forms of prayer that might be used for this purpose by both lay and religious. That such practices were also followed in Wales and England is suggested by a group of private prayer books of eighth- and early ninth-century date from western Mercia which contain prayers for protection of the Irish type; one of the manuscripts associated with Worcester contains a protective prayer said to be composed by a man with the British name Moucan.[180] Latin was the language ideally used to invoke God, but Anglo-Saxon priests were expected to teach the Lord's Prayer and the Creed in Old English,[181] and Adomnán records that even the most degenerate laymen could receive protection by singing songs in Gaelic in praise of Columba and calling on his name, for the saints could make intercessions with God on behalf of those who sought their aid.[182]

Another form of protection was contained by the wearing or possession of amulets. Anglo-Saxon inhumation burials of the sixth and early seventh centuries, especially of women, shows that the custom was well established among them in the pre-Christian period.[183] Amulets at this time might consist of the claws or bones of birds of prey or the teeth of animals such as wolves that might be worn on necklaces with beads of a variety of materials, some of which may also have been believed to have a protective function. Teeth, fossils and shells, some such as the Red Sea cowries imported from considerable distances, and other miscellaneous items such as objects of Roman origin might be worn in small bags at the waist. Such objects may have provided protection in life as well as death, but it is possible that some had a specific function in funereal and death rituals, such as the miniature combs and toilet implements that were included in pots containing cremations.[184] Towards the end of the period of furnished burial in the seventh century these types of amulets disappeared and were replaced by the wearing of crosses or objects inscribed with a cross, cylindrical copper-alloy containers and, in burials of children and young women, beaver-tooth pendants. It seems likely, as John Blair has argued, that all these objects had Christian connotations and represent a Christian substitute for pagan amulets.[185] The association of crosses is obvious, and has a high-ranking counterpart in the famous pectoral cross buried with St Cuthbert that was made of gold and garnets and may have contained a relic. Some of the cylindrical boxes contained textiles which were possibly examples of *brandea*, cloths that had been in contact with the corporeal relics of a saint. The beaver was associated in Christian commentary with the much-prized virtue of chastity (because of the similarity of the Latin word for chastity (*castitas*) with the word for beaver (*castor*)?) and so may have been deemed to be particularly appropriate for those who had died young.

In northern Britain we lack comparable furnished burials, but there are examples of the inclusion of white or painted pebbles in burials that may be evidence for a comparable amuletic tradition. Adomnán has Columba on one of his visits to Pictland take a pebble from the river Ness with the words 'Mark this white stone ... through which the Lord will bring about the healing of many sick people'.[186] Subsequently the *magus* Broichan was cured by drinking water in which the stone had been placed, or rather on which it miraculously floated. White quartzite pebbles, some painted with small circles or dots, are known from a number of sites in Shetland, Orkney and Caithness stretching back to the early centuries AD, but some of the later examples appear to have been Christianised by the addition of a cross.[187] The small slate disc from Dunadd inscribed *in nomine* (in the name of [the Lord]) may have been a comparable portable amulet, and scatterings of white quartzite pebbles over burials have been recorded from Whithorn and a number of sites in Wales and Ireland.[188] Stones might be included in the amuletic collections found with Anglo-Saxon female burials, and the use of stones is recommended for some cures in the later Anglo-Saxon medical collections such as Bald's *Leechbook*. A belief in the magical powers of certain stones, which seems to have been present in some parts of Britain at least before conversion, continued after Christianisation, perhaps aided by a verse from the Revelation of St John the Divine that presents a white stone as a symbol of salvation.[189]

If the interpretation of these examples is correct, it suggests a willingness among early missionaries to provide Christian substitutes for amulets whose power had been believed previously to stem from a different source, and a willingness by the population to accept them and presumably to trust in their efficiency. Archbishop Theodore allowed that one who was possessed by a demon could have curing stones or herbs, provided that no pagan incantation was said over them,[190] and so seems to echo Columba's endorsement of the healing properties of certain stones through God's power. However, such practices could be regarded as questionable by *de rigiste* commentators and towards the end of the eighth century Alcuin took a very different attitude and wrote to Archbishop Æthelheard complaining about a practice he had seen on his last visit to England of men wearing amulets for 'it is better to imitate the examples of the saints in the heart than to carry bones in little bags, to have gospel teachings in the mind than to wear them around the neck scribbled on scraps of parchment'.[191] The latter practice reveals the faith placed in the writing of holy script that is also suggested by the *in nomine* stone from Dunadd and implied in the incising of a cross as part of the ritual of the charms. It also recalls the question put by the thegn holding Imma who when his chains repeatedly fall off enquired whether he had 'any loosing letters' about him,[192] perhaps a reference to runes that may have been used in pre-Christian times for magical among other purposes. Runic script continued to be used alongside Latin scripts after the conversion of the Anglo-Saxons, and, though writing could be used for purely practical purposes, the recording of certain holy words accompanied by appropriate ritual might also acquire talismanic properties. One can only speculate whether the inscription of Pictish symbols might also have had magical properties that could have been adapted to Christian contexts following conversion.[193]

It would appear that the spread of Christianity was aided by some deliberate decisions by church leaders to emphasise certain areas of continuity between the new religion and previous religious practice. Such adaptations were in line with Pope Gregory's instructions to Mellitus and are also comparable with what seems to have occurred earlier during the conversion of the British and Irish to Christianity in the fourth and fifth centuries.[194] But although there may have been some deliberate substitutions, for instance of Christian for pagan amulets, not all adaptations to take account of native practice necessarily occurred in this way, but might be a natural by-product of incorporating the new religion into organised societies where religious intervention was expected in certain circumstances such as severe illness. It is not necessary to see such actions as a kind of 'dumbing-down' of Christianity to take account of the more magical expectations of native societies that risked compromising the integrity of the Christian religion. Nor is it necessary to suggest that there was a divide between a type of popular 'Christian magic' allowed to lay people, while the educated clergy followed more 'correct' forms.[195] Control of natural forces was an expectation of both pagan and Christian belief and there were certain areas of overlap in the rituals for achieving that which could allow for the substitution of prayers to God for incantations to the gods, for the cross in the place of pagan symbols. But there were also significant contrasts in the belief systems, and certain compromises that would have undermined the basis of Christian belief were eschewed.

Determined steps seem to have been undertaken to undermine some aspects of earlier practice. Burial mounds came to be seen as the abodes of dragons and undesirable spirits rather than the helpful ancestors and heroes of the pre-Christian period.[196] Aspects of pagan practice which had no Christian counterparts were banned as unacceptable 'magic', but the frequent references to certain practices in laws and penitentials from within this period and later show that they were hard to eliminate and were aspects of the old religion which the new could not fully satisfy. The nature of these practices can be summed up by an extract from the Anglo-Saxon council of *Clofesho* of 747 where bishops were urged to make clear on their diocesan circuits that the following 'pagan observances' were forbidden: 'diviners, soothsayers, auguries, auspices, amulets, enchantments or any other filth of the ungodly, and errors of the heathens'.[197] Fortune-telling and other means of seeing the future figure prominently, and seem to have been major aspects of Celtic and Germanic traditional religious practice in which observances were made from such things as the flight of birds, the fights of animals or from observation of sacrifices. Such practices were regarded as incompatible with the idea that only God could know or influence the course of events. On the continent by this time a form of ecclesiastical divination (*sortes sanctorum*) had been developed (and proscribed) in which the scriptures or other ecclesiastical writing were opened at random to provide guidance on a course of events.[198] *Theodore's Penitential* had also forbidden divination, and envisaged that the clergy were as likely to be as eager as laymen when it came to fore-seeing the future,[199] but its main concern was to forbid the calling upon or offering of sacrifices to pagan deities as part of rituals.[200] As we have seen, many practices, such as those concerned with healing, could be con-tinued with substitution of Christian ritual, but not those that sought to cause people harm or which involved incorporation of the body's effluvia (blood, urine, semen). It is apparent from *Theodore's Penitential* that the practitioners of forbidden incantations and divinations were likely to be women, and it has been suggested that certain Anglo-Saxon female burials with exceptional numbers of amulets could have been examples of such local 'wise women' for whom there was no equivalent role within the Christian church.[201] Later condemnations of such women and their activi-ties suggest that they continued to flourish and filled needs not met adequately by official religion.

By such legislation acceptable and unacceptable behaviour for Christians was defined, the unacceptable becoming 'magic' and the ousted deities or other supernatural beings whose help had been evoked in the past now outlawed as 'devils'. There was room for disagreement over exactly where the line was to be drawn on certain matters, the wearing of Christian amulets being a case in point where Alcuin, after he had spent some time in Carolingian Francia, seems to have taken a much harder line than many Anglo-Saxon clergy, but there does not seem to have been any major distinction between clerical and lay attitudes to the workings of religion as far as we can tell. Such a conclusion would be consistent with the views proposed in Chapter 3 where a considerable overlap in the culture of lay communities and those in religious communities was suggested, with the major contrast being between major teachers and thinkers such as Bede and Alcuin and the rest, rather than between laymen and clerics as such. The accommodation of Christianity to the needs of society, the nature of life within religious communities, the balance between learned and more popular culture all underwent several shifts in medieval society. The Carolingian Renaissance of the late eighth and ninth centuries was concerned with many of these issues that related to the correct ordering of Christian society, and was extremely influential in all areas of Britain. We therefore need to be careful not to assume that all practices that might appear to fit a 'primitive' stage of adoption of Christianity occurred at an early date. For example, an Anglo-Saxon manuscript of late tenth- or early eleventh-century date preserves a ceremony for blessing the fields to improve fertility that incorporates both Christian and more traditional rituals.[202] It could be seen as the type of thing that might have originated in the period before 800 when Christianity was first being adapted to the needs of society. However, it is also possible that it represents a further stage in the process made closer in date to the manuscript itself, for the tenth century in Anglo-Saxon England saw major developments in the provision of pastoral care.[203]

Another example of the problem of establishing the correct context for a development is the topic of holy wells.[204] Wells, generally associated with a local saint, were a common phenomenon throughout medieval Britain, and there are still a number that are considered to have some numinous quality even in areas which have been staunchly Protestant for many centuries. As wells and springs seems to have been important components of the pre-Christian religions of the British Isles, there has often been an assumption that holy wells are a good example of the Christianisation of traditional holy sites at the time of conversion. Two holy wells associated with Columba are recorded by Adomnán; one appeared miraculously on Ardnamurchan when Columba needed to baptise a boy, the other was already in existence in Pictland and worshipped by local people although its waters were doing them harm before Columba expelled its 'demons' and turned it into a healing well.[205] The latter seems to be a classic example of the Christianisation of a previously pagan site. However, the hagiographies written in Anglo-Saxon England in the period 600–800 do not show a comparable interest in holy wells. There are only two such miracles in the *Ecclesiastical History*; one attributed to the British martyr Alban at his place of execution and one to Cuthbert on Inner Farne;[206] no miracles of this type were attributed to Wilfrid or Guthlac. However, later medieval Lives of Anglo-Saxon saints often contain accounts of wells being miraculously created by their saintly subjects, and the phenomenon of a well springing up where the head of a decapitated saint fell is to be found in a large number of accounts of British saints. The creation of holy wells may have been a process with a long history that was not just restricted to periods of conversion. By the time the Anglo-Saxons and Picts were converted in the seventh century the tradition of holy wells was in existence among the Irish and probably the British, though that is not to say that all holy wells had been established that early. They do not seem to have been a significant feature of early Anglo-Saxon Christianity, at least not as reflected in the written Lives, and it may be significant that the two examples Bede provides are associated with the British Alban and with Cuthbert from the Dál Riatan foundation of Lindisfarne. Possibly springs and wells were not such significant pre-Christian holy sites for the Anglo-Saxons as they may have been for the British, Irish and Picts. But by the late Anglo-Saxon period holy wells were as much a phenomenon in Anglo-Saxon areas as Celtic, and had become part of a growing Christianisation of the landscape in which popular beliefs, oral and written traditions of saints and the desire of churchmen to ensure greater lay involvement with local churches may all have played a part.[207] The concept of holy wells may be traced back to pre-Christian religious practices, but that is unlikely to mean that all wells associated with saints had pagan origins even in Celtic areas. They became an established part of the Christian landscape and it came to be expected that a church would have a well associated with it (and the building of churches close to natural water supplies, of course, made sense for practical reasons as well).

Conclusion

We began Chapter 2 with the three phases of conversion identified by Ludo Milis: control of external collective behaviour; control of external individual behaviour; control of internal individual behaviour and consciousness.[208] As he stresses, these phases would partly have overlapped and different sectors of society might be subject to them at varying times. We do not possess the range of sources, particularly for some areas of early medieval Britain, that enable us to demonstrate conclusively that the whole of society had passed through these phases by 800. But we can say that it was the intention that all classes should have done so, and that most areas of Britain were provided with communities of native religious specialists that were a prerequisite for the more complete conversion of society. Penance, private prayer and other religious rituals such as fasting were expected to be followed by lay people as well as religious and would have led to the type of interiorisation of the moral code that was necessary for the final stage of conversion. Certain practices such as forms of burial and commemoration and the provision of amulets are visible in the material record as well as in written texts and can be traced throughout Britain for different levels of society with the implication that an understanding of the basics of Christian belief had permeated daily life (and death). Naturally there was a gulf in knowledge and understanding between a highly educated cleric such as Adomnán and people such as the Pictish hunter-gathers whom he depicts Columba meeting. But those who have seen early medieval conversion as superficial or the nature of early medieval Christianity compromised by its absorption of traditional culture may be unduly pessimistic.[209] The practice of religion is always going to reflect contemporary culture and one could argue that it is a sign that the final stages of conversion were being reached when there is evidence that people were integrating Christianity into their everyday life. Contemporary churchmen were aware of the dangers of adaptation to contemporary expectations, and there was not always agreement between religious specialists about what was and was not acceptable, but it was generally recognised that the Christian religion as did any other needed to be responsive to the needs of different groups within society and to be felt to be meeting their concerns. Early medieval societies were never going to be transformed completely into model Christian communities, but we may be justified in saying that by 800 a substantial number of people were aware of what Christian ideals were and had incorporated some of the rituals of Christianity into their everyday lives.

Notes

1 D. Bullough, 'Burial, community and belief in the early medieval west', in *Ideal and Reality in Frankish and Anglo-Saxon Society*, ed. P. Wormald (Oxford, 1983), 177–201.

2 C. Thomas, *Christianity in Roman Britain to AD 500* (London, 1981), 228–39; D. Petts, *Christianity in Roman Britain* (Stroud, 2003), 135–58; S. Pearce, *South-western Britain in the Early Middle Ages* (London, 2004), 77–134.

3 D. Petts, 'Cemeteries and boundaries in western Britain', in *Burial*, ed. Lucy and Reynolds, 24–46; Pearce, *South-western Britain*, 148–66.

4 D. Farwell and T. Molleson, *Poundbury Volume 2: The Cemeteries* (Dorchester, 1993).

5 C. Thomas, *And Shall These Mute Stones Speak? Post-Roman Inscriptions in Western Britain* (Cardiff, 1994). See Introduction, 22–5.

6 E. Alcock, 'Burials and cemeteries in Scotland', in *The Early Church in Wales and the West*, ed. N. Edwards and A. Lane (Oxford, 1992), 125–9; E. Proudfoot, 'The Hallowhill and the origins of Christianity in Scotland', in *Conversion and Christianity in the North Sea World*, ed. B. Crawford (St Andrews, 1998), 57–74; C. Webster, 'Square-ditched barrows in post-Roman Britain', *Archaeological Journal* 161 (2004), 63–79.

7 See Chapter 2, 128–31. Our knowledge of boundaries at different periods

is imprecise – what was apparently Pictish territory in the late seventh and eighth centuries could have been 'British' in the sixth century.

8 H. Geake, *The Use of Grave-Goods in Conversion-Period England c.600–c.850*, BAR 261 (Oxford, 1997).

9 A. Boddington, 'Models of burial, settlement and worship: the Final Phase reviewed', in *Anglo-Saxon Cemeteries: A Reappraisal*, ed. E. Southworth (Stroud, 1990), 177–99; Geake, *Use of Grave-Goods*.

10 See Chapter 2, 125–6.

11 H. Williams, 'An ideology of transformation: cremation rites and animal sacrifice in early Anglo-Saxon England', in *The Archaeology of Shamanism*, ed. N. Price (London, 2001), 193–212.

12 S. Burnell and E. James, 'The archaeology of conversion on the continent in the sixth and seventh centuries', *St Augustine*, ed. Gameson, 83–106.

13 J. Blair, *The Church in Anglo-Saxon Society* (Oxford, 2005), 51-4. For contrary views that barrow burial signalled a pagan, Scandinavian allegiance and a reaction against Christianity see M. Carver, 'Reflections on the meanings of monumental barrows in Anglo-Saxon England', in *Burial*, ed. Lucy and Reynolds, 132–43.

14 I Timothy ch. 6, v. 7

15 Bede, *Hist. Eccl.*, I, 33; R. Emms, 'The early history of St Augustine's abbey, Canterbury', *St Augustine*, ed. Gameson, 410–28, at 411–13.

16 M. Biddle and B. Kjølbye Biddle, 'The Repton stone', *Anglo-Saxon England* 14 (1985), 233–92.

17 A. Morton, 'Burial in Middle Saxon Southampton', in *Death in Towns: Urban Responses to the Dying and the Dead 100–1600*, ed. S. Bassett (Leicester, 1993), 68–77. An earlier furnished burial ground that dates to before the foundation of the *wic* is not considered here.

18 D.M. Hadley, 'Burial practices in northern England in the later Anglo-Saxon period', in *Burial*, ed. Lucy and Reynolds, 209–28, especially 212–14.

19 T. O'Loughlin, 'The tombs of the saints: their significance for Adomnán', in *Saints and Scholars: Studies in Irish Hagiography*, ed. J. Carey, M. Herbert and P. Ó Riain (Dublin, 2001), 1–14.

20 D. Longley, 'Orientation within early medieval cemeteries: some data from north-west Wales', *Antiquaries Journal* 82 (2002), 309–20.

21 O'Loughlin, 'Tombs of the saints'.

22 Bede, *Hist. Eccl.*, IV, 22.

23 Bede, *Hist. Eccl.*, V, 12; see also experiences of Fursa in III, 19.

24 Tangl no. 10; P. Sims-Williams, *Religion and Literature in Western England: 600–800* (Cambridge, 1990), 243–72.

25 H. Gittos, 'Creating the sacred: Anglo-Saxon rites for consecrating cemeteries', in *Burial*, ed. Lucy and Reynolds, 195–208; E. Zadora-Rio, 'The making of churchyards and parish territories in the early medieval landscape of France and England in the 7th–12th centuries; a reconsideration', *Medieval Archaeology* 47 (2003), 1–20.

26 Hadley, 'Burial practices', 210–14; Blair, *Church in Anglo-Saxon Society*, 228–45.

27 Adomnán, *V. Columbae*, I, 16

28 J. O'Sullivan, 'Iona: archaeological excavations, 1875–1996', in *Spes Scotorum*, 215–44, especially 236–7.

29 Bullough, 'Burial, community and belief', 176–7; Adomnán, *V.Columbae*, II, 39.

30 Bede, *Hist. Eccl.*, IV, 22.

31 P.J. Huggins, 'Excavations of a Belgic and Romano-British farm with Middle Saxon cemetery and churches at Nazeingbury, Essex, 1975–6', *Essex Archaeology and History* 10 (1978), 3rd series, 29–117; B. Yorke, *Nunneries and the Anglo-Saxon Royal Houses* (London, 2003), 18, 29, 113–14.

32 C. Etchingham, *Church Organisation in Ireland AD 650–1000* (Maynooth, 1999).

33 T. Charles-Edwards, *Early Christian Ireland* (Cambridge, 2000), 199–202.

34 *Vita Wulframi* Chapter 9, MGH *Scriptores Rerum Merovingicarum* 5, ed. W. Levison (Hannover, 1910), 668; I.N. Wood, *The Missionary Life: Saints and the Evangelisation of Europe 400–1050* (Harlow, 2001), 92–4.

35 T. Charles-Edwards, 'Boundaries in Irish law', in *Medieval Settlement: Continuity and Change*, ed. P. Sawyer (London, 1976), 83–7.

36 A. Reynolds, 'Burials, boundaries and charters in Anglo-Saxon England: a reassessment', in *Burial*, ed. Lucy and Reynolds, 171–94.

37 E. O'Brien, 'Pagan and Christian burials in Ireland during the first millennium AD: continuity and change', in *The Early Church in Wales and the West*, ed. N. Edwards and A. Lane (Oxford, 1992), 130–7.

38 Gittos, 'Creating the sacred', 205–8.

39 *Theodore's Penitential*, II, 1.4–5.

40 K. Sisam, 'Anglo-Saxon royal genealogies', *Proceedings of the British Academy* 39 (1953), 287–346.

41 Gittos, 'Creating the sacred'; Blair, *Church in Anglo-Saxon Society*, 463–71.

42 Zadora-Rio, 'The making of churchyards'.

43 Bede, *Hist. Eccl.*, I, 30.

44 *Councils*, Chapter 16, 368; Blair, *Church in Anglo-Saxon Society*, 176.

45 Wihtred Chapters 9–11; Ine Chapter 3; Attenborough, *Laws*, 26–7; 36–7.

46 *Councils*, Chapter 14, 367.

47 *Theodore's, Penitential*, II, 14.1

48 Bede, *Hist. Eccl.*, III, 23.

49 Adomnán, *V. Columbae*, I, 26.

50 Adomnán, *V. Columbae*, III, 41.

51 R. Meens, 'Pollution in the early Middle Ages: the case of the food regulations in penitentials', *Early Medieval Europe* 4 (1995), 3–19.

52 *Canones Adomnani* Chapters 8 and 1 respectively; *Cáin Adomonan and Canones Adomnani*, ed. and tr. P. Ó Néill and D.N. Dumville, 2 vols (Cambridge, 2003).

53 D. Ó Corráin, 'Irish vernacular law and the Old Testament', in *Ireland and Europe in the Early Middle Ages*, ed. P. Ní Chatáin and M. Richter (Stuttgart, 1984), 284–307; R. Meens, 'The uses of the Old Testament in early medieval canon law', in *The Uses of the Past in the Early Middle Ages*, ed. Y. Hen and M. Innes (Cambridge, 2000), 67–77.

54 Bede, *Hist. Eccl.*, I, 27 (especially question 8); R. Meens, 'A background to Augustine's mission to Anglo-Saxon England', *Anglo-Saxon England* 22 (1994), 5–17.

55 *Aldhelm: The Prose Works*, 158–9.

56 See further below, 248–56.

57 Meens, 'Uses of the Old Testament'; R. Meens, 'Questioning ritual purity', in *St Augustine*, ed. Gameson, 174–86.

58 Meens, 'Pollution in the early Middle Ages', 8–9.

59 D. Watts, 'Infant burials and Romano-British Christianity', *Archaeological Journal* 146 (1989), 372–83; S. Crawford, 'Children, death and the afterlife', *Anglo-Saxon Studies in Archaeology and History* 6 (1993), 83–92.

60 F. Paxton, *The Christianisation of Death* (London, 1990), 84–7.

61 N. Edwards, 'Celtic saints and early medieval archaeology', in *Local Saints*, ed. Thacker and Sharpe, 225–66, and see Chapter 3, 188–92.

62 D. Ó Corráin, 'Irish law and canon law', in *Ireland and Europe: The Early Church*, ed. P. Ni Chatháin and M. Richter (Stuttgart, 1984), 157–66; C. Fell, *Women in Anglo-Saxon England* (London, 1984), 56–73; W. Davies, 'Celtic women in the early Middle Ages', in *Images of Women in Antiquity*, ed. A. Cameron and A. Kuhrt (revised edn, London, 1993), 145–66; T. Charles-Edwards, *Early Irish and Welsh Kinship* (Oxford, 1993).

63 Yorke, *Nunneries*.

64 B. Yorke, *Kings and Kingdoms of Early Anglo-Saxon England* (London, 1990), 81–3, 136–42.

65 Bede, *Hist. Eccl.*, IV, 21; V. 24 (sa 697).

66 *Beowulf and the Fight at Finnsburg*, ed. F. Klaeber (3rd edn, Boston, 1950), lines 2032–2069; *The Finnsburh Fragment and Episode*, ed. D. Fry (London, 1974).

67 A. Woolf, 'Pictish matriliny reconsidered', *Innes Review* 49 (1998), 147–67; and see Chapter 1, 48–9.

68 J. Goody, *The Development of Family and Marriage in Europe* (Cambridge, 1983); Ó Corráin, 'Irish law and canon law'.

69 Gildas, *De Excidio*, Chapter 35.

70 Bede, *Hist. Eccl.*, II, 5–6.

71 Bede, *Hist. Eccl.*, I, 27; Chapter 5.

72 Ó Corráin, 'Irish law and canon law'.

73 Asser, Chapter 17.

74 *Charters of St Augustine's Abbey, Canterbury and Minster-in-Thanet*, ed. S. Kelly (Oxford, 1995), 37–8; *Theodore's Penitential* I, 14.2.

75 *Theodore's Penitential* II, 12.8.

76 *Canones Adomnani* Chapter 16; T. Charles-Edwards, 'The Penitential of Theodore and the *Iudicia Theodori*', in *Archbishop Theodore*, ed. M. Lapidge (Cambridge, 1995), 141–74.

77 Bede, *Hist. Eccl.*, IV, 19; see also *V. Wilfridi* ch, Chapters 19 and 22. C. Fell, 'Saint Æthelthryth: a historical-hagiographical dichotomy revisited', *Nottingham Medieval Studies* 38 (1994), 18–34; Yorke, *Nunneries*, 31–5, 153–4.

78 *Theodore's Penitential*, II, 14.1

79 *Historia Regum*, sa 762 and 792.

80 Anon., *V. Cuthberti*, III, 6; Bede, *V. Cuthberti*, Chapter 24; C. Ireland, 'Aldfrith of Northumbria and the Irish genealogies', *Celtica* 22 (1991), 64–78.

81 *Councils*, III, 453–4; *EHD I*, no. 191 (Chapter 12).

82 Yorke, *Kings and Kingdoms*, 115–18; J. Story, *Carolingian Connections: Anglo-Saxon England and Carolingian Francia, 750–870* (Aldershot, 2003), 168–80.

83 A. Thacker, 'Monks, preaching and pastoral care in England', in *Pastoral Care*, 137–70, at 154–6.

84 Bede, *Hist. Eccl.*, V, 12.

85 *Aldhelm: The Prose Works*, 55–67; S. O'Sullivan, 'Aldhelm's *De Virginitate*: patristic pastiche or innovative exposition?', *Peritia* 12 (1998), 271–95.

86 Boniface in his letter to Æthelbald (see below) tried to shame him into better behaviour by citing contemporary pagan punishment of adulterers and fornicators.

87 R. North, *Heathen Gods in Old English Literature* (Cambridge, 1997); N. Price, *The Viking Way: Religion and War in Late Iron Age Scandinavia* (Uppsala, 2002).

88 Tangl no. 73; Talbot, *Anglo-Saxon Missionaries*, 120–6; Yorke, *Nunneries*, 153–6.

89 Yorke, *Kings and Kingdoms*, 114–18.

90 Asser, Chapter 74; J. Nelson, 'Monks, secular men and masculinity *c.*900', in *Masculinity in Medieval Europe*, ed. D. Hadley (Harlow, 1999), 121–42.

91 Thacker, 'Monks, preaching and pastoral care', 156–62.

92 *Theodore's Penitential*, Chapter I, 2.16 and 3.5 respectively.

93 A.J. Frantzen, *The Literature of Penance in Anglo-Saxon England* (New Brunswick, 1983).

94 Charles-Edwards, 'Penitential of Theodore'.

95 Adomnán, *V. Columbae*, I, 21, 22, 30; II, 39.

96 B. Bedingfield, 'Public penance in Anglo-Saxon England', *Anglo-Saxon England* 31 (2002), 223–56.

97 Bede, *Hist. Eccl.*, IV, 15–16; V, 7; C. Stancliffe, 'Kings who opted out', in *Ideal and Reality in Frankish and Anglo-Saxon Society*, ed. P. Wormald (Oxford, 1983), 154–76. See also Chapter 2, 125–8.

98 See Chapter 3, 164–6 for discussion of why kings may have retired to monasteries and to Rome.

99 Bede, *Hist. Eccl.*, III, 14.

100 Bede, *Hist. Eccl.*, III, 24.

101 D. Rollason, *The Mildrith Legend: A Study in Early Medieval Hagiography in England* (Leicester, 1982).

102 *Councils*, III, 371–2, Chapter 26; C. Cubitt, *Anglo-Saxon Church Councils c.650–c.850* (Leicester, 1995), 110–12.

103 Bede, *Hist. Eccl.*, II, 16.

104 Gildas, *De Excidio*, Chapter 27.

105 Bede, *Hist. Eccl.*, III, 2; Adomnán, *V. Columbae*, I, 1.

106 Bede, *Hist. Eccl.*, IV, 16.

107 Bede, *Hist. Eccl.*, III, 6.

108 Bede, *V. Cuthberti*, Chapter 11; D. Kirby, 'Bede and the Pictish church', *Innes Review* 24 (1973), 6–25.

109 Bede, *Hist. Eccl.*, III, 24.

110 Bede, *Hist. Eccl.*, II, 20 and III, 1.

111 H. Edwards, 'Two documents from Aldhelm's Malmesbury', *Bulletin of the Institute of Historical Research* 59 (1986), 1–19; B. Yorke, *Wessex in the Early Middle Ages* (London, 1995), 61–2.

112 J.R. Davies, 'Church, property and conflict in Wales: AD 600–1100', *Welsh History Review* 18 (1996/7), 387–406.

113 M. Ní Dhonchadha, 'Birr and the Law of the Innocents' and 'The Law of Adomnán: a translation', in *Adomnán at Birr, AD 697. Essays in Commemoration of the Law of the Innocents*, ed. T. O'Loughlin (Dublin, 2001), 13–32 and 53–68 respectively.

114 Bede, *Hist. Eccl.*, IV, 26. The death of Ealdorman Berhtred of Northumbria in 698 at the hands of the Picts recorded in V, 24 implies at least one battle that took place during the reign of Aldfrith.

115 Bede, *Hist. Eccl.,* IV, 21.

116 *Theodore's Penitential* I, 4.1.

117 *Goddodin*, A8, 58–9, line 72.

118 *Theodore's Penitential* I, 4.6.

119 W. Davies, ' "Protected space" in Britain and Ireland in the Middle Ages', in *Scotland in Dark Age Britain*, ed. B. Crawford (St Andrews, 1996), 1–20.

120 N. Hughes and M. Owen, 'Twelfth-century Welsh hagiography: the *Gogynfeirdd* poems to saints', in *Celtic Hagiography and Saints' Cults*, ed. J. Cartwright (Cardiff, 2003), 45–76, especially 55–7.

121 See Chapter 3, 164–6.

122 See below, 236–44.

123 Attenborough, *Laws*, 36–7; *EHD* I, no. 32.

124 M. Grimmer, 'Britons and Saxons in pre-Viking Wessex', *Parergon* 19 (2002), 1–17; and see above Chapter 1, 41–3.

125 J.M. Wallace-Hadrill, *Early Germanic Kingship in England and on the Continent* (Oxford, 1971).

126 Bede, *Hist. Eccl.*, I, 32 and III, 2; for Constantine see R. Fletcher, *The Conversion of Europe* (London, 1977), 18–19, 22–5, 97–129.

127 Bede, *Hist, Eccl.*, I, 34.

128 Gildas, *De Excidio*, Chapters 37–63.

129 *V. Wilfridi*, Chapters 20 and 37.

130 I. Henderson, '*Primus inter pares*: the St Andrews sarcophagus and Pictish sculpture', in *The St Andrews Sarcophagus: A Pictish Masterpiece and its International Connections*, ed. S. Foster (Dublin, 1998); G. Henderson and. I. Henderson, *The Art of the Picts: Sculpture and Metalwork in Early Medieval Scotland* (London, 2004), 129–37, 197–205.

131 *Alfred the Great: Asser's Life of King Alfred and Other Contemporary Sources*, trans. S. Keynes and M. Lapidge (Harmondsworth, 1983), 153–60, 301–3.

132 Wallace-Hadrill, *Early Germanic Kingship*, 57; D. Ó Cróinín, *Early Medieval Ireland 400–1200* (London, 1995), 77–8.

133 P. Wormald, 'Bede, Beowulf and the conversion of the English aristocracy', in *Bede and Anglo-Saxon England*, ed. R.T. Farrell, BAR 46 (Oxford, 1978), 32–95.

134 D.H. Green, *The Carolingian Lord* (Cambridge, 1965).

135 T.A. Shippey, *Poems of Wisdom and Learning in Old English* (Cambridge, 1976), 112–19.

136 See Chapter 3, 178–9.

137 See Chapter 3, 164–6.

138 Attenborough, *Laws*, 4–61.

139 See Chapter 2, 118–21.

140 G. Henderson, *Vision and Image in Early Christian England* (Cambridge, 1999), 94–6.

141 P. Wormald, 'The age of Offa and Alcuin', in *The Anglo-Saxons*, ed. J. Campbell (Oxford, 1982), 101–31; Story, *Carolingian Connections*, 169–211.

142 A. Lane and E. Campbell, *Dunadd: An Early Dalriadic Capital* (Oxford, 2000).

143 Blair, *Church in Anglo-Saxon Society*, 204–12; A. Gannon, *The Iconography of Early Anglo-Saxon Coinage: Sixth to Eighth Centuries* (Oxford, 2003).

144 J. Nelson, 'Inauguration rituals', in *Early Medieval Kingship*, ed. P. Sawyer and I.N. Wood (Leeds, 1977), 50–71; M.J. Enright, *Iona, Tara, and Soissons: The Origins of the Royal Anointing Ritual* (Berlin, 1985).

145 Gildas, *De Excidio*, Chapter 20.

146 Adomnán, *V. Columbae*, III, 5; Adomnán of Iona, trans. Sharpe, n. 358.

147 R. Welander, D. Breeze and T.O. Clancy (eds), *The Stone of Destiny: Artefact and Icon* (Edinburgh, 2003); A. Pantos and S. Semple (eds), *Assembly Places and Practices in Medieval Europe* (Dublin, 2004); and see Chapter 2.

148 *ASC* sa 787; Nelson, 'Inauguration rituals'. Offa was successful in this, but Ecgfrith died after a reign of a few months.

149 *V. Wilfridi*, Chapters 24 and 63.

150 *V. Wilfridi*, Chapters 59 and 60.

151 D. Kirby, 'Northumbria in the time of Wilfrid', in *Saint Wilfrid at Hexham*, ed. D. Kirby (Newcastle, 1974), 1–34; D. Rollason, 'Hagiography and politics in early Northumbria', in *Holy Men and Holy Women: Old English Prose Saints' Lives and Their Contexts*, ed. P. Szarmach (Albany, 1996), 95–114. For what follows see also the *Historia Regum* under relevant years and Yorke, *Kings and Kingdoms*, 86–94.

152 *EHD I*, nos. 207 and 208.

153 M.J. Enright, 'Royal succession and abbatial prerogative in Adomnán's *Vita Columbae*', *Peritia* 4 (1985), 83–103; M. Tanaka, 'Iona and the kingship of Dál Riata in Adomnán's *Vita Columbae*', *Peritia* 17–18 (2003–4), 199–214.

154 T.O. Clancy, 'Philosopher king: Nechtan mac Der-Ilei', *Scottish Historical Review* 83 (2004), 125–49.

155 *AU* sa 732; M.O. Anderson, *Kings and Kingship in Early Scotland* (Edinburgh, 1980), 183–4.

156 N. Brooks, *The Early History of the Church of Canterbury* (Leicester, 1984), 120–5.

157 R. MacMullen, *Christianizing the Roman Empire (AD 100–400)* (New Haven, 1984).

158 D. Pelteret, *Slavery in Early Medieval England from the Reign of Alfred until the Twelfth Century* (Woodbridge, 1995).

159 Attenborough, *Laws*: Ine, Chapter 11.

160 Bede, *Hist. Eccl.*, IV, 13.

161 W. Davies, *Wales in the Early Middle Ages* (Leicester, 1982), 64–7.

162 Adomnán, *V. Columbae*, II, 33.

163 Gildas, *De Excidio*, Chapters 27 and 66.

164 Bede, *Hist. Eccl.*, III, 6.

165 See further in Chapter 3.

166 C. Clover, 'Regardless of sex: men, women and power in early northern Europe', *Speculum* 69 (1993), 363–87; S. Hollis, *Anglo-Saxon Women and the Church* (Woodbridge, 1992).

167 Ní Dhonchadha, 'Birr and the Law of the Innocents', 17–27; J. Hawkes, 'Columban Virgins: iconic images of the Virgin and Child in insular sculpture', in *Studies in the Cult of St Columba*, ed. C. Bourke (Dublin, 1997), 107–35.

168 Bede, *Hist. Eccl.*, IV, 19–20.

169 Yorke, *Nunneries, passim.*

170 Yorke, *Nunneries*, 162–5.

171 *V. Wilfridi*, Chapter 59.

172 Hollis, *Anglo-Saxon Women*, 179–207.

173 J. Blair, 'A handlist of Anglo-Saxon saints', in *Local Saints*, 495–565.

174 K. Jolly, *Popular Religion in Late Anglo-Saxon England: Elf Charms in Context* (Chapel Hill and London, 1996); M. Smyth, *Understanding the Universe in Seventh-Century Ireland* (Woodbridge, 1996).

175 Bede, *Hist. Eccl.*, V, 2–7.

176 M.L. Cameron, *Anglo-Saxon Medicine* (Cambridge, 1993).

177 Jolly, *Popular Religion*, 96–131.

178 Jolly, *Popular Religion*, 128–9.

179 *The Triumph Tree. Scotland's Earliest Poetry AD 550–1350*, ed. T.O. Clancy (Edinburgh, 1998), 100–1.

180 P. Sims-Williams, *Religion and Literature*, 273–327.

181 *Councils*, III, 366 (clause 10).

182 Adomnán, *V. Columbae*, I, 1.

183 A.L. Meaney, *Anglo-Saxon Amulets and Curing-Stones*, BAR 96 (Oxford, 1981).

184 H. Williams, 'Material culture as memory: combs and cremation in early medieval Britain', *Early Medieval Europe* 12 (2003), 89–128.

185 Blair, *Church in Anglo-Saxon Society*, 170–5.

186 Adomnán, *V. Columbae*, II, 33,

187 A. Ritchie, 'Painted pebbles in early Scotland', *Proceedings of the Society of Antiquaries of Scotland* 104 (1971–2), 297–301.

188 Lane and Campbell, *Dunadd*, 253–4.

189 Revelation II, 17: 'To him that overcometh will I give to eat of the hidden manna and will give to him a white stone, and in that stone a new name written, which no man knoweth, saving he that receiveth it'.

190 *Theodore's Penitential*, II, 10.

191 *Alcuini Epistolae*, nos 290–1, as cited by Blair, *Church in Anglo-Saxon Society*, 175.

192 Bede, *Hist. Eccl.*, IV, 22; see above.

193 Henderson and Henderson, *Art of the Picts*, 171–2.

194 See Chapter 2, 109–14.

195 As suggested in V. Flint, *The Rise of Magic in Early Medieval Europe* (Oxford, 1991) and J.C. Russell, *The Germanisation of Early Medieval Christianity: A Sociological Approach to Religious Transformation* (Oxford, 1994); on which see A. Murray, 'Missionaries and magic in Dark Age Europe', *Past and Present* 136 (1992), 186–205 and Jolly, *Popular Religion*, 9–34.

196 S. Semple, 'A fear of the past: the place of the prehistoric burial mound in the ideology of middle and later Anglo-Saxon England', *World Archaeology* 30 (1998), 109–26.

197 *Councils*, III, 363–4 (Chapter 3); as cited and translated in A.L. Meaney, 'Anglo-Saxon idolaters and ecclesiasts from Theodore to Alcuin: a source study', *ASSAH* 5 (1992), 103–25, at 112.

198 Meaney, 'Idolaters and ecclesiasts', 110–11.

199 *Theodore's Penitential*, I, 15, Chapter 4.

200 *Theodore's Penitential*, I, 4 Chapter 7; I, 14, Chapters 15–16; I, 15, Chapters 1–5.

201 *Theodore's Penitential*, I, 15, Chapter 4; Meaney, 'Idolaters and ecclesiasts', 105–7; T.M. Dickinson, 'An Anglo-Saxon "cunning woman" from Bidford-on-Avon', in *In Search of Cult*, ed. M. Carver (Woodbridge, 1993), 45–54.

202 Jolly, *Popular Religion*, 6–8.

203 Blair, *Church in Anglo-Saxon Society*, 452–504.

204 J. Rattue, *The Living Stream: Holy Wells in Historical Context* (Woodbridge, 1995).

205 Adomnán, *V. Columbae*, II, 10–11.

206 Bede, *Hist. Eccl.*, I, 7 and IV, 26.

207 Blair, *Church in Anglo-Saxon Society*, 375–82.

208 L. Milis, 'La conversion en profandeur: un procès sans fin', *Revue du Nord* 68 (1986), 187–98.

209 For example, Russell, *Germanisation of Early Medieval Christianity*; Flint, *The Rise of Magic*.

Conclusion

The period 600–800 is a significant one in the history of Britain, and rightly designated as the early Middle Ages, as it was in these centuries that many of the structures and institutions were established that were to determine the lives of the peoples of Britain in the rest of the medieval period and beyond. However, it is not an easy period to study as sufficient evidence is lacking in certain key areas and it can be hard to disentangle causes from effects. The origins of medieval Wales, Scotland and England, the politico-geographical organisation of Britain with which we are familiar, can be traced to this period, even if the final unity of the medieval kingdoms of England and Scotland was to be achieved at a later point. By 800 there were only 4 major Anglo-Saxon kingdoms (Northumbria, Mercia, the East Angles and Wessex) left of the 12 or so that existed in 600 (see Map 2). The East Angles probably had much the same borders as they did in 600, but the other three had expanded considerably by annexing smaller Anglo-Saxon kingdoms and British-held territories. Although the process of absorbing Cornwall into Wessex was not completed by 800, the western march with Wales had been more or less established by this date. Major advances had been made towards the establishment of the kingdom of Alba, precursor of the medieval kingdom of Scotland, through the bringing together of the kingdoms of the Picts and the Dál Riata under the rule of one dynasty with hereditary links to the royal houses of both. What is less clear, and currently the subject of some debate, is whether this was preceded in both Pictland and Dál Riata by the absorption of lesser Pictish and Dalriadic kingdoms to create larger units as in the Anglo-Saxon world. Although the core of medieval Scotland may have been well on its way to being achieved by 800, the full achievement of bringing all of northern Britain under one monarch was several centuries away. In 800 the British kingdom of Dumbarton was probably still in existence, and in the following century the political map would be changed considerably by Viking incursions and the establishment of independent Norse colonies within the future Scotland. There would be Scandinavian settlements in England as well, but these were less enduring as separate polities. The Vikings did much to enable the creation of a united England by removing the royal houses of Northumbria, Mercia and East Angles, but failing to defeat Alfred and his brothers in Wessex. The way was clear for Alfred's successors of the tenth century to bring all England under their control, and after some adjustment of the northern borders, it had the boundaries with which we are familiar today.

A review of the political developments between 600 and 800 naturally throws up the question of why the history of Wales seems to have been so different from that of England and Scotland. Not only was there no united Wales in 800, when it was divided between seven kingdoms, but there is little sign of the type of military overlordship that assisted the growth of larger kingdoms at the expense of smaller in Anglo-Saxon England, and is often assumed to have been a feature of Pictland and Dál Riata as well. This seems all the more surprising as Welsh kings appear to have been as much the leaders of armies as their counterparts in other areas of Britain, and often individually able to mount a fierce resistance to outside attacks as Powys did against Mercia in the eighth century. Gildas had complained about the military companions of contemporary British kings, but also about their failure since the successes of Ambrosius Aurelianus to combine against the Anglo-Saxons and about their readiness to fight one another. Wendy Davies's analysis of the evidence for early Welsh kingship could suggest that its military basis was differently constituted than those of other areas of Britain, and that Welsh kings in this period did not have a right to military service from their freemen and nobles.[1] Gildas called his fellow British *cives* 'citizens' and under the Roman empire its citizens did not have to perform military service so this expectation may have continued in the post-Roman provinces of the west of Britain. Some at least of the Irish who can be detected in western Britain in the fifth and sixth centuries, for instance through ogham inscriptions, may have been 'hired guns', but the ability of western British rulers to recruit foreign fighters may have been restricted by their relative poverty in the early Middle Ages; they may have been land rich, but probably lacked the movable wealth and 'treasure' that was so desirable in the early medieval world.[2] Imported items from the former Roman empire are known in Wales from the sixth century, but not from the seventh when such items were continuing to reach areas of western Scotland. Their absence may suggest some form of economic crisis that weakened the position of the western kings.[3]

None of this need mean that it was less desirable to be an ordinary inhabitant in Wales than in other areas of Britain, perhaps rather the contrary. Strong, centrist kings may appear as 'successful' in the sense that they ruled large areas and possessed great wealth, but they could also be extremely autocratic and vicious, and were able to use their military might to demand payments from their own subjects as much as from peoples they had conquered. References from charters, laws and narrative sources such as Bede's *Ecclesiastical History* suggest that land held by Anglo-Saxons was assessed in taxable hides by the seventh century, and there is the implication of locally based royal officials who knew who held what and what they owed. The *Senchus fer nAlban* holds out the possibility of organised renders that could help maintain royal power in Dál Riata. Scepticism has been expressed about the ability of the rulers of Pictland to mount this type of centrist control, but the possibility exists that structures in operation in the medieval kingdom of Scotland may also have been in place in its Pictish predecessors and could have had roots going back further into the Iron Age past.[4]

No one supervised the lives of their subjects more closely than the Roman empire and it is a moot point how much of the legacy of Roman rule remained to support its post-Roman heirs. This is part of the bigger question of how cataclysmic the end of Roman Britain was. One should perhaps remember here that it was British elites who decided they were better off outside the empire, rather than Roman authorities who made the final decision, though the British may not have appreciated, of course, some of the economic and other consequences of their actions. In British provinces and kingdoms those who took control in the fifth century may have based their authority on Roman precedents. But did any of this survive to benefit Anglo-Saxon elites? It is at least arguable, though almost impossible to prove, that settlement and provisioning of incoming Germans by British authorities provided infrastructures that continued to be utilised when the balance of power shifted. Four centuries of Roman rule not only left a legacy for areas that had been included in the province of *Britannia*, but also for those areas which had been excluded. It helped define, for instance, the border between Pictish and British territories in Scotland. Such decisions had themselves been influenced by the physical geography of Britain and the latter continued to be a significant factor in framing the lives of the inhabitants of Britain. It was an inescapable fact that areas of eastern and southern England were closer to the mainland of Europe than anywhere else in Britain and that there were therefore greater opportunities for those living in these areas to have easier access to foreign markets. Such contacts may have helped to underpin prosperous small kingdoms in the seventh century, but also benefited a much broader section of the community. Increasingly, specialised places for temporary trading and exchange are being recognised in the countryside of England south of the Humber.[5] Although few are in the same location as small Roman towns, they may have shared some of their functions and utilised the roads that had led to these Roman hubs. Patterns that had operated in the Roman period had in some ways reappeared in Britain by the seventh century and gave greater opportunities for a wider sector of the population in the east and south than in other areas of the island.

The rulers of early medieval Britain were aware of their legacy as the heirs of Rome. Among the more Romanised British elites who had come to power by rejecting Rome, especially those of the west, the association seems to have been, at least to begin with, a negative one. Reuse of hill-forts and prehistoric burial sites and some of the art forms that were adopted appear to look back to the pre-Roman past and an earlier period of British self-rule. In less Romanised areas of northern Wales and north Britain the new elites erected Roman-style memorial stones inscribed in Latin, a type of monument also especially favoured by Irish incomers to these areas and to Pictland (though not by those of Dál Riata). Anglo-Saxon kings, from the evidence of burials such as Sutton Hoo, Taplow and Prittlewell, borrowed regalia, such as elaborate belt-sets and standards, from the late Roman world though decorated in styles shared with Germanic elites in other parts of Europe. They showed awareness of physical remains of the Roman past and might incorporate these into their own power bases. Æthelbert of Kent seems to have based himself in the Roman *civitas* capital within his kingdom at Canterbury before the arrival of the mission led by Augustine, while the Northumbrian royal centre at Yeavering seems to include a unique building that resembled a section of a Roman amphitheatre.[6]

Christianity was, of course, part of that legacy from the Roman world as Gildas reminded those whom he addressed in his *De Excidio*. The Christian religion was one aspect of the Roman past that the British regimes did not want to reject and Gildas also suggests that it was an important part of British self-identity by the sixth century. British churchmen ensured that Christianity was spread to the less Romanised British areas, to Ireland and probably to southern parts of Pictland, but were unable or unwilling to make any impact in the Anglo-Saxon kingdoms. British missionary zeal was inherited by the Irish who penetrated further into Pictland and to many Anglo-Saxon kingdoms, though it was the combination of Frankish influence and a papal mission that were the main catalyst for religious change in the southern Anglo-Saxon kingdoms. The combination of papal and imperial authority was a heady mixture at the Anglo-Saxon and Pictish royal courts, and may have helped sway both Oswiu of Northumbria and Nechtan of the Picts to decide in favour of the Roman Easter. Not only Pictish and Anglo-Saxon churchmen, but also some Anglo-Saxon kings made the journey to Rome, with which they appear to have felt a strong bond.

The church was another means of reintroducing Roman technologies to the parts of early medieval Britain that had lost them. Reading and writing were among these, and the prestige and desirability of such skills is perhaps suggested by the fact that the Irish and Anglo-Saxons had already developed the distinctive ogham and runic scripts for writing in their own languages before conversion to Christianity. It is possible that the Pictish symbols should also be seen as a form of alphabet and represent the same kind of yearning for literacy and the forms of commemoration and authentication that it could bring. After conversion religious specialists had to master Latin and the most scholarly of them did so triumphantly, producing within a couple of generations some of the most talented and original authors in early medieval Europe. Through the works of people such as Adomnán, Aldhelm and Bede, a real love of learning shines through, as well as devotion to the new religion. The Picts unfortunately have left no such written evidence, but Pictish sculptures demonstrate that they drew and reflected on the same scholarly repertoire.

The Christian church reintroduced other practical skills. Masons and glaziers were brought to Anglo-Saxon kingdoms from Francia so that the Anglo-Saxons could have buildings erected in the Roman style, and at King Nechtan's request their skills were introduced into Pictland as well. The excavator of the northern British Christian centre at Whithorn has likened the arrival of clerics there to the impact of Cistercians many centuries later in opening up underexploited districts to new technologies.[7] New forms of ploughing, lime-production and the smelting of haematite ore are some of the processes he associated with the advent of Christianity at this site, and there have been similar arguments for the impact of ecclesiastical foundations on the Irish rural economy and land management.[8] But how far can we push the impact of the church on non-religious aspects of life in early medieval Britain? Recent studies have suggested that the minsters could have been the main agents which account for the flourishing of trade and reintroduction of coinage in seventh- and eighth-century England.[9] But one must be careful not to confuse cause and effect. There was a limit to what church foundations could achieve on their own. Ireland had many large and vigorous monastic foundations, but the Irish economy did not develop the international trading links that could be found in eastern England, nor did it use coinage. But it would be true to say, as John Blair has suggested, that the Anglo-Saxon minsters with their large, centrally managed estates were in an ideal position to make the most of the opportunities for trade and economic prosperity that existed in southern and eastern England in the seventh and eighth centuries, but which had their origins even earlier.[10] Finds from Anglo-Saxon cemeteries of the sixth century demonstrate that their denizens had the means and the opportunity to acquire non-essential items of foreign manufacture or origin, some of which, such as ivory rings and cowrie shells, had travelled considerable distances.[11]

Any assessment of the impact of Christianity in early medieval Britain must take account of the fact that, as in all Christian societies, it had to work within the established frameworks of power. The support of Anglo-Saxon and Pictish rulers was necessary to give the church the protection and patronage that the missionaries needed and the progress of the latter was aided by existing relations between overkings and underkings and by contacts formed through marriage and the reception of exiled princes. In Ireland and Anglo-Saxon England the principle was followed that every kingdom should have its own diocese (even if some Anglo-Saxon ones were subsequently subdivided), echoing the arrangements within Roman provinces where the diocese was in origin a unit of civilian administration which became the basis of church organisation as well. The same principle may have been followed in the Welsh kingdoms. It is therefore potentially a matter of some relevance to understanding the political structures of Pictland and Dál Riata that each of these provinces seems to have constituted one diocese (though possibly there were, or were at one time, separate dioceses for northern and southern Picts). The implication could be that these provinces were not divided among several kingdoms of similar status, but had developed a centralising overkingship at an early date within the early Middle Ages though any such conclusions can only be tentative and controversial.

When native churchmen took over from the missionaries those in positions of influence were drawn from the leading families of their respective kingdoms and some were kin of the royal houses. The Anglo-Saxons seem to have been unusual among the peoples of Britain in the number of major minsters that were commanded by princesses and former queens, though, of course, women could not hold positions which required ordination to the priesthood. Although some churchmen and churchwomen may have succeeded in completely withdrawing from the world in the spirit of the origins of monasticism, others – perhaps most – remained involved in the affairs of their families, which often meant the high politics of their respective kingdoms. Aspects of the way of life of the inmates of religious institutions did differ from that of their counterparts in the secular world: military service was replaced by the liturgical round. But excavations at Anglo-Saxon religious sites support the claims made by critical churchmen such as Bede, Aldhelm and Alcuin that many aspects of lay aristocratic culture were followed within them. Indeed, there is currently some debate about whether certain undocumented Anglo-Saxon sites should be interpreted as minsters or lay residences, and it is even possible that some were both, with a small minster attached to a residence of the family which controlled it.[12] Gildas had made comparable criticisms of worldly priests and bishops of his day. But even those who criticised the manner of living within some religious communities do not seem to have believed that churchmen should not have some political involvement. Bede's message was that secular leaders should be guided by their ecclesiastical advisers, but in endeavouring to do so many churchmen seem to have felt the need to adopt the standards and tactics that won friends and influence in the lay world.

Churchmen did, of course, inherit an established tradition of ecclesiastical culture in the western church, and could turn to the decisions of early church councils and evoke papal rulings to support their own policies. The reforming church councils held in Francia in the eighth and ninth centuries were also a major influence on Anglo-Saxon church leaders. However, the support systems of the universal church were puny compared to what they would be in later centuries. Kings could ignore even papal rulings with impunity if they felt the need to do so as Bishop Wilfrid discovered on more than one occasion. Only the Anglo-Saxons possessed an archiepiscopal organisation under which bishops and other major churchmen met in regular church synods under an archbishop to discuss and legislate on ecclesiastical matters, though how successful they were in getting such decisions implemented is difficult to assess. The fact that the leading archbishop was based in Kent, which was not a major power after the end of the seventh century, gave him a certain independence from lay control. Archbishops were able on occasion to stand up successfully to Mercian overlords in the eighth century, as when Archbishop Jaenbert prevented Offa from moving the archiepiscopal see to London that was more fully under Mercian control. Offa retaliated by persuading the pope to establish a third archiepiscopal see (the second was at York) at the Mercian see of Lichfield, but Archbishop Æthelheard had this suppressed after his death. Churchmen in other areas of medieval Britain without an archiepiscopal organisation could also agree to meet in ecclesiastical councils, as leading ecclesiastics of the former Roman province of *Britannia Prima* seem to have done when Augustine requested a meeting, and as seems to have happened in Pictland when the decision was made to adopt the Roman practice of calculating Easter.

Not all significant ecclesiastical groupings followed political boundaries. Most successful of the wider-based monastic confederations was that of Iona, which in the middle of the seventh century supervised from its centre in Dál Riata daughter houses in Ireland, Pictland and Northumbria. Irish and Anglo-Saxon churchmen travelled extensively in Britain and mainland Europe in the seventh and eighth centuries and such experiences and their interchanges with each other helped to foster common aspects of ecclesiastical culture in early medieval Britain. Certain common features of artwork in Britain and Ireland are designated 'insular' and debate still continues on whether certain manuscripts without clear ascriptions to any particular centre were produced in England, Scotland or Ireland. The one area that does not seem to have participated so fully in a shared insular ecclesiastical culture is Wales. Although due allowance has to be made for the shortage of contemporary evidence surviving from Wales, there are very few references to Welsh clergy travelling in Britain, Ireland or on the Continent in the many different types of sources that enable us to trace Irish and Anglo-Saxon travellers. The westward expansion of the Anglo-Saxons seems to have isolated Wales to at least a certain extent, an isolation that was perhaps both physical and mental. The recruitment of Asser at King Alfred's court appears to be without precedent, but such assumptions may be misleading. There are hints of earlier interactions, for instance in the inclusion of the prayer of the British Moucan in the Mercian 'Book of Cerne'. The Lichfield Gospels, which were at Llandeilo Fawr by the beginning of the ninth century when certain marginalia were added, are written in the script known as insular half-uncial, which was also used for the Lindisfarne Gospels, and has decoration in the insular style. It is usually argued that the Lichfield Gospels were made in England or Ireland and brought to Wales, but it is also possible that they were produced within Wales and are evidence for its participation in the broader ecclesiastical culture of Britain.[13]

There were limits to how far a common ecclesiastical culture could transcend political boundaries. Ionan influence in the Northumbrian church was ended when King Oswiu decided to side with the other Anglo-Saxon kingdoms over the calculation of Easter and to place the church of his kingdom under the jurisdiction of Canterbury. It was not just a rejection of church customs that were not in conformity with Rome, but a cultural realignment. A modest religious way of life that Bede recognised as being in the spirit of the founders of monasticism was replaced by one more open to continental influences in which God was honoured through the display of ecclesiastical wealth in stone churches decorated with paintings and vessels of gold and silver, many of them imported from Rome itself. Although there were some shared features of insular art, there were also some marked regional differences. The sculptural forms of Northumbria and Pictland are, for instance, quite distinctive and reflect not just the work of different schools of masons, but the differing tastes of their patrons from the two kingdoms. Pictish sculptors continued to utilise the system of symbols and ways of portraying animals that had originated before conversion to Christianity and which arguably were part of the identity of the Pictish elite.

There were therefore ways in which the Christian church could reinforce the distinctive cultures that seem to have been fostered in the ruling circles of the four peoples of early medieval Britain, but it is unlikely that such identities were, as has sometimes been proposed, largely the invention of learned churchmen though such commentators may have given them a new interpretation. Gildas and Bede both saw not just their own individual provinces, but the entire British and Anglo-Saxon peoples to which they belonged as having a special identity as a Chosen People of the Christian God in a way that distinguished them from the other peoples of Britain. The origins of British and Anglo-Saxon difference stretched back to the fifth century and were proclaimed in the very different material culture of their territories.[14] After the conversion of the Anglo-Saxons, differences over church custom provided an additional dimension that gave Anglo-Saxons justification, they appear to have believed, for their advance westwards and the annexation of British churches in order to 'reform' them. The Columban church may have rejected some worldly trappings, but successive abbots followed their founder in cultivating close links with various regimes and in particular furthered the interests of the Cenél Conaill lineage of the northern Uí Neill in Ireland and beyond and that of Cenél Gabráin in Dál Riata. But one of the most intriguing, though unfortunately poorly recorded, examples of such cooperation is the Ionan involvement in the creation of a new political identity that was in process at the end of our period and led after 900 to the replacement of Pictland by the kingdom of Alba. Iona was part of the gradual Gaelicisation of Pictland that led up to and continued after the formation of Alba; the transfer of part of Columba's relics to Dunkeld in the ninth century helped ensure his promotion as the patron saint of the new people of Alba.[15] The exact weight that should be given to the roles of the kings and the abbots of Iona is hard to discern from the scanty sources which are available, but we are probably safe to assume that it was a mutually supportive effort and a classic example of the intertwining of the interests of church and state that was so characteristic of early medieval Britain – and, one might add, of the whole of early medieval Europe.

Such matters may have been of less consequence to the peasant cultivators of early medieval Britain who made up the bulk of the population. Family and their immediate localities were likely to have been more significant for them than broader political identities, though no one is likely to have been completely immune from the demands of lordship or the repercussions of war. What we are probably safe in saying is that by 800 Christianity had become part of the personal identity of practically everyone in Britain. The degree of knowledge and understanding may have varied considerably, as may have access to priests and churches, but burial evidence suggests a widespread impact of the basics of Christian belief and a desire to be under the protection of the Christian God in life and in death. Ruling elites seem to have taken seriously their obligation to organise the conversion of their subjects, though knowledge of Christianity and its rituals may also have been spread through regular interaction of peasant communities for trade and other social purposes that no doubt transcended political and religious boundaries. Naturally not all aspects of previous religious practice disappeared; people were still likely to consult the local wise women or try to foresee the future, though they were probably less likely by 800 to call upon the pagan gods for assistance. Christianity had not transformed early medieval society in Britain by 800, but it had become an integral part of that society and one of the structures which supported it.

Notes

1 W. Davies, *An Early Welsh Microcosm* (London, 1978), 102–16; W. Davies, *Wales in the Early Middle Ages* (Leicester, 1982), 68–71, 125–40.

2 H. Pryce, 'Ecclesiastical wealth in early Wales', in *The Early Church in Wales and the West*, ed. N. Edwards and A. Lane (Oxford, 1992), 22–32.

3 E. Campbell, 'The archaeological evidence for external contacts: imports, trade and economy in Celtic Britain AD 400–800', in *External Contacts and the Economy of Late Roman and Post-Roman Britain*, ed. K. Dark (Woodbridge, 1996), 83–96.

4 W. Davies, 'Celtic kingship in the Early Middle Ages', in *Kings and Kingship in Medieval Europe*, ed. A.J. Duggan (London, 1993), 101–24; A. Grant, 'The construction of the early Scottish state', in *The Medieval State. Essays Presented to James Campbell*, ed. J.R. Maddicott and D.M. Palliser (London, 2000), 47–71.

5 T. Pestell and K. Ulmschneider (eds), *Markets in Early Medieval Europe: Trading and 'Productive' Sites 650–850* (Macclesfield, 2003).

6 W. Filmer-Sankey, 'The "Roman emperor" in the Sutton Hoo Ship Burial', *Journal of the British Archaeological Association* 149 (1996), 1–9; L. Webster and M. Brown (eds), *The Transformation of the Roman World* (London, 1997).

7 P. Hill, *Whithorn and St Ninian: The Excavation of a Monastic Town 1984–91* (Stroud, 1997), especially 28–9.

8 C. Doherty, 'The monastic town in early medieval Ireland', in *The Comparative History of Urban Origins in Non-Roman Europe*, ed. H.B. Clarke and A. Simms, BAR International Series 255 (Oxford, 1985), 45–75.

9 K. Ulmschneider, *Markets, Minsters and Metal-Detectors: The Archaeology of Middle Saxon Lincolnshire and Hampshire Compared*, BAR 307 (Oxford, 2000); A. Gannon, *The Iconography of Early Anglo-Saxon Coinage: Sixth to Eighth Centuries* (Oxford, 2003).

10 J. Blair, *The Church in Anglo-Saxon Society* (Oxford, 2005), 251–68.

11 J.W. Huggett, 'Imported grave goods and the early Anglo-Saxon economy', *Medieval Archaeology* 32 (1988), 63–96.

12 T. Pestell, *Landscapes of Monastic Foundation: The Establishment of Religious Houses in East Anglia, c.650–1200* (Woodbridge, 2004), 18–64.

13 D. Jenkins and M.E. Owen, 'The Welsh marginalia in the Lichfield Gospels, part 1', *CMCS* 5 (1983), 37–66.

14 J. Hines, 'Welsh and English: mutual origins in post-Roman Britain?', *Studia Celtica* 34 (2000), 81–104; B. Ward-Perkins, 'Why did the Anglo-Saxons not become more British?', *English Historical Review* 115 (2000), 513–33.

15 J. Bannerman, 'The Scottish take-over of Pictland and the relics of Columba', in *Spes Scotorum*, 71–94; D. Broun, 'Dunkeld and the origin of Scottish identity', in *Spes Scotorum*, 95—111.

Appendix 1 Timeline of main events and people

Year	England and Wales	Dál Riata	Pictland
597	Arrival of Augustine at Canterbury	Death of Columba	
603		Battle of Degastan; defeat of King Áedán	
c.613	Battle of Chester		
616	Death of K. Æthelbert of Kent. Battle of River Idle – death of K. Æthelfrith and accession of Edwin in Northumbria		
c. 625	Death of K. Raedwald of East Angles		
633	Battle of Hatfield; Edwin slain by British K. Caedwalla and K. Penda of Mercia		
634	Accession of Oswald in Northumbria after battle of Heavenfield		
635		B. Aidan from Iona founded Lindisfarne	
642	Oswald killed by Penda at battle of Maserfelth; accession of his brother Oswiu in Bernicia	Death of K. Domnall Brecc at battle of Strath Carron	
653			Accession of Talorcan, son of K. Eanfrith of Northumbria

Year	England and Wales	Dál Riata	Pictland
655	Oswiu slew Penda at the battle of the Winwaed and became king of all Northumbria		
664	Synod of Whitby	Iona monks leave Lindisfarne	
669	Arrival of AB Theodore of Canterbury		
670	Death of Oswiu; accession of Ecgfrith		
672			Accession of Bridei, son of Beli (K. of Dumbarton?)
674	Benedict Biscop founded Wearmouth		
675	Death of K. Wulfhere of Mercia; accession of his brother Æthelred	Adomnán appointed abbot of Iona	
678	Expulsion of B. Wilfrid of Northumbria		
679	K. Æthelred defeated K. Ecgfrith at the battle of the River Trent		
684	K. Ecgfrith ordered raid on Brega in Ireland		
685			K. Bridei defeated and killed K. Ecgfrith at Nechtansmere
686	Accession of Aldfrith in Northumbria and Caedwalla in Wessex	Adomnán's first visit to Northumbria	
687	Death of B. Cuthbert of Lindisfarne		
688	Accession of K. Ine of Wessex	Adomnán's second visit to Northumbria	

Year	England and Wales	Dál Riata	Pictland
697		Promulgation of Law of the Innocents; Adomnán completed *Life of Columba*	Accession of Bridei, son of Derelei
704/5		Death of Adomnán	
706	Death of B. Aldhelm of Sherborne		Accession of Nechtan, son of Derelei
709	Death of B. Wilfrid		
716	Accession of Æthelbald of Mercia		
717			Nechtan expelled Ionan monks who would not accept Roman Easter
719		K. Selbach slew his brother Ainbellach	
729			Accession of K. Onuist
731	Bede completed *Ecclesiastical History*		
735	Death of Bede		
739			Onuist drowned Talorcan, son of K. of Atholl
741		Major attack from K. Onuist	
747	Council of *Clofesho*		
750	K. Cuthred of Wessex 'rose against' Æthelbald and Onuist		Onuist defeated by Britons of Dumbarton
757	Murder of K. Æthelbald of Mercia; accession of K. Offa		
761			Death of K. Onuist; succession of his brother Bridei

Year	England and Wales	Dál Riata	Pictland
768	Britons of Wales adopt Roman Easter	K. Áed Find invaded Pictland	K. Ciniod fought with Áed
786	Visitation of papal legates to provinces of Canterbury and York		
787	Ecgfrith son of Offa anointed as king		
789			Accession of K. Constantine
793	Attack on Lindisfarne by Vikings		
796	Deaths of K. Offa and K. Ecgfrith of Mercia		

Appendix 2 Pictish kings from king lists P and Q to 837

1 Bridei, son of Mailcon 556–84
2 Gartnait, son of Domelch 584–602
3 Nectu/Nechtan, grandson of Uerb 602–21
4 Cinioch, son of Lutrin 621–31
5 Gartnait, son of Uuid 631–5
6 Bridei, son of Uuid 635–41
7 Talorc, brother of Bridei 641–53
8 Talorcan, son of Eanfrith 653–7
9 Gartnait, son of Domnall 657–63
10 Drest, brother of Gartnait 663–72
11 Bridei, son of Beli 672–93
12 Taran, son of Entifidich 693–7
13 Bridei, son of Derelei 697–706
14 Nechtan, son of Derelei 706–24
15 Drest 724–9
16 Alpin 726–8
   [Nechtan second reign – 9 months 728–9]
17 Onuist, son of Uurguist 729–61
18 Bridei, son of Uurguist 761–63
19 Ciniod, son of Uuredech 763–75
20 Alpin, son of Uuroid 775–80
   [N.B. chronology of kings 780–9 is uncertain and disputed]
21 Drest, son of Talorcan 780
22 Talorcan, son of Drostan 780–2
23 Talorcan, son of Onuist 782
24 Conall, son of Tadg 785–9
25 Constantine, son of Uurguist 789–820
26 Onuist, son of Uurguist 820–34
27 Drest, son of Constantine 834–7

Adapted from M.O. Anderson, *Kings and Kingship in Early Scotland* (Edinburgh, 1980)

Appendix 3 Kings of Northumbria from Æthelfrith to Eardwulf

Æthelfrith, son of K. Æthelric of Bernicia, 592/3–616

Edwin, son of K. Ælle of Deira, 616–33

Eanfrith, son of K. Æthelfrith, 633–4 [Bernicia]
Osric, son of Ælfric, 633–4 [Deira]

Oswald, son of K. Æthelfrith, 633–42

Oswiu, son of K. Æthelfrith, 642–55 [Bernicia], 655–70 [Northumbria]
Oswine, son of K. Osric, 644–51 [Deira]
Oethelwald, son of K. Oswald, 651–5 [Deira]

Ecgfrith, son of K. Oswiu, 670–86

Aldfrith, son of K. Oswiu, 686–705

Osred I, son of K. Aldfrith, 706–16

Cenred, son of Cuthwine, 716–18

Osric, son of K. Aldfrith, 718–29

Ceolwulf, son of Cuthwine, 729–37

Eadberht, son of Eata, 737–58

Oswulf, son of K. Eadbert, 758

Æthelwald Moll, 758–65

Alhred, son of Eanwine, 765–74

Æthelred, son of K. Æthelwald Moll, 774–9

Ælfwald, son of K. Oswulf, 779–88

Osred II, son of K. Alhred, 788–92

Eardwulf, son of Eardwulf, 796–806

Appendix 4 Kings of Mercia from Penda to Coenwulf

Penda, son of Pybba, d. 655

[Oswiu of Northumbria 655–8]

Wulfhere, son of K. Penda, 658–75

Æthelred, son of K. Penda, 675–704

Cenred, son of K. Wulfhere, 704–9

Ceolred, son of K. Æthelred, 709–16

Æthelbald, son of Alwih, 716–57

Beornred, 757

Offa, son of Thingfrith, 757–96

Ecgfrith, son of K. Offa, 796

Coenwulf, 796–821

For detailed lists of the kings of all the Anglo-Saxon kingdoms see D.N. Dumville, 'The local rulers of England to AD 927', in *The Handbook of British Chronology*, ed. E.B. Fryde, D.E. Greenway, S. Porter and I. Roy (3rd edn, London, 1986), 1–25

Appendix 5 The Union of the Bernician and Deiran royal houses through marriage

Deira

Bernicia

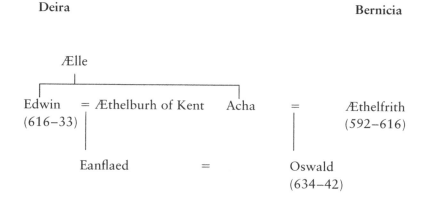

Ælle

Edwin = Æthelburh of Kent   Acha   =   Æthelfrith
(616–33)   (592–616)

Eanflaed   =   Oswald
                    (634–42)

Appendix 6 Two rival theories for the descent of the Pictish kings Constantine (789–820) and Onuist, the sons of Uurguist/Fergus

(NB the names Uurguist and Fergus are the same in Pictish and Gaelic respectively)

(a) Hypothetical Pictish descent

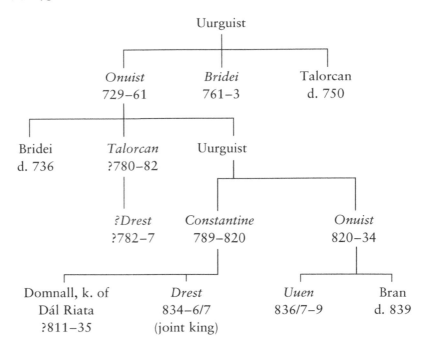

Kings of the Picts are italicised

From D Broun, 'Pictish kings 761–839: integration with Dál Riata or separate development?', in *The St Andrews Sarcophagus: A Pictish Masterpiece and its International Connections*, ed. S. Foster (Dublin, 1998), 71–83.

(b) Hypothetical Dál Riatan descent

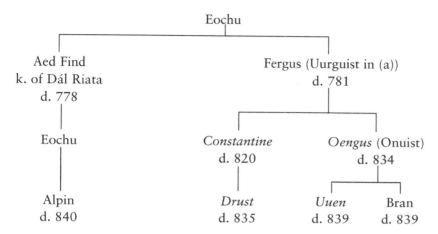

For ease of comparision the descendants of Fergus/Uurguist have been given in Pictish form and rulers are italicised as in (a)

Adapted from J. Bannerman, 'The Scottish take-over of Pictland and the relics of Columba', in *Spes Scotorum*, 71–94

Bibliography

Primary Written Sources

Adomnán of Iona, *Life of St Columba*, trans. R. Sharpe (Harmondsworth, 1995)

Adomnan's Life of St Columba, ed. A.O. Anderson and M.O. Anderson (2nd edn, Oxford, 1991)

Æthelwulf, *De Abbatibus*, ed. A. Campbell (Oxford, 1967)

Agricola and Germany by Tacitus, trans. A.R. Birley (Oxford, 1999)

Alcuini, 'Epistolae', in *MGH Epistolae* IV, vol. 2, ed. E. Dümmler (Berlin, 1895)

Aldhelm: The Poetic Works, ed. M. Lapidge and J. Rosier (Woodbridge, 1985)

Aldhelm: The Prose Works, ed. M. Lapidge and M. Herren (Ipswich, 1979)

Alfred the Great: Asser's Life of King Alfred and Other Contemporary Sources, trans. S. Keynes and M. Lapidge (Harmondsworth, 1983)

The Anglo-Saxon Chronicle, ed. D. Whitelock, with D.C. Douglas and S.I. Tucker, (London, 1961)

Anglo-Saxon Missionaries in Germany, trans. C.H. Talbot (London, 1954)

'The Annals of Tigernach', ed. W. Stokes, *Revue Celtique* 16 (1895), 374–419 and 17 (1896), 6–33, 119–263

The Annals of Ulster (to AD 1131), ed. and trans. S. Mac Airt and G. Mac Nicoaill, part 1 (Dublin, 1983)

Asser's Life of King Alfred, ed. W.H. Stevenson (Oxford, 1904)

Bede's Ecclesiastical History of the English People, ed. B. Colgrave and R.A.B. Mynors (Oxford, 1969)

Bede, *Venerabilis Bedae Opera Historica*, ed. C. Plummer, 2 vols (Oxford, 1896)

Beowulf and the Fight at Finnsburg, ed. F. Klaeber (3rd edn, Boston, 1950)

S. Bonifatii et Lulli Epistolae, MGH Epistolae Selecta I, ed. M. Tangl (Berlin, 1916)

Cáin Adomnan and Canones Adomnani, ed. and trans. P. Ó Néill and D.N. Dumville, 2 vols (Cambridge, 2003)

Charters of St Augustine's Abbey, Canterbury and Minster-in-Thanet, ed. S. Kelly (Oxford, 1995)

Charters of Selsey, ed. S. Kelly (Oxford, 1998)

Councils and Ecclesiastical Documents Relating to Great Britain and Ireland: II, The Churches of Ireland and Scotland 350–1188. III, The English Church 595–1066, ed. A.W. Haddan and W. Stubbs (Oxford, 1871)

Culhwch ac Olwen, ed. R. Bromwich and D. Simon Evans (Cardiff, 1992)

The Dream of the Rood, ed. M. Swanson (2nd edn, Exeter, 1987)

The Earliest Life of Gregory the Great, ed. B. Colgrave (Lawrence, 1968)

English Historical Documents, I, c.500–1042, ed. and trans. D. Whitelock (2nd edn, London, 1979)

Felix's Life of Saint Guthlac, ed. B. Colgrave (Cambridge, 1956)

The Finnsburh Fragment and Episode, ed. D. Fry (London, 1974)

Gildas: The Ruin of Britain and Other Documents, ed. and trans. M. Winterbottom (Chichester, 1978)

The Gododdin: The Oldest Scottish Poem, ed. K.H. Jackson (Edinburgh, 1969)

The Gododdin: Text and Context from Dark-Age North Britain, ed. and trans. J.T. Koch (Cardiff, 1997)

Gregory of Tours, *Decem Libri Historiarum*, ed. B. Krusch and W. Levison, *MGH Scriptores rerum Merovingicarum* I (Hanover, 1951)

Iona: the Earliest Poetry of a Celtic Monastery, ed. T.O. Clancy and G. Márkus (Edinburgh, 1995)

J.F. Kenney, *Sources for the Early History of Ireland: Ecclesiastical* (New York, 1929)

The Laws of the Earliest English Kings, ed. and trans. F.L. Attenborough (Cambridge, 1922)

The Life of Bishop Wilfrid by Eddius Stephanus, ed. B. Colgrave (Cambridge, 1927)

The Llandaff Charters, ed. W. Davies (Aberystwyth, 1979)

Medieval Handbooks of Penance, ed. J.T. McNeill and H.M. Garner (rpr. New York, 1979), 130–5

Nennius: British History and the Welsh Annals, ed. and trans. J. Morris (Chichester, 1980)

Nicholas Roscarrock's Lives of the Saints: Cornwall and Devon, ed. N. Orme, Devon and Cornwall Record Society, new series 35 (1992)

Poems of Wisdom and Learning in Old English, ed. T.A. Shippey (Cambridge, 1976)

St Patrick: His Writings and Muirchu's Life, ed. A.B.E. Hood (Chichester, 1978)

P. Sawyer, *Anglo-Saxon Charters: An Annotated List and Bibliography* (London, 1968)

Tacitus: The Germania, ed. J.G.C. Anderson (Oxford, 1938)

The Triumph Tree. Scotland's Earliest Poetry AD 550–1350, ed. T.O. Clancy (Edinburgh, 1998)

Two Lives of Saint Cuthbert, ed. B. Colgrave (Cambridge 1940)

La Vie ancienne de Saint Samson de Dol, ed. P. Flobert (Paris, 1997)

Vita Wulframi, MGH Scriptores Rerum Merovingicarum 5, ed. W. Levison (Hanover, 1910)

William of Malmesbury, *The Deeds of the Bishops of England*, trans. D. Preest (Woodbridge, 2002)

Secondary Sources

Aist, R., Clancy, T., O'Loughlin, T. and Wooding, J (eds), *Adomnán of Iona: Theologian – Lawmaker – Peacemaker* (Dublin, forthcoming)

Aitchison, N. *The Picts and Scots at War* (Stroud, 2003)

Alcock, E. 'Burials and cemeteries in Scotland', in *The Early Church in Wales and the West*, ed. N. Edwards and A. Lane (Oxford, 1992), 125–9

Alcock, L. *Cadbury Castle Somerset: The Early Medieval Archaeology* (Cardiff, 1995)

Alcock, L. *Kings and Warriors, Craftsmen and Priests in Northern Britain AD 550–850* (Edinburgh, 2003)

Aldhouse-Green, M. 'Gallo-British deities and their shrines', in *A Companion to Roman Britain*, ed. M. Todd (Oxford, 2004), 192–219

Alexander, L.M. 'The legal status of the native Britons in late seventh-century Wessex as reflected by the Law Code of Ine', *Haskins Society Journal* 7 (1995), 31–8

Allen, J.R. *The Early Christian Monuments of Scotland* (Edinburgh, 1903)

Anderson, M.O. *Kings and Kingship in Early Scotland* (Edinburgh, 1980)

Armit, I. *Celtic Scotland* (London, 1997)

Arnold, C. and Davies, J.L. *Roman and Early Medieval Wales* (Stroud, 2000)

Bailey, R.N. *Viking-Age Sculpture in Northern England* (London, 1980).

Bannerman, J. *Studies in the History of Dalriada* (Edinburgh, 1974)

Bannerman, J. 'The Scottish take-over of Pictland and the relics of Columba', in *Spes Scotorum, 71–94*

Barnwell, P. '*Hlafaeta, ceorl, hid* and *scir*': Celtic, Roman or Germanic?', *ASSAH* 9 (1996), 58–61

Barrow, G.W.S. *The Kingdom of the Scots* (London, 1973)

Barrow, G.W.S. *Saint Ninian and Pictomania* (Whithorn, 2004)

Bartlett, R. 'Symbolic meanings of hair in the Middle Ages', *TRHS*, 6th series (1994), 43–60

Bassett, S. 'Lincoln and the Anglo-Saxon see of Lindsey', *Anglo-Saxon England* 18 (1989), 1–32

Bassett, S. 'Church and diocese in the West Midlands: the transition from British to Anglo-Saxon control', in *Pastoral Care, 13–40*

Bassett, S. 'How the West was won: the Anglo-Saxon take-over of the West Midlands', *ASSAH* 11 (2000), 107–18.

Bazelmans, J. *By Weapons Made Worthy: Lords, Retainers and Their Relationship in Beowulf* (Amsterdam, 1999)

Bedingfield, B. 'Public penance in Anglo-Saxon England', *Anglo-Saxon England* 31 (2002), 223–56

Biddle, M. and Kjølbye Biddle, B. 'The Repton stone', *Anglo-Saxon England* 14 (1985), 233–92

Bidwell, P. *The Legionary Bath-House and Basilica and Forum at Exeter* (Exeter, 1979)

Binchy, D.A. *Celtic and Anglo-Saxon Kingship* (Oxford, 1970)

Blair, J. 'Anglo-Saxon pagan shrines and their prototypes', *ASSAH* 8 (1995), 1–28

Blair, J. 'Ecclesiastical organization and pastoral care in Anglo-Saxon England', *Early Medieval Europe* 4 (1995), 193–212

Blair, J. 'A saint for every minster? Local cults in Anglo-Saxon England', in *Local Saints*, 455–94

Blair, J. 'A handlist of Anglo-Saxon saints', in *Local Saints*, 495–565

Blair, J. *The Church in Anglo-Saxon Society* (Oxford, 2005)

Blair, J. and Sharpe, R. (eds), *Pastoral Care Before the Parish* (Leicester, 1992)

Blair, P.H. 'The Northumbrians and their southern frontier', *Archaeologia Aeliana*, 4th series 26 (1948), 98–126

Blair, P.H. *The World of Bede* (London, 1970, revised edn, 1990)

Boddington, A. 'Models of burial, settlement and worship: the Final Phase reviewed', in *Anglo-Saxon Cemeteries: A Reappraisal*, ed. E. Southworth (Stroud, 1990), 177–99

Bonner, G. (ed.), *Famulus Christi* (London, 1976)

Bonner, G., Rollason, D. and Stancliffe, C. (eds), *St Cuthbert, His Cult and His Community to AD 1200* (Woodbridge, 1989)

Bonner, G. 'The pelagian controversy in Britain and Ireland', *Peritia* 16 (2002), 144–55

Bowen, E.G. *Saints, Seaways and Settlements in the Celtic Lands* (Cardiff, 1969)

Bradley, R. 'Time regained: the creation of continuity', *Journal of British Archaeological Association* 140 (1987), 1–17

Breeze, D. *Roman Scotland: Frontier Country* (London, 1996)

Breeze, D. and Dobson, B. *Hadrian's Wall* (4th edn, London, 2000)

Brenan, M. *Hanging Bowls and their Contexts*, BAR 220 (Oxford, 1991)

Brooks, N. 'The development of military obligations in eighth- and ninth-century England', in *England Before the Conquest*, ed. P. Clemoes and K. Hughes (Cambridge, 1971), 69–84

Brooks, N. *The Early History of the Church of Canterbury* (Leicester, 1984)

Brooks, N. 'The creation and early structure of the kingdom of Kent', in *The Origins of Anglo-Saxon Kingdoms*, ed. S. Bassett (Leicester, 1989), 55–74

Brooks, N. 'The formation of the Mercian kingdom', in *The Origins of Anglo-Saxon Kingdoms*, ed. S. Bassett (Leicester, 1989), 159–70

Brooks, N. *Bede and the English* (Jarrow lecture, 1999)

Broun, D. 'The literary record of St Nynia: fact or fiction?', *Innes Review* 42 (1991), 143–50

Broun, D. 'Pictish kings 761–839: integration with Dál Riata or separate development?', in *The St Andrew Sarcophagus. A Pictish Masterpiece and its International Connections*, ed. S. Foster (Dublin, 1998), 71–83

Broun, D. 'Dunkeld and the origin of Scottish identity', in *Spes Scotorum*, 95–111

Broun, D. *The Irish Identity of the Kingdom of the Scots* (Woodbridge, 1999)

Broun, D. 'The seven kingdoms in *De situ Albaniae*: a record of Pictish political geography or imaginary map of Alba', in *Alba: Celtic Scotland in the Medieval Era*, ed. E.J. Cowan and R.A. McDonald (East Linton, 2000), 24–42

Broun, D. 'Kentigern', *Oxford Dictionary of National Biography* (Oxford, 2004)

Broun, D. 'Alba: Pictish homeland or Irish offshoot?' (forthcoming)

Broun, D and Clancy, T.O. (eds), *Spes Scotorum: Hope of Scots. Saint Columba, Iona and Scotland* (Edinburgh, 1999)

Brown, M. *The Lindisfarne Gospels: Society, Spirituality and the Scribe* (London, 2003)

Brown, P. *The Cult of Saints: Its Rise and Function in Latin Christianity* (Chicago, 1981)

Brown, P. *The Rise of Western Christendom: Triumph and Diversity* AD *200–1000* (Oxford, 1996)

Bruce-Mitford, R.L.S. *The Sutton Hoo Ship-Burial*, 3 vols (London, 1975–83)

Brugmann, B. 'Britons, Angles, Saxons, Jutes and Franks', in *The Anglo-Saxon Cemetery at Mill Hill, Deal, Kent*, ed. K. Parfitt and B. Brugmann (London, 1997), 110–24

Bullough, D. 'Burial, community and belief in the early medieval west', in *Ideal and Reality in Frankish and Anglo-Saxon Society*, ed. P. Wormald (Oxford, 1983), 177–201

Burnell, S. and James, E. 'The archaeology of conversion on the continent in the sixth and seventh centuries', *St Augustine*, ed. Gameson, 83–106

Byrne, F.J. *Irish Kings and High Kings* (London, 1973)

Caldwell, D.H. 'Finlaggan, Islay: stones and inauguration ceremonies', in *The Stone of Destiny: Artefact and Icon*, ed. R. Welander, D.J. Breeze and T.O. Clancy (Edinburgh, 2003), 61–76

Cambridge, E. and Rollason, D. 'The pastoral organization of the Anglo-Saxon church: a review of the "minster hypothesis" ', *Early Medieval Europe* 4 (1995), 87–104

Cameron, K. 'Eccles in English place-names', in *Christianity in Britain, 300–700*, ed. M. Barley and R. Hanson (Leicester, 1968), 87–92

Cameron, M.L. *Anglo-Saxon Medicine* (Cambridge, 1993)

Campbell, E. 'The archaeological evidence for external contacts: imports, trade and economy in Celtic Britain AD 400–800', in *External Contacts and the Economy of Late Roman and Post-Roman Britain*, ed. K. Dark (Woodbridge, 1996), 83–96

Campbell, E. 'Were the Scots Irish?', *Antiquity* 75 (2001), 285–92

Campbell, E. 'Royal inauguration in Dál Riata and the Stone of

Destiny', in *The Stone of Destiny: Artefact and Icon*, ed. R. Welander, D.J. Breeze and T.O. Clancy (Edinburgh, 2003), 43–60

Campbell, J. *Essays in Anglo-Saxon History* (London, 1986)

Campbell, J. 'Elements in the background to the Life of St Cuthbert and his early cult', in *St Cuthbert, His Cult and His Community to* AD *120*, ed. G. Bonner, D. Rollason and C. Stancliffe (Woodbridge, 1989), 3–19

Carey, J. 'Varieties of supernatural contact in the Life of Adomnán', in *Saints and Scholars: Studies in Irish Hagiography*, ed. J. Carey, M. Herbert and P. Ó Riain (Dublin, 2001), 49–62

Carey, J. 'Werewolves in Medieval Ireland', *CMCS* 44 (2002), 37–72

Cartwright, J. (ed.), *Celtic Hagiography and Saints' Cults* (Cardiff, 2003)

Carver, M. (ed.), *The Age of Sutton Hoo* (Woodbridge, 1992)

Carver, M. 'Reflections on the meanings of monumental barrows in Anglo-Saxon England', in *Burial*, ed. Lucy and Reynolds, 132–43

Carver, M. 'An Iona of the East: the early medieval monastery at Portmahomack, Tarbat Ness', *Medieval Archaeology* 48 (2004), 1–30

Cassidy, B. (ed.), *The Ruthwell Cross* (Princeton, 1992)

Chadwick, N.K. *Celt and Saxon; Studies in the Early British Border* (Cambridge, 1963), 138–66

Chambers, R.A. 'The late and sub-Roman Cemetery at Queensford Farm, Dorchester-on-Thames (Oxon)', *Oxoniensia* 52 (1987), 35–69

Charles-Edwards, T. 'The seven bishop-houses of Dyfed', *Bulletin of the Board of Celtic Studies* 24 (1970–2), 247–62.

Charles-Edwards, T. 'Kinship, status and the origin of the hide', *Past and Present* 56 (1972), 3–33

Charles-Edwards, T. 'Boundaries in Irish law', in *Medieval Settlement: Continuity and Change*, ed. P. Sawyer (London, 1976), 83–7

Charles-Edwards, T. 'The distinction between land and moveable wealth in Anglo-Saxon England', in *Medieval Settlement: Continuity and Change*, ed. P. Sawyer (London, 1976), 180–7

Charles-Edwards, T. 'The social background to Irish *peregrinatio*', *Celtica* 11 (1976), 43–59

Charles-Edwards, T. 'Bede, the Irish and the Britons', *Celtica* 15 (1983), 42–52

Charles-Edwards, T. 'Early medieval kingships in the British Isles', in *The Origins of Anglo-Saxon Kingdoms*, ed. S. Bassett (London, 1989), 28–39

Charles-Edwards, T. *Early Irish and Welsh Kinship* (Oxford, 1993)

Charles-Edwards, T. 'Palladius, Prosper, and Leo the Great: mission and primatial authority', in *Saint Patrick, AD 493–1993*, ed. D.N. Dumville (Woodbridge, 1993), 1–18

Charles-Edwards, T. 'Language and society among the insular Celts, 400–1000', in *The Celtic World*, ed. M. Green (London, 1995), 703–36

Charles-Edwards, T. 'The Penitential of Theodore and the *Iudicia Theodori*', in *Archbishop Theodore*, ed. M. Lapidge (Cambridge, 1995), 141–74

Charles-Edwards, T. ' "The Continuation of Bede", sa 750; High-kings, kings of Tara and "Bretwaldas" ', in *Seanchas: Studies in Early Medieval Irish, Archaeology, History and Literature in Honour of Francis J. Byrne*, ed. A.P. Smyth (Dublin, 2000), 137–45

Charles-Edwards, T. *Early Christian Ireland* (Cambridge, 2000)

Charles-Edwards, T. 'Érlam: the patron saint of an Irish church', in *Local Saints*, 267–90

Charles-Edwards, T. 'Nations and kingdoms: a view from above', in *After Rome*, ed. T. Charles-Edwards (Oxford, 2003), 23–58

Chase, C. (ed.), *The Dating of Beowulf* (Toronto, 1981)

Clancy, T.O. 'Columba, Adomnán, and the cult of the saints in Scotland, in *Spes Scotorum*, 3–34

Clancy, T.O. 'The real St Ninian', *Innes Review* 52 (2001), 1–28

Clancy, T.O. 'Scottish saints and national identities in the early Middle Ages', in *Local Saints*, 397–421

Clancy, T.O. 'Philosopher king: Nechtan mac Der-Ilei', *Scottish Historical Review* 83 (2004), 125–49

Cleary, A.S. Esmonde, *The Ending of Roman Britain* (London, 1989)

Clover, C. 'Regardless of sex: men, women and power in early northern Europe', *Speculum* 69 (1993), 363–7

Corney, M. *The Roman Villa at Bradford-on-Avon: The Investigations of 2003* (Bradford-on-Avon, 2004)

Corning, C. 'The baptism of Edwin, king of Northumbria: a new analysis of the British tradition', *Northern History* 36 (2000), 5–15

Cramp, R. 'Monastic sites' in *The Archaeology of Anglo-Saxon England*, ed. D. Wilson (London, 1996), 202–52

Crawford, S. 'Children, death and the afterlife', *ASSAH* 6 (1993), 83–92

Cubitt, C. 'The 747 council of *Clofesho*' in *Pastoral Care*, 193–211

Cubitt, C. *Anglo-Saxon Church Councils c.650–c.850* (Leicester, 1995)

Cubitt, C. 'Sites and sanctity: revisiting the cults of murdered and martyred kings', *Early Medieval Europe* 9 (2000), 53–83

Cubitt, C. 'Universal and local saints in Anglo-Saxon England', in *Local Saints*, 423–54

Cubitt, C. 'The clergy in early Anglo-Saxon England', *Historical Research* 78 (2005), 273–87

Daniels, R. 'The Anglo-Saxon monastery at Church Close, Hartlepool, Cleveland', *Archaeological Journal* 145 (1988), 158–210

Dark, K. *Civitas to Kingdom: British Political Continuity 300–800* (London, 1994)

Dark, K. *Britain and the End of the Roman Empire* (Stroud, 2000)

Dark, S.P. 'Palaeoecological evidence for landscape continuity and change in Britain ca, AD 400–800', in *External Contacts and the Economy of Late Roman and Post-Roman Britain*, ed. K. Dark (Woodbridge, 1996), 23–52

Davidson, H.E. *The Lost Beliefs of Northern Europe* (London, 1993)

Davies, J.R. 'Church, property and conflict in Wales, AD 600–1100', *Welsh History Review* 18 (1996/7), 387–406

Davies, J.R. 'The Book of Llandaf; a twelfth-century perspective', *Anglo-Norman Studies* 21 (1998), 31–46

Davies, J.R. 'The Saints of south Wales and the Welsh church', *Local Saints*, 360–95

Davies, J.R. *The Book of Llandaf and the Norman Church in Wales* (Woodbridge, 2003)

Davies, W. *An Early Welsh Microcosm* (London, 1978)

Davies, W. *The Llandaff Charters* (Cardiff, 1979)

Davies, W. 'The Latin charter-tradition in western Britain, Brittany and Ireland in the early medieval period', in *Ireland in Early Mediaeval Europe*, ed. D. Whitelock, R. McKitterick and D.N. Dumville (Cambridge, 1982), 258–80

Davies, W. *Wales in the Early Middle Ages* (Leicester, 1982)

Davies, W. 'The myth of the Celtic church', in *The Early Church in Wales and the West,* ed. N. Edwards and A. Lane (Oxford, 1992), 12–21

Davies, W. 'Celtic women in the early Middle Ages', in *Images of Women in Antiquity*, ed. A. Cameron and A. Kuhrt (revised edn, London, 1993), 145–66

Davies, W. 'Celtic kingship in the Early Middle Ages', in *Kings and Kingship in Medieval Europe*, ed. A.J. Duggan (London, 1993), 101–24

Davies, W. ' "Protected space" in Britain and Ireland in the Middle Ages', in *Scotland in Dark Age Britain*, ed. B. Crawford (St Andrews, 1996), 1–20

Davies, W. and Fouracre, P. (eds), *The Settlement of Disputes in Early Medieval Europe* (Cambridge, 1986)

Davies, W. and Vierck, H. 'The contexts of Tribal Hidage: social aggregates and settlement patterns', *Frühmittelalterliche Studien* 8 (1974), 233–93

Detsicas, A.P. and Hawkes, S.C. 'Finds from the Anglo-Saxon cemetery at Eccles, Kent', *Antiquaries Journal* 53 (1973), 281–6

Dickinson, T.M. 'An Anglo-Saxon "cunning woman" from Bidford-on-Avon', in *In Search of Cult*, ed. M. Carver (Woodbridge, 1993), 45–54

Dickinson, T.M. 'Early Saxon saucer brooches: a preliminary overview', *ASSAH* 6 (1993), 11–44

Doherty, C. 'The monastic town in early medieval Ireland', in *The Comparative History on Urban Origins in Non-Roman Europe*, ed. H.B. Clarke and A. Simms, BAR International Series 255 (Oxford, 1985), 45–75

Donaldson, G. 'Scottish bishops' sees before the reign of David I', *Proceedings of the Society of Antiquaries of Scotland* 87 (1952–3), 106–17

Dransart, P. 'Saints, stones and shrines: the cults of Sts Moluag and Gerardine in Pictland', in *Celtic Hagiographies and Saints' Cults*, ed. J. Cartwright (Cardiff, 2003), 232–48

Drinkwater, J. and Elton, H. (eds), *Fifth-Century Gaul: A Crisis of Identity?* (Cambridge, 1992)

Driscoll, S.T. 'Power and authority in early historic Scotland: Pictish symbol stones and other documents', in *State and Society: The Emergence and Development of Social Hierarchy and Political Centralization*, ed. J. Gledhill, B. Bender and M.T. Larsen (London, 1988), 215–35

Driscoll, S.T. 'Church archaeology in Glasgow and the kingdom of Strathclyde', *Innes Review* 49 (1998), 95–114

Dumville, D.N. 'Kingship, genealogies and regnal lists', in *Early Medieval Kingship*, ed. P. Sawyer and I.N. Wood (Leeds, 1977), 72–104

Dumville, D.N. 'Gildas and Uinniau', in *Gildas: New Approaches*, ed. M. Lapidge and D.N. Dumville (Woodbridge, 1984), 207–14

Dumville, D.N. 'Some British aspects of the earliest Irish Christianity', in *Ireland and Europe: The Early Church*, ed. P.N. Chatháin and M. Richter (Stuttgart, 1984), 16–24

Dumville, D.N. 'The local rulers of England to AD 927', in *The Handbook of British Chronology*, ed. E.B. Fryde, D.E. Greenway, S. Porter and I. Roy (3rd edn, London, 1986), 1–25

Dumville, D.N. (ed.), *Saint Patrick AD 493–1993* (Woodbridge, 1993)

Dumville, D.N. *Saint David of Wales* (Cambridge, 2001)

Dumville, D.N. 'Ireland and North Britain in the earlier Middle Ages: contexts for *Míniugud Senchasa fher*', in *Rannsachadh na Gàidhlig 2000*, ed. C.O. Baoill and N.R. McGuire (Aberdeen, 2002), 185–211

Duncan, A.A.M. *The Making of Scotland* (Edinburgh, 1975)

Duncan, A.A.M. 'Bede, Iona and the Picts', in *The Writing of History in the Middle Ages. Essays Presented to Richard William Southern*, ed. R.H.C. Davis and J.M. Wallace-Hadrill (Oxford, 1981), 1–42

Edwards, H. 'Two documents from Aldhelm's Malmesbury', *Bulletin of the Institute of Historical Research* 59 (1986), 1–19

Edwards, N. 'Celtic saints and early medieval archaeology', in *Local Saints*, 225–65

Edwards, N. and Lane, A. (eds), *The Early Church in Wales and the West*, Oxbow monograph 16 (Oxford, 1992)

Emms, R. 'The early history of St Augustine's abbey, Canterbury', in *St Augustine*, ed. Gameson, 410–28

Enright, M.J. *Iona, Tara, and Soissons: The Origins of the Royal Anointing Ritual* (Berlin, 1985)

Enright, M.J. 'Royal succession and abbatial prerogative in Adomnán's *Vita Columbae*', *Peritia* 4 (1985), 83–103

Etchingham, C. *Church Organisation in Ireland* AD 650–1000 (Maynooth, 1999)

Fahy, D. 'When did Britons become Bretons?', *Welsh History Review* 2 (1964–5), 111–24

Faith, R. *The English Peasantry and the Growth of Lordship* (London, 1997)

Farwell, D. and Molleson, T. *Poundbury Volume 2: The Cemeteries* (Dorchester, 1993)

Faulkener, N. *The Decline and Fall of Roman Britain* (Stroud, 2000)

Faull, M.I. 'The post-Roman period', in *West Yorkshire: An Archaeological Survey to* AD 1500, ed. M.I. Faull and S. Moorhouse (Wakefield, 1981), 171–224

Featherstone, P. 'The Tribal Hidage and the ealdormen of Mercia', in *Mercia: An Anglo-Saxon Kingdom in Europe*, ed. M. Brown and C. Farr (London, 2001), 23–34

Fell, C. *Women in Anglo-Saxon England* (London, 1984)

Fell, C. 'Saint Æthelthryth: a historical-hagiographical dichotomy revisited', *Nottingham Medieval Studies* 38 (1994), 18–34

Filmer-Sankey, W. 'The "Roman emperor" in the Sutton Hoo Ship

Burial', *Journal of the British Archaeological Association* 149 (1996), 1–9

Filppula, M., Klemola, J. and Pitkänen, H. (eds), *The Celtic Roots of English* (Joensuu, 2002)

Finberg, H.P.R. *Lucerna* (London, 1964)

Finberg, H.P.R. (ed.), *The Agrarian History of England and Wales 1.2: AD 43–1042* (Cambridge, 1972)

Fletcher, R. *The Conversion of Europe* (London, 1977)

Flint, V. *The Rise of Magic in Early Medieval Europe* (Oxford, 1991)

Foot, S. 'Parochial ministry in early Anglo-Saxon England: the role of monastic communities', *Studies in Church History* 26 (1989), 43–54

Foot, S. ' "By water in the spirit": the administration of baptism in early Anglo-Saxon England', in *Pastoral Care*, 171–92

Foot, S. 'Anglo-Saxon minsters: a review of terminology', in *Pastoral Care*, 212–25

Foot, S. *Veiled Women*, 2 vols (Aldershot, 2000)

Forsyth, K. *Language in Pictland*, Studia Hameliana 2 (Utrecht, 1997)

Forsyth, K. 'Some thoughts on Pictish symbols as a formal writing system', in *The Worm, the Germ and the Thorn: Pictish and Related Studies Presented to Isabel Henderson*, ed. D. Henry (Balgavies, 1997), 85–98

Forsyth, K. 'Literacy in Pictland', in *Literacy in Medieval Celtic Societies,* ed. H. Pryce (Cambridge, 1998), 39–61

Forsyth, K. 'Evidence of a lost Pictish source in the *Historia Regum Anglorum*', in *Kings, Clerics and Chronicles in Scotland 500–1297*, ed. S. Taylor (Dublin, 2000), 19–34

Foster, S. *Picts, Gaels and Scots* (London, 1996)

Foster, S. (ed.), *The St Andrews Sarcophagus: A Pictish Masterpiece and its International Connections* (Dublin, 1998)

Frantzen, A.J. *The Literature of Penance in Anglo-Saxon England* (New Brunswick, 1983)

Fraser, J. 'Northumbrian Whithorn and the making of St Ninian', *Innes Review* 53 (2002), 40–59

Fraser, J. 'Adomnán, Cumméne Ailbe, and the Picts', *Peritia* 17–18 (2003–4), 183–98

Frend, W.H.C. *The Archaeology of Early Christianity: A History* (London, 1996)

Frend, W.H.C. 'Roman Britain, a failed promise', in *The Cross Goes North: Processes of Conversion in Northern Europe, AD 300–1300*, ed. M. Carver (York, 2003), 79–91

Frere, S. *Britannia: A History of Roman Britain* (3rd edn, London, 1987)

Gameson, R. (ed.), *St Augustine and the Conversion of England* (Stroud, 1999)

Gannon, A. *The Iconography of Early Anglo-Saxon Coinage: Sixth to Eighth Centuries* (Oxford, 2003)

Geake, H. *The Use of Grave-Goods in Conversion-Period England c.600–c.850*, BAR 261 (Oxford, 1997)

Geary, P. *Before France and Germany: The Creation and Transformation of the Merovingian World* (Oxford, 1988)

Geary, P. *The Myth of Nations: The Medieval Origins of Europe* (Princeton, 2002)

Gelling, M. *Signposts to the Past: Place-names and History in England* (London, 1978)

Gelling, M. *The West Midlands in the Early Middle Ages* (London, 1992)

Gillett, A. (ed.), *On Barbarian Identity: Critical Approaches to Ethnicity in the Early Middle Ages* (Turnhout, 2002)

Giot, P.-R., Guigon, P. and Merdrignac, B. *The British Settlement of Brittany* (Stroud, 2004)

Gittos, H. 'Creating the sacred: Anglo-Saxon rites for consecrating cemeteries', in *Burial*, ed. Lucy and Reynolds, 195–208

Godfrey, J. 'The place of the double monastery in the Anglo-Saxon minster system', in *Famulus Christi*, ed. G. Bonner (London, 1976), 344–50

Goetz, H.-W., Jarnut, J. and Pohl, W. (eds), *Regna and Gentes. The Relationship between Late Antique and Early Medieval Peoples and Kingdoms in the Transformation of the Roman World* (Leiden, 2003)

Goffart, W. *The Narrators of Barbarian History* (Princeton, 1988)

Goody, J. *The Development of Family and Marriage in Europe* (Cambridge, 1983)

Grant, A. 'The construction of the early Scottish state', in *The Medieval State. Essays Presented to James Campbell*, ed. J.R. Maddicott and D.M. Palliser (London, 2000), 47–71

Green, D.H. *The Carolingian Lord* (Cambridge, 1965)

Green, M. *The Gods of the Celts* (Gloucester, 1986)

Green, M. *Exploring the World of the Druids* (London, 1997)

Grimmer, M. 'Britons and Saxons in pre-Viking Wessex', *Parergon* 19 (2002), 1–17

Hadley, D.M. 'Burial practices in northern England in the later Anglo-Saxon period', in *Burial*, ed. Lucy and Reynolds, 209–28

Hall, T.A. *Minster Churches in the Dorset Landscape*, BAR 304 (Oxford, 2000)

Halsall, G. *Warfare and Society in the Barbarian West, 450–900* (London, 2003)

Hamerow, H. *Early Medieval Settlements: The Archaeology of Rural Communities in North-West Europe 400–900* (Oxford, 2002)

Handley, M. 'The early medieval inscriptions of western Britain', in *The Community, the Family and the Saint: Patterns of Power in Early Medieval Europe*, ed. J. Hill and M. Swan (Turnhout, 1998), 339–62

Härke, H. 'The Anglo-Saxon weapon burial rite', *Past and Present* 126 (1990), 22–43

Harrington, C. *Women in a Celtic Church: Ireland 450–1150* (Oxford, 2002)

Harrison, K. *The Framework of Anglo-Saxon History to AD 900* (Cambridge, 1976)

Hase, P. 'The mother churches of Hampshire', in *Minsters and Parish Churches*, ed. J. Blair (Oxford, 1988), 45–66

Hawkes, J. 'Columban Virgins: iconic images of the Virgin and Child in insular sculpture', in *Studies in the Cult of St Columba*, ed. C. Bourke (Dublin, 1997), 107–35

Hawkes, J. 'Symbolic lives: the visual evidence', in *The Anglo-Saxons from the Migration Period to the Eighth Century: An Ethnographic Perspective*, ed. J. Hines (Woodbridge, 1997), 311–44

Headeager, L. 'Cosmological endurance: pagan identities in early Christian Europe', *European Journal of Archaeology* 1 (1998), 382–96

Henderson, G. *Vision and Image in Early Christian England* (Cambridge, 1999)

Henderson, G. and I. Henderson, *The Art of the Picts: Sculpture and Metalwork in Early Medieval Scotland* (London, 2004)

Henderson, I. '*Primus inter pares*: the St Andrews sarcophagus and Pictish sculpture', in *The St Andrews Sarcophagus: A Pictish Masterpiece and its International Connections*, ed. S. Foster (Dublin, 1998)

Henig, M. *The Art of Roman Britain* (London, 1995)

Henig, M. and Lindley, P. (eds), *Alban and St Albans: Roman and Medieval Architecture, Art and Archaeology*, BAA Conference Transactions 24 (2001)

Herbert, M. *Iona, Kells and Derry: The History and Hagiography of the Monastic Familia of Columba* (Dublin, 1996)

Herren, M. 'Gildas and early British monasticism', in *Britain 400–600: Language and History*, ed. A. Bammesberger and A. Wollmann (Heidelberg, 1990), 65–83.

Herren, M. and Brown, S.A. *Christ in Celtic Christianity: Britain and Ireland from the Fifth to the Tenth Century* (Woodbridge, 2002)

Higgitt, J. 'The Pictish Latin inscription at Tarbat in Ross-shire', *Proceedings of the Society of Antiquaries of Scotland* 112 (1982), 300–21

Higham, N.J. 'New light on the Dark Age landscape: the description of Britain in the *De Excidio Britanniae* of Gildas', *Journal of Historical Geography* 17 (1991), 363–72

Higham, N.J. *Rome, Britain and the Anglo-Saxons* (London, 1992)

Higham, N.J. *The English Conquest: Gildas and Britain in the Fifth Century* (Manchester, 1994)

Higham, N.J. *The Convert Kings: Power and Religious Affiliation in Early Anglo-Saxon England* (Manchester, 1997)

Higham, N.J. 'Britons in northern England in the early Middle Ages: through a thick glass darkly', *Northern History* 38 (2001), 5–25

Hill, D. *An Atlas of Anglo-Saxon England* (Oxford, 1981)

Hill, D. and Cowie, R. (eds), *Wics: The Early Medieval Trading Centres of Northern Europe* (Sheffield, 2001)

Hill, D. and Metcalf, D.M. (eds), *Sceattas in England and on the Continent*, BAR 128 (Oxford, 1984)

Hill, P. *Whithorn and St Ninian: The Excavation of a Monastic Town 1984–91* (Stroud, 1997)

Hillaby, J. 'Early Christian and pre-conquest Leominster: an exploration of the sources', *Transactions of the Woolhope Naturalists' Field Club* 45 (1987), 557–685

Hines, J. *The Scandinavian Character of Anglian England in the Pre-Viking Period*, BAR 124 (Oxford, 1984)

Hines, J. 'The becoming of the English: identity, material culture and language in early Anglo-Saxon England', *ASSAH* 7 (1994), 49–59

Hines, J. 'Welsh and English: mutual origins in post-Roman Britain?', *Studia Celtica* 34 (2000), 81–104

Hines, J. 'Society, community and identity', in *After Rome*, ed. T. Charles-Edwards (Oxford, 2003), 61–101

Hodges, R. *Dark Ages Economics: The Origins of Towns and Trade* AD *600–1000* (London, 1982)

Hollis, S. *Anglo-Saxon Women and the Church* (Woodbridge, 1992)

Hooper, N. 'The Aberlemno stone and cavalry in Anglo-Saxon England', *Northern History* 29 (1993), 188–96

Hope-Taylor, B. *Yeavering: An Anglo-British Centre of Early Northumbria* (London, 1972)

Howlett, D. 'The provenance, date and structure of *De Abbatibus*', *Archaeologia Aeliana* 5th series 3 (1975), 121–30

Howlett, D. *The Celtic Latin Tradition of Biblical Style* (Dublin, 1995)

Howlett, D. *Cambro-Latin Compositions: Their Competence and Craftsmanship* (Dublin, 1998)

Huggett, J.W. 'Imported grave goods and the early Anglo-Saxon economy', *Medieval Archaeology* 32 (1988), 63–96

Huggins, P.J. 'Excavations of a Belgic and Romano-British farm with

Middle Saxon cemetery and churches at Nazeingbury, Essex, 1975–6', *Essex Archaeology and History* 10 (1978), 3rd series, 29–117

Hughes, K. *The Church in Irish Society* (London, 1966)

Hughes, K. 'Where are the writings of early Scotland?', in *Celtic Britain in the Early Middle Ages*, ed. D.N. Dumville (Woodbridge, 1980), 1–21

Hughes, N. and Owen, M. 'Twelfth-century Welsh hagiography: the *Gogynfeirdd* poems to saints', in *Celtic Hagiography and Saints' Cults*, ed. J. Cartwright (Cardiff, 2003), 45–76

Ireland, C. 'Aldfrith of Northumbria and the Irish genealogies', *Celtica* 22 (1991), 64–78

Jackson, A. *The Symbol Stones of Scotland: A Social Anthropological Resolution of the Problem of the Picts* (Stromness, 1984)

Jackson, K.H. *Language and History in Early Britain* (Edinburgh, 1953)

Jackson, K.H. 'On the northern British section in Nennius', in *Celt and Saxon: Studies in the Early British Border*, ed. N.K. Chadwick (Cambridge, 1963), 20–62

James, E. 'Bede and the tonsure question', *Peritia* 3 (1984), 83–93

James, E. 'The origins of barbarian kingdoms: the continental evidence', in *The Origins of Anglo-Saxon Kingdoms*, ed. S. Bassett (Leicester, 1989), 40–52

James, E. *Britain in the First Millennium* (London, 2001)

Jenkins, D. and Owen, M.E. 'The Welsh marginalia in the Lichfield Gospels, part 1', *CMCS* 5 (1983), 37–66

Jochens, J. 'Late and peaceful: Iceland's conversion through arbitration in 1000', *Speculum* 74 (1999), 621–55

John, E. *Land Tenure in Early England* (Leicester, 1960)

John, E. 'The point of Woden', *ASSAH* 5 (1992), 127–34

Jolly, K. *Popular Religion in Late Anglo-Saxon England: Elf Charms in Context* (Chapel Hill and London, 1996)

Jones, B. and Mattingly, D. *An Atlas of Roman Britain* (Oxford, 1990)

Jones, G.R.J. 'Multiple estates and early settlements', in *Medieval Settlement*, ed. P. Sawyer (London, 1976), 11–40

Jones, P. and Pennick, N. *A History of Pagan Europe* (London, 1995)

Keynes, S. 'Raedwald the Bretwalda', in *Voyage to the Other World: The Legacy of Sutton Hoo*, ed. C.B. Kendall and P.S. Wells (Minneapolis, 1992), 103–23

Keynes, S. 'Episcopal lists', in *Blackwell Encyclopaedia*, 172–4

King, A. 'Rural settlement in southern Britain', in *A Companion to Roman Britain*, ed. M. Todd (Oxford, 2004), 349–70

Kirby, D. 'Bede's native sources for the *Historia Ecclesiastica*', *Bulletin of the John Ryland's Library* 48 (1966), 341–71

Kirby, D. 'Bede and the Pictish church', *Innes Review* 24 (1973), 6–25

Kirby, D (ed.), *Saint Wilfrid at Hexham* (Newcastle, 1974)

Kirby, D. 'Northumbria in the time of Wilfrid', in *Saint Wilfrid at Hexham*, ed. D. Kirby (Newcastle, 1974), 1–34.

Kirby, D. *The Earliest English Kings* (London 1991)

Lamb, R. 'Pictland, Northumbria and the Carolingian empire', in *Conversion and Christianity in the North Sea World*, ed. B. Crawford (St Andrews, 1998), 41–56

Lancaster, L. 'Kinship in Anglo-Saxon society, parts I and II', *British Journal of Sociology* 9 (1958), 230–50, 359–77

Lane, A. and Campbell, E. *Dunadd: An Early Dalriadic Capital* (Oxford, 2000)

Lapidge, M. 'Gildas's education and the Latin culture of sub-Roman Britain', in *Gildas: New Approaches*, ed. M. Lapidge and D.N. Dumville (Woodbridge, 1984), 27–50

Lapidge, M. (ed.), *Archbishop Theodore: Commemorative Studies of his Life and Influence* (Cambridge, 1995)

Lapidge, M. *et al.* (eds), *The Blackwell Encyclopaedia of Anglo-Saxon England* (Oxford, 1999)

Lapidge, M. 'Libraries' and 'Schools', in *Blackwell Encyclopaedia*, 285–6 and 407–9

Lapidge, M. and Dumville, D.N. (eds), *Gildas: New Approaches* (Woodbridge, 1984)

Laporte, J.-P. and Boyer, R. *Trésors de Chelles: Sépultures et Reliques de la Reine Bathildis et de l'Abbesse Bertille* (Chelles, 1991)

Leigh, D. 'Ambiguity in Anglo-Saxon Style I art', *Antiquaries Journal* 64 (1984), 34–42

Le Jan, R. 'Convents, violence and competition for power in seventh-century Francia', in *Topographies of Power in the Early Middle Ages*, ed. M. de Jong, F. Theuws and C. van Rhijn (Leiden, 2001), 243–69

Levison, W. *England and the Continent in the Eighth Century* (Oxford, 1946)

Lloyd, J.E. *A History of Wales from the Earliest Times to the Edwardian Conquest*, 2 vols (3rd edn, London, 1939)

Longley, D. 'Orientation within early medieval cemeteries: some data from north-west Wales', *Antiquaries Journal* 82 (2002), 309–20

Loveluck, C. 'Wealth, waste and conspicuous consumption: Flixborough and its importance for middle and late rural settlement studies', in *Image and Power in the Archaeology of Early Medieval Britain*, ed. H. Hamerow and A. MacGregor (Oxford, 2001), 79–130

Lowe, C.E. 'New light on the Anglian minster at Hoddom', *Transactions of the Dumfries and Galloway Natural History and Antiquarian Society* 3rd series, 66 (1991), 11–35

Lucy, S. *The Early Anglo-Saxon Cemeteries of East Yorkshire*, BAR 282 (Oxford, 1998)

Lucy, S. and Reynolds, A. (eds), *Burial in Early Medieval England and Wales* (London, 2002)

McCarthy, M. 'Carlisle and St Cuthbert', *Durham Archaeological Journal* 14–15 (1999), 59–67

McCarthy, M. 'Rheged: an early historic kingdom near the Solway', *Proceedings of the Society of Antiquaries of Scotland* 132 (2002), 357–81

McCone, K. 'Werewolves, cyclopes, *díberga* and *fianna*: juvenile delinquency in early Ireland', *CMCS* 12 (1986), 1–22

MacDonald, A. *Curadán, Boniface and the Early Church of Rosemarkie* (Groom House Museum, 1992)

MacDonald, A. 'Aspects of the monastic landscape in Adomnán's *Life of Columba*', in *Saints and Scholars: Studies in Irish Hagiography*, ed. J. Cary, M. Herbert and P. Ó Riain (Dublin, 2001), 15–30

MacLean, D. 'Maelrubai, Applecross and the late Pictish contribution west of Druimalban', in *The Worm, the Germ and the Thorn:*

Pictish and Related Studies Presented to Isabel Henderson, ed. D. Henry (Balgavies, 1997), 173–87

McManus, D. *A Guide to Ogam* (Maynooth, 1991)

MacMullen, R. *Christianizing the Roman Empire (AD 100–400)* (New Haven, 1984)

McNeill, P. and Nicholson, R. (eds), *An Historical Atlas of Scotland c.400–c.1600* (St Andrews, 1975)

Macquarrie, A. 'The career of Saint Kentigern of Glasgow: *vitae, lectiones* and glimpses of fact', *Innes Review* 37 (1986), 3–24

Macquarrie, A. 'Early Christian religious houses in Scotland: foundation and function', in *Pastoral Care*, 110–33

Macquarrie, A. 'The Kings of Strathclyde, *c.*400–1018', in *Medieval Scotland. Crown, Lordship and Community. Essays Presented to G.W.S. Barrow*, ed. A. Grant and K.J. Stringer (Edinburgh, 1993), 1–19

Macquarrie, A. '*Vita Sancti Servani*: the Life of St Serf', *Innes Review* 44 (1993), 122–52

Macquarrie, A. *The Saints of Scotland* (Edinburgh, 1997)

MacQueen, J. *St Nynia* (2nd edn, Edinburgh 1990)

Maddicott, J.R. 'Plague in England in the seventh century', *Past and Present* 156 (1997), 7–54

Maddicott, J.R. 'Two frontier states: Northumbria and Wessex', in *The Medieval State. Essays Presented to James Campbell*, ed. J.R. Maddicott and D.M. Palliser (London, 2000), 25–45

Maddicott, J.R. 'Prosperity and power in the age of Bede and Beowulf', *Proceedings of the British Academy* 117 (2002), 49–71

Manchester, K. *The Archaeology of Disease* (Bradford, 1983)

Markus, R.A. 'Pelagianism: Britain and the continent', *Journal of Ecclesiastical History* 37 (1986), 191–204

Markus, R.A. *The End of Ancient Christianity* (Cambridge, 1990)

Markus, R.A. *Gregory the Great and his World* (Cambridge, 1997)

Mayr-Harting, H. *The Coming of Christianity to Anglo-Saxon England* (3rd edn, London, 1991)

Meaney, A.L. *Anglo-Saxon Amulets and Curing Stones*, BAR 96 (Oxford, 1981)

Meaney, A.L. 'Anglo-Saxon idolaters and ecclesiasts from Theodore to Alcuin: a source study', *ASSAH* 5 (1992), 103–25

Meek, D.E. *The Quest for Celtic Christianity* (Edinburgh, 2000)

Meens, R. 'A background to Augustine's mission to Anglo-Saxon England', *Anglo-Saxon England* 22 (1994), 5–17

Meens, R. 'Pollution in the early Middle Ages: the case of the food regulations in penitentials', *Early Medieval Europe* 4 (1995), 3–19

Meens, R. 'Questioning ritual purity', in *St Augustine*, ed. Gameson, 174–86

Meens, R. 'The uses of the Old Testament in early medieval canon law', in *The Uses of the Past in the Early Middle Ages*, ed. Y. Hen and M. Innes (Cambridge, 2000), 67–77

Metcalf, D.M. *Thrymsas and Sceattas in the Ashmolean Museum, Oxford*, 3 vols (Oxford, 1993–4)

Milis, L. 'La conversion en profandeur: un procès sans fin', *Revue du Nord* 68 (1986), 187–98

Millett, M. *The Romanisation of Britain: An Essay in Archaeological Interpretation* (Cambridge, 1990)

Moisl, H. 'The Bernician royal dynasty and the Irish in the seventh century', *Peritia* 2 (1983), 103–26

Morris, R. *Churches in the Landscape* (London, 1989)

Morton, A. 'Burial in Middle Saxon Southampton', in *Death in Towns: Urban Responses to the Dying and the Dead 100–1600*, ed. S. Bassett (Leicester, 1993), 68–77

Murray, A. 'Missionaries and magic in Dark Age Europe', *Past and Present* 136 (1992), 186–205

Museum of London Archaeology Service, *The Prittlewell Prince: The Discovery of a Rich Anglo-Saxon Burial in Essex* (London, 2004)

Nelson, J. 'Inauguration rituals', in *Early Medieval Kingship*, ed. P. Sawyer and I.N. Wood (Leeds, 1977), 50–71

Nelson, J. 'Queens as Jezebels: the careers of Brunhild and Balthild in Merovingian history', in *Studies in Church History*, Subsidia 1 (London, 1978), 31–77

Nelson, J. 'Monks, secular men and masculinity *c.*900', in *Masculinity in Medieval Europe*, ed. D. Hadley (Harlow, 1999), 121–42

Ní Dhonchadha, M. 'Birr and the Law of the Innocents' and 'The Law of Adomnán: a translation', in *Adomnán at Birr, AD 697. Essays in Commemoration of the Law of the Innocents*, ed. T. O'Loughlin (Dublin, 2001), 13–32 and 53–68

Nock, A.D. *Conversion* (Oxford, 1933)

North, R. *Heathen Gods in Old English Literature* (Cambridge, 1997)

O'Brien, E. 'Pagan and Christian burials in Ireland during the first millennium AD: continuity and change', in *The Early Church in Wales and the West*, ed. N. Edwards and A. Lane (Oxford, 1992), 130–7

Ó Carragáin, É. 'The Ruthwell crucifixion poem in iconographical and liturgical contexts', *Peritia* 6–7 (1987–8), 1–71

Ó Corráin, D. 'Irish regnal succession; a reappraisal', *Studia Hibernica* 11 (1971), 7–39

Ó Corráin, D. 'Nationality and kingship in pre-Norman Ireland', in *Nationality and the Pursuit of National Independence*, ed. T.W. Moody (Belfast, 1978), 1–35

Ó Corráin, D. 'Irish law and canon law', in *Ireland and Europe: The Early Church*, ed. P. Ni Chatháin and M. Richter (Stuttgart, 1984), 157–66

Ó Corráin, D. 'Irish vernacular law and the Old Testament', in *Ireland and Europe in the Early Middle Ages*, ed. P. Ní Chatháin and M. Richter (Stuttgart, 1984), 284–307

Ó Cróinín, D. *Early Medieval Ireland 400–1200* (London, 1995)

Okasha, E. *Corpus of Early Inscribed Stones of South-West Britain* (London, 1993)

Oliver, L. *The Beginnings of English Law* (Toronto, 2002)

O'Loughlin, T. 'The exegetical purpose of Adomnán's *De Locis Sanctis*', *CMCS* 24 (1992), 37–53

O'Loughlin, T. (ed.), *Adomnán at Birr, AD 697. Essays in Commemoration of the Law of the Innocents* (Dublin, 2001)

O'Loughlin, T. 'The tombs of the saints: their significance for Adomnán', in *Saints and Scholars: Studies in Irish Hagiography*, ed. J. Carey, M. Herbert and P. Ó Riain (Dublin, 2001), 1–14

Olson, L. *Early Monasteries in Cornwall* (Woodbridge, 1989)

Olson, L. and Padel, O.J. 'A tenth-century list of Cornish parochial saints', *CMCS* 12 (1986), 33–71

Orchard, A. *The Poetic Art of Aldhelm* (Cambridge, 1994)

Orchard, A. 'Enigmata', in *Blackwell Encyclopaedia*, 171–2.

Orchard, A. 'Latin and the vernacular languages', in *After Rome*, ed. T. Charles-Edwards (Oxford, 2003), 191–219

O'Reilly, J. 'Reading the scriptures in the *Life of Columba*', in *Studies in the Cult of Saint Columba*, ed. C. Bourke (Dublin, 1997), 80–106

Ó Riain, P. 'St Finnbarr: a study in a cult', *Journal of the Cork Historical and Archaeological Society* 82 (1977), 63–82

O'Sullivan, D. 'Space, silence and shortages on Lindisfarne: the archaeology of asceticism', in *Image and Power in the Archaeology of Early Medieval Britain*, ed. H. Hamerow and A. MacGregor (Oxford, 2001), 33–52

O'Sullivan, J. 'Iona: archaeological excavations, 1875–1996', in *Spes Scotorum*, 215–44

O'Sullivan, S. 'Aldhelm's *De Virginitate*: patristic pastiche or innovative exposition?', *Peritia* 12 (1998), 271–95

Owen-Crocker, G. *Dress in Anglo-Saxon England* (Manchester, 1986)

Padel, O.J. 'A new study of the *Gododdin*', *CMCS* 35 (1998), 45–55

Padel, O.J. 'Local saints and place-names in Cornwall', in *Local Saints*, 303–60,

Page, R. *Norse Myths* (London, 1990)

Page, R. 'Anglo-Saxon paganism: the evidence of Bede', in *Pagans and Christians: The Interplay between Christian Latin and Traditional Germanic Cultures in Early Medieval Europe*, ed. T. Hosfra, L. Houwen and A. MacDonald (Groningen, 1995), 99–130

Page, R. *Runes and Runic Inscriptions* (Woodbridge, 1995)

Pantos, A. and Semple, S. (eds), *Assembly Places and Practices in Medieval Europe* (Dublin, 2004)

Paxton, F. *The Christianisation of Death* (London, 1990)

Pearce, S. *South-western Britain in the Early Middle Ages* (London, 2004)

Pelteret, D. *Slavery in Early Medieval England from the Reign of Alfred until the Twelfth Century* (Woodbridge, 1995)

Pestell, T. *Landscapes of Monastic Foundation: The Establishment of Religious Houses in East Anglia, c.650–1200* (Woodbridge, 2004)

Pestell, T. and Ulmschneider, K. (eds), *Markets in Early Medieval Europe: Trading and 'Productive' Sites 650–850* (Macclesfield, 2003)

Petts, D. 'Cemeteries and boundaries in western Britain', in *Burial*, ed. Lucy and Reynolds, 24–46

Petts, D. *Christianity in Roman Britain* (Stroud, 2003)

Picard, J. 'The purpose of Adomnán's *Vita Columbae*', *Peritia* 1 (1982), 160–77

Powlesland, D. 'Early Anglo-Saxon settlements, structures, form and layout', in *The Anglo-Saxons from the Migration Period to the Eighth Century: An Ethnographic Perspective*, ed. J. Hines (Woodbridge, 1997), 101–24

Preston-Jones, A. 'Decoding Cornish churchyards', in *The Early Church in Wales and the West*, ed. N. Edwards and A. Lane (Oxford, 1992), 104–24

Price, N. *The Viking Way: Religion and War in Late Iron Age Scandinavia* (Uppsala, 2002)

Prinz, E. *Frühes Monchtum in Frankenreich* (2nd edn, Munich, 1988)

Proudfoot, E. 'The Hallowhill and the origins of Christianity in Scotland', in *Conversion and Christianity in the North Sea World*, ed. B. Crawford (St Andrews, 1998), 57–74

Pryce, H. 'Ecclesiastical wealth in early Wales', in *The Early Church in Wales and the West*, ed. N. Edwards and A. Lane (Oxford, 1992), 22–32

Pryce, H. 'Pastoral Care in Early Medieval Wales', in *Pastoral Care*, 41–62

Pryce, H. (ed.), *Literacy in Medieval Celtic Societies* (Cambridge, 1998)

Radford, C.A.R. 'The Celtic monastery in Britain', *Archaeologia Cambrensis* 111 (1962), 1–24

Raftery, B. *Pagan Celtic Ireland: The Enigma of the Irish Iron Age* (London, 1994)

Rahtz, P. 'Excavations on Glastonbury Tor', *Archaeological Journal* 127 (1971), 1–81

Rahtz, P. 'Pagan and Christian by the Severn Sea', in *The Archaeology and History of Glastonbury Abbey*, ed. L. Abrams and J.P. Carley (Woodbridge, 1991), 3–37

Randsborg, K. *The First Millennium AD in Europe and the Mediterranean* (Cambridge, 1991)

Rattue, J. *The Living Stream: Holy Wells in Historical Context* (Woodbridge, 1995)

RCHM Scotland, *Argyll Vol. 3: Mull, Tiree, Coll and Northern Argyll* (Edinburgh, 1980)

RCHM Scotland, *Pictish Symbol Stones. An Illustrated Gazetteer* (Edinburgh, 1999)

Reynolds, A. 'Burials, boundaries and charters in Anglo-Saxon England: a reassessment', in *Burial*, ed. Lucy and Reynolds, 171–94

Reynolds, S. *Kingdoms and Communities in Western Europe, 900–1300* (Oxford, 1984)

Riché, P. *Education and Culture in the Barbarian West from the Sixth through to the Eighth Century*, trans. J. Contreni (Columbia, 1976)

Ritchie, A. 'Painted pebbles in early Scotland', *Proceedings of the Society of Antiquaries of Scotland* 104 (1971–2), 297–301

Ritchie, A. (ed.), *Govan and its Early Medieval Sculpture* (Stroud, 1994)

Ritchie, A. *Iona* (London, 1997)

Rivet, A.L.F. and Smith, C. *The Place-Names of Roman Britain* (Cambridge, 1979), 39–40

Rollason, D. *The Mildrith Legend: A Study in Early Medieval Hagiography in England* (Leicester, 1982)

Rollason, D. *Saints and Relics in Anglo-Saxon England* (Oxford, 1989)

Rollason, D. 'Hagiography and politics in early Northumbria', in *Holy Men and Holy Women: Old English Prose Saints' Lives and Their Contexts*, ed. P. Szarmach (Albany, 1996), 95–114

Rollason, D. *Northumbria 500–1000: Creation and Destruction of a Kingdom* (Cambridge, 2003)

Runciman, W. 'Accelerating social mobility: the case of Anglo-Saxon England', *Past and Present* 104 (1984), 3–30

Russell, J.C. *The Germanisation of Early Medieval Christianity: A Sociological Approach to Religious Transformation* (Oxford, 1994)

Salway, P. *Roman Britain* (Oxford, 1981)

Samson, R. 'The re-interpretation of the Pictish symbols', *Journal of the British Archaeological Association* 145 (1992), 29–65

Scull, C. 'Social archaeology and Anglo-Saxon kingdom origins', *The Making of Kingdoms*, ed. T.M. Dickinson and D. Griffiths, *ASSAH* 10 (1999), 7–24

Sellar, W.D.H. 'Warlords, holy men and matrilineal succession', *Innes Review* 36 (1985), 29–43

Semple, S. 'A fear of the past: the place of the prehistoric burial mound in the ideology of middle and later Anglo-Saxon England', *World Archaeology* 30 (1998), 109–26

Sharpe, R. 'Hiberno-Latin *Laicus*, Irish *Láech* and the Devil's Men', *Ériu* 30 (1979), 75–92

Sharpe, R. 'Armagh and Rome in the seventh century', in *Ireland and Europe: The Early Church*, ed. P.N. Chatháin and M. Richter (Stuttgart, 1984), 58–72

Sharpe, R. 'Gildas as a Father of the church', in *Gildas: New Approaches*, ed. M. Lapidge and D.N. Dumville (Woodbridge, 1984), 193–205.

Sharpe, R. 'Some problems concerning the organisation of the early medieval church in Ireland', *Peritia* 3 (1984), 230–70

Sharpe, R. 'The thriving of Dalriada', in *Kings, Clerics and Chronicles in Scotland: 500–1297*, ed. S. Taylor (Dublin, 2000), 47–61

Sharpe, R. 'Martyrs and saints in late antique Britain', in *Local Saints*, 75–154

Sims-Williams, P. 'Gildas and the Anglo-Saxons', *CMCS* 6 (1983), 1–30

Sims-Williams, P. 'The settlement of England in Bede and the "Chronicle" ', *Anglo-Saxon England* 12 (1983), 1–41

Sims-Williams, P. *Religion and Literature in Western England: 600–800* (Cambridge, 1990)

Sims-Williams, P. 'The death of Urien', *CMCS* 32 (1996), 25–56

Sims-Williams, P. 'The uses of writing in early medieval Wales', in *Literacy in Medieval Celtic Society*, ed. H. Pryce (Cambridge, 1998), 15–38

Sims-Williams, P. 'The five languages of Wales in pre-Norman inscriptions', *CMCS* 44 (2002), 1–36

Sisam, K. 'Anglo-Saxon royal genealogies', *Proceedings of the British Academy* 39 (1953), 287–346

Smith, I. 'The origins and development of Christianity in north Britain and southern Pictland', in *Church Archaeology: Research Directions for the Future*, ed. J. Blair and C. Pyrah (London, 1996), 19–42

Smyth, A.P. *Warlords and Holy Men: Scotland* AD *800–1000* (London, 1984)

Smyth, M. *Understanding the Universe in Seventh-Century Ireland* (Woodbridge, 1996)

Sorensen, P. Meulengracht 'Religions old and new', in *The Oxford Illustrated History of the Vikings*, ed. P. Sawyer (Oxford, 1997), 202–24

Southern, P. 'The army in late Roman Britain', in *A Companion to Roman Britain*, ed. M. Todd (Oxford, 2004), 393–48, at 404–5

Speake, G. *Anglo-Saxon Animal Art and its Germanic Background* (London, 1980)

Stacey, R.C. 'Texts and society', in *After Rome*, ed. T. Charles-Edwards (Oxford, 2003), 221–57

Stafford, P (ed.), *The Blackwell Companion to Early Medieval Britain*, (Oxford, forthcoming)

Stancliffe, C. 'From town to country: the Christianisation of the Touraine 370–600', in *The Church in Town and Countryside*, ed. D. Baker (London, 1979), 43–59

Stancliffe, C. 'Kings who opted out', in *Ideal and Reality in Frankish and Anglo-Saxon Society*, ed. P. Wormald (Oxford, 1983), 154–76

Stancliffe, C. 'The British church and the mission of Augustine', in *St Augustine*, ed. Gameson, 107–51

Stancliffe, C. *Bede, Wilfrid and the Irish* (Jarrow lecture, 2003)

Stenton, F.M. 'The foundations of English history', in *Preparatory to Anglo-Saxon England*, ed. D.M. Stenton (Oxford, 1970), 116–26

Stenton, F.M. *Anglo-Saxon England* (3rd edn, Oxford, 1971)

Stevens, W.M. 'Easter controversy', in *Blackwell Encyclopaedia*, 155–7

Stoodley, N. *The Spindle and the Spear: A Critical Enquiry into the Construction and Meaning of Gender in the Early Anglo-Saxon Inhumation Burial Rite* BAR 288 (Oxford, 1999)

Story, J. *Carolingian Connections: Anglo-Saxon England and Carolingian Francia, 750–870* (Aldershot, 2003)

Swift, C. *Ogam Stones and the Earliest Irish Christians* (Maynooth, 1997)

Tanaka, M. 'Iona and the kingship of Dál Riata in Adomnán's *Vita Columbae*', *Peritia* 17–18 (2003–4), 199–214

Taylor, S. 'Place-names and the early church in eastern Scotland', in *Scotland in Dark Age Britain*, ed. B. Crawford (St Andrews, 1996), 93–110

Taylor, S. 'Seventh-century Iona abbots in Scottish place-names', in *Spes Scotorum*, 35–70

Thacker, A. 'Monks, preaching and pastoral care in England', in *Pastoral Care*, 137–70

Thacker, A. '*Membra disjecta*: the division of the body and the diffusion of the cult', in *Oswald: Northumbrian King to European Saint*, ed. C. Stancliffe and E. Cambridge (Stamford, 1995), 97–127

Thacker, A. '*Loca sanctorum*: the significance of place in the study of the saints', in *Local Saints*, 1–44

Thacker, A. 'The making of a local saint', in *Local Saints*, 45–74

Thacker, A. 'Wilfrid', in *Oxford Dictionary of National Biography* (Oxford, 2004), 944–50

Thacker, A. and Sharpe, R. (eds), *Local Saints and Local Churches in the Early Medieval West* (Oxford, 2002)

Thomas, C. 'The interpretation of the Pictish symbols', *Archaeological Journal* 120 (1963), 31–97

Thomas, C. *Christianity in Roman Britain to AD 500* (London, 1981)

Thomas, C. '"Gallici nautae de Galliarum provinciis": a sixth/seventh-century trade with Gaul reconsidered', *Medieval Archaeology* 34 (1990), 1–26

Thomas, C. *And Shall These Mute Stones Speak? Post-Roman Inscriptions in Western Britain* (Cardiff, 1994)

Thompson, A.H. (ed.), *Bede: His Life, Times and Writings* (Oxford, 1935)

Todd, M. 'The latest inscriptions of Roman Britain', *Durham Archaeological Journal* 14–15 (1999), 53–8

Todd, M. (ed.), *A Companion to Roman Britain* (Oxford, 2004)

Tristram, H.L.C. 'Why don't the English speak Welsh?', in *Britons in Anglo-Saxon England*, ed. N. Higham (forthcoming)

Ulmschneider, K. *Markets, Minsters and Metal-Dectectors: The Archaeology of Middle Saxon Lincolnshire and Hampshire Compared*, BAR 307 (Oxford, 2000).

Veitch, K. 'The Columban church in northern Britain, 664–712: a reassessment', *Proceedings of the Society of Antiquaries of Scotland* 127 (1997), 627–47

Venclová, N. 'The venerable Bede, druidic tonsure and archaeology', *Antiquity* 76 (2002), 458–71

Vince, A. (ed.), *Pre-Viking Lindsey* (Lincoln, 1993)

Wainwright, F.T. *The Problem of the Picts* (Perth, 1955)

Wallace-Hadrill, J.M. *Early Germanic Kingship in England and on the Continent* (Oxford, 1971)

Ward-Perkins, B. 'Why did the Anglo-Saxons not become more British?', *English Historical Review* 115 (2000), 513–33

Watson, W.J. *The Celtic Place-Names of Scotland* (Edinburgh, 1926)

Watts, D. 'Infant burials and Romano-British Christianity', *Archaeological Journal* 146 (1989), 372–83

Watts, D. *Religion in Late Roman Britain: Forces of Change* (London, 1998)

Webster, C. 'Square-ditched barrows in post-Roman Britain', *Archaeological Journal* 161 (2004), 63–79

Webster, L. and Backhouse, J. (eds), *The Making of England: Anglo-Saxon Art and Culture AD 600–900* (London, 1991)

Webster, L. and Brown, M. (eds), *The Transformation of the Roman World* (London, 1997)

Welander, R., Breeze, D. and Clancy, T.O. (eds), *The Stone of Destiny: Artefact and Icon* (Edinburgh, 2003)

White, R. and Barker, P. *Wroxeter: Life and Death of a Roman City* (Stroud, 1998)

Will, R., Forsyth, K., Clancy, T.O. and Charles-Edwards, G. 'An eighth-century inscribed cross-slab in Dull, Perthshire', *Scottish Archaeological Journal* 25 (2003), 57–72.

Williams, H. 'Placing the dead: investigating the location of wealthy barrow burials in seventh-century England', in *Grave Matters: Eight Studies of First Millennium AD Burials in Crimea, England and Southern Scandinavia,* ed. M. Rundkvist, BAR International Series 781 (Oxford, 1999), 57–86

Williams, H. 'An ideology of transformation: cremation rites and animal sacrifice in early Anglo-Saxon England', in *The Archaeology of Shamanism,* ed. N. Price (London, 2001), 193–212

Williams, H. 'Material culture as memory: combs and cremation in early medieval Britain', *Early Medieval Europe* 12 (2003), 89–128

Williamson, T. *The Origin of Hertfordshire* (Manchester, 2000)

Willmott, T. *Birdoswald: Excavations of a Roman Fort on Hadrian's Wall and its Successor Settlements, 1987–92* (London, 1997)

Wilson, D. *Anglo-Saxon Paganism* (London, 1992)

Wood, I.N. *The Merovingian North Sea* (Alingsås, 1983).

Wood, I.N. *The Merovingian Kingdoms: 450–751* (London, 1994)

Wood, I.N. 'The mission of Augustine of Canterbury to the English', *Speculum* 69 (1994), 1–17

Wood, I.N. *The Most Holy Abbot Ceolfrith* (Jarrow, 1995)

Wood, I.N. 'Northumbrians and Franks in the age of Wilfrid', *Northern History* 31 (1995), 10–21

Wood, I.N. 'Pagan religions and superstitions east of the Rhine from the fifth to the ninth century', in *After Empire: Towards an Ethnology of Europe's Barbarians,* ed. G. Ausenda (Woodbridge, 1995), 253–79

Wood, I.N. *The Missionary Life: Saints and the Evangelisation of Europe, 400–1050* (Harlow, 2001)

Wood, I.N. 'The final phase', in *A Companion to Roman Britain,* ed. M. Todd (Oxford, 2004), 428–42

Wood, P.N. 'On the little British kingdom of Craven', *Northern History* 32 (1996), 1–20

Woodward, A. *Shrines and Sacrifice* (London, 1992)

Woolf, A. 'Pictish matriliny reconsidered', *Innes Review* 49 (1998), 147–67

Woolf, A. 'The Verturian hegemony: a mirror in the north', in *Mercia. An Anglo-Saxon Kingdom in Europe*, ed. M.P. Brown and C.A. Farr (London; 2001), 106–11

Woolf, A. 'The Britons: from Romans to Barbarians', in *Regna and Gentes: The Relationship between Late Antique and Early Medieval Peoples and Kingdoms in the Transformation of the Roman World*, ed. H.-W. Goetz, J. Jarnut and W. Pohl (Leiden, 2003), 344–80

Woolf, A. 'The age of sea-kings: 900–1300', in *The Argyll Book*, ed. D. Omand (Edinburgh, 2004), 94–109

Woolf, A. 'Caedualla *rex Brettonum* and the passing of the Old North', *Northern History* 41 (2004), 5–24

Woolf, A. 'Onuist son of Uurguist: *tyrannus carnifex* or a David of the Picts?', *Æthelbald and Offa: Two Eighth-Century Kings of Mercia*, ed. D. Hill and M. Worthington, BAR 383 (Oxford, 2005)

Woolf, A. 'Dún Nechtain, Fortriu and the geography of the Picts' (forthcoming)

Woolf, A. 'Early historic Scotland to 761', in *The Shorter History of Scotland*, ed. R. Oram (Edinburgh, forthcoming)

Wormald, P. 'Bede and Benedict Biscop', in *Famulus Christi*, ed. G. Bonner (London, 1976), 141–69

Wormald, P. '*Lex scripta* and *Verbum regis*: legislation and Germanic kingship', in *Early Medieval Kingship*, ed. P. Sawyer and I.N. Wood (Leeds, 1977), 105–38

Wormald, P. 'Bede, Beowulf and the conversion of the English aristocracy', in *Bede and Anglo-Saxon England*, ed. R.T. Farrell, BAR 46 (Oxford, 1978), 32–95

Wormald, P. 'The age of Offa and Alcuin', in *The Anglo-Saxons*, ed. J. Campbell (Oxford, 1982), 101–31

Wormald, P. 'Bede, the *Bretwaldas* and the origin of the *gens Anglorum*', in *Ideal and Reality in Frankish and Anglo-Saxon Society*, ed. P. Wormald *et al.* (Oxford, 1983), 99–129

Wormald, P. *Bede and the Conversion of England: The Charter Evidence* (Jarrow, 1984)

Wormald, P. 'Celtic and Anglo-Saxon kingship: some further thoughts', in *Sources of Anglo-Saxon Culture*, ed. P. Szarmach (Kalamazoo, 1986), 151–83

Wright, N. 'Gildas's geographical perspective: some problems', in *Gildas: New Approaches*, ed. M. Lapidge and D.N. Dumville (Woodbridge, 1984)

Yeoman, P. 'Pilgrims to St Ethernan: the archaeology of an early saint of the Picts and Scots', in *Conversion and Christianity in the North Sea World*, ed. B. Crawford (St Andrews, 1998), 75–92

Yorke, B. 'Joint kingship in Kent *c*.560 to 785', *Archaeologia Cantiana* 99 (1983), 1–19

Yorke, B. *Kings and Kingdoms of Early Anglo-Saxon England* (London, 1990)

Yorke, B. 'Fact or fiction? The written evidence for the fifth and sixth centuries AD', *ASSAH* 6 (1993), 45–50

Yorke, B. *Wessex in the Early Middle Ages* (London, 1995)

Yorke, B. 'The reception of Christianity at the Anglo-Saxon royal courts', in *St Augustine*, ed. Gameson, 152–73

Yorke, B. 'Political and ethnic identity: a case study of Anglo-Saxon practice', in *Social Identity in Early Medieval Britain*, ed. W.O. Frazer and A. Tyrrell (London, 2000), 69–90

Yorke, B. 'Gregory of Tours and sixth-century Anglo-Saxon England', in *The World of Gregory of Tours*, ed. K. Mitchell and I.N. Wood (Leiden, 2002), 113–30

Yorke, B. 'The adaptation of the royal courts to Christianity', in *The Cross Goes North: Processes of Conversion in Northern Europe, AD 300–1300*, ed. M. Carver (York, 2003), 243–58

Yorke, B. 'Anglo-Saxon gentes and regna', in *Regna and Gentes: The Relationship between Late Antique and Early Medieval Peoples and Kingdoms in the Transformation of the Roman World*, ed. H.-W. Goetz, J. Jarnut and W. Pohl (Leiden, 2003), 381–408

Yorke, B. *Nunneries and the Anglo-Saxon Royal Houses* (London, 2003)

Yorke, B. 'Adomnán at the court of King Aldfrith', in *Adomnán of Iona: Theologian – Lawmaker – Peacemaker*, ed. R. Aist, T. Clancy, T. O'Loughlin and J. Wooding (Dublin, forthcoming).

Yorke, B. 'Boniface's insular background', in *Bonifatius Congressband* (Mainz, forthcoming).

Yorke, B. 'The origin myths of Anglo-Saxon kingdoms', in *Myths,*

Charters and Warfare in Anglo-Saxon England. Essays in Honour of Nicholas Brooks, ed. J. Barrow and A. Wareham (forthcoming)

Youngs, S. *'The Work of Angels': Masterpieces of Celtic Metalwork, 6th–9th Centuries* AD (London, 1989)

Zadora-Rio, E. 'The making of churchyards and parish territories in the early medieval landscape of France and England in the 7th–12th centuries: a reconsideration', *Medieval Archaeology* 47 (2003), 1–20

Index

Lightning Source UK Ltd.
Milton Keynes UK
UKOW06f0408150515

251596UK00003B/54/P